The Hunger Winter

In this pioneering study, Ingrid de Zwarte examines the causes and demographic impact of the 'Hunger Winter' that occurred in the Netherlands during the final months of German occupation in the Second World War. She offers a comprehensive and multifaceted view of the socio-political context in which the famine emerged and considers how the famine was confronted at different societal levels, including the responses by Dutch, German, and Allied state institutions, affected households, and local communities. Contrary to highly politicised assumptions, she argues that the famine resulted from a culmination of multiple transportation and distribution difficulties. Although Allied relief was postponed for many crucial months and official rations fell far below subsistence level, successful community efforts to fight the famine conditions emerged throughout the country. She also explains why German authorities found reasons to cooperate and allow relief for the starving Dutch. With these explorations, *The Hunger Winter* offers a radically new understanding of the Dutch famine and provides a valuable insight into the strategies and coping mechanisms of a modern society facing catastrophe.

Ingrid de Zwarte is Assistant Professor of Rural and Environmental History at Wageningen University.

T0349751

Studies in the Social and Cultural History of Modern Warfare

General Editor
Jay Winter, *Yale University*

Advisory Editors
David Blight, *Yale University*
Richard Bosworth, *University of Western Australia*
Peter Fritzsche, *University of Illinois, Urbana-Champaign*
Carol Gluck, *Columbia University*
Benedict Kiernan, *Yale University*
Antoine Prost, *Université de Paris-Sorbonne*
Robert Wohl, *University of California, Los Angeles*

In recent years the field of modern history has been enriched by the exploration of two parallel histories. These are the social and cultural history of armed conflict, and the impact of military events on social and cultural history.

Studies in the Social and Cultural History of Modern Warfare presents the fruits of this growing area of research, reflecting both the colonisation of military history by cultural historians and the reciprocal interest of military historians in social and cultural history, to the benefit of both. The series offers the latest scholarship in European and non-European events from the 1850s to the present day.

A full list of titles in the series can be found at:
www.cambridge.org/modernwarfare

The Hunger Winter

Fighting Famine in the Occupied Netherlands, 1944–1945

Ingrid de Zwarte

Wageningen University

CAMBRIDGE
UNIVERSITY PRESS

CAMBRIDGE
UNIVERSITY PRESS

Shaftesbury Road, Cambridge CB2 8EA, United Kingdom

One Liberty Plaza, 20th Floor, New York, NY 10006, USA

477 Williamstown Road, Port Melbourne, VIC 3207, Australia

314–321, 3rd Floor, Plot 3, Splendor Forum, Jasola District Centre, New Delhi – 110025, India

103 Penang Road, #05–06/07, Visioncrest Commercial, Singapore 238467

Cambridge University Press is part of Cambridge University Press & Assessment, a department of the University of Cambridge.

We share the University's mission to contribute to society through the pursuit of education, learning and research at the highest international levels of excellence.

www.cambridge.org
Information on this title: www.cambridge.org/9781108819213

DOI: 10.1017/9781108872515

First published 2020
First paperback edition 2022

A catalogue record for this publication is available from the British Library

Library of Congress Cataloging-in-Publication data
Names: Zwarte, Ingrid de, 1988– author.
Title: The hunger winter : fighting famine in the occupied Netherlands,
    1944–1945 / Ingrid de Zwarte, Wageningen University, the Netherlands.
Other titles: Fighting famine in the occupied Netherlands, 1944–1945
Description: Cambridge, UK ; New York : Cambridge University Press, [2020]
    | Series: Studies in the social and cultural history of modern warfare | Includes
    bibliographical references and index.
Identifiers: LCCN 2020003340 (print) | LCCN 2020003341 (ebook) |
    ISBN 9781108836807 (hardback) | ISBN 9781108819213 (paperback) |
    ISBN 9781108872515 (epub)
Subjects: LCSH: Netherlands–History–German occupation, 1940–1945.
    | World War, 1939–1945–Food supply–Netherlands. | World War,
    1939–1945–Civilian relief. | Food supply–Netherlands–History–20th century. |
    Famines–Netherlands–History–20th century.
Classification: LCC D802.N4 Z93 2020 (print) | LCC D802.N4 (ebook) |
    DDC 940.53/492–dc23
LC record available at https://lccn.loc.gov/2020003340
LC ebook record available at https://lccn.loc.gov/2020003341

ISBN   978-1-108-83680-7   Hardback
ISBN   978-1-108-81921-3   Paperback

For the victims, the survivors, and all those who came to their aid

Contents

Illustrations

Figures

Maps

Tables

Acknowledgements

This book is the product of a long journey, and I am grateful for the opportunity to acknowledge the many people who have helped me along the way. My PhD research at the University of Amsterdam and NIOD Institute for War, Holocaust and Genocide Studies (NIOD), on which this book is based, would not have been possible without my dedicated and inspiring supervisors Peter Romijn and Ralf Futselaar, whose positive influence on my work cannot be overestimated. I count myself very fortunate to have been a student of both and hope that our collegial relationship continues for many years to come.

My amazing colleagues from universities at Amsterdam, Rotterdam, Oxford, and Wageningen have always offered me the opportunity to engage in intellectual conversation amidst a pleasantly informal and amicable atmosphere. I am most grateful to them for providing a stimulating environment to exchange ideas and discuss research. In no particular order, I would like to extend my gratitude to Liz Buettner, James Kennedy, Mieke Aerts, Samuël Kruizinga, Geert Janssen, Eveline Buchheim, Gerard Trienekens, Hans Blom, Ewout Frankema, Frank van Vree, Patricia Clavin, and Bob Moore for commenting on earlier parts of this work and encouraging me to turn my thesis into a book.

Near the end of my PhD project, I was very fortunate to spend an inspiring semester at Columbia University. I am grateful to Volker Berghahn for facilitating this stay and for kindly welcoming me to Columbia's European Institute. Thankful acknowledgement also goes out to Adam Tooze for hosting me there, and to Francois Carrel-Billiard and Tess Drahman for making all the arrangements. My stay at Columbia would not have been possible without L. H. Lumey, whom I met through our shared interest in the Hunger Winter and who invited me to work with him at Columbia's Department of Epidemiology. He has helped me tremendously in finding new data and refining my argumentation. I am also indebted to Peter Ekamper, Frans van Poppel, and Govert Bijwaard from the Netherlands Interdisciplinary Demographic Institute (NIDI), who allowed me to build on their innovative research and graciously made additional calculations from their data for this study. Of course, all mistakes and misinterpretations that nevertheless remain are completely my own.

My thanks go out as well to the librarians and archivists who helped me find my way to the books and sources that are the foundation of this book. Archivists and staff from the NIOD, National Archives of the Netherlands in The Hague, and local archives in Amsterdam, Rotterdam, The Hague, Utrecht, Leiden, Haarlem, Delft, Schiedam, Purmerend, Zaandam, Gouda, Den Bosch, Assen, Groningen, and Leeuwarden helped me enormously during my quest. The generous support from archivists and staff at the Bundesarchiv in Berlin-Lichterfelde, National Archives in Kew, London, National Archives and Record Administration in College Park, Maryland, and United Nations Archives and Record Centre in New York City was indispensable as well. Part of this archival research would have never been possible without the help of my brilliant research assistant Debbie Varekamp, who zealously managed to work through more material in three months than most historians could have done in half a year.

This book could also not have been written without the generous financial support of the Niels Stensen Foundation, which funded my postdoctoral fellowship at the Oxford Centre for European History in 2018–2019. The editors at Cambridge University Press have been incredibly supportive in the writing and publishing process, in particular Michael Watson and Emily Sharp. Thankful acknowledgement also goes out to the two anonymous reviewers for their thoughtful reading of the manuscript, constructive criticism, and extremely helpful suggestions. I am also indebted to Job Lisman and Mai Spijkers at Prometheus, which published a Dutch popularised version of this work in 2019 and generously gave me permission to work on an English monograph. The permission granted by the NIOD, NIDI, Nederlands Fotomuseum, Leiden University Libraries, Zijper Museum, Studio Christa Jesse, and The Map Archive to use their illustrations is gratefully acknowledged as well. Heartfelt thanks also go to Harco Gijsbers for his kind assistance with selecting photographs, and to Marguérite Corporaal and our NWO-funded research project 'Heritages of Hunger' (NWA.1160.18.197) for financially supporting the use of third-party materials in this book.

On a much more personal level, there are some important people without whom I could have never finished this research project – or perhaps even started it in the first place. My dear friends have always been there for me, and I am grateful for their patience in letting me go on about my research and for all the moments they reminded me that there is more to life than work. I am beyond thankful for sharing my life and work with Tim, whose love and dedication seems to know no limits and who means more to me than he could possibly know. My greatest debt is to my family: my sister Sonja and my parents Jan and Marianne, who have always unconditionally supported me in all my endeavours, including this one.

Lastly, over the years, I have been fortunate to meet and learn from dozens of people who have shared their personal experiences of the war and famine with me – this book would not have been the same without them. The list of people who contributed to this study through fascinating conversations, interviews, and personal documentation on the Hunger Winter is endless. Here, I would like to mention Frans Nieuwenhuis, Richard C. Hall, Jan and Ine Spier, and Joop van Diepen for their valuable contributions. I hope this book helps to enlighten the complex history of the Hunger Winter and does justice to their memories and experiences. This book is dedicated to the famine's victims and survivors, as well as to all those who came to their aid.

Abbreviations

ANP	*Algemeen Nederlands Persbureau* (Netherlands National News Agency)
BBC	British Broadcasting Corporation
BMI	body mass index
CBS	*Centraal Bureau voor de Statistiek* (Statistics Netherlands)
CCD	*Crisis Controle Dienst* (Crisis Control Service)
CDK	*Centraal Distributiekantoor* (Central Rationing Office)
CEB	*Centraal Evacuatie Bureau* (Central Evacuation Office)
CK	*Centrale Keukens* (Communal Kitchens)
CRV	*Centrale Reederij Voedselvoorziening* (Central Shipping Company for the Food Supply)
FAD	food availability decline
FAO	Food and Agriculture Organisation
GP	general practitioner
gr	gram
ha	hectare
HARK	*Hulpactie Rode Kruis* (Relief Aid Red Cross)
hl	hectolitre
HOA	*Hulporganisatie Amsterdam* (Aid Organisation Amsterdam)
ICRC	International Committee of the Red Cross
IKB	*Interkerkelijk Bureau voor Noodvoedselvoorziening* (Interdenominational Bureau for Emergency Nutrition
IKO	*Interkerkelijk Overleg* (Interdenominational Counsel)
kcal	kilocalorie
kg	kilogram
KLV	*Kinderlandverschickungen* (Evacuation of children to the countryside)
NC	*Nationale Commissie tot Uitzending van Nederlandsche Kinderen 1945* (National Committee for the Evacuation of Dutch Children 1945)
NGO	non-governmental organisation

NIDI	Netherlands Interdisciplinary Demographic Institute
NIOD	NIOD Institute for War, Holocaust and Genocide Studies
NMA	Netherlands Military Authority
NSB	*Nationaal-Socialistische Beweging* (National Socialist Movement)
NSV	*Nationalsozialistische Volkswolfahrt* (National Socialist People's Welfare)
NVB	*Nederlandse Vrouwenbeweging* (Dutch Women's Movement)
NVD	*Nederlandse Volksdienst* (Dutch People's Service)
NVH	*Nederlands Volksherstel* (Dutch People's Reconstruction Movement)
OHNS	*Onderlinge Hulp Noodtoestand Schooljeugd* (Mutual Aid Emergency Situation Schoolchildren)
OKW	*Oberkommando der Wehrmacht* (High Command of the Armed Forces)
pc	piece
POW	prisoner of war
PVC	*Provinciale Voedselcommissaris* (Provincial Food Commissioner)
RAF	Royal Air Force
RBVVO	*Rijksbureau voor de Voedselvoorziening in Oorlogstijd* (Directorate of Food Supply during Wartime)
RBVVVO	*Rijksbureau voor de Voorbereiding van de Voedselvoorziening in Oorlogstijd* (Directorate for the Preparation of the Food Supply during Wartime)
SHAEF	Supreme Headquarters Allied Expeditionary Force
SiPo und SD	*Sicherheitspolizei und Sicherheitsdienst* (Security Police and Security Service)
SS	*Schutzstaffel* (Protection Squadron)
UN	United Nations
UNRRA	United Nations Relief and Rehabilitation Administration
USAAF	United States Army Air Forces
UVV	*Unie voor Vrouwelijke Vrijwilligers* (Union for Female Volunteers)
VBNA	*Vereniging ter Behartiging van de Nederlandsche Aardappelhandel* (Dutch Potato Trade Association)

Maps

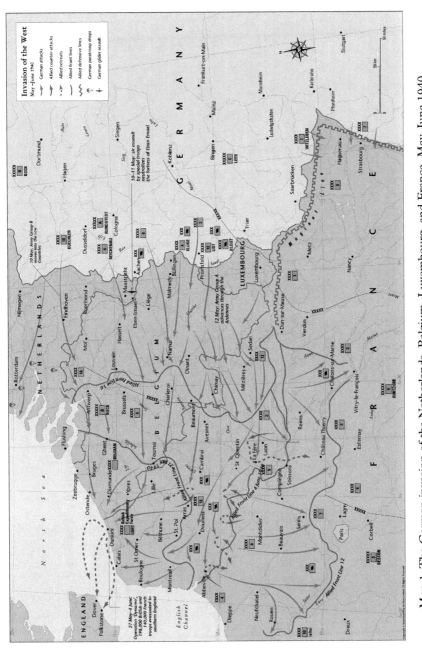

Map 1 The German invasion of the Netherlands, Belgium, Luxembourg, and France, May–June 1940.

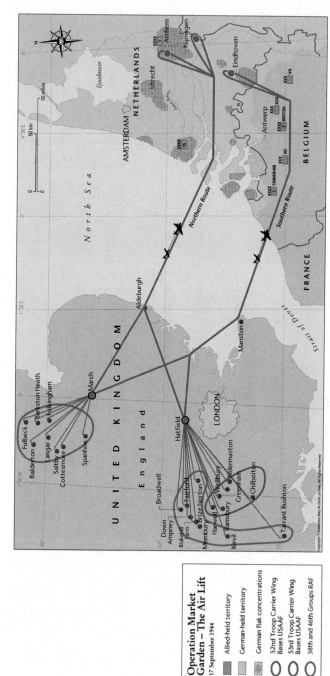

Map 2 Operation Market Garden, the airlift, 17 September 1944.

Map 3 The liberated and occupied areas in early 1945 – urban areas western provinces in darker grey.

Introduction

The Dutch famine of 1944–1945, popularly known in the Netherlands as the 'Hunger Winter', is one of the major European World War II famines and has been central to the Dutch collective memory of the German occupation since the country's liberation in May 1945.[1] The food crisis took place in the urbanised western Netherlands during the final months of the German occupation when the Allies had already liberated the southern part of the country. After November 1944, official daily rations for the once well-nourished Dutch dropped below an already meagre 750 calories per capita, decreasing to less than 370 calories just before the German surrender in May 1945. While the Dutch had also experienced problems with the food supply during the First World War, widespread hunger and famine-related mortality had not reoccurred since the European Potato Failure in the mid-nineteenth century.[2] On the contrary, in the 1940s the Netherlands enjoyed a highly developed economy, modern health care system, and strong civil society: as Stephen Devereux has stated, 'those who suffered during the famine were probably the wealthiest, best educated and most mobile victims of any famine in history'.[3]

Thanks to the advanced registration practices in the Netherlands, the physiological consequences of the famine have been well documented. The Hunger Winter has provided epidemiologists with a unique 'natural experience' to study the long-term effects of prenatal exposure to malnutrition on health in later life and is one of the most important cases for testing the 'fetal origins hypothesis'. Studies on the 'Dutch Hunger Winter Cohort' have revealed that prenatal famine exposure changed

---

[1] For decades, the Hunger Winter featured more prominently in the Dutch collective memory of the German occupation than the Holocaust. David Barnouw, *De Hongerwinter* (Hilversum: Verloren, 1999), 76; Hein A. M. Klemann, 'De Hongerwinter', in *Een Open Zenuw: Hoe Wij Ons de Tweede Wereldoorlog Herinneren*, eds. Madelon de Keizer and Marije Plomp (Amsterdam: Bert Bakker, 2010), 256–264.

[2] Daniel Curtis et al., 'Low Countries', in *Famine in European History*, eds. Guido Alfani and Cormac Ó Gráda (Cambridge: Cambridge University Press, 2017), 123–133.

[3] Stephen Devereux, *Theories of Famine* (New York: Harvester Wheatsheaf, 1993), 159.

the epigenetic profile of the survivors and that those who were born or conceived during the crisis suffer from higher risks for conditions such as obesity, diabetes, and schizophrenia.[4] While the long-term effects of the Hunger Winter were dire, actual casualties in the western Netherlands remained relatively low compared with other famines of the twentieth century, with famine-related mortality among the 2.6 million people who were affected reaching approximately 20,000 in 1944–1945.[5] How, then, did the Dutch survive these famine conditions until liberation in May 1945?

Thus far, no clear answer to this question has been formulated. Indeed, while we continue to learn about the tremendous physiological impact of the Dutch Hunger Winter, much less is known about how and why the famine evolved the way it did. Due to a significant lack of non-Dutch publications on the Hunger Winter, international literature still reproduces profound misunderstandings about the famine, particularly where the role of the German occupier is concerned. For similar reasons, even less is known about the social consequences of the famine and efforts to confront the crisis. This book is the first attempt to fully document these causes and effects of the Dutch famine.

The focus of this book is on the social and political responses to the Dutch famine. While previous studies on the Hunger Winter have generally only considered the role of the failing state and of self-serving individuals, I argue that this orthodox view on food provisioning has overlooked vital forms of societal resilience and agency – actions that played a decisive role in the course and impact of the famine. To correct such myopic understandings, this study considers a wider range of responses by investigating Dutch, German, and Allied state institutions, the affected households, and local communities. By revealing the

---

[4] L. H. Lumey and Frans van Poppel, 'The Dutch Famine of 1944–45 as a Human Laboratory: Changes in the Early Life Environment and Adult Health', in *Early Life Nutrition and Adult Health and Development: Lessons from Changing Dietary Patterns, Famines, and Experimental Studies*, eds. Lumey and Alexander Vaiserman (New York: Nova Science Publishers, 2013), 59–76. These studies are discussed elaborately in Chapter 3.

[5] For example, in occupied Greece in 1941–1944 (±250,000–450,000), besieged Leningrad 1941–1944 (±700,000), and the Warsaw ghetto in 1940–1942 (±58,000–98,000). By comparison, in early 1942 in besieged Leningrad, the same number of deaths was recorded weekly. Violetta Hionidou, *Famine and Death in Occupied Greece, 1941–1944* (Cambridge: Cambridge University Press, 2006), 158; Nadezhda Cherepenina, 'Assessing the Scale of Famine and Death in Besieged Leningrad', in *Life and Death in Besieged Leningrad, 1941–1944*, eds. John Barber and Andrei Dzeniskevich (Basingstoke: Palgrave Macmillan, 2005), 43–44, 62–65; Charles G. Roland, *Courage under Siege: Starvation, Disease, and Death in the Warsaw Ghetto* (Oxford: Oxford University Press, 1992), 98.

interactions among various levels and actors and the effectiveness of their efforts, this book offers a comprehensive and multifaceted view of the socio-political context in which the famine emerged and was confronted.

At the same time, this book also examines the broader question of how a modern society with a highly developed economy such as the Netherlands coped with food shortage and famine. The Hunger Winter provides an excellent case for studying responses to modern war-induced famines in general, not least because of the relative abundance of archival materials left in its wake. By taking a wider comparative view, it identifies important similarities and differences between the Dutch famine and other food crises that occurred in Nazi-occupied Europe, revealing how and why the German occupier found reasons to cooperate and allow relief in the Dutch case. By doing so, this study aims to further our understanding of the hunger politics of Nazi Germany and of the functioning of modern societies facing famine.

Famine as a Weapon in Nazi-Occupied Europe

The Dutch Hunger Winter forms an integral part of the history of Nazi-occupied Europe. Since the 'new imperial turn' in German historiography scholars have begun to view Nazi Germany in the period 1933–1945 as an empire with race, culture, and economics as its defining elements. Although there were great discontinuities with prior 'traditional' German colonialism in Africa, Asia, and the Pacific in the years 1884–1918, its expansionism also showed continuities in terms of the ideology of territorial acquisitions and violent repressive measures, not to mention the resemblances to the attitude and behaviours of other imperial powers such as Great Britain. What set Nazi imperialism apart, however, was its late timing, its fixation on European territories, and, most importantly, its genocidal racial doctrine.[6] Empire and imperialism can be useful categories for thinking about fascism, particularly because they help to frame the relationship between Nazi Germany and the occupied peoples as that of coloniser versus the colonised.

This imperialistic perspective is especially useful when considering the hunger politics pursued by Nazi Germany in its occupied territories. Food became a crucial element in the policies of the Nazi leadership, which connected the constant need for labour with the brutal ideological

---

[6] Uta G. Poiger, 'Imperialism and Empire in Twentieth-Century Germany', *History and Memory* 17 (2005): 117–143; Mark Mazower, *Hitler's Empire: How the Nazis Ruled Europe* (New York: Allen Lane, 2008); Shelly Baranowski, *Nazi Empire: German Colonialism and Imperialism from Bismarck to Hitler* (Cambridge: Cambridge University Press, 2011).

imperative for genocide.[7] Throughout the war, the Nazi agricultural sector struggled to produce ample food to provide adequate rations for German civilians and the *Wehrmacht*. This was exacerbated by the necessity of feeding the growing number of forced labourers with barely enough food to continue productivity for the German war economy.[8] The very inception of the foreign labour programme in the spring of 1940 had also derived from this food conundrum as, with the absence of German farmers, bringing in foreign workers became imperative for the cultivation of the land. At the height of this programme, in the autumn of 1944, the number of forced labourers had grown to an astonishing 7.9 million: equivalent to 20 per cent of the German workforce. At that moment, over 300,000 of them were Dutchmen.[9]

In the pursuit of German '*Lebensraum*' (living space) and agricultural self-sufficiency, Adolf Hitler and the Nazi leadership were convinced that 'useless mouths' needed to be exterminated. In the first weeks of 1941, the Reich Ministry of Food and the *Wehrmacht* agreed on the Hunger Plan, which called for the deliberate starvation of 20–30 million Soviet civilians. However, as war conditions changed over the winter of 1941–1942 and German food supplies dropped to dangerous levels, the Nazi leadership abandoned the impossible plan of killing millions of civilians in Eastern Europe and turned their attention towards the largest coercive labour and genocidal programmes ever seen. In the Nazi empire's quest for food, countries deemed inferior were plundered of their resources, most notably, Ukraine and Poland.[10]

The spring of 1942 saw a return to the principles of the Hunger Plan but now coupled to the programme of racial genocide, beginning with the murder of all Jews in Poland and followed by those of the other occupied countries. In addition to the hundreds of thousands of Jews who starved to death in ghettos and concentration camps, an estimated three million Soviet prisoners of war (POWs) were deliberately starved as

---

[7] Adam Tooze, *The Wages of Destruction: The Making and Breaking of the Nazi Economy* (London: Allen Lane, 2006), 520, 538–539; Gesine Gerhard, *Nazi Hunger Politics: A History of Food in the Third Reich* (Lanham: Rowman & Littlefield, 2015).

[8] Lizzie Collingham, *The Taste of War: World War Two and the Battle for Food* (London: Allen Lane, 2011), 155–164.

[9] Tooze, *The Wages of Destruction*, 517; Ben A. Sijes, *De Arbeidsinzet: De Gedwongen Arbeid van Nederlanders in Duitsland*, 2nd ed. (The Hague: Nijhoff, 1990), 624. Contrary to the situation in other occupied countries, there were hardly any women among these Dutch forced labourers.

[10] Karel C. Berkhoff, *Harvest of Despair: Life and Death in Ukraine under Nazi Rule* (Cambridge, MA: Belknap Press of Harvard University Press, 2004); Martin Winstone, *The Dark Heart of Hitler's Europe: Nazi Rule in Poland under the General Government* (New York: I. B. Tauris & Co. Ltd, 2015).

part of the Nazi famine policies.[11] The central idea was to support only workers who were fundamentally contributing to the economic future of the Third Reich. Also, emerging from this compromise between racial ideology and economic pragmatism was the policy of '*Vernichtung durch Arbeit*' (destruction through labour), which was established in concentration camps from 1942 onward.[12] Food and famine thus became two of Nazi Germany's prime weapons of war and repression in occupied Europe.

The Dutch Hunger Winter has been subsequently regarded by scholars to be the result of similar Nazi hunger politics. Despite Germany's focus on Eastern Europe as a source of plunder, it has been demonstrated that Western Europe contributed more to its wartime food supply than the entire Soviet Union. While the Hunger Winter was the only full-blown famine that struck in Western Europe, in the process of creating a self-sufficient empire, hunger was also exported to countries such as Norway, Belgium, and France by means of exploitation and low rations. Indeed, people across occupied Europe suffered from food shortages; in particular, the famine in occupied Greece in 1941–1944 added substantially to the suffering experienced by the population in Eastern Europe.[13] As Hermann Göring stated in a meeting with the leaders of occupied Europe on 6 August 1942: 'The Fuhrer repeatedly said, and I repeat after him, if anyone has to go hungry, it shall not be the Germans but other peoples.'[14]

---

[11] Gerhard Hirschfeld, 'Chronology of Destruction', in *Policies of Genocide: Jews and Soviet Prisoners of War in Nazi Germany*, ed. Hirschfeld (Boston: Allan & Unwin, 1986), 145–156; Christian Gerlach, *Krieg, Ernährung, Völkermord: Deutsche Vernichtuinspolitiek im Zweiten Weltkrieg* (Zürich: Pendo Verlag, 2001), 154–156; Hirschfeld, 'Food and Genocide: Nazi Agrarian Politics in the Occupied Territories of the Soviet Union', *Contemporary European History* 18 (2009): 45–65; Timothy Snyder, *Bloodlands: Europe between Hitler and Stalin* (London: Vintage, 2011), 162–182; Alex de Waal, *Mass Starvation: The History and Future of Famine* (Cambridge: Polity Press, 2018), 101–105.

[12] Tooze, *The Wages of Destruction*, 513–551; Tooze, 'The Economic History of the Nazi Regime', in *The Short Oxford History of Germany: Nazi Germany*, ed. Jane Caplan (Oxford: Oxford University Press, 2008), 168–195; Nikolaus Wachsmann, *KL: A History of Nazi Concentration Camps* (New York: Farrar, Straus and Giroux, 2015).

[13] Polymeris Voglis, 'Surviving Hunger: Life in the Cities and the Countryside during the Occupation', in *Surviving Hitler and Mussolini: Daily Life in Occupied Europe*, eds. Robert Gildea, Olivier Wieviorka, and Anette Warring (Oxford: Berg, 2006), 16–41; Tatjana Tönsmeyer, 'Supply Situations: National Socialist Policies of Exploitation and Economies of Shortage in Occupied Societies during World War II', in *Coping with Hunger and Shortage under German Occupation in World War II*, eds. Tatjana Tönsmeyer, Peter Haslinger, and Agnes Laba (London: Palgrave Macmillan, 2018), 3–23.

[14] Cited in Collingham, *The Taste of War*, 156.

According to many studies, the Dutch Hunger Winter fits in perfectly with Göring's words. The German occupier allegedly prohibited all food transportation to the western Netherlands from September 1944 onward, thereby deliberately creating the conditions for famine.[15] 'The intention was cynical and brutal – to starve the Dutch into submission', Devereux stated.[16] It has even been assumed that the Germans cut off food supplies as well as all other basic necessities such as gas, electricity, and water in the Netherlands during the final months of war.[17] According to these studies, the Dutch famine was the result of a collective punishment measure by the Nazis that was unique in the Western European context or, as Ian Buruma explained, 'Slavic peoples had been subjected to this treatment, but not Western Europeans'.[18]

In Dutch historiography, these views on the role of the German occupier in the Netherlands were abandoned about three decades ago in favour of a new perspective. Studies have convincingly demonstrated the relatively favourable economic position enjoyed by the 'Germanic' Netherlands in the years 1940–1944 compared to the rest of occupied Europe, which assured that the Dutch diet maintained quantitative and qualitative sufficiency until September 1944.[19] This economic view of the German occupation of the Netherlands also caused a shift in considerations of the causes of the famine. While earlier studies placed the blame on the German occupier, Dutch historiography has negated these assumptions by bringing other contributing factors to the fore; namely, the devastating consequences of the national railway strike, which was instigated by the Dutch government-in-exile in London in September 1944 to support the Allied war effort, and a period of winter frost that lasted from late December 1944 until the end of January 1945. Dutch

[15] E.g., Walter B. Maas, *The Netherlands at War: 1940–1945* (London: Abelard-Schuman, 1970), 205; Wallace R. Aykroyd, *The Conquest of Famine* (London: Chatto & Windus, 1974), 98–103; Zena Stein, Mervyn Susser, and Gerhard Saenger, *Famine and Human Development: The Dutch Hunger Winter of 1944–1945* (New York: Oxford University Press, 1975), 44; Voglis, 'Surviving Hunger', 22; Mazower, *Hitler's Empire*, 280–281; Kevin Lowe, *Savage Continent: Europe in the Aftermath of World War II* (London: Viking, 2012), 34–37.
[16] Devereux, *Theories of Famine*, 160.   [17] Collingham, *The Taste of War*, 176.
[18] Ian Buruma, *Year Zero: A History of 1945* (New York: The Penguin Press, 2013), 54.
[19] J. C. H. Blom, 'Nazificatie en Exploitatie', in *De Organisatie van de Bezetting*, eds. Henk Flap and Wil Arts (Amsterdam, Amsterdam University Press, 1997), 17–30; Gerard M. T. Trienekens, *Tussen ons Volk en de Honger: De Voedselvoorziening 1940–1945* (Utrecht: Stichting Matrijs, 1985), 53–63, 201–202; 409–414; Klemann, *Nederland 1938–1948: Economie en Samenleving in Jaren van Oorlog en Bezetting* (Amsterdam: Boom, 2002). See also: Klemann, 'Did the German Occupation (1940–1945) Ruin Dutch Industry?' *Contemporary European History* 17 (2008): 457–481; Klemann, 'Die niederländische Wirtschaft von 1938 bin 1948 im Griff von Krieg und Besatzung', *Jahrbuch für Wirtschaftsgeschichte* 1 (2001): 53–76.

historians have argued that the government in London 'exacerbated hunger' by refusing to terminate the railway strike that had led to no or minimal gain at the expense of a humanitarian disaster.[20] Some have even stated that, while the German occupation was the underlying cause of the famine, the Dutch railway strike and the failed Allied invasion were the famine's causal triggers.[21]

In this book, I argue that monocausal and highly politicised explanations, focusing on either the German food blockade or the Dutch railway strike, do not do justice to the unfolding of events that eventually led to famine in the occupied western Netherlands. Certainly, the fate of the war was the determining factor – the underlying cause – but the causal triggers of the Dutch famine were much more complex. As Devereux has elegantly phrased it: 'Famines are too complicated to be explained by one single factor.'[22] Understanding famine in the occupied Netherlands, therefore, means examining the context of war and occupation as well as all contributory economic, social, and natural factors. This not only applies for discerning the complex events and interactions that eventually cumulated into famine, but also for determining all political and social efforts that mitigated its effects.

Coping with Hunger and Famine

A new understanding of famine causation in the occupied Netherlands also enables investigation of human behaviour during the crisis. Previous studies have commonly assumed that the Hunger Winter was a period of far-reaching social disintegration, in which most people were left to fend for themselves.[23] Where does this prevailing view come from? And how does this view on Dutch behaviour align with general knowledge of social responses to famine? The central question of this new understanding

---

[20] Trienekens, *Tussen ons Volk en de Honger*, 383; Klemann, *Nederland 1938–1948*, 465–466; Ralf D. Futselaar, *Lard, Lice and Longevity: A Comparative Study on the Standard of Living in Occupied Denmark and the Netherlands, 1940–1945* (Amsterdam: Aksant, 2008), 33.

[21] Chris van der Heijden, *Grijs Verleden: Nederland en de Tweede Wereldoorlog*, 10th ed. (Amsterdam: Olympus, 2009), 316.

[22] Devereux, 'Famine in the Twentieth Century', IDS Working Paper 105 (Brighton: IDS, 2000), 15, 29. See also: Ó Gráda, *Famine: A Short History* (Princeton: Princeton University Press, 2009), 9–13; Robert W. Davies and Stephen G. Wheatcroft, *The Years of Hunger: Soviet Agriculture, 1931–1933* (Basingstoke: Palgrave Macmillan 2004), xiii–xx, 441.

[23] E.g., G. J. Kruijer, *Sociale Desorganisatie. Amsterdam tijdens de Hongerwinter* (Meppel: J. A. Boom & Zoon, 1951); Trienekens, *Tussen ons Volk en de Honger*, 375; Jeroen L. van der Pauw, *Rotterdam in de Tweede Wereldoorlog* (Amsterdam: Boom, 2006), 637; Futselaar, *Lard, Lice and Longevity*, 77–78.

therefore focuses on what people at various levels of society did when faced with the threat of famine. Before discussing this issue further, it is first necessary to clarify some of the terms and concepts central to this study: 'famine', 'food crisis', 'food shortage', 'food poverty', 'food deprivation', 'hunger', and, first of all, 'Hunger Winter'.

The term 'hunger winter' first appeared in Dutch newspapers during the final days of occupation. Around this time, the resistance press used it in a general sense to describe the hardships of previous months: the capitalised name 'Hunger Winter' was actually a post-war construct.[24] In scholarly writings, use of the term is rather ambiguous as historians have used it as both a periodisation, which refers to the last eight months of occupation following the Allied Operation Market Garden (i.e., September 1944–May 1945), and at the same time, as a synonym for 'famine', the exact duration of which commonly remains unmentioned.[25] To exemplify the arbitrary use of the term, the Wikipedia article on the Hunger Winter states that it lasted from November 1944–April 1945, implying that the famine ended before the country was liberated.[26]

Despite its problematic usage, Hunger Winter has become an integral part of Dutch collective memory and popular culture, comparable to 'An Gorta Mór' (1845–1850) in Ireland or 'Holodomor' in Ukraine (1932–1933); thus, its use should not be rejected. In this book, I adopt the popular definition of the term Hunger Winter, which does not align with a defined period or measurable famine but refers to the whole event and all its consequences. In other words, Hunger Winter in this study is used to refer to the food and fuel crisis emerging in the western Netherlands in the autumn of 1944, the circumstances of which eventually led to famine.

Building on seminal studies by Cormac Ó Gráda, Paul Howe, and Stephen Devereux, 'famine' is defined as a shortage of food or purchasing power directly leading to excess mortality from starvation, hunger-induced diseases, and fertility decline. These measurable indicators distinguish famine from a more moderate 'food crisis', in which there are also serious problems with the food supply, but elevated mortality is not necessarily linked to food deprivation. Common symptoms of an 'early-stage famine' (i.e., in cases when food shortages result in

---

[24] See, for example: 'Nogmaals Handhaaft Zelfdiscipline', *De Nieuwe Amsterdammer*, 20 April 1945; 'Nieuwsberichten', *Trouw*, 5 May 1945.

[25] E.g., Henri A. van der Zee, *The Hunger Winter: Occupied Holland 1944–45* (London: Jill Norman & Hobhouse, 1982); Trienekens, *Tussen ons Volk en de Honger*; Devereux, *Theories of Famine*; Barnouw, *De Hongerwinter*; Klemann, *Nederland 1938–1948*; Lowe, *Savage Continent*; Buruma, *1945*.

[26] https://nl.wikipedia.org/wiki/Hongerwinter. Accessed on 13 June 2017.

measurable detrimental effects but supplies are not yet fully depleted) are rising prices, black-market trade, food riots, increase in crimes against property, and rise in temporary migration – all of which are investigated in this book.[27] Examining these indicators provide new insight into the geography and chronology of the Dutch famine, allowing me to place the famine in a prolonged period defined as food crisis.[28] Instead of ending with the liberation of the country in May 1945, as is common in literature on the Hunger Winter, this book focuses on the entire crisis period between the first responses to the impending food crisis in September 1944 and the dismantling of emergency organisations over the summer of 1945. The terms food crisis and famine will be used accordingly to demarcate the difference in food situation in a certain place or time.

Applying the clear definitions provided by Sara Millman and Robert Kates of the three levels at which a scarcity of food may manifest itself, 'food shortage' is defined as the insufficient availability of food within a bounded region: insufficiency being understood as relative to the usual or expected supplies. 'Food poverty' applies to the circumstance in which a certain household cannot obtain enough food to fulfil the nutritional needs of all members of the household – the smallest organisational unit within which individuals routinely share food. At the lowest level, 'food deprivation' refers to the inadequacy of individual food intake to satisfy individual needs. A clear distinction among these three levels is imperative; for example, it is perfectly possible for a household coping with food poverty to have some of its members living in food deprivation while others do not, or alternately, for food poverty to occur in a society without food shortage.[29] At each of these levels of aggregation, factors other than actual scarcity can also operate, such as conflict and competition or shifts in the distribution of rights to food: the so-called entitlements. As will be explained later, it was the entitlements that ultimately determined which groups or individuals were most affected by the food shortage.

Following these more or less measurable qualifications, 'hunger' is probably the most difficult concept to define. Generally, hunger refers

---

[27] Paul Howe and Devereux, 'Famine Intensity and Magnitude Scales: A Proposal for an Instrumental Definition of Famine', *Disasters* 28 (2004): 353–372; Devereux, 'Famine in the Twentieth Century', 4; Ó Gradá, *Famine*, 3–6.

[28] Hionidou argues the same for the food crisis and famine in occupied Greece. Hionidou, *Famine and Death in Occupied Greece*, 32–33.

[29] Sara Millman and Robert W. Kates, 'Towards Understanding Hunger', in *Hunger in History: Food Shortage, Poverty and Deprivation*, ed. Lucile F. Newman (Cambridge: Cambridge University Press, 1990), 11–15. An excellent study on household inequality in times of food shortage is: Jeremy Lise and Shannon Seitz, 'Consumption Inequality and Intra-Household Allocations', *Review of Economic Studies* 78 (2011): 328–355.

to physiological, quantitative malnutrition: the inadequacy in individual dietary food intake relative to the kind and quantity of food required for growth, physical and mental activity, and for the maintenance of good health: such a definition makes the term synonymous to food deprivation.[30] Similar to the latter, hunger is, by definition, individual and independent of larger social units. While this physiological hunger is difficult to measure, psychological hunger or 'feeling hungry' is impossible to calculate.[31] Yet both the physiological and the psychological aspects of hunger can be determinants of human behaviour. As this book focuses on responses to the famine, it is imperative not to define hunger in only a narrow, physiological way. Therefore, this study's definition of hunger includes all psychological experiences and social behaviour in relation to food deprivation.

If we consider what historians have argued about social behaviour during the Dutch famine, it seems as if hunger dissolved virtually all expressions of solidarity and sense of community. While early post-war studies had noticed the resilience of civil society during the famine,[32] community responses have been largely overlooked in most later historical studies on the Dutch wartime food supply. Indeed, studies on the Hunger Winter have generally stressed that the collapse of central food rationing caused society to disintegrate by provoking self-preserving behaviour among the population.[33] After September 1944, ordered society is said to have disappeared and neither the authority of resistance

---

[30] Millman and Kates, 'Towards Understanding Hunger', 3.

[31] Futselaar, *Lard, Lice and Longevity*, 204–223; Ann G. Carmichael, 'Infection, Hidden Hunger and History', in *Hunger in History: The Impact of Changing Food Production and Consumption Patterns on Society*, eds. Robert I. Rotberg and Theodore K. Rabb (Cambridge: Cambridge University Press, 1983), 51–68.

[32] Cornelis Banning, 'Food Shortage and Public Health, First Half of 1945', *Annals of the American Academy for Political and Social Sciences* 245 (1946): 94–95. See also: Banning, 'De Gezondheidstoestand in Nederland: De Algemeene Sterfte en Sterfte door Verhongering', *Nederlandsch Tijdschrift voor Geneeskunde* XXVII (1945): 311–315; Banning, 'Voeding en Voedingstoestand', in *Medische Ervaringen in Nederland tijdens de Bezetting, 1940–1945*, ed. Ite Boerema (Groningen: Wolters, 1947), 235–267; Jan M. Romein, 'The Spirit of the Dutch People during the Occupation', *Annals of the American Academy of Political and Social Science* 245 (1946): 177; George C. E. Burger et al., eds., *Malnutrition and Starvation in Western Netherlands: September 1944–July 1945*, part I (The Hague: General State Printing Office, 1948), 21–22. The most elaborate exposition of community responses to the famine can be found in De Jong, although he only listed some of these efforts anecdotally, thereby refraining from interpretation. Loe de Jong, *Het Koninkrijk der Nederlanden in de Tweede Wereldoorlog*, 10b (The Hague: Martinus Nijhoff, 1981), 231–234.

[33] Kruijer, *Sociale Desorganisatie*, 52–59; Van der Zee, *De Hongerwinter*, 56–57; Trienekens, *Tussen ons Volk en de Honger*, 381; Trienekens, *Voedsel en Honger in Oorlogstijd 1940–1945: Misleiding, Mythe en Werkelijkheid* (Utrecht: Kosmos Z & K, 1995), 104; Barnouw, *De Hongerwinter*, 48–50; Bart van der Boom, *Den Haag in de Tweede*

groups nor the churches – not even the Dutch government-in-exile – was capable of controlling the situation.[34] The basic assumption has been that, when the state failed to allocate food at subsistence level, civil society proved incapable of maintaining social cohesion. Following the same line of reasoning, the only significant famine relief reaching the starving Dutch during the crisis was sent by external and state actors – the International Committee of the Red Cross (ICRC) and, significantly, the Allies in the final days before liberation.

This common characterisation of the Dutch famine as a period of far-reaching social disintegration seems especially odd when taking into account the general knowledge about social behaviour during famines. Following pioneering studies such as the Minnesota Semi-Starvation Experiment (1944–1945) and the General Adaptation Syndrome study of the human body's reaction to stress (1950s), social scientists have identified generalisable patterns and sequences in the adaptation of famine coping strategies.[35] Generally speaking, in the first stages of famine, most people display a hyper-activation and intensified inter-action with others in virtually every sphere; in the second stage, increasing energy deficits force a decrease in activity and social ties begin to erode; in the final stage, only personal survival comes first. In other words, a shift occurs from a social orientation to individual needs as food deprivation persists.[36] This last stage of famine is what Pitrim Sorokin has famously described as the 'evaporation' of normal rationality and sociability under the stress of hunger.[37]

Was the Dutch famine truly such an extreme, long-lasting famine, in which solidarity and sense of community 'evaporated'? In this book,

Wereldoorlog (Den Haag: Seapress, 1995), 231; Van der Heijden, *Grijs Verleden*, 320; Klemann, *Nederland 1939–1948*, 561; Futselaar, *Lard, Lice and Longevity*, 77–78.

[34] Klemann, *Nederland 1938–1948*, 561.

[35] Ancel Keys et al., *The Biology of Human Starvation*, 2 vols. (Minneapolis: s.n., 1950); Hans Seyle, *The Stress of Life* (New York: McGraw-Hill, 1956).

[36] Derrick B. Jelliffe and Eleanor F. Patrice Jelliffe, 'The Effects of Starvation on the Function of the Family and of Society', in *Famine: A Symposium Dealing with Nutrition and Relief Operations in Times of Disaster*, eds. Gunnar Blix, Yngve Hofvander, and Bo Vahlquist (Upsala: The Swedish Nutrition Foundation, 1971), 58; Robert Dirks, 'Social Responses during Severe Food Shortages and Famine', *Current Anthropology* 21 (1980): 21–43; R. Brooke Thomas, Sabrina H. B. H. Paine, and Barrett P. Brento, 'Perspectives on Socio-Economic Causes of and Responses to Food Deprivation', *Food & Nutrition Bulletin* 11 (1989): 41–54.

[37] Pitrim A. Sorokin, *Hunger as a Factor in Human Affairs* (Gainesville: University Presses of Florida, 1975). See also: Sorokin, *Man and Society in Calamity: The Effects of War, Revolution, Famine, Pestilence upon Human Mind, Behavior, Social Organization and Cultural Life*, 4th ed. (New York: E. P. Dutton & Co., 1946).

I first investigate the scope and intensity of the famine, which provides the necessary background for examining responses to the crisis. If the Hunger Winter was not an extreme-stage famine, but rather an early-stage one, then societal resilience should logically be considered when examining coping strategies during the famine. All food crises challenge social structures by eroding hospitality, solidarity, and community, but they can also bring out the best in people. Stories about charitable relief efforts and local self-help entities in times of widespread hunger are as numerous as their negative counterparts.[38] These communal coping strategies and mutual support networks have indeed been the subject of many studies on pre-modern and modern famines alike, most notably following E. P. Thompson's famously coined concept of the 'moral economy'.[39] Recently, the focus in World War II studies has also begun to shift from policies of exploitation to self-organisation and collective coping strategies.[40] This scholarly consensus about reciprocity and cooperation as acknowledged coping strategies in the early phases of famine accentuates the importance of reintegrating community responses into the history of the Hunger Winter.

Vulnerability and Resilience

The relevance of investigating responses to the famine lies not only in ascertaining the mechanisms of policy-making and human behaviour but also in revealing the efficacy of various actions. It has been demonstrated that, in times of famine, death and survival are always partly biologically determined and partly the result of social processes operating at different levels of society. From state to household levels, human actions

---

[38] Ó Gráda, *Famine*, 47–48.

[39] Most importantly: E. P. Thompson, 'The Moral Economy of the English Crowd in Eighteenth Century', *Past & Present* 50 (1971): 76–136; James C. Scott, *The Moral Economy of the Peasant: Rebellion and Subsistence in Southeast Asia* (New Haven, Yale University Press, 1976); David Arnold, *Famine: Social Crisis and Historical Change* (Oxford: Blackwell, 1988), 73–86; Eric Vanhaute and Thijs Lambrecht, 'Famine, Exchange Networks and the Village Community: A Comparative Analysis of the Subsistence Crises of the 1740s and 1840s in Flanders', *Continuity and Change* 26 (2011): 155–186; Thierry Bonzon and Belinda Davies, 'Feeding the Cities', in *Capital Cities at War: London, Paris, Berlin 1914–1919*, eds. Jay Winter and Jean-Louis Robert (Cambridge: Cambridge University Press, 1997), 309. On African famines and communal coping, a special issue of *IDS* was dedicated in 1993: Jeremy Swift, 'Understanding and Preventing Famine and Famine Mortality', *IDS Bulletin* 24 (1993): 1–15; Alayne Adams, 'Food Insecurity in Mali: Exploring the Role of the Moral Economy', *IDS Bulletin* 24 (1993): 41–45.

[40] Tönsmeyer et al., eds., *Coping with Hunger and Shortage under German Occupation*.

ultimately determine how available food resources are divided.[41] In compliance with these observations, this book also relates to the connection between responses to famine and their measurable impact. This enquiry requires an examination of all formal and informal food distribution systems – not just at state and individual levels, but incorporating community efforts operating between these levels as well.

The association between social relations and vulnerability to famine correlates with the 'entitlements theory' coined by economist and philosopher Amartya Sen. Until the late 1970s, the dominant view on famine causation was still very much in line with Thomas Malthus's *Essay on the Principle of Population* (1798). In this famous essay, Malthus argued that population increase is limited by natural resources and that famine is nature's intervention mechanism to regulate population growth and balance the demand for food with available supplies.[42] Sen has challenged this view of famine as an event triggered by food availability decline (FAD). A paradigm shift occurred after the publication of *Poverty and Famines* (1981), in which Sen demonstrated that historical famines were not always triggered by FAD but could also be the result of market failures. His 'entitlement approach' showed the inability of certain groups of people to command enough food for subsistence, irrespective of food availability. In his theory, Sen distinguished four legal ways of acquiring food: production, trade, labour, and gifts or transfers. Accordingly, individuals and households face starvation when their specific entitlement set fails to provide them with adequate access to food.[43]

While Sen's study has been challenged for his empirical basis as well as for his rejection of the FAD approach,[44] his reconceptualisation of the nature of famine has been widely acknowledged. The Dutch Hunger Winter has also been considered to accord with the entitlement approach, which has led to the hypothesis that people who only held buying entitlements (i.e., official rations) were most likely to succumb

---

[41] Joan P. W. Rivers, 'The Nutritional Biology of Famine', in *Famine*, ed. Geoffrey A. Harrison (Oxford: Oxford University Press, 1988), 92–93; George Kent, *The Politics of Children's Survival* (New York: Praeger, 1991), 2–3.

[42] Thomas Malthus, *An Essay on the Principle of Population, as It Affects the Future Improvement of Society* (London: J. Johnson, 1798).

[43] Amartya Sen, *Poverty and Famines* (Oxford: Clarendon Press, 1981). See also: Sen, 'Starvation and Exchange Entitlements: A General Approach and Its Application to the Great Bengal Famine', *Cambridge Journal of Economics* 1 (1977): 33–59. Another influential study approaching famine as market failures is: Martin Ravallion, *Markets and Famines* (Oxford: Clarendon Press, 1987).

[44] Devereux, 'Famine in the Twentieth Century', 9, 20; Devereux, 'Sen's Entitlement Approach: Critiques and Counter-Critiques', *Oxford Development Studies* 29 (2001): 245–263; Meghnad Desai, 'The Economics of Famine', in *Famine*, 112–114.

first.[45] Because the entitlement theory includes the legal and moral framework upon which distributive networks rest, the approach is a useful tool. It tells us that vulnerability can be seen as the socio-economic space that is delineated by three domains: market disturbances, coping thresholds, and social security limitations.[46] However, the essentially economic theory primarily explains how certain groups of people fail to acquire sufficient food supplies. By examining the underlying mechanisms and strategies at various levels of society this study aims to add why this distribution was organised in particular ways as well.

In this book, I assess responses to the famine from the household to the international level. Not only politics, but social relations, culture, and institutions should be taken into account when investigating famine responses. As Ó Gráda has argued: 'Effective and compassionate governance might lead to competitive markets, sanctions against corruption, and well-directed relief. Healthy endowments of social capital might mean less crime, and a greater willingness to help one's neighbour or community.'[47] In light of these words, one might ask: How did various actors involved in the crisis respond to the food shortage? Who benefited from these efforts and which groups of people were left out? How was the effectiveness of various applied strategies perceived and measured, and how did they adapt in the course of the famine? In order to investigate these challenging and fundamental questions about the impact and effectiveness of famine responses, this book includes the famine's demographic impact, revealing which groups of people were most and least affected physiologically by the conditions. These quantitative observations provide the background against which the qualitative investigation into social and political responses to the famine can be considered.

A New Perspective

While the vast amount of studies on the long-term consequences of the Dutch Hunger Winter continues to add to our understanding of the physiological impact of the famine, much remains unknown about how the crisis unfolded the way it did. Seventy-five years after the end of

---

[45] Futselaar, *Lard, Lice and Longevity*, 77–78.

[46] Michael J. Watts and Hans G. Bohle, 'Hunger, Famine and the Space of Vulnerability', *GeoJournal* 30 (1993): 119.

[47] Ó Gradá, *Famine*, 13. Fiona Watson's chapter on why no famine struck in besieged areas of Bosnia in the years 1992–1995 is a good example of this approach. Fiona Watson, 'Why are There no Longer "War Famines" in Contemporary Europe? Bosnia Besieged, 1992–1995', in *The New Famines: Why Famines Persist in an Era of Globalization*, ed. Devereux (London: Routledge, 2007), 269–289.

World War II, this question is in urgent need of reconsideration. In this book, I examine the causes and measurable effects of the famine as well as the efforts of households, communities, and state institutions to fight these famine conditions during the final months of the German occupation. In doing so, I propose a shift from a monocausal explanatory framework to one that reveals the multiple dimensions of the famine, thereby enhancing our understanding of German occupation policies during World War II and of modern famines in general.

In exploring this new perspective, this study builds on the vast literature that regards food politics not as a top-down process, but views consumers and civil society as active players in the food system.[48] Understanding these responses also means understanding the dynamics of the occupational regime, and recognition of the complexities that characterised the relationships among the occupiers, populations, and liberators in wartime and the direct post-war period. The concept of 'legitimacy' provides a valuable means of approaching these complexities of interaction, which is understood as the informal set of values that exists within political cultures and dynamically shapes rulers and ruled alike.[49] This approach allows for examining how notions of what constituted legitimate government influenced the ways in which political actors, individuals, and communities responded to the famine conditions, and how these responses in their turn shaped political and social environments.

The issues this study aims to address require a wide variety of sources. To reveal decision-making at the international and national level, I have consulted archival documents from the NIOD Institute for War, Holocaust and Genocide Studies, the National Archives in The Hague, the National Archives in Kew, London, the National Archives and Records Administration in College Park, Maryland, the United Nations Archives and Records Centre in New York City, and the Bundesarchiv in Berlin-Lichterfelde. To reveal community responses, I have consulted local archives located throughout the Netherlands. For the investigation of household and individual coping strategies, ego documents such as

---

[48] E.g., Frank Trentmann and Flemming Just, 'Introduction', in *Food and Conflict in Europe in the Age of the Two World Wars*, eds. Trentmann and Just (Basingstoke: Palgrave Macmillan, 2006), 2; Liz Young, 'World Hunger: A Framework for Analysis', *Geography* 81 (1996): 97–100; Antoon Vrints, 'Alles is Van Ons: Anonieme Brieven over de Voedselvoorziening in Nederland tijdens de Tweede Wereldoorlog', *BMGN-Low Countries Historical Review* 126 (2011): 25–51; Bonzon and Davies, 'Feeding the Cities'.

[49] Martin Conway and Peter Romijn, 'Political Legitimacy in Mid-Twentieth-Century Europe: An Introduction', in *The War for Legitimacy in Politics and Culture, 1936–1946*, eds. Conway and Romijn (Oxford and New York: Berg, 2008), 1–27.

diaries, memoires, and correspondence materials have also made a vital contribution. Materials from private collections, graciously lent to me by people who have experienced the famine first hand, have also been of crucial value, bringing an indispensable personal dimension to this study. Although I have chosen not to use oral history materials systematically for reasons of feasibility and reliability, the conversations I shared with survivors have greatly added to the focus of my study. Finally, thanks to the Netherlands Interdisciplinary Demographic Institute, I have also examined demographic data, enabling me to answer crucial questions about the specifics of death and survival during the Hunger Winter.

The book is divided into eight chapters. The specific order reflects current explanatory models that solely focus on the role of the state and the individual, revealing the lacuna in historiography by not including community responses in the analyses. Chapter 1 situates the crisis in its historical context and gives an essential background to the most important events during the German occupation of the Netherlands prior to the famine. Chapter 2 investigates the causes of the famine and development of the crisis. Chapter 3 is devoted to the famine's demographic impact; most notably, mortality, fertility, and the long-term physiological effects. The government policies on the central level by the Dutch food administration and German civil authorities are central to Chapter 4. Chapter 5 takes state intervention to a higher level by exploring the politics and practices of Allied relief. Chapter 6 zooms in on individual and household coping strategies and investigates important famine markers such as crime, black-market trade, food expeditions, and the hunt for fuel. The final two chapters investigate community responses to the crisis. Chapter 7 provides a detailed account of the emergence of local self-help entities, the constitution of the main NGO during the famine, local child-feeding initiatives as well as women's food protests. Chapter 8 investigates the evacuation of Dutch children out of the famine-affected areas, providing a case in point for the positive outcomes of community efforts in the face of disaster.

With these explorations, I hope this book contributes to a new understanding of the Dutch Hunger Winter and provides insight into the strategies and coping mechanisms of a modern society facing catastrophe.

1   Historical Contexts

The Netherlands before the German Occupation

For the historical contexts of the Dutch wartime food supply, we must go back in history to the beginning of the evolution of the agricultural sector in the second half of the nineteenth century. Following the globalisation of the food industry, the Netherlands became a highly specialised food exporting country. The Dutch agricultural sector relied heavily on the import of cereals, fertiliser, and fodder while exporting high value-added horticultural, arable (to be processed), and animal products. After initial successes on the international market, the Netherlands suffered a major agricultural crisis in the years 1878–1895, which led the Dutch to reconsider their agricultural position. The Dutch government began to invest in agricultural training and introduced protective legislation for export products, but farmers could count on limited financial state support. As a result, agricultural organisations institutionalised and professionalised rapidly during the crisis. New developments in water management and fertilisers contributed considerably to the sector's recovery, as did the introduction of new feed grains and other feed concentrates. The establishment of agricultural cooperatives, enabling farmers to get better prices for their products and giving them access to new technology and knowledge, similarly played a pivotal role in this Dutch agricultural transition.[1]

The highly specialised and import-dependent Dutch agricultural sector, however, made the country vulnerable to worldwide crises, as became apparent during the First World War.[2] While the Netherlands remained neutral throughout the war, its economy and agriculture

---

[1] Paul Brassley, 'Food Production and Food Processing in Western Europe, 1850–1990', in *Exploring the Food Chain: Food Production and Food Processing in Western Europe, 1850–1990*, eds. Yves Segers, Jan Bieleman, and Erik Buyst (Turnhout: Brepols Publishers, 2009), 283; Bieleman, *Boeren in Nederland: Geschiedenis van de Landbouw 1500–2000* (Amsterdam: Boom, 2008), 30–32, 271–287.

[2] Trienekens, *Tussen ons Volk en de Honger*, 1.

suffered heavily from the increased export demands from the belligerent states. The dire threat the British and German exports posed to domestic supplies finally forced the Dutch government to become involved in the agricultural sector. The government introduced price ceilings and established export rules and permits, but was able to leave the executive tasks largely to private commissions. However, by mid-1916, it became clear that a centralised approach was impossible to circumvent. In August 1916, the state rather reluctantly designed a Rationing Law, which became the legal basis for the first nationwide rationing system.[3] In 1917, the already difficult food position in the Netherlands was further aggravated by the German unrestricted submarine warfare obstructing imports. The import of cereals, fodder, coal, and fertiliser almost came to a complete standstill; meanwhile, the country was simultaneously dealing with more than 100,000 refugees.[4] In the end, the war circumstances led to a full-fledged command economy with production arrangements, food rationing, and price regulations, which together only just averted a severe food crisis like the one experienced in neighbouring Belgium.[5]

The end of the war would usher in a period of overproduction and price fall. While the Dutch government was still reluctant to interfere in agricultural affairs, the competition on the European market and withdrawal of German demand, combined with extremely low wages, eventually forced governmental agencies to intervene again. From the late 1920s onward, the state set up financial support programmes for farmers in sectors that were making a loss: a rescue policy that was followed by the introduction of protectionist legislation covering almost all sectors of agricultural production. In order to coordinate the new legislation, the Dutch government introduced an Agricultural Crisis Law in May 1933, which was implemented in July 1934. This law authorised ministers to regulate food prices and quality, transportation, as well as inspection and disciplinary action. To the farmers' dismay, individual freedom of

---

[3] Dirk H. Peereboom Voller, *Distributiewetgeving in Nederland* (Groningen: Rijksuniversiteit Groningen, 1945); Maartje Abbenhuis-Ash, *The Art of Staying Neutral: The Netherlands in the First World War, 1914–1918* (Amsterdam: Amsterdam University Press, 2006), 187–189; Thimo de Nijs, 'Food Provision and Food Retailing in The Hague, 1914–1930', in *Food and Conflict in Europe*; Samuël F. Kruizinga, *Overlegeconomie in Oorlogstijd: De Nederlandse Overzee Trustmaatschappij en de Eerste Wereldoorlog* (Zuthpen: Walburg Press, 2012), 107–203.

[4] Evelyn U. de Roodt, *Oorlogsgasten: Vluchtelingen en Krijgsgevangenen in Nederland tijdens de Eerste Wereldoorlog* (Zaltbommel: Europese Bibliotheek, 2000), 137–210; Abbenhuis-Ash, *The Art of Staying Neutral*, 304.

[5] Marie W. F. Treub, *Herinneringen en Overpeinzingen* (Haarlem: H. D. Tjeenk Willink & Zoon NV, 1931), 320; Kruizinga, *Overlegeconomie in Oorlogstijd*, 251–255. Giselle Nath, *Brood Willen we Hebben! Honger, Sociale Politiek en Protest tijdens de Eerste Wereldoorlog in België* (Antwerpen: Manteau, 2013).

economic trade was once again replaced by – according to them – a not very successful command economy.[6]

By 1937, the Netherlands had overcome the agricultural crisis, giving Dutch administrators just sufficient room to prepare for yet another war. The Dutch population had grown during the interwar years from 6.5 to 8.7 million, making the Netherlands one of the most densely populated countries in Western Europe. About half of this number lived in the three western provinces of North Holland, South Holland, and Utrecht: the largest conurbations were also located in these provinces.[7] The country simultaneously upheld one of the highest standards of living with an average working-class diet in 1936 consisting of approximately 3,000 kcal daily per capita. At the same time, arable land had increased by only 7 per cent, which also meant that agricultural production lagged behind the rapid population growth.[8]

Since the Netherlands was still anything but self-sufficient, these numbers were the cause of much concern to government administrations. That same year, Minister of Economic Affairs Maximilien Steenberghe established the Directorate for the Preparation of the Food Supply during Wartime (*Rijksbureau voor de Voorbereiding van de Voedselvoorziening in Oorlogstijd*: RBVVVO). This new body was placed under the direction of agricultural engineer Stephanus L. Louwes, who belonged to an old-established family of gentleman-farmers and had been involved in the agricultural crisis politics since the 1920s.[9] The first objective of Louwes's RBVVVO was to shape an organisation that could regulate and control the food system from production to allocation; the second was to accumulate food stocks that could cover the period in which Dutch agriculture had to transition to self-sufficiency.

The new rationing system had to be substantially different from the previous one for several interrelated reasons. After the implementation of the 1916 Rationing Law, the Dutch government had acted as the main

---

[6] Bieleman, *Boeren in Nederland*, 290–294; Hilde Krips-van der Laan, *Praktijk als Antwoord: S. L. Louwes en het Landbouwcrisisbeleid*, Historia Agriculturae XVI (Groningen: Nederlands Agronomisch-Historisch Instituut, 1985), 40–48; Krips-van der Laan, 'Honderd Jaar Landbouwgeschiedenis 1880-1980', *Kleio-Didactica* 29 (1994): 21.

[7] In 1930, over 65 per cent of the Dutch population lived in urban areas, making the Netherlands a strongly urbanised country. Jan Bank and Maarten van Buuren, *1900: Hoogtij van Burgerlijke Cultuur, Nederlandse Cultuur in Europese Context* (The Hague: Sdu Publishers, 2000), 133.

[8] Trienekens, *Tussen ons Volk en de Honger*, 2; Futselaar, *Lard, Lice, and Longevity*, 81.

[9] Stephanus L. Louwes, 'De Voedselvoorziening', in *Onderdrukking en Verzet* II, ed. Johannes J. van Bolhuis (Arnhem: Van Loghum Slaterus, 1950), 607–608; Krips-van der Laan, *S. L. Louwes en het Landbouwcrisisbeleid*, 13–22, 35–39; Trienekens, *Tussen ons Volk en de Honger*, 10–12.

buyer and distributor of foodstuffs. Inexperienced and dissatisfied with these tasks, the Dutch government's rationing system became highly bureaucratic. Moreover, the malfunctioning system led to extremely high costs and prices, which had a destructive effect on trade and businesses.[10] Therefore, in the new system, the government would play a regulatory role only, while the different agricultural sectors would be allowed to manage the production of their foodstuffs themselves. Official legislation would ensure full documentation of rules and regulations, thereby mitigating unrest and corruption. According to Louwes, who was a highly esteemed member of the agricultural community, it was of the utmost importance that farmers should cooperate voluntarily: the new system had to be based on mutual trust, not force.[11] The foundation for this preparatory work was the 1933 Agricultural Crisis Law and the ensuing complex Agricultural Crisis apparatus. By September 1938, an impressive nine agricultural emergency acts had come into force, including a new Rationing Law.[12]

Parallel with the mobilisation of the Dutch armed forces at the outbreak of the Second World War, preparations for food supply were put into effect in late 1939. One of the first measures taken was the introduction of a rationing scheme that redirected the consumption of fodder to protect much-needed cereals. Regulations for production and distribution were not yet necessary; nonetheless, the rationing system consolidated by constituting a Central Rationing Office (*Centraal Distributiekantoor*: CDK), dividing the country into rationing districts, and by distributing the first ration cards among the population. Another important measure concerned state requisitioning of private stocks from importers and factories, by which means reserves of cereals, fodder, and oils from imports could be stockpiled. A national rationing scheme was also put into effect, even though this was initiated more as a trial than as a consequence of actual scarcity. On 12 October 1939, sugar became the first product 'on a stamp'. In the months that followed, the German

---

[10] Kruizinga, '"Heere God! Straf Posthema!" F. E. Posthuma (1874–1943)', in *Nederland Neutraal: De Eerste Wereldoorlog 1914–1918*, eds. Wim Klinkert, Kruizinga, and Paul Moeyes (Amsterdam: Boom, 2014), 242–279; Trienekens, *Tussen ons Volk en de Honger*, 15–16.

[11] Krips-van der Laan, *S. L. Louwes en het Landbouwcrisisbeleid*, 68–69; Trienekens, *Tussen ons Volk en de Honger*, 15.

[12] National Archives The Hague [NA], 2.21.238 Archief S. L. Louwes, inv.no. 117, Report by Louwes on his policies during the German occupation, 1945, 1; M. J. L. Dols and D. J. A. M. van Arcken, 'Food Supply and Nutrition in the Netherlands during and immediately after World War II', *The Milbank Memorial Fund Quarterly* 24 (1946): 326; Louwes, 'De Voedselvoorziening', 608; Trienekens, *Tussen ons Volk en de Honger*, 18–24. The Rationing Law was reinforced in 1939.

Wehrmacht conquered Poland, Norway, and Denmark, pressuring the Dutch government to accelerate measures concerning the food supply with successful results. By the time Germany invaded the Netherlands in May 1940, the rationing system had already been fully developed and tested.[13]

Occupation and the New Balance of Power

On 10 May 1940, Germany attacked the Netherlands. That early morning, the German *Luftwaffe* bombed the country's military airfields, followed by airborne landings near The Hague, Rotterdam, and Moerdijk. The German ground force led by Field Marshal Fedor von Bock simultaneously invaded the Netherlands from the east. As part of *Fall Gelb*, Belgium, France, and Luxembourg were attacked that very same day (see Map 1).[14] Realising that their position in the Netherlands would be severely endangered, on 13 May, Queen Wilhelmina and the Dutch cabinet fled to London, where they would function as a government-in-exile until the spring of 1945. State authority was transferred to commander-in-chief of the Dutch armed forces, General Henri Winkelman. Winkelman's poorly equipped army of about 280,000 men was quickly outnumbered. On 14 May, Germany crushed the last Dutch resistance by bombing the inner city of Rotterdam, killing 850 civilians.[15] The next day, after only five days of war, General Winkelman was forced to sign the instrument of surrender.

Three days after Dutch surrender, Hitler signed a decree that appointed the occupied Netherlands with a German civil administration. The decision to install a civil administration resulted from both military and ideological considerations. A military administration was installed in occupied Belgium because of the strategic value of the Belgian coastline. The Netherlands, on the other hand, was considered less strategically important but had considerably greater ideological potential for Nazi Germany. The Nazi leadership contemplated incorporating the 'Germanic' Dutch into the Third Reich and, to achieve this goal, a period of education and Nazification under German supervision would be

---

[13] Dols and Van Arcken, 'Food Supply and Nutrition', 326; Louwes, 'De Voedselvoorziening', 610, 622; Trienekens, *Tussen ons Volk en de Honger*, 26, 41–42.

[14] For an extensive overview of the five days of war in the Netherlands in May 1940: Herman Amersfoort and Piet Kamphuis, eds., *Mei 1940: De Strijd op Nederlands Grondgebied*, 4th ed. (Amsterdam: Boom, 2012).

[15] Van der Pauw, *Rotterdam in de Tweede Wereldoorlog*, 84–89; Susan Hogervorst and Patricia van Ulzen, *Rotterdam en het Bombardement: 75 Jaar Herinneren en Vergeten* (Amsterdam: Boom, 2015).

imperative.[16] On 29 May 1940, the Austrian lawyer and Nazi politician Arthur Seyss-Inquart was inaugurated as the country's *Reichskommissar,* who was to function as the highest civil administrator with support of his own government and German police and judicial institutions. These German institutions would operate parallel to, and in command of, Dutch police and justice services. *General der Flieger* Friedrich Christiansen was appointed as *Wehrmachtbefehlshaber* alongside Seyss-Inquart for all affairs relating to war and defence. He would also be authorised to issue measures with the force of law, if deemed necessary for the execution of his military tasks or for the 'military safety' in the Netherlands.[17]

Seyss-Inquart, who was mockingly referred to by the Dutch as '*zes-en-een-kwart*' (six and a quarter), for his limping and as a play on his name, was given the order to treat the Dutch carefully and correctly, in line with Nazi Germany's ideological and economic objectives in the country. He received two specific instructions from Hitler: not to let the living standard in the Netherlands drop below German levels and to merge Dutch industry with the German war economy. According to Hitler, the Dutch needed to be won over by National Socialism so that they would voluntarily restructure society along ideological lines, which shows the relatively 'privileged' position the supposedly 'Aryan' Dutch were given by the Nazi leadership among the occupied people of Europe.[18]

The German civil administration in the occupied Netherlands was relatively small and its main function was supervisory. The day-to-day running of the country remained in the hands of Dutch civil servants, directed by Dutch secretary generals of the former ministries, who had been instructed to stay in office in the event of a military defeat and occupation as long as this benefitted the Dutch population more than the occupying regime.[19] The occupying authorities gave the secretary

---

[16] Bob Moore, 'The Netherlands, 1940-45', in *The Civilian in War: Occupation and the Home Front in World War II,* ed. Jeremy Noakes (Exeter: Exeter University Press, 1992), 129.

[17] Jennifer L. Foray, 'The "Clean *Wehrmacht*" in the German-Occupied Netherlands, 1940–5', *Journal of Contemporary History* 45 (2010): 769.

[18] De Jong, *Het Koninkrijk* 4 (The Hague: Martinus Nijhoff, 1972), 46–104; Piet de Rooy, *Republiek van Rivaliteiten: Nederland sinds 1813* (Amsterdam: Mets & Schilt, 2002), 197–198; Johannes Koll, *Arthur Seyss-Inquart und die deutsche Besatzungspolitik in den Niederlanden 1940–1945* (Vienna: Böhlau Verlag, 2015). Occupied Norway was also appointed a civil administration, albeit with considerable differences: Richard Petrow, *The Bitter Years: The Invasion and Occupation of Denmark and Norway, April 1940–May 1945* (New York: Morrow, 1974), 102–117.

[19] Trienekens, 'The Food Supply in The Netherlands during the Second World War', in *Food, Science, Policy and Regulation in the Twentieth Century: International and Comparative Perspectives,* eds. David F. Smith and Jim Phillips (London: Routledge, 2000), 118;

generals increased control over the lower administrative echelons, as well as the veto right, and the force of law, albeit under German super-vision.[20] These supervising tasks were placed under four German *Generalkommissare* (general commissioners) who were simultaneously representatives of the occupying regime and head of their own depart-ments.[21] By 1941, Seyss-Inquart's Reich Commissariat employed about 1,600 workers, civil servants, and office personnel, not including members of German police and other security services.[22]

In compliance with Hitler's orders, the German authorities' main priority in the occupied Netherlands was exploitation of its economy, technology, and, eventually, colonies.[23] These priorities differed greatly from those in the eastern occupied territories. As Voglis has explained: 'In Western Europe the German policy aimed at maintenance and adjustment of the pre-war structures to the new needs with a view of rationally exploiting the resources, whereas in Eastern and southeastern Europe the Nazi policy consisted of requisitions of the agricultural pro-duction and raw materials.'[24] As part of these more sophisticated exploit-ation strategies, it was in Germany's best interest to retain Dutch experts who knew how to maximise agricultural production and set up an effi-cient wartime rationing system. It was for this reason that, throughout the occupation, responsibility for the food supply remained in the hands of two Dutch senior bureaucrats who had played a leading role in the country's economic and agricultural affairs since the 1930s – Secretary General of Economic Affairs (head of the Department of Agriculture and Fisheries as well as of the Department of Trade, Industry and Shipping) Hans Max Hirschfeld and Stephanus Louwes, who was now Director General of Food Supply (*Rijksbureau voor de Voedselvoorziening in Oorlog-stijd*: RBVVO). They were the ones who would henceforth negotiate between the Dutch and German interests in the field of food and nutri-tion policies.

Romijn, *Burgemeesters in Oorlogstijd: Besturen tijdens de Duitse Bezetting* (Amsterdam: Balans, 2006), 50–57.
[20] Werner Warmbrunn, *The Dutch under German Occupation, 1940–1945* (Stanford: Stanford University Press, 1963), 37.
[21] These were Management and Justice (*Verwaltung und Justiz*; Friedrich Wimmer), Finance and Economy (*Finanz und Wirtschaft*; Hans Fischbock), Security (*Sicherheitswesen*; Hanss Albin Rauter) and 'Special Issues' (*besonderen Verwendung*; Fritz Schmidt).
[22] Warmbrunn, *The Dutch under German Occupation*, 36; Hirschfeld, *Bezetting en Collaboratie: Nederland tijdens de Oorlogsjaren 1940–1945 in Historisch Perspectief* (Haarlem: H. J. W. Brecht, 1991), 23–24.
[23] Blom, 'Nazificatie en Exploitatie'; Trienekens, *Tussen ons Volk en de Honger*, 54–63.
[24] Voglis, 'Surviving Hunger', 17.

The new rationing apparatus was also largely a continuation of the pre-war organisation, with the main exception that all regulations were subordinate to the German *Hauptabteilung Ernährung und Landwirtschaft*, which in practise did little to disturb the Dutch food officials in executing their tasks.[25] Louwes's wartime RBVVO was founded upon the Agricultural Crisis Organisation and the cluster of statutory trade organisations that had originated as a result of these measures since the mid-1930s. This meant that Louwes was well acquainted with all the leading figures in the agricultural sector. Their trust and commitment only grew during the occupation because of Louwes's anti-German reputation. Even Seyss-Inquart had once allegedly addressed Louwes as 'the legal leader of the Illegality'.[26]

Other pre-war measures continued as well. The Provincial Food Commissioners, appointed in August 1939, remained competent for the agricultural organisation and inspection apparatus of their province. Local authority over each rationing district, which mostly overlapped with municipal boundaries, rested with local office-holders. The Central Rationing Office (CDK) in Zwolle remained responsible for all affairs related to food allocation. As a result of these measures, the size of the bureaucratic food system grew immensely. Even without taking into account the thousands of people working for local distribution offices, during the occupation about 20,000 civil servants worked for the food supply.[27]

Immediately after the surrender to Nazi Germany, this Dutch food administration took all necessary measures to maintain the food supply at the highest possible level. The reserves of cereals, fats, and fodder that the Directorate of Food Supply had set aside before the war, equalling 80–90 per cent of an annual harvest, proved to be of indispensable value. In addition, as a result of the loss of exports, there was a considerable surplus of vegetables. The loss of food imports, however, still required an extensive agricultural transformation, which entailed an acute and severe reduction in the pig and poultry population to save cereals for human consumption. In addition, the cultivation of crops needed to increase with a specific focus on carbohydrates, resulting in the growth of potato

---

[25] Direct supervision of this *Hauptabteilung* was exercised by the *Generalkommissar für Finanz und Wirtschaft*, Fischböck. Until January 1942, the *Hauptabteilung* was called *Geschäftsgruppe Ernährung und Landwirtschaft*. Trienekens, *Tussen ons Volk en de Honger*, 43–44.

[26] Trienekens, *Tussen ons Volk en de Honger*, 68–70; Trienekens, *Voedsel en Honger in Oorlogstijd*, 39.

[27] Trienekens, *Tussen ons Volk en de Honger*, 23, 53, 68–70; Trienekens, *Voedsel en Honger in Oorlogstijd*, 39, 45, 52.

cultivation and also of rye and rapeseed. A large proportion of agricultural activity thus had to switch from raising animals to the tillage of crops, which was combined with the large-scale ploughing up of pastures – a strategy the Dutch government had also pursued during the First World War. Louwes concisely captured this transition by stating that 'the nutrition of the Dutch people had to be lowered in quality in order to stay more or less quantitatively sufficient'.[28]

The new rationing system needed to be refined to fit different biological needs. A special nutritional department at the Directorate of Food Supply led by Dutch nutrition expert M. J. L. Dols created classifications according to age and profession that had to ensure the fairest allocation of food possible. Workers doing heavy labour were entitled to considerably larger rations than other adult workers; children received smaller rations but relatively higher proportions of fats and proteins, and young or expecting mothers were entitled to larger allotments of milk in particular as well as other animal-source foodstuffs. Of course, in practice, intra-household allocation ultimately determined individual consumption. Supplementary rations were also allocated to the sick and people doing work considered to be detrimental to their health. The elderly could not count on extra rations, according to Louwes, because the German occupier deemed them 'economically unproductive'.[29] Farmers were allowed to consume part of their own produce and were not given coupons for the foodstuffs they produced themselves, which meant that their wartime diets did not change to such an extent as those of the urbanites. Still, the overall social distribution of food during the German occupation was more 'fair' than it had been before the war.[30]

Instead of being able to buy and consume unrestrictedly, rationing essentially enforced rigid buying entitlements. Similar to the situation in many other German-occupied territories and Great Britain, consumers depended upon purchase permits, which were granted on the basis of the above-mentioned calculations of individual needs and actual supplies.[31] Each Dutch person received a personal ration card with a certain number of coupons that could be used within a specific rationing period, which

---

[28] NA, 2.21.238, inv.no. 117, Report Louwes, 7; Dols and Van Arcken, 'Food Supply and Nutrition', 327.

[29] Louwes, 'De Voedselvoorziening', 622.

[30] Burger et al., *Malnutrition and Starvation*, 67; Trienekens, 'The Food Supply', 122; Futselaar, *Lard, Lice, and Longevity*, 69.

[31] Alexander Loveday, *Wartime Rationing and Consumption*, Economic Intelligence Service of the League of Nations (Geneva: League of Nations, 1942), 13; Zweiniger-Bargielowska, *Austerity in Britain: Rationing, Controls, and Consumption 1939–1955* (Oxford: Oxford University Press, 2000).

were announced in local newspapers. Officially, no rationed article could
be bought or sold without these coupons. Unofficially, however, most
people supplemented their rations by growing or gathering their own
food, buying food directly from farmers or on urban black markets: this
was exactly how the Dutch food authorities had envisioned it.

Illustration 1 Director General of Food Supply S. L. Louwes (second
from the left) tastes food at a soup kitchen in The Hague, 1941.

To support the rationing scheme, in the second half of 1940 the
RBVVO established a Communal Kitchen system (*Centrale Keukens*:
CK). The purpose of the CK was to provide hot meals for those not able
to cook at home, in return for part of the rationing coupons and a small
payment. The CK also focussed on providing coupon-free meals for
those in need of extra feeding, such as factory and company workers,
but also students and schoolchildren. National Socialist involvement
made participation in the CK's civilian feeding highly unpopular. In
the years 1942–1944, a mere 100,000 adults and children participated
in the CK. Up until the Hunger Winter, the CK's main task was to
provide over 450,000 labourers in the Netherlands with coupon-free
meals to ensure their economic productivity.[32]

[32] Dols, J. P. van Loon, and H. Zoethout, 'De Centrale Keukens in de Jaren 1940–1945',
Voeding 7 (1946): 67–75; Dols and Van Arcken, 'Food Supply and Nutrition', 327–328.

In addition to the new rationing scheme, a pre-war agreement between the Public Health Division of the Department of Social Affairs, Department of Economic Affairs, and the RBVVO resulted in the formation of the so-called Food Council. This council became the major advisory committee for the Dutch food administration. Special sub-committees of the Food Council studied the relation between rations and public health and subsequently devised rations for the sick.[33] Another sub-committee conducted scientific research into food processing; for instance, in the milling extraction of grains and the preparation of synthetic vitamin C, which indicates how advanced the Netherlands was in the field of food science in the 1940s. Yet another division produced brochures with recipes and cooking methods, helping 'housewives' to cope with the numerous rationing regulations at household levels.[34]

Although all aspects of daily life were affected by the occupation, for most people, the reality of the German occupation failed to meet their initial anxieties and fears. The first large-scale symbolic resistance took place on 29 June 1940, the birthday of Prince Bernhard – husband of Crown Princess Juliana – with people all over the country demonstrating their allegiance to the House of Orange by wearing carnations, his favourite flower. Almost everyone began to listen to Radio Orange, a 15-minute broadcast in Dutch over the BBC, starting in July 1940 with a radio address by the Queen herself, who became a symbol of the Dutch resistance. For some groups, however, the occupation created an immediate and permanent threat. Already in the autumn of 1940, the Germans began to exclude Jews from public life and positions of influence, including universities, resulting in student strikes and protests.[35] The occupying regime also initially interned Dutch army veterans, although they were treated relatively well and most of them were released again in June 1940. Yet even for Dutch veterans, Jews, communists, social democrats,

---

[33] Commissie tot Onderzoek van de Voedings- en Gezondheidstoestand van de Nederlandse Bevolking, *Rapport Betreffende het Onderzoek naar de Voedings- en Gezondheidstoestand van de Nederlandse Bevolking in de Jaren 1941–1945, uitgezonderd de z.g. Hongerwinter (1944–1945), Deel 1A Voeding* (The Hague: Commissie tot Onderzoek van de Voedings- en Gezondheidstoestand van de Nederlandse Bevolking, 1952–1958).
[34] A. P. den Hartog, 'Nutrition Education in Times of Food Shortages and Hunger: War and Occupation in the Netherlands, 1939–1945', in *Food and War in Twentieth Century Europe*, eds. Ina Zweiniger-Bargielowska, Rachel Duffett, and Alain Drouard (Farnham: Ashgate, 2011), 183–200; C. van den Berg, 'Over het Ontstaan van de Voedingsorganisatie T.N.O. en van de Voedingsraad en over het Werk van deze Laatste Gedurende de Bezetting', *Voeding* 26 (1965): 299–308; R. B. M. Rigter, 'De Gezondheids- en Voedingsraad in Oorlogstijd', in *Geneeskunde en Gezondheidszorg in Nederland 1940–1945*, eds. Marius J. van Lieburg and Wijnandus W. Mijnhardt (Amsterdam: Rodopi, 1992), 228–239.
[35] Warmbrunn, *The Dutch under German Occupation*, 35.

and other 'vulnerable' groups, in the first months following the German invasion, daily life seemed to return to a form of normality.[36]

This return to normalcy was in part facilitated by the fact that only a small minority of the Dutch population supported National Socialism. In June 1940, the *Nationaal-Socialistische Beweging* (National Socialist Movement: NSB), founded in 1931 by Anton A. Mussert, only had 27,000 members.[37] Other political parties and organisations with a party-based character were subjected to restrictions and bans but, in July 1940, the Germans did allow the establishment a new broad-based political and social movement, called the *Nederlandse Unie* (Dutch Union), hoping this would facilitate collaborations with the Dutch. The Dutch Union wanted to accommodate the realities of the German occupation. It also aimed to prevent the NSB from claiming authority and to dispose of the social divisions that had supposedly weakened the Dutch democracy. At its peak, the movement had about 800,000 members, roughly 9 per cent of the total population. Contrary to what the occupier had envisioned, most of the rank and file joined in support of national revival and as protest against, rather than support of, National Socialist rule.[38]

Although profound changes initially seemed few, under the influence of German rule the social and economic structure of the Netherlands changed considerably. The opening of the German market and the growing need for food and services due to the loss of imports caused an enormous increase in labour demand. National Socialist policies concerning command economy and social legislation were gradually implemented, ending a large percentage of the pre-war unemployment (about 325,000 registered in May 1940, excluding 70,000 demobilised soldiers) and introducing wage control, fixed rents, prices, and leases. From June 1940 until March 1942, about 227,000 men who could not find a job in the Netherlands were sent to work in Germany, including some who volunteered for economic or ideological reasons.[39] Because of these economic developments, many small farmers and retailers derived more income after 1940. Indeed, the first 15 months of occupation

---

[36] For the phases of the occupation period, I largely adopt the clear phases described by Warmbrunn, *The Dutch under German Occupation*, 11–17. See also: Hirschfeld, *Bezetting en Collaboratie*, 30–50; Bob Moore, 'The Netherlands', 126–149.

[37] At its height, in the third quarter of 1941, these numbers had grown to 75,000. De Jong, *Het Koninkrijk* 6, 382–383.

[38] Wichert ten Have, *De Nederlandse Unie: Aanpassing, Vernieuwing en Confrontatie in Bezettingstijd, 1940–1941* (Amsterdam: Prometheus, 1999).

[39] Of this group, 61,000 men returned to the Netherlands in 1942. Sijes, *De Arbeidsinzet*, 77, 117; Trienekens, 'The Food Supply', 121–122.

showed the best economic figures since the Depression.[40] Working-class people were also (on average) better off than before the war thanks to employment, entitlements to good rations, and a national health insurance system from 1941 onwards. Only civil servants with no connection to the countryside benefitted little from the new economic situation.[41]

Nazification and Persecution

The first phase of mutual adaptation to the occupation ended in February 1941.[42] Following heightening tensions and violence between National Socialists and Jewish fighting squads in the city centre of Amsterdam and after consultation with *Reichsführer SS* Heinrich Himmler, on 22–23 February, *Reichskommissar* Seyss-Inquart and *Höhere SS- und Polizeiführer* Hanns Albin Rauter ordered the public arrest and deportation of 425 young Jewish men. This in turn, on 25–26 February, prompted a general strike in Amsterdam and neighbouring towns led by workers, including many communists – the first and largest general strike in any German-occupied territory against the persecution of the Jews.[43] The strike was violently repressed by the Germans. It provoked Rauter to authorise Christiansen to declare martial law, thereby enabling the military to punish disobedience against the occupying regime by death. For the Dutch, the brutal German retaliation was a clear sign that the occupation had entered into a new phase.[44]

In the two years after the 'February strike', the social and political climate between civilians and occupier deteriorated rapidly. This second phase of the occupation was marked by increasing Nazification of Dutch political and civil institutions, accompanied by the exclusion and prosecution of Jews, Roma, Sinti, and other minority groups. The growing demand for cooperation with SS police organisations in enforcing these repressive measures would undo the *Wehrmacht*'s initial inclination to remain a neutral and apolitical – or 'clean' – military power. In addition to these domestic developments, there were crucial international shifts in the war, with the Soviet Union and United States entering the war on the

---

[40] Klemann, 'Did the German Occupation Ruin Dutch Industry?'; Klemann, 'Die niederländische Wirtschaft'.

[41] Futselaar, *Lard, Lice and Longevity*, 138.

[42] Warmbrunn, *The Dutch under German Occupation*, 12; Hirschfeld, *Bezetting en Collaboratie*, 37; Moore, 'The Netherlands', 129–130.

[43] Katje Happe, *Veel Valse Hoop: De Jodenvervolging in Nederland in 1940–1945* (Amsterdam: Atlas Contact, 2018), 76–84.

[44] Warmbrunn, *The Dutch under German Occupation*, 106–111; Moore, 'The Netherlands', 130; Hirschfeld, *Bezetting en Collaboratie*, 37–38.

Allied side in June and December 1941, and the loss of the Dutch East Indies to the Japanese forces in March 1942. These war developments led to escalating politics of 'Nazification' and repression in the Netherlands.[45]

While Seyss-Inquart initially left Dutch governance structures largely untouched, in 1941 he gradually implemented authoritarian principles, by giving department heads increased regulatory powers and appointing National Socialists to government posts. In August 1941, the 'Leadership principle' effectively abolished municipal and provincial self-government and gave mayors and provincial commissioners extended authority over lower ranks. The appointed mayors were placed under supervision of the provincial commissioners and were dependent on the directions of the secretary general of the department concerned. Consequently, provincial commissioners became subordinate to Seyss-Inquart as the highest civil authority in the country. This direct, hierarchal chain from Seyss-Inquart to mayors guaranteed the occupier a system of institutionalised control.[46] By September 1943, the German civil administration had replaced 8 of the 11 provincial commissioners and 341 of the 850 Dutch mayors with 'reliable', pro-German men, including those of all large cities.[47]

The occupation regime made increasing use of the NSB to nazify, or 'co-ordinate', Dutch society by placing its members in government posts. However, Seyss-Inquart did not grant any executive power to Mussert's NSB as a political organisation as he held no high regard for the party or its leader. The German military similarly did not want to be associated with Mussert or other Dutch collaborators, as popular hostility towards these 'traitors' would undermine their military objectives and interests. Mussert wanted to become the representative of the Dutch people and constitute a 'Greater Netherlands' within the German Reich, which included Flanders, but was never taken very seriously. As a concession for his loyalty to the Reich, in December 1941, Mussert was allowed to take the oath of loyalty before Hitler. A year later, he was allowed to call himself 'Leader of the Dutch people' and was given an advisory position with Seyss-Inquart although, in practice, he was merely a puppet of the occupation authorities.[48] The aspirations of the widely supported Dutch Union to counteract the NSB's influence in Dutch politics were brought

---

[45] Hirschfeld, *Bezetting en Collaboratie*, 37–38; Foray, 'The "Clean *Wehrmacht*"', 769–772.
[46] Warmbrunn, *The Dutch under German Occupation*, 37.
[47] Hirschfeld, *Bezetting en Collaboratie*, 38–41; Romijn, *Burgemeesters in Oorlogstijd*, passim.
[48] Hirschfeld, *Bezetting en Collaboratie*, 38–39; Foray, 'The "Clean *Wehrmacht*"', 775–776; Emerson Vermaat, *Anton Mussert en zijn Conflict met de SS* (Soesterberg: Aspekt, 2011), 30–34, 65–70.

to an abrupt halt in December 1941, when the occupier forbade all political organisations except the NSB.[49] Even then, the NSB continued to receive limited support by the Dutch population.

In addition to government structures, the organisation of daily life also changed considerably during the second phase of the occupation. The years 1941–1942 witnessed the most intensive effort to shape the Netherlands into the German image and to socially engineer Dutch public life. Before the war, the Dutch social order had been characterised by a division of communities along ideological and denominational lines. In the mid-1930s, the term 'pillarisation' (*verzuiling*) was coined to describe this phenomenon, which in a rather ahistorical way romanticised the supposedly unique Dutch quality of a segmented society with four large communities – orthodox Protestants, Catholics, social democrats, and liberals – living in peaceful coexistence.[50] Based on their own norms and values, each of these socio-denominational communities built up an extensive network of foundations, associations, and organisations that virtually encompassed all aspects of daily life.[51] Those who were critical of the Dutch political system saw the quick defeat to Nazi Germany in May 1940 as the ultimate failure of this old social system – a view often expressed by the Dutch Union and in the illegal resistance press.[52]

Already in the months leading up to the second phase of the occupation, National Socialist organisations comparable to organisations in the Third Reich had aimed to overthrow this pillarised system. Following the example of the German *Nationalsozialistische Volkswohlfahrt* (NSV), two National Socialist welfare organisations were established in the Netherlands: Winter Aid (*Winterhulp*) in October 1940 and the Dutch People's Service (*Nederlandse Volksdienst*: NVD) in July 1941. Both organisations aimed to coordinate all social work through local governments, churches, and private organisations, thereby endeavouring to replace the pillarised Dutch welfare system.[53] By late 1941, thousands of denominational and

[49] Ten Have, *De Nederlandse Unie*, 482–483.

[50] Blom, 'Vernietigende Kracht en Nieuwe Vergezichten: Het Onderzoeksproject Verzuiling op Lokaal Niveau Geëvalueerd', in *De Verzuiling Voorbij: Godsdienst, Stand en Natie in de Lange Negentiende Eeuw*, eds. Blom and Jaap Talsma (Amsterdam: Het Spinhuis, 2000), 207.

[51] The liberals, or 'neutrals', however, remained much more loosely connected. Peter van Dam, *Staat van Verzuiling: Over een Nederlandse Mythe* (Amsterdam: Wereldbibliotheek, 2011), 23–38; De Rooy, *Republiek van Rivaliteiten*, 147–148; De Rooy, 'Een Zoekende Tijd: De Ongemakkelijke Democratie, 1913–1949', in *Land van Kleine Gebaren: Een Politieke Geschiedenis van Nederland 1780-2012*, 8th rev. ed., eds. Remieg Aerts et al. (Amsterdam: Boom, 2013), 218–220.

[52] De Rooy, 'Een Zoekende Tijd', 258–261.

[53] *De Nederlandsche Volksdienst: Wat beoogt de N.V.D. en waar ligt het Verschil tussen den N.V.D. en Winterhulp Nederland?* (S.l.: s.n., 194X); Josje Damsma and Erik Schumacher,

ideological associations and foundations had been liquidated, including many youth organisations and sport clubs. Although most formerly religion-based organisations dissolved officially, in practice the German occupying regime did not have the numbers nor the means to stop their unofficial continuation.[54]

In the same period, the German administration intensified its efforts to segregate and concentrate the Jewish population, about 140,000 of whom were considered to be 'full Jews' under the Nuremberg Laws. The establishment of a Jewish Council in Amsterdam in February 1941, as part of a Europe-wide scheme to designate Jewish leaders whom the Germans could deploy in the administration of Jewish Affairs, and the relative order in the Netherlands facilitated the administrative operation that led to the segregation and deportation of Dutch Jews. From April 1942 onwards, Jews were forced to wear the Star of David in public. Two months later, the Central Agency for Jewish Emigration (*Zentralstelle für jüdische Auswanderung*) informed the Jewish Council that the Reich had decided to send Jews to Germany for work, with the first group planning to leave before the middle of July. The council was tasked with selecting the Jews based on files from the registry offices. Those not living in Amsterdam were, for the greater part, forced to move there, after which they were sent to Dutch transit camps in Westerbork and Vught.[55] Despite this administrative facilitation of deportations, resistance was also present. For example, Walter Süskind – a member of the Jewish Council and leader of the deportation centre Hollandsche Schouwburg – managed with the aid of some of his colleagues and resistance groups to smuggle over 600 Jewish children out of a nursery, who had been designated for deportation.[56]

In general, after the February strike, the Dutch resistance slowly grew and became better organised. In addition to communists and social democrats, churches gained a larger role in the organised resistance, benefitting from their large pre-war social and political networks.[57] Initially, clergymen mostly provided mere guidance on ideological issues

---

Hier Woont een NSB'er: Nationaalsocialisten in Bezet Amsterdam (Amsterdam: Boom, 2010), 82–84; Romijn, *Burgemeesters in Oorlogstijd*, 202–216.

[54] Warmbrunn, *The Dutch under German Occupation*, 43–47.

[55] De Jong, *Het Koninkrijk* 6, 226–372.

[56] De Jong, *Het Koninkrijk* 6, 258; Happe, *De Jodenvervolging in Nederland*, 238–239.

[57] In 1930, there were three Christian denominations in the Netherlands with sizable numbers: Catholics made up 36.4 per cent of the population, the Dutch Reformed Church (*Nederlands Hervormde Kerk*) 34.4 per cent, and the Reformed Churches (*Gereformeerde Kerken*) 8 per cent. Only 14 per cent of the population did not belong to any religion.

and practical matters arising from occupation policies; but, increasingly, they also began to act as spokesmen for their communities through pastoral letters, interviews with Dutch and German authorities, and in open letters addressed to the occupier. Some churches basically became resistance organisations, collecting funds, using lay groups to conceal clandestine organisations, and encouraging and allowing pastors and priests to join underground movements. While the resistance of churches came with sacrifices, their societal position grew stronger and more united during the occupation. Other groups also organised themselves against Nazification and persecution, most notably students and physicians.[58] The Dutch food authorities, including Louwes, managed to clandestinely support the supply of foodstuffs to these illegal organisations so that people in hiding were generally able to secure food.[59]

Illustration 2 People waiting in line at the Amsterdam Rationing Office.

Although there was still no real scarcity in this phase, food rationing meant a major transition for the Dutch, most importantly because the wartime diet radically changed compared to consumption patterns before the war. By April 1941, following the introduction of the potato

[58] Warmbrunn, *The Dutch under German Occupation*, 153–164; Jeroen Kemperman, *Oorlog in de Collegebanken: Studenten in het Verzet 1940–1945* (Amsterdam: Boom, 2018).
[59] Trienekens, 'The Food Supply', 123.

coupon, nearly all foodstuffs were included in the rationing system, with the exception of fruit, vegetables, and fish.[60] For increasingly more luxury products such as coffee, tea, and sugar, inferior surrogates found their way into the household. Animal products such as cheese, full-cream milk, and meat made way for potatoes and vegetables, and the beloved white bread was replaced by brown 'government' bread. In addition, blackout regulations, queuing, curfews, limited availability of public transport, and shortages of fuel, textiles, and shoes were now beginning to affect the daily lives of most people.[61]

Exploitation and Coercion

In the spring of 1943, the occupation entered into a third phase, one that was marked by increased repression, violence, and economic exploitation, and consequently, of resistance. These deteriorating circumstances were partly the result of wider measures in occupied Europe following the German military defeats at Stalingrad and in the Mediterranean, and their subsequent need for additional manpower.[62] The direct domestic cause was the announcement by *Wehrmachtbefehlshaber* Christiansen on 29 April 1943 that 300,000 Dutch army veterans would be re-interned, with the intention of sending them for forced labour to Germany. The announcement prompted a second general strike in the Netherlands, which lasted locally up till the first week of May 1943. Contrary to the February strike in 1941, when the bulk of strikes comprised industrial and municipal workers in the western urban areas, the Dutch rural population in the northern, eastern, and central parts of the Netherlands took the lead in a strike that eventually involved an estimated half million people. The strike provoked Rauter to temporarily declare a police state of siege, thereby pre-empting Christiansen's declaration of martial law, which resulted in about 200 summary executions.[63] It was at this stage that the Germans abandoned their plans to Nazify and incorporate the Netherlands into the Third Reich, which made it less important for the occupier to treat the Dutch as equals.[64]

One month before the strike, in March 1943, Hitler had declared a state of total war mobilisation for all occupied territories and appointed Himmler as Reich Minister of the Interior. This resulted in a power shift

---

[60] De Jong, *Het Koninkrijk* 7, 151.
[61] De Jong, *Het Koninkrijk* 7, 1–269; Klemann, *Nederland 1938–1948*, 453–463.
[62] Warmbrunn, *The Dutch under German Occupation*, 13.
[63] Warmbrunn, *The Dutch under German Occupation*, 116–117; De Jong, *Het Koninkrijk* 7, 799–862; Foray, 'The "Clean *Wehrmacht*"', 783.
[64] Moore, 'The Netherlands', 130.

towards the radical wing, and measures by the SS becoming more brutal and repressive. Rauter, as *Generalkommissar für das Sicherheitswesen* and *Höhere SS- und Polizeiführer*, was in command of the SS, SD, Waffen-SS and German police in the Netherlands; he thus indirectly controlled Dutch police, for which, until September 1944, he commanded about 10,000 German men. In this period, conflicts between the *Reichskommissar* and the SS in the Netherlands grew considerably, due to the increasing power of Rauter's SS and his conviction that, as a tool of the Führer, they were placed above the state and party. At the same time, *Wehrmachtsbefehlshaber* Christiansen was determined to assert his own authority and that of the *Wehrmacht* over the Dutch people. This change in attitude, among other things, included the increasing use of reprisal actions against civilians as a means of punishing acts of resistance.[65]

Illustration 3 Left to right: Schumann, Christiansen, Seyss-Inquart, Mussert, and Rauter, 1943.

Connected to the mounting repression was the deportation of the remaining Jews from transit camps and prisons to concentration and extermination camps in the East. In September–October 1943, the leaders of the Jewish Council were among the last to be deported from

---

[65] Hirschfeld, *Bezetting en Collaboratie*, 44–45 Foray, 'The "Clean *Wehrmacht*"', 783.

Amsterdam. Of the approximately 107,000 Dutch Jews deported from the Netherlands, about 5,200 returned after the war, meaning that 101,800 were killed or perished in concentration camps. In total, an estimated 36,000 Jews survived the war – 16,000 in hiding, 3,000 because they managed to flee abroad, and about 10,000 because they lived in 'mixed' marriages. Other surviving groups were considered to be of 'mixed-blood' or Protestant Jews.[66] With about 75 per cent of the Jewish population not surviving the war, the number and percentage of Jewish victims in the Netherlands was the highest in all of Western Europe.[67]

Of the estimated 350,000 people in hiding by September 1944, Jews thus only made up a small percentage. The vast majority comprised adult men who wanted to avoid the *Arbeitseinsatz*. From 1943 onwards, *Reichsmarschall* Hermann Göring demanded increasingly more Dutch men for the German war economy and to work on fortifying projects. However, because voluntary drafting proved highly insufficient, the occupying regime resorted to measures of coercion. Not just the unemployed, but all men between the ages of 18–35 years working in professions that the occupier deemed 'non-essential' to the war effort were ordered to enlist for the *Arbeitseinsatz*. Many of these men went into hiding, either by simply not enlisting and hiding indoors or moving away from home. Nevertheless, by 1944, approximately 300,000 Dutchmen were forced to work in Nazi Germany; during the entire occupation, these numbers totalled about half a million.[68]

With so many people in hiding, the German occupying regime began to deploy new strategies of exclusion. Previously, the German desire to introduce a separate rationing system for Jewish citizens had been successfully stalled by the Dutch food authorities, but in late 1943 they were unable to resist the German demand to introduce new rationing cards. The introduction of these second rationing cards (*Tweede Distributiestamkaart*) was a clear attempt to deprive people who were hiding foodstuffs. With the second rationing cards, food rationing became tied to personal identification, which ensured that the German authorities could make

[66] Nine hundred Jews were still in transit camp Westerbork at the time of liberation. De Jong, *Het Koninkrijk* 8, 708; De Jong, *Het Koninkrijk* 12, 54–55.

[67] In occupied Belgium and Norway, about 40 per cent of the pre-war Jewish population lost their lives, France an estimated 25 per cent and in Denmark less than 2 per cent. Pim Griffioen and Ronald Zeller, *Jodenvervolging in Nederland, Frankrijk en België: Overeenkomsten, Verschillen en Oorzaken* (Amsterdam: Boom, 2011), 17. See also: Marnix Croes and Peter Tammes, *'Gif Laten wij niet Voortbestaan'. Een Onderzoek naar de Overlevingskansen van Joden in de Nederlandse Gemeenten, 1940–1945* (Amsterdam: Aksant, 2004), 29.

[68] Sijes, *De Arbeidsinzet*, 624.

food another important device in their overall system of exclusion and repression.[69]

With no valid papers or ration cards, national and local resistance groups took priority in providing for the material needs of people in hiding. After the April/May strike, falsifying identity cards and robbing rationing offices developed into two of the main priorities for Dutch resistance groups. In the summer of 1944, the *Landelijke Organisatie voor Hulp aan Onderduikers* (National Organisation for Aid to Hiders) distributed an impressive 220,000 ration cards a month. The *Landelijke Knokploegen* (National Action Groups) grew from 300 official members in early 1944 to about 1,500 by September of that year. Their primary task was to obtain ration cards and other official documents by force but also to destroy sensitive materials such as population records. Although still not a considerable number, by September 1944, the 'active resistance' had grown to some 25,000 people.[70] Similar to elsewhere in Europe, farms became popular places for resistance fighters to go into hiding, and clandestine production and trade were vital for their operations.[71]

Increasingly, generally law-abiding Dutch citizens now also became involved in the shadow economy. In a similar fashion to other countries coping with rationing and controls, when rations of certain goods became too small to satisfy the demand, the black market thrived and further decreased supplies on the legal market. Not everybody could afford 'black' products. Between 1938 and 1939 and the first half of 1944, the cost of living increased by 50 per cent while real wages decreased by 13 per cent. At the same time, many people were faced with the issue of excess purchasing power as legally little was available to buy – other than food – and wages could therefore not always be spent.[72]

Broadly speaking, there were two types of black-market trade: trade in scarce supplies and trade in ration coupons that could be exchanged for supplies. The considerable illegal price differences for foodstuffs between city and countryside made this coupon trade attractive for both lower- and middle-class families, who could trade their 'luxury' coupons for more staple foods in the countryside than in the city.[73] In general,

---

[69] Warmbrunn, *The Dutch under German Occupation*, 13; De Jong, *Het Koninkrijk* 5, 434; Romijn, *Burgemeesters in Oorlogstijd*, 225–233.

[70] Warmbrunn, *The Dutch under German Occupation*, 187–196; De Jong, *Het Koninkrijk* 10b, 744–746; Moore, 'The Netherlands', 142–143.

[71] Klemann, *Nederland 1938–1948*, 218.

[72] Jan J. Woltjer, *Recent Verleden: Nederland in de Twintigste Eeuw* (Amsterdam: Balans, 1992), 182–183. Jan Luiten van Zanden, *Een Klein Land in de 20ᵉ Eeuw: Een Economische Geschiedenis van Nederland 1914–1995* (Zeist: Het Spectrum, 1997), 163–170.

[73] Claus B. Christensen and Futselaar, 'Zwarte Markten in de Tweede Wereldoorlog: Een Vergelijking Tussen Nederland en Denemarken', in *Thuisfront: Oorlog en Economie in de*

however, black-market trade remained relatively limited until the autumn of 1944 – at least in comparison to other occupied countries in Western Europe. Roughly 20–25 per cent of the total agricultural production was clandestinely retained by farmers and channelled into the black market. Most of these clandestinely produced and traded foodstuffs benefitted the countryside population: only a small proportion flowed into the large conurbations in the west and into occupied Belgium.[74]

Another part of the Dutch agricultural production crossed the German border. Wild estimations during and after the war spoke of 80–90 per cent of total production disappearing to the east, which fitted perfectly with the image of the German occupier who had systematically plundered the Netherlands of its resources. Although at the beginning of the occupation a large part of the Dutch reserves of fats, coffee, and cocoa was forcibly exported to Germany, in the following years the exports remained relatively low. The actual exports (in kcal) to Germany had been a mere 3.9 per cent in 1942–1943 and only 3.3 per cent in 1943–1944 and comprised mostly of vegetables and seeds.[75] The authorities in Germany continuously pressed for a substantial volume of imports from the Netherlands but the Dutch food officials' relatively good relations with the German *Hauptabteilung Ernährung und Landwirtschaft* in the Netherlands assisted in the limitation of these exports.[76] While, from 1943 onwards, *Reichsmarschall* Göring demanded increasingly more Dutch men and materials for the German war economy, the German civil authorities became less inclined to meet these demands, focusing on maintaining domestic order instead. Certainly, Louwes and Hirschfeld both put great effort into providing the German civil authorities with arguments in their export negotiations with Berlin. Keeping the official rations in the Netherlands slightly below those in

Twintigste Eeuw, Jaarboek van het Nederlands Instituut voor Oorlogsdocumentatie, eds. Klemann and Dirk Luyten (Zutphen: Walburg Press, 2003), 95–99; Futselaar, *Lard, Lice and Longevity,* 158–191; Futselaar, 'Incomes, Class, and Coupons: Black Markets for Food in the Netherlands during the Second World War', *Food & History* 8 (2010): 171–198.

[74] Klemann, '"Die Koren Onthoudt, wordt Gevloekt onder het Volk ..." De Zwarte Markt in Voedingswaren 1940-1948', *BMGN – Low Countries Historical Review* 115 (2000): 536–546; Futselaar, *Lard, Lice and Longevity,* 180–183.

[75] Trienekens, *Tussen ons Volk en de Honger,* 201–202. Trienekens, 'The Food Supply', 118–120.

[76] NIOD Institute for War, Holocaust and Genocide Studies [NIOD], 212a Archief H.M. Hirschfeld, inv.no. 102, Letter from Louwes to Hirschfeld on food situation, 11 January 1944.

Germany and underreporting agricultural production were two key strategies they pursued to minimise export demands.[77]

Due to the economic changes, the position of the agricultural sector changed immensely and agrarians gained a more prominent position in Dutch society. Between 1938 and 1946, the number of agrarian businesses increased by 6 per cent to about 393,000. The transformation of the agricultural sector and dependency on farmers to provide for Dutch needs brought the agrarians new opportunities and was accompanied by bonuses and rising prices for their products. Simultaneously, the growing fuel shortages meant that the sector could not wholly depend on machines and had to shift to more manual labour. From 1942, agrarians also benefitted from higher wages and increasing profits from the black market. While it was well-known that farmers structurally underreported their harvests, Dutch food authorities allowed a limited black-market share and administratively covered the losses with the idea that this would benefit the population more than it did the occupier.[78]

Despite the mounting exploitation and repression, the extensive Dutch preparations of the wartime food supply and advanced rationing institutions, combined with the secondary nature of the black market and relatively low export demands, ensured that the rations could prevent a serious food crisis until the autumn of 1944. However, the meagre war diet increasingly lacked animal products and fats and thus generated a widespread sense of impoverishment and hunger among the Dutch, which many people voiced at the time and recalled vividly after the war.[79] There has been considerable debate about the actual nutritional value of this wartime diet. Trienekens has concluded that the Dutch diet was not only quantitatively and qualitatively sufficient until September 1944 but, according to modern nutritional standards, was even 'healthier' than the pre-war diet because of the lower fat intake and increased consumption of vegetables and fibres.[80] By contrast, Futselaar has argued that there were indeed serious nutritional shortcomings much earlier on. These measurable micronutrient deficiencies caused a high incidence of infectious disease and increased mortality among children in particular, contradicting the image of a nutritious and healthy wartime diet.[81] Data on the height and weight of schoolchildren in Amsterdam indicate that in March 1944, 13-year-old children were on average three

---

[77] NA, 2.21.238, inv.no. 117, Report Louwes, 9; Louwes, 'De Voedselvoorziening', 615–616; Klemann, *Nederland 1938–1948*, 493–494.

[78] Klemann, *Nederland 1938–1948*, 217–221.

[79] De Jong, *Het Koninkrijk* 7, 1–269; Klemann, *Nederland 1938–1948*, 453–463.

[80] Trienekens, *Tussen ons Volk en de Honger*, 409–414.

[81] Futselaar, *Lard, Lice and Longevity*.

Table 1.1 *Daily rations (kcal) in the occupied Netherlands per age group and profession per year, 1941–1944*[a]

Age/profession	1941	1942	1943	1944
0–3 years	1,701	1,672	1,638	1,541
4–13 years	2,016	2,011	2,010	1,843
14–20 years	2,062	2,157	2,203	1,972
>21 years	1,836	1,784	1,778	1,590
Long hours	2,040	2,015	2,086	1,885
Heavy work	2,480	2,416	2,427	2,170
Very heavy work	3,358	3,286	3,252	2,907

[a] 1941 only quarter II–IV; 1944 only quarter I–III.
Source: Table based on Ministry of Agriculture, Fisheries, and Food Supply, Section Statistics, in: Burger et al., *Malnutrition and Starvation* II, Appendix 1a–1b.

kilograms lighter and two centimetres shorter than before the war, which certainly points towards deficiencies in caloric intake.[82]

Unfortunately, it is very difficult to reconstruct consumption levels during the war. We are, however, fortunate that the Directorate of Food Supply kept excellent records of official rations during this period, which provide a good indication of the minimum consumption levels among different groups. From the beginning of the occupation, Dutch food officials factored in that households would supplement their official rations with food from informal and extra-legal channels, adding an estimated 10–20 per cent in calorific value. As Table 1.1 demonstrates, Dutch rations fluctuated seasonally but stayed more or less stable up to 1943, a year with a good harvest. The decline in foodstuffs in 1944 affected children's rations less than adult's rations, but overall the official diets of all age groups had already significantly deteriorated before the Allied invasion in September 1944.

Comparing the situation in the Netherlands with other European countries in the same period (Table 1.2), one observes that the Dutch rations were only slightly lower than those in Germany and the Protectorate of Bohemia and Moravia: again, a clear indication that the Dutch maintained a 'privileged' position among the occupied countries and enjoyed a well-functioning rationing system. Additionally, the comparatively high rations in the Netherlands also show that Hitler's explicit orders for not treating the non-Jewish Dutch any differently than

---

[82] J. Tuntler, 'Onderzoek naar Den Voedingstoestand van Schoolkinderen te Amsterdam 1935-45', *Tijdschrift voor Sociale Geneeskunde* 23 (1945): 106–124.

Table 1.2 *Daily rations (kcal) average adult consumers in nine European countries, 1941–1944*

Country	1941	1942	1943	1944
Germany	2,020	1,940	1,990	2,000
Protectorate	1,950	1,875	1,800	1,760
Netherlands	1,800	1,785	1,845	1,765
Finland	1,650	1,375	1,640	1,775
Norway	1,580	1,445	1,445	1,445
Belgium	1,375	1,325	1,365	1,555
France	1,230	1,110	1,065	1,135
Poland	1,290	1,235	1,135	1,160
Italy	1,160	1,020	930	990

Source: Lindberg, *Food, Famine and Relief 1940–1946*, 21.

German citizens of the Third Reich were indeed followed during the first four years of occupation. Most other occupied territories in Western and Eastern Europe had to cope with much less: the main exception was self-sufficient occupied Denmark.[83] For example, neighbouring Belgium already had to deal with food shortage and hunger as early as the winter of 1940–1941 as it was much less prepared for a self-sufficient wartime food supply. Shortages of food and other primary resources started in France in the first year of the war as well. After the French army's defeat and signing of the armistice in June 1940, Nazi Germany demanded that agricultural and industrial products be sent to Germany as part of 'occupation costs' and exploitation strategies. To make matters worse, the northern and coastal regions of France that produced the majority of the country's coal, steel, textiles, cereals, milk, sugar, and meat, were now occupied by German troops.[84]

As evident from Tables 1.1 and 1.2, in 1944 the changing war conditions began to seriously affect the Dutch food system. The *Wehrmacht* not only demanded more food to consume but, as part of their military operations, restricted fishing and shipping, and inundated arable land.

[83] John Lindberg, *Food, Famine and Relief 1940–1946* (Genève: United Nations, 1946), 21; Klemann and Sergei Kudryashov, *Occupied Economies: An Economic History of Nazi-Occupied Europe, 1939–1945* (London: Berg, 2012), 380. For more on food rationing in occupied Denmark, see: Futselaar, *Lard, Lice and Longevity*, 64–87.

[84] Voglis, 'Surviving Hunger', 17–20; Shannon L. Fogg, *The Politics of Everyday Life in Vichy France: Foreigners, Undesirables, and Strangers* (Cambridge: Cambridge University Press, 2009), 4–5. Loss of its colonial possessions in late 1942 was another detrimental turning point in France's food supply. Allan Mitchell, *Nazi Paris: The History of an Occupation, 1940–1944* (New York: Berghahn Books, 2008), 110–111.

Eager to prevent or delay an Allied invasion, by the summer of 1944 the *Wehrmacht* had inundated over 50,000 hectares of land around Rotterdam and Amsterdam in addition to large swathes of cultivated land in the province of Zeeland.[85] All these disrupting measures accelerated after the liberation of Brussels and Antwerp (3–4 September). On 4 September, Seyss-Inquart announced a State of Emergency (*Ausnahmezustand*), which essentially entailed that any form of resistance against the occupier would be answered immediately with armed force. The state of alert was accompanied by utter chaos. On 5 September, tens of thousands of Germans and Dutch National Socialists fled the country on what became known as 'Crazy Tuesday' (*Dolle Dinsdag*).[86] The remaining *Wehrmacht* soldiers confiscated transportation means, machines, fuel, and foodstuffs: anything that could be utilised in the expected battle for the Netherlands. What was left of the Dutch economy and centralised food system instantly disintegrated.[87]

---

[85] De Jong, *Het Koninkrijk* 10a, 55; Trienekens, *Tussen ons Volk en de Honger,* 46.
[86] De Jong, *Het Koninkrijk* 10a, 57, 175–176, 180–204; Romijn, *Burgemeesters in Oorlogstijd,* 571.
[87] NIOD, 216h Departement Landbouw en Visserij, inv.no. 87, Minutes meeting RBVVO, 9-10 September 1944; Press releases on food supply, 7–9 September 1944; NA, 2.21.238, inv.no. 117, Report Louwes, 16.

2 Causes of the Famine

Why did famine strike the Netherlands? Considering that the crisis occurred in one of the most highly developed countries in Europe, the most logical explanation would be that food shortage and subsequent famine in the occupied western Netherlands was a product of total war. Similar to other famines brought about by Nazi rule, such as in the Warsaw ghetto in 1940–1942, occupied Greece in 1941–1944, and besieged Leningrad in 1941–1944, the war not only played a major causal role, but it was also the main reason why famine could not be prevented or alleviated in time.[1] Yet, identifying war and enemy occupation as the underlying cause still largely fails to explain exactly what happened in the occupied Netherlands during the final months of war – or more importantly – to clarify who or what was responsible for the shortages that quickly escalated into famine conditions.

Historiography on the Dutch Hunger Winter has been divided over this question. In line with popular Dutch belief, many international studies have presumed that the German occupying forces played a malevolent role in creating the conditions that produced famine. According to this view, the German occupier brutally imposed a food blockade upon the western Netherlands with the intention of breaking the national railway strike and all expressions of Dutch resistance with it. Some scholars have even assumed that this food blockade was maintained throughout the final eight months of war.[2] Dutch historiography, on the other hand, has put more emphasis on the devastating consequences of the national railway strike, which was instigated by the Dutch government-in-exile in London in September 1944 to support the Allied advance. These scholars have argued that the government exacerbated hunger by refusing to terminate

---

[1] Devereux, *Theories of Famine*, 148; Voglis, 'Surviving Hunger', 16–41; Roland, *Courage under Siege.*

[2] E.g., Maas, *The Netherlands at War*, 205; Aykroyd, *The Conquest of Famine*, 98–103; Collingham, *The Taste of War*, 176; Buruma, *Year Zero*, 54; Voglis, 'Surviving Hunger', 22.

a strike that quite evidently served little military purpose for the Allies.[3] In doing so, both of these highly politicised narratives have placed human culpability, or even intent, at the centre of their accounts.

This chapter offers a new perspective on famine causation in the occupied Netherlands. Instead of blaming the German blockade or the continuation of the Dutch railway strike, this chapter demonstrates that the famine resulted from a culmination of various transportation and distribution problems – both intentional and unintentional. To understand the complex events that adversely affected the Dutch food system, I show that internal conflicts and power struggles within the German occupying authorities as well as in Dutch-Allied relations proved to be of crucial importance in these transportation problems. This examination of the causes of the famine not only contributes to the pressing question of why 2.6 million people in the occupied western Netherlands faced hunger in the final months of war, but also provides an indispensable context for examining subsequent responses to this crisis.

Famine as a Weapon

On Sunday 17 September 1944, the Allies launched the largest airborne operation up to that time – Operation Market Garden (see Map 2). Led by Field Marshal Bernard Montgomery, Market Garden intended to encircle the industrial heart of Germany, the Ruhr, while simultaneously achieving a quick liberation of the Netherlands. At first all seemed to work according to plan, as the Allies managed to secure Dutch bridges across the rivers Waal and Meuse. But the offensive over the river Rhine, near the city of Arnhem, proved to be the proverbial 'bridge too far'. The Germans counterattacked and by 25 September the last Allied troops had to retreat from Arnhem.[4] Operation Market Garden had failed, and the Northern provinces would remain occupied until the spring of 1945 (see Map 3). In the following months, the people in the still-occupied part of the country not only experienced intensified German repression, but also suffered the consequences of losing three major food-producing provinces in addition to their only domestic mining area.

---

[3] Trienekens, *Tussen ons Volk en de Honger*, 383; Klemann, *Nederland 1938–1948*, 465–466; Van der Heijden, *Grijs Verleden*, 316; Futselaar, *Lard, Lice and Longevity*, 33.

[4] Dwight D. Eisenhower, *Eisenhower's Own Story of the War: The Complete Report by the Supreme Commander General Dwight D. Eisenhower on the War in Europe from the Day of Invasion to the Day of Victory* (New York: Arco Publishing Company, 1946), 67–68; J. J. Gulmans, 'Operatie Market Garden', in *De Bevrijding van Nederland, 1944–1945: Oorlog op de Flank*, eds. Christ Klep and Ben Schoenmaker (The Hague: Sdu Koninginnegracht Publishers, 1995), 118–124, 137–149; Antony Beevor, *Arnhem: The Battle for the Bridges, 1944* (London: Viking, 2018).

Illustration 4 Operation Market Garden, American paratroopers from
the 101st Airborne Division land near Grave, 17 September 1944.

In order to support the Allied war effort and hinder German military
activities, on 17 September, the Dutch government-in-exile in London
instigated a national railway strike. This was by no means an impromptu,
spontaneous action. As early as May 1943, the Dutch Council of the
Resistance (*Raad van Verzet*) had brought the option of a railway strike to
the attention of the government.[5] Prime Minister Pieter S. Gerbrandy
subsequently discussed this with the Allied Headquarters, and they too
indicated that they favoured this kind of ground support. However, the
actual strike was a direct request from Supreme Commander General
Dwight D. Eisenhower's Allied Headquarters in 1944, not an idea of the
exiled government itself. According to the Head of the Dutch intelligence service in London, Cees Fock, the government's announcement of
the strike via Dutch broadcast on the BBC was actually planned to

---

[5] Adolf J. C. Rüter, *Rijden en Staken: De Nederlandse Spoorwegen in Oorlogstijd* (The Hague:
Martinus Nijhoff, 1960), 219. The Dutch Railways at the time were a highly contested
institution, mainly resulting from their collaboration with the German authorities in
transporting Jews and political prisoners to and from the transit camp Westerbork.

precede the Allied invasion of Dutch territory, thereby following the example of the extensive French railway sabotage preceding the Normandy invasion. But because both Gerbrandy and Minister of War Otto van Lidth de Jeude had not responded to his call in time, the announcement had to be postponed until the evening broadcast.[6] In any case, the government's announcement of the strike was highly successful: close to all 30,000 employees of the Dutch Railways left their jobs and went into hiding.[7] Consequently, no Dutch trains ran in the occupied areas until the liberation in May 1945.

Because of the strike, the food supply in the occupied areas suddenly depended on inland shipping and road transportation alone. This transition was not a smooth one. Sixty per cent of the transportation of coal had, up till then, depended on the railways, and a similar percentage of perishable products, such as potatoes, had always been transported by train.[8] To add to the confusion, the timing of all these events could not have been worse. In September, the annual depletion of stockpiles should have been compensated by the new potato harvest. Moreover, the embattled German authorities continued to confiscate all means of transportation in addition to foodstuffs and fuel. Contributing to these difficulties was the fact that the occupier had been using much farmland for the construction of airfields and military fortifications or otherwise flooding valuable cultivated land to delay the Allied advance. As a result, the occupied areas only kept meagre food stocks, sufficient for just a few weeks of rationing.[9] At the same time, Dutch officials had to cope with grave difficulties transporting these supplies from the agricultural northeast to consumers in the west, which was inhabited by 4.3 million people – 2.6 million of whom resided in the large urban areas.[10] In

---

[6] Cees L. W. Fock, 'De Nederlandse Regering in Londen en de Spoorwegstaking', *De Gids* 188 (1955): 348–356. In his official response, Gerbrandy stated that he did spend the night at his hotel, but that he attended church that morning, this being the reason why he missed Fock's initial call. Pieter S. Gerbrandy, 'Nogmaals: De Nederlandse Regering en de Spoorwegstaking', *De Gids* 119 (1956): 39–41. See also: Rüter, *Rijden en Staken*, 220–222; Cees Fasseur, *Eigen Meester, Niemands Knecht: Het Leven van Pieter Sjoerds Gerbrandy, Minister-President van Nederland in de Tweede Wereldoorlog* (Amsterdam: Balans, 2014), 412.

[7] For a detailed description of the course of the strike, see: Rüter, *Rijden en Staken*, 227–235.

[8] Rüter, 'De Nederlandse Spoorwegen', in *Onderdrukking en Verzet* IV, 635–636.

[9] NA, 2.21.238, inv.no. 117, Report Louwes, 17; NIOD, 212a, inv.no. 160, 'The liberation of the West of the Netherlands'. See also: Bob Moore, 'The Western Allies and Food Relief to the Occupied Netherlands, 1944–1945', *War & Society* 10 (1992): 108–109.

[10] Centraal Bureau voor de Statistiek, *Jaarcijfers voor Nederland 1943–1946* (Utrecht: W. de Haan, 1948), 5.

September 1944, the three western provinces themselves produced only sufficient bread grain for one month, potatoes for up to three weeks, and margarine for two weeks.[11]

The German occupier responded to the railway strike with threats and violent measures. The German *Beauftragte* for the railways presented the Dutch Railways board with an ultimatum: the strikers had to resume work within a week or otherwise their families would be taken prisoner. In their absence, the *Wehrmacht* would burn their houses and take other civilians captive. At the same time, Dutch food officials Hirschfeld and Louwes received notice from Seyss-Inquart's headquarters that, if the strike continued, the occupier would cut off all food supplies to cities in the west, confiscate any leftover stocks, and close all stores for the public. On Friday 22 September, the *Wehrmacht* put their words into action by destroying the Amsterdam port installations.[12] A simultaneously released press statement from the German-controlled ANP press agency warned strikers of the consequences of a 'self-imposed famine'.[13] The threat of famine was now actively deployed to break the Dutch resistance.

On 22 September, the same day the *Wehrmacht* destroyed the Amsterdam port installations, the head of the German *Hauptabteilung Ernährung und Landwirtschaft* Jürgen von der Wense called Hirschfeld and Louwes for an emergency consultation: this was at the request of Seyss-Inquart. Von der Wense, who had been on good terms with the Dutch officials throughout the occupation, expressed sincere concerns for the future of urban dwellers in the west. He revealed there were serious disputes between the German civil and military authorities concerning Seyss-Inquart's threats of a transportation embargo and that it was the food officials' responsibility to help terminate the strike. A heated discussion followed. Louwes and Hirschfeld argued that the Dutch people had always behaved in an exemplary fashion while under occupation, but now they had entered a new phase in the war. Both men also asserted that, given the severe disruption of infrastructure in combination with Allied bombings before 17 September, from 18 September onwards, no railway traffic would have been possible anyway. Moreover, the Allies had ordered the strike and therefore they should be the ones terminating it. Hirschfeld and Louwes pointed out that they had never refrained from making difficult discussions during the occupation, but that calling off

---

[11] National Archives and Records Administration, College Park, Maryland [NARA], Record Group 331, Entry 2, Box 117, Memorandum Ambassador Michiels, 28 September 1944.

[12] NIOD, 212a, inv.no. Note Hirschfeld on meeting with Von der Wense, 23 September 1944; De Jong, *Het Koninkrijk* 10b, 7–13.

[13] NIOD, 212a, inv.no. 164, Press release ANP Dittmar, 22 September 1944.

the strike would mean an immediate loss of the legitimacy of their positions. And so, they refused.[14]

On 27 September, Seyss-Inquart retaliated by cutting off all food transports from the northeast to the west. The embargo on all inland shipping was accompanied by the large-scale confiscation of transportation means, ships, fuel, and foodstuffs. To further disrupt communication in the occupied areas, the *Wehrmacht* terminated all postal services, telegraph and telephone lines. In addition to the harbours in Amsterdam, the Germans detonated over three kilometres of quays in the port of Rotterdam, although this was done against the advice of the German Admiralty in the Netherlands. Large vessels in both cities were sunk in order to block any passageway remaining.[15] Louwes remarked after the war on these events: 'From this date originates the bitter battle for the very existence of our people, famine in optima forma.'[16]

Illustration 5 Demolition of the Rotterdam harbour, 1944.

News of the German embargo soon reached the Dutch government, where the continuation of the railway strike became the object of serious dispute. With the loss of the battle of Arnhem, the strike had suddenly acquired dubious value. Most importantly, the impact of the strike on German transports had shown itself to be limited. Minister of Water Management and Transport in London, Willem Albarda, was inclined to

[14] NIOD, 212a, inv.no. 162, Note Hirschfeld.
[15] NIOD, 001 *Wehrmachtsbefehlshaber in den Niederlanden*, inv.no. 656, *Kriegestagebuch Marinebefehlshaber Vizeadmiral* Stange, September 1944.
[16] NA, 2.21.238, inv.no. 117, Report Louwes, 18; De Jong, *Het Koninkrijk* 10b, 8.

terminate the strike but his colleague, Minister for War Lidth de Jeude, reminded the council that it was not up them to make this decision. This should rather be left to the Supreme Headquarters Allied Expeditionary Force (SHAEF), which had actually given the order. The Allied Headquarters itself indicated that the railway strike in the western Netherlands could be called off but that continuation east of the Arnhem-Apeldoorn line was imperative from the military point of view. The Dutch government, however, considered a partial resumption of work by the strikers quite impossible because this could easily provoke German retaliation measures. Even though Seyss-Inquart asserted he would refrain from prosecuting the strikers, the Dutch ministers claimed fear of German retaliations as their general argument to persist across the board; so, on 2 October 1944, the government-in-exile called for the continuation of the railway strike.[17]

The government's distrust of the German intentions had been fuelled not only by the demolitions and confiscations, but also by the mounting repression in the occupied areas. One day before London called for continuation of the strike, *Wehrmachtbefehlshaber* Christiansen had ordered a raid on the town of Putten (Gelderland), as retaliation for an attack on German *Wehrmacht* officials by a local resistance group, which killed one German officer. Six men and a young woman were executed on the spot and 659 other men from Putten were deported to camp Amersfoort, 601 of whom were later deported to concentration camp Neuengamme. Of the original 601, only 49 survived.[18]

German Interests Divided

The constraints on both railway traffic and inland shipping proved devastating for the food supply. To make matters worse, the increasing fuel shortages resulted in the disconnection of electricity and gas for private use in October and November to save fuel for vital economic services.[19] Realising that deprivation of all basic necessities would lead to social chaos, the German occupier soon rescinded some of its more extreme retaliation measures. More specifically, it was *Wehrmachtbefehlshaber* Christiansen who fearfully anticipated that widespread hunger in the urbanised west would lead to disorder, riots, and disease, which the

---

[17] Rüter, *Rijden en Staken*, 257, 276–280; Fock, 'De Nederlandse Regering', 352.
[18] Of these 49 survivors, five died shortly after the war. Madelon de Keizer, *Putten: De Razzia en de Herinnering* (Amsterdam: Bakker, 1998).
[19] Waterlands Archief [WA], 0056 Gemeente Purmerend, inv.no. 1482, Minutes city council, 1 November 1944; De Jong, *Het Koninkrijk* 10b, 25–28.

German army dreaded while fighting the Allies in the south of the country. 'Trouble in the rear' was the last thing Christiansen desired now that the Netherlands had turned into an active battlefield.[20]

Pressured by the *Wehrmacht*, on 16 October 1944 Seyss-Inquart partially lifted the shipping embargo. The Dutch food officials evidently knew of the dispute between the German civil and military authorities prior to this decision as a report by Hirschfeld from October 1944 demonstrates:

> The Dutch authorities have concluded, notwithstanding the great difficulties the west of the country faces due to the embargo, not to cooperate with actions that would terminate the strike. The German authorities most likely recognised the danger of hunger insurgency in the west, especially in the large cities, posing a threat to the rear of the German army. Apparently, that is why the embargo, for now only concerning potatoes, has been lifted.[21]

The official reason for lifting the shipping embargo stated that the German authorities wanted to salvage the potato harvest in the northeastern provinces. The German authorities even released about 7,000 Dutchmen, who were forcibly working on German fortification projects in the northeast, to work the potato fields.[22] A little less than a month later, on 8 November 1944, Seyss-Inquart fully lifted the embargo. The duration and impact of the German blockade of the western Netherlands should therefore not in any way be compared to the German blockade of Leningrad in the years 1941–1944, which lasted for almost 900 days.[23] During his Nuremberg trial, the former *Reichskommissar* stated that the embargo had always been intended as a temporary measure to break the railway strike and that he had never planned to impose famine on the Dutch population. The real fault, according to Seyss-Inquart, lay with

[20] NIOD, 212a, inv.no. 162, Note by Hirschfeld on meeting with Von der Wense, 23 September 1945. See also: Private archive Dr J. C. Hooykaas, Final report of the Central IKB, 1945; transcript in: P. V. J. van Rossem, *Het Ontstaan van het Inter Kerkelijk Bureau en zijn Organisatie* (Amsterdam: s.n., 1984), 52–61; Secret telegram Fock in London, 17 November 1944, from *Nieuwe Rotterdamsche Courant*, 23 April 1955; transcript in: Van Rossem, *Het Ontstaan van het Inter Kerkelijk Bureau en zijn Organisatie* , 2; J. Ravesloot, *De Houding van de Kerk in de Bezettingstijd, 1940–1945* (S.l.: s.n., 1946), 30.

[21] NIOD, 212a, inv.no. 117, Correspondence on the potato harvest, 1944. See also: Minutes meeting Harvesting Operation, 16 October 1944; inv.no. 167, Diary Hirschfeld, 16 October 1944.

[22] NIOD, 212a, inv.no. 167, Report meeting Department of Trade and Industry, 16 October 1944. Hirschfeld also testified to this at Seyss-Inquart's Nuremberg trial: NIOD, 458 Collectie Proces van Neurenberg, inv.no. 27, Hearing Hirschfeld at Nuremberg Trial Seyss-Inquart, 14 June 1946, 11685.

[23] Anna Reid, *Leningrad: The Epic Siege of World War II, 1941–1944* (New York: Walker & Company, 2011); Snyder, *Bloodlands*, 172–174.

the *Wehrmacht*: 'In practice, traffic was never interrupted through my embargo, but rather – and I believe witnesses will confirm me in this – that the fact of the confiscation of ships [by the *Wehrmacht*] was the cause.'[24]

Not everybody trusted the occupier's ulterior motives – for good reason. One of the major issues contributing to the growing shortages was the considerable growth in clandestine production and trade, which now reached 40 per cent of total production.[25] Fearing German confiscations or searching for quick profits, farmers and transporters increasingly withheld their produce from the central rationing system and traded it for money and valuables on the black market instead.[26] The vast expansion of the black market made it extremely difficult for the food administration to restore the food supply after the embargo was lifted. Another factor contributing to the Dutch food officials' struggle to regain trust in the rationing system was that the Dutch government in London as well as various resistance groups continuously undermined the officials' authority, calling upon the Dutch to never trust collaborations with the German occupier, even if this seemed to be in the best interest of the food supply.[27]

These warnings were, of course, not entirely unfounded. Once the German civil authorities and Dutch food officials started cooperating again, the *Wehrmacht* intensified its hunt for adult men. In line with Berlin's strategy of 'withdrawal from military service with the enemy' (*Entziehung vom Wehrdienst beim Feind*), the *Wehrmacht* sought to eliminate all 'able-bodied' men – approximately 600,000 in the west – by forcing them to work for the German war effort.[28] On 10–11 November 1944, just after Seyss-Inquart had lifted the embargo, the Germans rounded up 52,000 of the 70,000 men aged 17–40 in the cities of Rotterdam and Schiedam and sent most of them to Germany. On 21 November, another raid followed in The Hague, Voorburg, and Rijswijk. This time, the Germans managed to capture 'only' 13,000 men because many others had gone into hiding. It has been said that Amsterdam was not targeted because of rumours about typhus among

---

[24] NIOD, 458, inv.no. 25, 11431. See also: 11493, 11499–11500; Wilco Gieling, *Seyss-Inquart* (Soesterberg: Aspekt, 2009), 229.

[25] Klemann, *Nederland 1938–1948*, 212

[26] NA, 2.21.238, inv.no. 117, Report Louwes, 18; Klemann, 'De Zwarte Markt', 546–549.

[27] NIOD, 212a, inv.no. 167, Diary Hirschfeld, 16–19 October 1944; inv.no. 117, 119; GAR, inv.no. 1855, Poster warning against potato harvesting campaign, October 1944.

[28] NIOD, 458, inv.no. 23, Transcripts of the trial of Seyss-Inquart, 10 June 1946, 11408. Sijes, *De Arbeidsinzet*, 540; De Jong, *Het Koninkrijk* 10b, 96–110.

the population, but Louwes stated that the capital city was spared because he managed to convince the German civil authorities that the rationing system would simply collapse if all adult men would be taken away from their posts, or otherwise go into hiding. The overextension of the *Wehrmacht*, which the *Oberkommando der Wehrmacht* (OKW) expected to battle the Allies and, at the same time, quell domestic disturbances, likely also played a role. From September to December 1944, at least 120,000 men were seized in the still-occupied areas: this loss of manpower evidently caused the rationing system to further disintegrate.[29]

The raids on adult men fuelled the distrust among the Dutch and provoked the population to take matters into their own hands. A local resistance group in Leeuwarden, for example, made it their goal 'to withdraw as much food as possible from the German banditry by allocating the supplies outside of the rationing system to those most in need'.[30] This kind of grassroots food redistribution severely disrupted the central rationing system. Municipal administrations, especially Amsterdam, similarly began hoarding food for their own citizens at the expense of central rationing. Shopkeepers contributed to the anarchical situation by trading their supplies instead of collecting ration coupons. To protect the food system from total collapse and restore the central rationing system, the food authorities recognised that they needed the support of farmers and transporters as well as city councils.[31] The only way to achieve this was by cooperating with the German civil authorities, who were more amenable to working with the Dutch food authorities; however, this was a policy that increasingly diverged from the military directives from Berlin.

On 5 December 1944, the establishment of the Central Shipping Company for the Food Supply (*Centrale Reederij Voedselvoorziening*: CRV) became the embodiment of the rapprochement between German civil authorities and Dutch food officials. As we will see in Chapter 4, this company became the core of the central rationing system during the final months of occupation. By then, the conditions had reached famine proportions as reflected in both official rations, dropping below a mere 750 kcal per day for adults after 26 November 1944 (Figure 2.1), and

---

[29] NA, 2.21.238, inv.no. 117, Report Louwes, 19; Sijes, *De Arbeidsinzet*, 552; Sijes, *De Razzia van Rotterdam: 10–11 November 1944* (The Hague: Nijhoff, 1951); Foray, 'The "Clean *Wehrmacht*"', 785.

[30] Tresoar, 350 Vereniging Friesland 1940–1945, inv.no. 689, Kroniek 1940–1945 by Y. Ypma.

[31] NA, 3.11.30.05, inv.no. 65, Report on food supply, 19 December 1944.

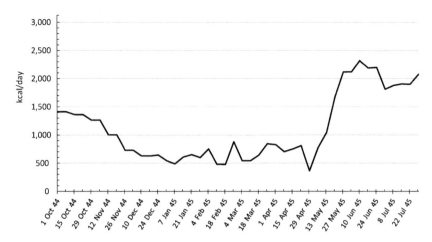

Figure 2.1 Weekly adult rations in kcal per day in the western Netherlands, October 1944–July 1945.
Source: NA, 2.11.23.02, inv.no. 192, Reports on rationing in the Netherlands, 1946

the accompanying rising mortality rates and reduced fertility. In December, official institutions began calling the crisis an 'undeniable famine'.[32]

On 14 December, Hirschfeld and Seyss-Inquart met for the first time in private after almost four and a half years of occupation. This meeting became a turning point in the crisis. In their private conversation, the *Reichskommissar* spoke of the possibility of keeping the west out of future military activities – 'neutralising the west' – and restoring Dutch authority. Hirschfeld wrote in his war diary on this meeting: 'It should be said that Dr Seyss-Inquart had gone into the matter with great care and offered his assistance to prevent or alleviate the menacing famine. The German faction also feels responsible.'[33] Several other important meetings between the German civil authorities, Dutch food officials, and representatives from the organised industries followed, in which Seyss-Inquart expressed similar views. During these meetings, they also discussed the possibility of Dutch vessels retrieving coal from Germany as

---

[32] NA, 2.11.30.05, inv.no. 65, Report RBVVO food position, 19 December 1945; NIOD, 212a, inv.no. 167, Diary Hirschfeld, 3 January 1945.
[33] NIOD, 212a, inv.no. 167, Diary Hirschfeld, 15 December 1944. Hirschfeld confirmed this change in attitude during the Nuremberg trials as well: NIOD, 458, inv.no. 27, Hearing Hirschfeld at Nuremberg Trial Seyss-Inquart, 14 June 1946, 11686, 11696.

well as food relief by the International Red Cross.[34] As will be explained in Chapters 4 and 5, due to serious miscommunications, Seyss-Inquart's plans to neutralise part of western Holland from military activities failed to reach London, delaying serious negotiations until the spring of 1945.

The Final Struggle

Shortly after inland shipping had resumed, food and fuel transportations were profoundly hindered once again. This time, weather conditions aggravated the situation with a heavy frost period that lasted from 23 December 1944 until 30 January 1945. Because the *Wehrmacht* and *Kriegsmarine* had confiscated large numbers of vessels and tugboats, there was minimal shipping activity to keep the waterways open. Most inland routes froze over and only those few harbours of interest to the *Kriegsmarine* remained navigable in January.[35] On 12 January 1945, the CRV warned that 'the backlog since September 1944, due to the embargo, the confiscations of large supplies of cereals, the loss of three surplus provinces [in the liberated south], and the troubles with harvesting, *cannot* be fixed, especially not now the frost has set in'.[36] By now, the German civil authorities as well as the *Sicherheitspolizei und Sicherheitsdienst* (*Sipo und SD*) in the Netherlands communicated with Berlin using the terms 'famine' (*Hungersnot*) and 'emergency situation' (*Notlage*) to refer to the situation in the western provinces.[37]

With an average daily mean temperature of -1.6 Celsius in January,[38] weather circumstances cannot be described as an extremely severe winter as is often assumed in literature. Yet combined with the fuel shortages, German transportation requisitions, and the railway strike, the frost period accelerated famine conditions in the west. Adverse weather conditions had also played a role earlier during the crisis as heavy rains in November had stagnated the harvest of potatoes and sugar beets in the northeast, producing a much poorer harvest than usual.[39] In January 1945, official rations dropped to approximately 500 calories per capita in the west, which resulted in increasing numbers of famine-related

---

[34] NIOD, 212a, inv.no. 167, Diary Hirschfeld, 16–22 December 1944. See also: De Jong, *Het Koninkrijk* 10b, 1228–1231.

[35] NIOD, 216h, inv.no. Report CRV, 24 January 1945; Hans M. Hirschfeld, 'De Centrale Reederij voor de Voedselvoorziening', *Economie* 10 (1946): 1–2.

[36] NIOD, 216h, inv.no. 312, Report meeting 12 January 1945.

[37] Bundesarchiv Berlin Lichterfelde [BA], NS 19 Stab Reichsführer SS, 2429, Telegram 10 January 1945; BA, R70NL Polizeistellen in den Niederlanden, 54, Report on illegal press in the Netherlands, 6 February 1945.

[38] www.knmi.nl/klimatologie/daggegevens/index.cgim. Accessed 10 October 2014.

[39] *Jaarverslag van Amsterdam 1944* (Amsterdam: Stadsdrukkerij, 1946), 51.

deaths and diseases. People demolished tramlines, bridges, and empty houses to collect firewood, while black-market trade, looting, and theft became widespread. The complete lack of wood also created considerable difficulties burying the dead. Corpses sometimes remained above ground for weeks. The municipality of Amsterdam subsequently devised 'reusable coffins'; meanwhile, many had to be buried in sheets or even in paper.[40]

Communication with the German occupier now became of vital importance to the Dutch food officials, both in further centralising the rationing system and fighting the shadow economy, but also in arranging external relief for the starving urban dwellers. Conflicts between the German civil and military authorities continued in this period, especially concerning the usage of transportation means to feed the Dutch. At the international level, these negotiations were even more troublesome. Pressured by the Dutch government, the Allies had been debating relief since October 1944.[41] Yet relief planning and military strategies – most notably maintaining the economic blockade to keep supplies out of German hands – inevitably proved to be in conflict with each other, just as they had been elsewhere in occupied Europe.[42] After three months of negotiation, the first relief ships from the Swedish Red Cross managed to dock in the harbour of Delfzijl (Groningen) in early January, followed by four shipments from the Swedish and International Red Cross in February and March. Although limited in size, these shipments were of indispensable value for the western population, which is visible in the corresponding slight rise in rations in February, March, and April 1945 (Figure 2.1).[43]

The frost period also aggravated the dispute between the Netherlands and London on the continuation of the railway strike. The Dutch food officials became caught in a bitter conflict between Seyss-Inquart, who still desired to break the strike, and the Dutch government-in-exile, which refused to call the strikers back to work again. Although, in practice, the government had no say in the food system, Hirschfeld and

---

[40] Stadsarchief Amsterdam [SA], 391 Gemeentelijke Bureau voor Lijkbezorging, 1945; C. Feltkamp, *De Begrafenismoeilijkheden in 1945 te Amsterdam: Het Opheffen van den Achterstand in het Begraven door het Gemeentelijke Bureau voor Lijkbezorging* (Amsterdam: Stadsdrukkerij Amsterdam, 1945).

[41] Many documents on these negotiations can be found in: NARA, RG 331, Entry 2, Box 118; The National Archives London [TNA], PREM 3/221/12; PREM 4/29/12. See Chapter 5.

[42] Hionidou, *Famine and Death in Occupied Greece*, 16; Ronald W. Zweig, 'Feeding the Camps: Allied Blockade Policy and the Relief of Concentration Camps in Germany, 1944–45', *The Historical Journal* 41 (1998): 825–851.

[43] NA, 2.21.238, inv.no. 117, Report Louwes, 19.

Louwes knew that maintaining good relations with London was of the utmost importance for their political legitimacy. Nevertheless, in a telegram of 19 January 1945, they pleaded with London to either allow them to act or to take full responsibility for the consequences:

The Heads of Food Supply therefore request a statement addressed to them, that the Government accepts chaos and starvation as inevitable consequences of their decision and persists fully with this policy, or that they provide the Heads with the freedom and responsibility to act with discretion.[44]

At the same time, the Contact Committee of the government in the liberated south and resistance groups in the occupied areas still insisted on continuation of the strike. Persuaded by their arguments, the Dutch government responded to the food officials on 23 January, saying that 'giving in would lead to the least desirable outcome'.[45] On 25 January, the government announced that the strike would continue – a decision that was, and still is, highly disputed by many people in the Netherlands.[46]

The rejection from London strengthened the relations between the food officials and the German civil authorities. In particular, the head of the *Hauptabteilung Ernährung und Landwirtschaft* Von der Wense and Seyss-Inquart's *Beauftragte* for The Hague and the province of South Holland Ernst A. Schwebel played a significant role in mitigating famine conditions in the west. Although Seyss-Inquart publicly blamed the Allied invasion for the suffering and deprivation, behind the scenes he too demonstrated that he was fully aware of his precarious negotiating position. Early in 1945, he allowed some railway traffic for the civilian food supply, including a couple of German-driven trains to deliver potatoes to Communal Kitchens in the large conurbations.[47]

By now the Dutch food officials had become profoundly irritated with their own government. On 4 February 1945, the Directorate of Food Supply sent a message to London, stating that the Germans had offered to allow ten trains a week carrying potatoes and cereals, provided that Dutch manpower was used. The government reluctantly responded they

---

[44] NIOD, 233b Regering in Londen, inv.no. 18, Telegram food authorities to government, 19 January 1945.

[45] NIOD, 233b, inv.no. 18, Telegram Contact Commission to government in London, 17 January 1945; Telegram government to RBVVO, 23 January 1945.

[46] Including by historians. See, for example: Rüter, *Rijden en Staken*, 399–404; Trienekens, *Tussen ons Volk en de Honger*, 377; Klemann, *Nederland 1938–1948*, 465.

[47] Arthur Seyss-Inquart, *Wat nu? Vragen in Donkere Uren Aan Het Nederlandsche Volk Gesteld*, published radio speech 7 January 1945 (S.l.: s.n., 1945); Hirschfeld, 'De Centrale Reederij', 12; NIOD, 212a, inv.no. 116, Note meeting International Red Cross, Dutch Red Cross, and German Red Cross, 14 February 1945; NIOD, 216h, inv.no. 312, minutes CRV, 12 January 1945, 15 February 1945. See also: Trienekens, *Tussen ons Volk en de Honger*, 378.

would consider the proposal, but only if the Allies and the Contact Committee of the organised resistance approved.[48] Not coincidentally, a few days earlier a thaw had set in, thereby eliminating the immediate need to terminate the strike. While historians have rightfully criticised the January–February decisions to refuse to call off the strike, it should be considered that it was far from certain that railway transportation would have resumed otherwise. Even before the Allied invasion, railway traffic had been seriously constrained by Allied air raids. For example, on 5 August 1944, a train near Halfweg (North Holland) was shot by fighter aircraft, killing 13 people and leaving 48 heavily wounded. A month later, near Diemen (North Holland) 36 people were killed by Allied fighters.[49] The Head of the Intelligence Service Fock repeatedly referred to this in post-war statements, convincingly arguing that the combination of a demolished infrastructure and Allied airplanes firing at anything that moved would have made railway traffic nearly impossible during the final months of occupation anyway.[50]

By the beginning of February, most waterways had become accessible again. The dominating issue now was collecting transportation means and foodstuffs as well as providing the fuel necessary to enable this transportation. During the early months of 1945, the coal stocks had been virtually depleted and new supplies completely depended on occasional transport from Germany. On 8 February, Hirschfeld wrote a pressing letter to *Beauftragte* Schwebel, in which he envisioned that 'now the frost has disappeared and waterways are accessible again, the food supply will collapse due to coal shortages'.[51] Meanwhile, the *Wehrmacht* continued to confiscate supplies meant for civil use and redirected coal transportations to Germany. The fuel shortages that ensued not only threatened food transportation but also the polders, which would flood if the pumping mills were not sufficiently fuelled.[52] Many factories had to shut down in the final phase of the war in order to save fuel. The German-imported coal only just managed to power the pumping mills

---

[48] NIOD, 233b, inv.no. 33, Telegram RBVVO to Dutch government, 4 February 1945; Telegram Dutch government to the Netherlands, 6 February 1945.
[49] *Jaarverslag van Amsterdam 1944*, 36.
[50] Fock, 'De Nederlandse Regering'; Fock, Radio-interview VPRO 'De Hongerwinter', 8 October 1985, http://www.npogeschiedenis.nl/speler.POMS_VPRO_078920.html. Accessed 4 April 2016. Ambassador Michiels stated similarly in his memorandum to the Ministry of Economic Warfare that even if railway traffic were to continue, insufficient stocks of coal were available to ensure transports. NARA, 331, Entry 2, Box 117, Memorandum Michiels, 28 September 1944.
[51] NIOD, 212a, inv.no. 28, Letter Hirschfeld to Schwebel on coal position, 8 February 1945.
[52] NIOD, 216h, inv.no. 312, Report CRV, 14 March 1945.

and Communal Kitchens – the latter did not even last to the end of the occupation.

In late March, the Allies finally crossed the river Rhine, and, in their advance to encircle the German industrial heartland, liberated the north-eastern provinces. In only a few days' time, the three western provinces became totally isolated from the rest of the country, which proved to be one final blow to their already critical food situation. Not only did all food transports cease, but the rapid Allied advance also led to severe repressive measures from the German military authorities. On 2 April, Seyss-Inquart informed Hirschfeld that he had received orders from the OKW to inundate the west as part of its 'scorched earth' strategy. The *Reichskommissar*, however, asserted that he was willing to defy this order and negotiate with General Johannes Blaskowitz, the new German commander-in-chief of the northwestern Netherlands, provided that the Allies refrained from attacking the west. Seyss-Inquart had consulted on this matter with Reich Minister for Armaments and War Production Albert Speer on 1 April, who had received the same order for Germany and agreed with him that the command to inundate should not be carried out. Seyss-Inquart assured Hirschfeld that, due to the German army's isolation in the west, the OKW could not enforce these military demands anyway.[53]

In the final weeks of the war, Seyss-Inquart undoubtedly recognised his perilous situation and replaced his deeply rooted animosity towards the Allies with a more conciliatory approach. After his meeting with Hirschfeld on 2 April, several important secret meetings followed between Seyss-Inquart and representatives of the Dutch government in the occupied territory. During these meetings, an informal truce was proposed in which the Germans would refrain from further demolitions, inundations, and assaults, and give full support for food relief. In return, the Allies would refrain from attacking the west.[54] These negotiations on food relief fell safely within the parameters of legitimate discussion but, in reality, began to coincide with negotiations on the terms of surrender. And while the German *Wehrmacht* nonetheless inundated land between Muiden and Utrecht as well as the Wieringermeerpolder in fear of Allied landings, Seyss-Inquart remained amenable enough to allow aerial food drops and relief shipments.[55] On 28 and 30 April, the first meetings

---

[53] NIOD, 458, inv.no. 24, Nuremberg Trial Seyss-Inquart, 11 June 1946, 11427; NIOD, 212a, inv.no. 167, Diary Hirschfeld, 2 April 1945.

[54] NARA, 331, Entry 2, Box 118, Message Netherlands Interior Forces to SHAEF, 14 April 1945; Brief for parleys on relief of Holland, 23 April 1945.

[55] NARA, 331, Entry 2, Box 118, Message Netherlands Interior Forces to SHAEF, 15, 18 April 1945.

between the Germans and the Allies took place, resulting in the Achter-veld Agreement whereby the terms of food relief were discussed. Mean-while, on 29 April the legendary food drops commenced that would become symbolic of the liberation of the Netherlands. On 5 May, Blas-kowitz agreed to the terms of surrender of his armed forces. As is demonstrated in the following chapters, it would take the country months to recover from the suffering and deprivation. The interim Netherlands Military Authority finally lifted the emergency situation in the western Netherlands on 9 July 1945.[56]

Conclusion

Investigating the chronology of the food crisis, we have seen how the famine clearly resulted from a complex culmination of political and warfare events (e.g., war, railway strike, embargo, destroyed infrastruc-ture, postponement of emergency food aid), economic factors (e.g., import dependency), geography (e.g., separation of production food-stuffs and fuel and main consumption areas), natural conditions (winter frost) and social responses (e.g., the growth of the shadow economy, lack of trust in food administration). By exploring all these adverse exogenous shocks, this chapter has shown how various factors contributed to the transportation failure that led to famine conditions in the Netherlands. This observation does not absolve the belligerent states for ultimate responsibility for the famine; however, it does negate German intent in causing famine: in any case, after October 1944. Throughout these complex interactions of contributory factors, it is notable that a small number of key figures played pivotal roles in the decision-making pro-cesses. Interestingly enough, this tells us that, for the greater part during these final months of occupation, it was not an overarching conflict between German and Dutch-Allied administrations, but their internal disputes and negotiations that influenced the course of the famine. As the next chapters demonstrate, for all parties involved, the food situation was a powerful negotiating tool in times of war. In order to understand these responses, we first turn to the demographic impact of the famine, revealing the chronology and geography of the crisis as well as those most affected by the shortage.

---

[56] Willem H. van Baarle, Sla*g om B2: Een Herinnering in Woord en Beeld aan het Commissariaat Noodvoorziening* (The Hague: Mouton, 1945).

3   Effects on Mortality, Fertility, and Health in Later Life

Upon examination, most patients stand out because of their pale facial complexion and sunken cheeks. Their fatigue is expressed in their faces, in their posture, and in the slowness of their movements. Many doze off once they are seated in anticipation of examination, leaning heavily on their chair's armrests while getting up again. Most are mentally slow as well. One would expect a certain rebellion or irritability, which do occur, but mostly one sees an attitude of resignation and indifference towards what is to come. During examination of the body, the horrifying emaciation is evident from their bony ribs and shoulder blades, as well as skinny arms and legs, the latter only if oedema does not prevail.[1]

Before the Hunger Winter, most Dutch physicians had no experience whatsoever in treating famine diseases such as hunger oedema or cachexia. Similar to doctor C. L. de Jongh from The Hague, who gave this graphic description of 'hunger patients', medical practitioners in the occupied Netherlands faced the difficult task of combating these unfamiliar disorders whilst dealing with extreme shortages of not only food and fuel, but of medicines and medical instruments as well. Such working conditions had been unthinkable in the highly developed Netherlands of the interwar period.[2] Awareness of the extraordinary circumstances in which they had to operate prompted doctors to document the changing public health conditions, offering a powerful impression of the physiological impact of famine upon a twentieth-century society.[3]

---

[1] C. L. de Jongh, 'Ziekteverschijnselen door den Hongersnood Veroorzaakt', in *Medische Ervaringen*, 234.

[2] In 1939, mortality in the Netherlands was 8.7 per 1,000 population, life expectancy 65.7 years, mortality of infants below 1 year 33.7 per 1,000 live births, and tuberculosis mortality 4.11 per 10,000 population – rates that were more favorable than in most other Western-European countries at that time. Banning, 'Food Shortage and Public Health', 93; G. D. Hemmes, 'Besmettelijke Ziekten: Epidemiologie en Praeventieve Maatregelen', in *Medische Ervaringen*, 105; Henriette A. Bosman-Jelgersma, 'De Nederlandse Farmacie tijdens de Tweede Wereldoorlog', in *Geneeskunde en Gezondheidszorg in Nederland*, 217–219.

[3] Boerema, 'Inleiding', in *Medische Ervaringen*, 7–9.

Examination of this physiological impact poses certain methodological difficulties for the historian. Firstly, food deprivation is hard to measure due to its inherently individual nature. Likewise, levels of undernutrition based on the overall incidence of famine-related diseases are also difficult to ascertain as the relevant materials on this subject remain largely anecdotal. To overcome these obstacles and enable investigation of the scope and intensity of the Dutch famine, this chapter focuses on measurable, quantitative indicators such as mortality, fertility, and long-term biological consequences. An exploration of this demographic evidence helps reveal the chronology and geography of the famine and those groups of people that were most and least affected by the food shortage. Together, these aspects form an underlying framework that is necessary for the study of socio-political responses to the famine and their effectiveness. In addition, the outcomes of this demographic inquiry help determine the spatial and temporal focus of the following chapters on responses to the famine.

To gather knowledge on the scope and intensity of the Dutch famine, this chapter largely builds on recent research by Ekamper et al. (2017), who used previously unavailable data files from Statistics Netherlands (CBS) to estimate war-related deaths in the Netherlands in the period 1944–1945.[4] The Netherlands Interdisciplinary Demographic Institute (NIDI) has graciously made additional calculations and estimations from this data set for this study, enabling me to answer questions about the specifics of death and survival during the Hunger Winter.

Numbers and Places

How many people died during the famine? This seemingly simple question has, unfortunately, no clear answer. Dutch historians remain ambiguous in their estimations of 'famine-related deaths' in the large conurbations of the three western provinces, home to some 2.6 million people, citing anywhere between 10,000 and 'tens of thousands'.[5] This wide range of estimations is not unique to the Dutch famine, but rather a

---

[4] Peter Ekamper et al., 'War-Related Excess Mortality in The Netherlands, 1944–45: New Estimates of Famine- and Non-Famine-Related Deaths from National Death Records', *Historical Methods: A Journal of Quantitative and Interdisciplinary History* 50 (2017): 113–128.

[5] Dols and Van Arcken, 'Food Supply and Nutrition', 352; De Jong, *Het Koninkrijk* 10b, 219; Trienekens, *Tussen ons Volk en de Honger*, 401–407; Barnouw, *De Hongerwinter*, 52; Klemann, *Nederland 1938–1948*, 467; Futselaar, *Lard, Lice and Longevity*, 46–47; Futselaar, 'The Mystery of the Dying Dutch: Can Micronutrient Deficiencies Explain the Difference between Danish and Dutch Wartime Mortality?' in *Food and Conflict in Europe*, 193–222.

reoccurring methodological issue for famine studies in general.[6] Estimating mortality during famines begins with differentiating between excess mortality, war-related mortality, and famine-related mortality as well as providing a clear delineation of its time period and geographical focus. Methodologically speaking, to estimate population losses during a famine, it is necessary to estimate a 'baseline mortality' – mortality without the famine – based on population structure, fertility, and seasons. Even then, it remains difficult to estimate how many of these extra deaths were directly or indirectly related to malnutrition and starvation.[7]

Early estimations of famine-related mortality were all based on municipal statistics. Banning, in 'Food Shortage and Public Health' (1946), based his estimate of 10,000 on deaths that were officially reported as resulting 'from hunger'. At the time, 4,961 of these hunger deaths had been reported in seven towns in the western Netherlands: Amsterdam and The Hague among them. Banning estimated this number to double when statistics of the remaining towns in the western Netherlands would become available.[8]

The best-known estimation of excess deaths during the Hunger Winter derives from a publication by the CBS (October 1945). This report compared the absolute number of deaths in twelve municipalities in the western Netherlands with a population over 25,000 in the first half of 1944 with those in the first half of 1945, and calculated a difference of about 16,000 excess deaths in 1945 (Table 3.1).[9] Being the only available data for a long period of time, this publication generated a domino effect, with many publications reiterating the same numbers. Most authors, however, corrected their estimations of the 16,000 deaths to include a larger region and time window – the most well-known being the number

---

[6] See, for example: Ó Gráda, *Eating People Is Wrong, and Other Essays on Famine, Its Past and Its Future* (Princeton: Princeton University Press, 2015), 131; Davies and Wheatcroft, *The Years of Hunger*, 401; Andrea Graziosi, 'The Soviet 1931–1933 Famines and the Ukrainian Holodomor: Is a New Interpretation Possible, and What Would Its Consequences Be?' in *Hunger by Design: The Great Ukrainian Famine in Its Soviet Context*, ed. Halyna Hryn (Cambridge, MA: Harvard University Press, 2008), 1–20; Felix Wemheuer, *Famine Politics in Maoist China and The Soviet Union* (New Haven: Yale University Press, 2014).

[7] For more on estimating population losses, see: Jacques Vallin et al., 'A New Estimate of Ukrainian Population Losses during the Crises of the 1930s and 1940s', *Population Studies* 56 (2002): 249–264.

[8] 2,316 were reported in Amsterdam and 2,095 in The Hague. Banning, 'Food Shortage and Public Health', 99. In a previous article, Banning made a slightly different reporting: Banning, 'De Gezondheidstoestand in Nederland', 312.

[9] CBS, *Geboorte en Sterfte in Eenige Groote Gemeenten in het Westen des Lands: 1e Halfjaar 1945 Vergeleken met 1ᵉ Halfjaar 1944*, Announcement no. 1006 (S.l.: s.n., 1945).

Table 3.1 *Numbers of deaths in 12 municipalities in the first half year of 1944 and 1945*

Municipality	Number of deaths First half year		Ratio (1944 = 100)	Difference
	1944	1945		
Amsterdam	4,401	9,737	221	5,336
Rotterdam	3,255	7,854	241	4,599
The Hague[a]	2,389	5,811	243	3,422
Leiden	625	1,130	180	505
Hilversum	495	839	169	344
Delft	424	863	204	439
Dordrecht	424	603	142	179
Schiedam	396	737	186	341
Gouda	287	519	181	232
Voorburg	188	449	239	261
Vlaardingen	180	369	205	189
Rijswijk	91	211	232	120
Total	13,155	29,122	221	15,967

[a] Exclusive of 530 casualties from 'acts of war' (bombing Bezuidenhout 3 March 1945).
Source: Table based on CBS, *Geboorte en Sterfte*, 5, ordered by number of deaths in 1944.

put forward by De Jong, who estimated that 22,000 people died because of the famine.

While the 1945 CBS statistics shown in Table 3.1 lack information on baseline mortality and population structure, two important observations can be made from these statistics. First of all, the three largest cities – Amsterdam, Rotterdam, and The Hague – suffered the most fatalities in 1945 in absolute terms. The CBS statistics also reveal that the number of deaths in some smaller towns in close proximity to the large cities rose to similar proportions: cases in point being Rijswijk, Voorburg, Delft, and Vlaardingen. However, the numbers also have severe limitations. Firstly, several affected cities in the western provinces are excluded, such as Utrecht and Haarlem.[10] Secondly, comparing the number of deaths between the first half of 1944 and first half of 1945 is not an ideal indication of excess deaths: due to the circumstances of war, mortality in 1944 was far from normal. Thirdly, the CBS statistics refer to place of death, not place of residence, which may have led to distortions given the large numbers of people frequently moving during the famine.

[10] According to Banning, in Utrecht the difference between deaths in the first half of 1944 and first half of 1945 was 953, or with a ratio of 186 (1944 = 100). Banning, 'Occupied Holland: I Public Health', *British Medical Journal* 1 (1947): 540.

Illustration 6 Protestant church 'Zuiderkerk' in Amsterdam converted into a morgue, 1945.

The study by Ekamper et al. was the first to analyse a new data source, which has subsequently enabled new estimations of war-related excess deaths in the Netherlands. Instead of being limited to the use of aggregated annual data at the national level or information from selected municipalities, this study utilised the previously unavailable electronic Cause of Death Registry (*Doodsoorzakenstatistiek*) from the CBS, containing information on cause of death, month of death, age, sex, place of death, and place of residence. The excess deaths are estimated as deviations from monthly age- sex-, and region-specific mortality in 1946–1947, and are adjusted for seasonal trends. By estimating the number of deaths under normal circumstances and subtracting this estimate from the observed number of deaths in the presence of the famine and other war-related events, this method is far more accurate than previous estimates. In the study, the Netherlands was categorised according to three geographic locations: the 'Urban West' comprising six large cities in the western

Table 3.2 *Estimates of war-related excess deaths in the Netherlands in selected time periods by region*[a]

Region	September 1944–July 1945	September 1944–May 1945	January 1945–July 1945	January 1945–May 1945
Urban West	22,871	21,013	20,238	18,380
Rural West	12,427	11,001	10,138	8,712
Rest Netherlands	26,497	23,569	14,411	11,483
Total	61,795	55,583	44,787	38,575

[a] Excluding 16,400 deaths in the period of January 1944–July 1945 missing information on region and/or month of death.
Source: Table based on Ekamper et al., 'War-Related Excess Mortality', 124.

Netherlands heavily affected by famine – Amsterdam, Rotterdam, The Hague, Leiden, Haarlem and Utrecht; the 'Rural West', made up of smaller towns and rural areas in the three western provinces; and the remainder of the Netherlands, combined under the term 'Rest Netherlands'. The aim was thus to investigate war-related mortality across the entire country, allowing for a more precise estimation of the effects of famine as well as military activities in the years 1944–1945.[11]

The Ekamper study shows that the estimated total number of war-related excess deaths among civilians in the period from January 1944 to July 1945 was close to 91,000.[12] For the purpose of investigating famine-related mortality, it is relevant to zoom in on the urban and rural west and limit the observation period to the crisis months September 1944–July 1945 (Table 3.2), as previous studies have indicated that, even after liberation, people still died as a consequence of the famine. Using this scope, Ekamper et al. arrived at over 35,000 excess deaths: almost 23,000 of these deaths occurred in the six largest famine-affected cities.[13] Based on their analysis, including causes of death, Ekamper et al. concluded that some earlier estimates of famine-related deaths were probably not too far off.

Local differences in excess deaths can be investigated when dividing the famine-affected urban west into separate localities. The mortality patterns in Figures 3.1a–f are calculated by the NIDI as deviations from the reference period 1946–1947, taking seasonal mortality fluctuations into

---

[11] Ekamper et al., 'War-Related Excess Mortality'. For more on their data and methods, see pages 117–119.
[12] These statistics do not include individuals who were deported and died abroad, such as Jewish citizens, political prisoners, and those who were forced to work in Germany. Ekamper et al., 'War-Related Excess Mortality', 125–126.
[13] These numbers do not include deaths with inconclusive death records.

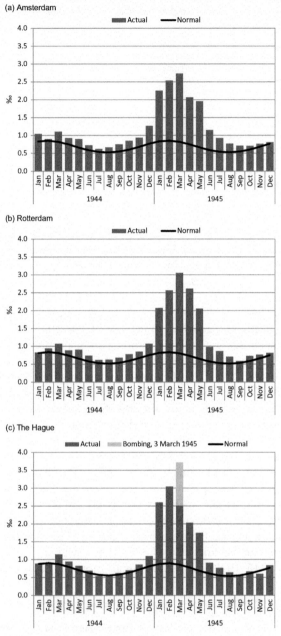

Figure 3.1 The actual and estimated 'normal'[a] number of deaths per 1,000 of the population, by year and month of death, and by city, 1944–1945.

[a]Estimated from post-war pattern 1946–1947.

Source: Calculations by NIDI using non-public microdata from Statistics Netherlands

(d) Utrecht

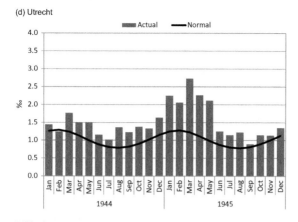

(e) Haarlem

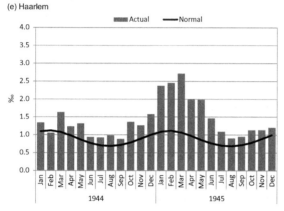

(f) Leiden

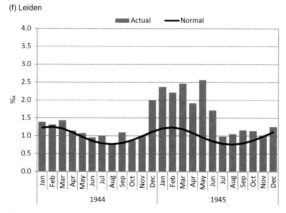

Figure 3.1 (*cont.*)

account. Looking at the six famine cities within the urban west separately, it becomes evident that famine followed a different chronology and intensity in each town. In most cities, the largest increase in number of deaths per 1,000 population was in January 1945 – corresponding with the period of winter frost – rising to a peak in March 1945. In all cities, actual deaths in June 1945 were still well above normal, which can be seen as a lagged effect of the famine in the conurbations. This could have also partly resulted from people being hospitalised in the large cities after the war.

The proportional rise of deaths was most marked in The Hague and Rotterdam, closely followed by Amsterdam. The difference in proportional rise of deaths with the other three, smaller cities – Utrecht, Haarlem, and Leiden – in part derived from their higher normal mortality patterns, especially so for Utrecht. Another striking difference is that the deaths in Amsterdam, Rotterdam, and The Hague were largely concentrated in the months of January–May 1945 while in Utrecht, Haarlem, and especially Leiden, the high mortality pattern started earlier and continued for a longer period after liberation. This suggests that the famine – and/or subsequent relief – ran a different course in these cities.

Age- and Sex-Specific Mortality

Questions about who died during the famine are similarly in need of reassessment. New data that include the age and gender composition of mortality yield new insight into the famine's impact upon different groups of people. Before differentiating between age groups, Figure 3.2 shows monthly deaths per 1,000 population in the urban and rural west, as well as in the rest of the Netherlands. It clearly reveals strongly elevated mortality rates in the urban west from early December 1944 onward, reaching a peak in March 1945 and quickly dropping after May 1945, only to reach normal levels again in the summer of 1945. This trend was particularly strong among men. Overall, mortality among both men and women in the rural west corresponds with urban mortality patterns although it was much less pronounced. The peaks in deaths outside the west, in October 1944 and April 1945, correspond with war activities surrounding the liberation of the south and northeast Netherlands.

Figures 3.3a–f show the death rates categorised by age group and sex. In all age groups, the highest monthly rates in the urban west were seen between January and May 1945, reaching a peak in March 1945. Focusing on the age distribution of mortality in the urban west, the figures show that, in absolute terms, the most affected age groups were infants and men and women over the age of 55 – especially men aged 70 years or over: the mortality of this last group reached 40 per 1,000 population in March

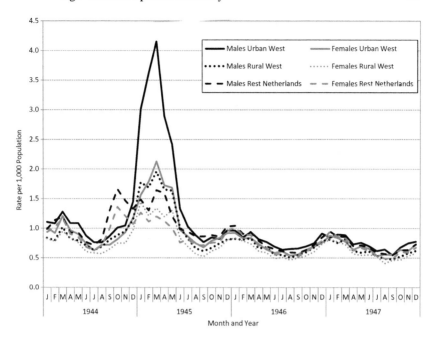

Figure 3.2 Deaths per 1,000 population, by region, sex, and year and month of death, 1944–1947.
Reprinted from Ekamper et al., 'War-Related Excess Mortality', 120

1945 compared to 10 per 1,000 during the same month in 1946–1947. In relative terms, adult men between the ages of 25–54 suffered a fourfold increase in deaths compared to the usual pattern. About the same increase can be detected among male infants and males 70 years or over. In all age groups, men were significantly more affected than women. In total, male deaths outnumbered female deaths by approximately two to one. Male and female deaths in the rural west followed similar patterns but on a much smaller scale. This female mortality advantage has also been detected in other modern famines, and can partly be explained physiologically by the fact that women have a much higher proportion of body fat and a lower proportion of muscle than men.[14] These age- and sex-specific mortality patterns largely parallel evidence from comparable modern famines as well as statements made in previous studies on the Hunger Winter.

[14] On the sex bias during famines, see: Rivers, 'Women and Children Last: An Essay on Sex Discrimination in Disasters', *Disasters* 6 (1982): 256–276; Kari Pitkänen, 'Famine Mortality in Nineteenth Century Finland: Is There a Sex Bias?' In *Famine Demography: Perspectives from the Past and Present*, eds. Tim Dyson and Ó Gráda (Oxford: Oxford University Press, 2002), 65–92; Ó Gráda, *Famine*, 98–101.

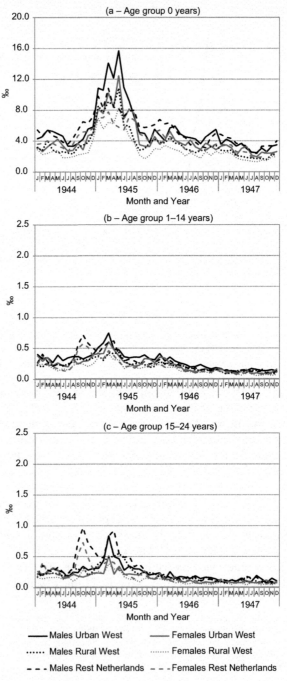

Figure 3.3 Deaths per 1,000 population, by region, sex, and age, 1944–1947.
Reprinted from Ekamper et al., 'War-Related Excess Mortality', 122

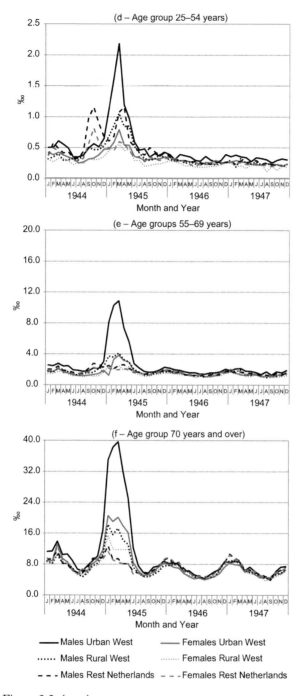

Figure 3.3 (*cont.*)

Another important conclusion to be drawn from Figures 3.3a–f is that the overall lowest death rates were seen among children and young adults; in particular, the age group of 1–14 years.[15] In this age group, death rates reached 0.7 per 1,000 population for boys and 0.6 for girls against roughly 0.4 in normal times. For teenagers and young adults, death rates were slightly higher, especially considering they had the lowest baseline of all ages, reaching 0.8 for men and 0.5 for women at the height of the famine. Although the absolute rise in death rate is relatively low, the proportional increase is still 50 per cent compared to the normal rates for the ages 1–14 years and about 100 per cent for 15–24 years. However, in both age groups, monthly death rates for men in the famine-struck urban west were matched by those in the rest of the country, leading to the assumption that starvation had relatively little impact on mortality in these age groups.[16]

The low death rates of Dutch children during the famine become even more evident when broken down in smaller age groups.[17] Figures 3.4a–c show that children aged 1–4 years experienced a peak in death rates in March 1945, which corresponds with Figure 3.3b and with overall mortality patterns in the urban west. By contrast, the patterns for the age groups 5–9 years and 10–14 years show quite a different form. Death rates of these children in the urban west were hardly affected during the famine period, both in absolute and in proportional terms. Most importantly, death rates of urban children in the western Netherlands show parity with those in the rural west, and remain well below the monthly death rates in the non-famine rest of the Netherlands.

These findings differ from evidence from other famines, including comparable modern European famines.[18] For example, children aged

---

[15] Since the turn of the century, school child mortality in the Netherlands had decreased by 85 per cent, infant mortality by 88 per cent, and pre-school child mortality by as much as 92 per cent, causing child mortality rates in the Netherlands to be among the most favourable in the Western world before World War II. J. H. de Haas, *Kindersterfte in Nederland/Child Mortality in the Netherlands* (Assen: Van Gorcum, 1956).

[16] Shortly after the war, Banning noticed this as well, but this observation has not been reconsidered since. Banning, 'De Gezondheidstoestand in Nederland'; Banning, 'Voeding en Voedingstoestand', 41.

[17] Because the numbers would otherwise become too small, boys and girls could not be differentiated, and 1947 is not included. To overcome the paucity of the data, the NIDI calculations require at least ten observations per month.

[18] E.g., Ó Gradá, *Famine: A Short History*, 101–102; Ó Gradá, *Black '47 and Beyond: The Great Irish Famine in History, Economy, and Memory* (Princeton: Princeton University Press, 2000), 90–91; Waal, 'Famine Mortality: A Case Study of Darfur, Sudan, in 1984–1985', *Population Studies* 43 (1989): 5–24; Pitkänen and James H. Mielke, 'Age and Sex Differentials in Mortality during Two Nineteenth Century Population Crises', *European Journal of Population* (1993): 1–32; Adamets, 'Famine in Nineteenth- and Twentieth-Century Russia: Mortality by Age, Cause, and Gender', in *Famine Demography*, 158–180.

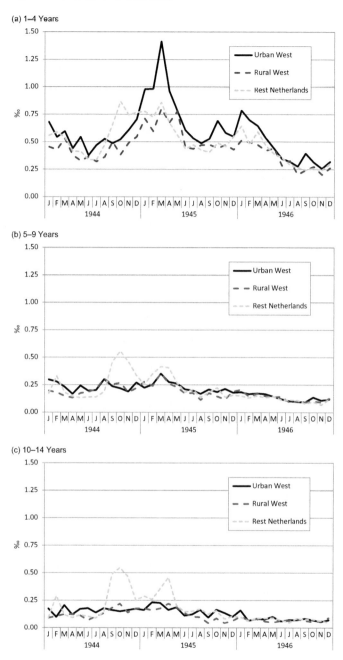

Figure 3.4 Deaths per 1,000 population, by region, and year and month of death, per age group, 1944–1946.
Source: Calculations by NIDI using non-public microdata from Statistics
Netherlands

5–14 years on the Greek islands Syros and Mykonos suffered approximately tenfold increases in mortality during the famine of 1941–1943, with the ages 5–9 years on Mykonos even yielding a ratio of 50 compared to the average number of deaths in 1936–1939. However, Hionidou has also revealed an anomalous pattern for the island Chios, where the ratio of famine to pre-famine deaths showed parity for the 10 to 14 age group – comparable to the patterns of Dutch children mentioned above. Hionidou attributed this exception in mortality to the meals provided to children through school soup kitchens.[19] Similarly, Davies and Wheatcroft have explained that in the case of the Ukrainian famine children continued to dominate as victims of the famine from late 1932 until April 1933, after which the pattern changed considerably. This was most likely due to the extensive food assistance supplied to children and the 'actions of some of the hardworking, fit people themselves'.[20]

Considering the current knowledge about child mortality during famines, these demographic insights into child death rates during the Dutch Hunger Winter suggest that their resilience to the famine conditions was perhaps not a product of physiological defence but rather caused by policy or socio-cultural factors.

Causes of Death

Causes of death is the final aspect of famine mortality this chapter explores. In general, all major types of diseases (apart from cancer) tend to increase during famines. However, the character of famine mortality has shifted radically in the twentieth century following medical breakthroughs in the treatment and prevention of disease. Broadly speaking, scholars investigating famine mortality make a distinction between 'modern western' famines and 'traditional' or 'non-western' famines. In the first category, famine occurs in developed economies with effective public health regimes and is often a product of war. Characteristic of these famines is limited epidemic outbreaks with a large part of the mortality increase directly related to malnutrition, including actual starvation. Famine victims in this category succumb to nutritional-sensitive diseases brought on by impaired immunity such as TB and dysentery, along with diseases of the circulatory and digestive system. The World War II famines in occupied Greece, the Warsaw ghetto, and besieged Leningrad are all examples of this type of famine. In 'traditional' and recent non-western famines, excess deaths are often caused by the

[19] Hionidou, *Famine and Death in Occupied Greece*, 168–172.
[20] Davies and Wheatcroft, *The Years of Hunger*, 418–419.

disruption of social life, increased mobility, and a deterioration in levels of hygiene. These circumstances produce outbreaks and the spread of seemingly unrelated diseases such as cholera, malaria, and influenza in addition to infamous famine killers such as dysentery.[21]

The causes of death during the Dutch Hunger Winter correspond with trends in other European World War II famines. The Netherlands was spared major epidemics; this can largely be attributed to the fact that the country enjoyed a modern health care system and that measures for preventing the spread of infectious disease had been part of daily routine until the crisis.[22] In their exploration into the causes of excess mortality for people of all ages in 1944–1945, Ekamper et al. concluded that the most common death was due to 'external causes': these included injuries and other war-related events. In absolute numbers, these deaths accounted for about 40 per cent of excess deaths among men in the western cities and over half the deaths outside the west. Among these deaths, one in five was reported as due to hunger.[23]

Starvation was an important killer in the Hunger Winter, and Dutch doctors officially reported 8,305 cases of hunger deaths in the years 1944–1945. The first deaths from malnutrition (officially 'hunger or thirst') were reported in November 1944 and rose sharply from January 1945 onward until finally attaining a maximum in March of that year. The last hunger deaths were reported in July, almost two months after liberation: the lingering vestiges of the famine. In agreement with earlier scholarly observations, male deaths from hunger were reported three to four times more often than female deaths with the same cause. The main victims of hunger comprised elderly people – almost 80 per cent of reported hunger mortality was experienced by men and women over 55 years of age. Less than 0.5 per cent was made up by children in the age group 5–14 years. Hunger deaths were also reported outside the urban west (16 per cent) and even outside the western provinces (2 per cent).[24] This supports the

---

[21] Hionidou, 'Why Do People Die in Famines? Evidence from Three Island Populations', *Population Studies* 56 (2002): 74; Ó Gráda, 'Making Famine History', *Journal of Economic Literature* 45 (2007): 21–22; Ó Gráda, *Eating People Is Wrong*, 145–146; Ó Gráda, *Famine*, 108–121; Dyson and Ó Gráda, 'Introduction', in *Famine Demography*, 2; Alfani and Ó Gráda, 'Famines in Europe: An Overview', in *Famine in European History*, 13.

[22] Ó Gráda, *Famine*, 112; Ó Gráda, *Black '47 and Beyond*, 97–98; Hionidou, *Famine and Death in Occupied Greece*, 212–219.

[23] The majority of war-related deaths included homicide, military service, civil casualties, and legal executions. Ekamper et al., 'War-Related Excess Mortality', 122–123.

[24] Calculations by NIDI using non-public microdata from Statistics Netherlands; Ekamper et al., 'War-Related Excess Mortality', 128.

argument that part of the excess mortality outside of the six large conurbations in the western Netherlands was related to the famine conditions and should thus be included in estimates about the famine's impact and in the investigation of subsequent responses.

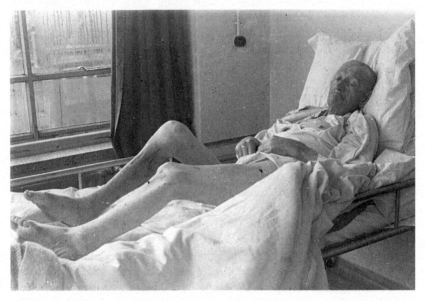

Illustration 7 Hospitalised man with hunger oedema, 1945.

The role of literal starvation during the Dutch famine is also revealed by the incidence of oedema. In most cities, hunger oedema was first diagnosed in January 1945 but did not take long before it became widespread. The Allied Medical Feeding Teams estimated that in May 1945 – a mere four months later – there were 200,000–250,000 people in the western Netherlands suffering from the condition. Most cases were found in the three largest cities of Amsterdam, Rotterdam, and The Hague, but some smaller towns were severely affected as well. After the war, approximately 280,000 people were classified by doctors as undernourished. Three thousand of these were being committed to hospital, 275 of whom died from the delayed consequences of starvation after liberation in May 1945.[25] The medical teams noticed that other deficiency diseases were largely absent, such as scurvy (vitamin

[25] Johannes Bok, *De Kliniek der Hongerziekte: Een Klinische Studie tijdens de Hongerwinter 1944–1945 te Rotterdam* (Leiden: H. E. Stenfert Kroese, 1949), 24, 120; Burger et al., *Malnutrition and Starvation* I, 52–53, 81–86.

C deficiency), rickets (vitamin D and calcium deficiency), beriberi (vitamin B1 deficiency) and night-blindness (vitamin A deficiency). This suggests that the deficiencies were mostly the result of protein malnutrition, and not caused by a lack of vitamins, which was likely related to the ample consumption of vegetables during the famine.[26]

Documentation from doctors and health authorities provides more insight into the socio-economic profile of these famine victims. Banning found that, in The Hague, deaths in working-class households were much more likely to be from malnutrition than in middle- or upper-class households. In the 'prosperous' class, only 24 people reportedly died from malnutrition in the first quarter of 1945, of whom 12 died in the last week of February 1945.[27] The Medical Feeding Teams reported on the adult cases of starvation: 'The cases were mainly of the lower income and social class. It was notable, that there were a considerable number of the vagrant class of low mental capabilities. There was a strong suggestion that these and others with limited wits had not the drive and ingenuity to make the best of the circumstances too difficult for them.'[28] The report concluded that the destitute, elderly people living alone or in pensions – 'bachelors, widowers, spinsters, and widows' – and people residing in institutions, such as prisons and psychiatric wards, fared worst during the famine. The Head of the Amsterdam Department of Statistics similarly observed that most hunger deaths occurred among widowers and boarders, thereby implicitly referring to the importance of a social safety net during the Hunger Winter.[29]

On the victims who resided in institutions much remains unknown. A recent study on psychiatric ward De Willem Arntsz Hoeve in Den Dolder (Utrecht), which was controlled by a national-socialist board, has revealed that during the famine 477 of the 1,400 patients died. Of these deaths, 178 were officially registered as having been caused by hunger. Even in the weeks after liberation, many patients from this institution died as a consequence of the famine.[30] At the moment, the NIOD is conducting further research into the specifics of mortality in other psychiatric wards in the Netherlands during the German occupation.

[26] Burger et al., *Malnutrition and Starvation* I, 78, 107–108, 165; Trienekens, *Tussen ons Volk en de Honger*, 400; Trienekens, *Voedsel en Honger in Oorlogstijd*, 96.

[27] Banning, 'Food Shortage and Public Health', 104–107; Wheatcroft and Ó Gráda, 'The European Famines of World Wars I and II', in *Famine in European History*, 264.

[28] Burger et al., *Malnutrition and Starvation* I, 84.

[29] M. G. Neurdenburg, 'Algemeene Statistiek der Mortaliteit en der Morbiditeit', in *Medische Ervaringen*, 402.

[30] Marco Gietema and Cecile aan de Stegge, *Vergeten Slachtoffers: Psychiatrische Inrichting de Willem Arntsz Hoeve in de Tweede Wereldoorlog* (Amsterdam: Boom, 2016).

Not all excess mortality during the famine was the direct result of malnutrition. The second most common cause of death in the years 1944–1945 was from infective and parasitic diseases, which had been on the rise since the beginning of the occupation. The overall medical shortages and other difficulties in hospitals in all regions during the final months of war likely contributed to this trend.[31] Contemporary physicians had also asserted that diseases such as typhus and tuberculosis spread much faster because of the increased contact between people and deteriorating levels of hygiene.[32] Most importantly, these physicians argued that food expeditions caused an unusual frequency of contact between city and countryside; queuing increased direct personal contact; and the thousands of evacuees brought with them diseases (including venereal diseases) that spread easily in the small living quarters. For example, in the town of Spijkenisse, near Rotterdam, a lack of clean water resulted in 192 cases of typhus, of which 17 were fatal.[33] Surgeon Ite Boerema added that adult men, in particular, died of these diseases, as many of them were in hiding from the German occupier and refused to call a doctor when they fell ill.[34] Deaths from ill-defined conditions were the third most reported cause of death, which highlights the wartime stresses on registration practices and emphasises the point that we should refer to all these reported causes of death with utmost caution.[35]

The primary causes of death, of course, differed per age group and the Amsterdam statistics illustrate this very well. During the famine period, the most commonly reported cause of death among infants in Amsterdam was congenial defects, together with diarrhoea and enteritis. The primary cause of death for adults was external causes (including hunger), but significant increases in deaths from diseases of the circulatory and digestive system, as well as tuberculosis, were also reported. For children ages 1–4 years, the main cause of death was external

---

[31] Boerema, 'Inleiding', 12–14; T. Huizinga, 'Geneesmiddelenverzorging', in *Medische Ervaringen*, 187–193; Bok, *De Kliniek der Hongerziekte*, 26.

[32] Futselaar has negated these assumptions by pointing to the direct post-war period, in which crowding and hygiene were equally adverse but the associated diseases had disappeared. Futselaar, *Lard, Lice and Longevity*, 194–197.

[33] Hemmes, 'Besmettelijke Ziekten', 105–110, 120–123; Bok, *De Kliniek der Hongerziekte*, 94–95, 101.

[34] Boerema, 'Inleiding', 10.

[35] Ekamper et al., 'War-Related Excess Mortality', 121–123. See also: CBS, *De Sterfte in Nederland naar Geslacht, Leeftijd en Doodsoorzaken, 1921–1955* (Zeist: W. de Haan, 1957), 40; Neurdenburg, 'Algemeene Statistiek der Mortaliteit en der Morbiditeit', 383–384.

causes, accompanied by diphtheria, diarrhoea, enteritis, and other undefined infectious diseases. By contrast, children in the age group 5–14 years died mainly from external causes – common in normal times as well – but mostly from diphtheria. It is important to note here that mortality from diphtheria had already risen well before the Hunger Winter, reaching the height of its wrath in the summer of 1943 and was thus not directly related to the famine conditions.[36] To examine the specifics of these patterns, however, further investigation into child mortality in other Dutch cities throughout the German occupation is required.

Effects on Births and Fertility

Averted births as well as rebound in births following the famine's wake should be included in the demographic reckoning as well. The effects brought about by the famine upon fertility and fecundity, respectively defined as the 'demonstrated capacity to reproduce' and the 'predisposition for reproducing', are as much part of the famine's demography as mortality.[37] For Dutch historians, the ways in which the famine affected fertility have remained outside their visual field. The only general observation, based on reports by contemporary doctors, is that about half of the women in the urban west experienced amenorrhea during the famine.[38] In contrast to historians, epidemiologists and demographers have given the effects of famine upon fertility their undivided interest, as

---

[36] *Maandbericht van het Bureau van Statistiek der Gemeente Amsterdam* 1944–46. See also: Futselaar, *Lard, Lice and Longevity*, 50–59. The increase in diphtheria morbidity and mortality in the Netherlands was connected to a European-wide epidemic wave, but also to the cessation of mass immunisation during the occupation years. In 1945, two-thirds of the children aged 6 months to 12 years were not immmunised. G. Stuart, 'Note on Diphtheria Incidence in Certain European Countries', *British Medical Journal* 2 (1945): 614.

[37] Definition by Stein and Susser, 'Fertility, Fecundity, Famine: Food Rations in the Dutch Famine 1944/45 Have a Causal Relation to Fertility, and Probably Fecundity', *Human Biology* 47 (1975): 132. See also: Ó Gráda, *Famine*, 102–108.

[38] Clement A. Smith, 'Effects of Maternal Undernutrition upon the Newborn Infant in Holland, 1944–1945', *Journal of Paediatrics* 30 (1947): 234; Smith, 'Effects of War-Time Starvation in Holland upon Pregnancy and Its Product', *American Journal of Obstetrics & Gynecology* 53 (1947): 599–608; Burger et al., *Malnutrition and Starvation*, 77; A. J. M. Holmer, 'Verloskunde en Vrouwenziekten', in *Medische Ervaringen*, 141; T. L. W. van Ravesteyn, *Studies over de Follikelrijping: Histologisch Onderzoek over de Follikel van de Graaf in de Praeovulatiephase, Klinisch Onderzoek over de Oorlogsamenorrhoe te 's-Gravenhage in 1944 en 1945, met een Inleiding over de Geschiedenis van het Onderzoek van de Follikel van De Graaf*, Thesis Rijksuniversiteit Utrecht (1946).

population losses due to birth deficits affect their study of the long-term consequences of the Dutch famine.[39] Fertility is subsequently included in this chapter because it is a significant indicator of the scope and impact of the famine and, again, it simultaneously forms a vital background for interpreting responses to the crisis conditions.

In the occupation years prior to the famine, there was a significant increase in the number of births, rising by 17 per cent between 1939 and 1944. This increase has been explained as the result of employment growth from the beginning of the war and the subsequent income improvements, which benefitted the formerly unemployed, small farmers, and retailers in particular. This rise in births in the occupied Netherlands is, in part, also a reflection of the relatively favourable food situation in the country. In neighbouring Belgium, for example, the birthrate decreased substantially during the occupation, which has been said to be a result of the much less effectively organised food supply and the lower availability of industrial raw materials.[40]

The food crisis immediately affected birth rates in the Netherlands. Figures 3.5–3.7 show the number of births in three of the four largest cities in the western Netherlands before, during, and after the famine. These figures are based on monthly and weekly municipal statistics published after the war, in the case of Rotterdam and Utrecht, and during the war for Amsterdam. Births in these three cities show quite similar patterns. Births dropped from June 1945 onwards (conception in September 1944), stagnated a little for the following two months and then fell rapidly to a low point in October 1945–January 1946. In this last low-birth phase, conception would have occurred during the famine months January–April 1945. In all cities, the absolute low was reached in November 1945 (conception in February 1945). In Amsterdam and Utrecht, the number of births declined twofold compared to pre-crisis levels; in Rotterdam, the number of births dropped to about a third of 'normal' numbers.[41] The end of the war also brought an end to this

[39] Stein and Susser, 'Fertility, Fecundity, Famine'; Thomas van den Brink, 'Birth Rate Trends and Changes in Marital Fertility in the Netherlands after 1937', *Population Studies* 4 (1950): 314–332. See also: Vallin et al., 'New Estimate of Ukrainian Population Losses'.

[40] Trienekens, 'The Food Supply', 123–124.

[41] In The Hague, birth rates followed a similar pattern, decreasing during the last five months of 1945 to approximately half of their normal numbers. Holmer, 'Verloskunde en Vrouwenziekten', 155. As a point of comparison, in besieged Leningrad in 1942, the number of births dropped to about 5 per cent of the number before the famine. A. N. Antonov, 'Children Born during the Siege of Leningrad in 1942', *Journal of Pediatrics 30* (1947): 250–259.

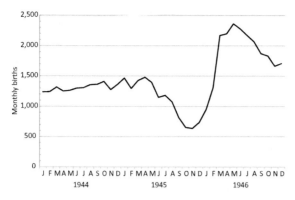

Figure 3.5 Monthly births in Amsterdam, January 1944–December 1946.
Source: Statistische Maandberichten Gemeente Amsterdam (1944–1946)

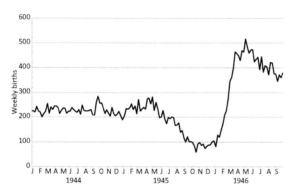

Figure 3.6 Weekly births in Rotterdam, January 1944–September 1946.
Source: Statistische Mededeelingen der Gemeente Rotterdam (1946)

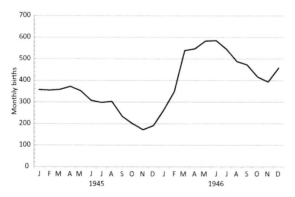

Figure 3.7 Monthly births in Utrecht, January 1945–December 1946.
Source: Statistische Berichten der Gemeente Utrecht (1946)

decline. In March 1946, birth rates rose to exceptional heights again: in line with the liberation of the country in May 1945 and the return of food supplies.[42] These high rebound birth rates continued for about eight months and in numbers that more than compensated for the lost births during the famine period. After this point, birth rates continued to remain above pre-crisis levels.

As strong as the correlation between nutrition and conception here may seem, other contributing factors should not be dismissed. Evidence from other famines shows that, in addition to lower libido, impotence, and amenorrhea caused by reduced food intake, the stress of war, and physical separation of spouses can be decisive factors.[43] In the Dutch case, these factors are reflected in the birth patterns. For instance, conceptions declined from September 1944 onward (birth in June 1945) when the Allies landed on Dutch soil but malnutrition had not yet prevailed. The fact that Rotterdam witnessed a sharper decline in births than Amsterdam and Utrecht should be explained by the large raid on adult men in that city in November 1944, which saw 52,000 men between the ages of 17 and 40 seized by the occupier. Moreover, Amsterdam and Utrecht experienced quite similar birth patterns even though Amsterdam was more adversely affected by the famine than Utrecht in terms of mortality. Most significantly, the rapid recovery rate after the liberation indicates that any physiological effects were offset shortly after this time. This recovery rate would likely have been more gradual if more severe physiological effects of malnutrition upon the female and male reproduction system had to be reversed. This suggests that the Dutch case corresponds with other early-stage famines, in which psychological and contingent causes had a significant impact with the outcome that births were postponed rather than lost.[44]

In addition to birth rates, the famine also profoundly affected pregnancy in the urban west. In his 1947 pioneering study on the effects of malnutrition upon the infant at birth, Clement Smith was the first to conclude that maternal nutrition affected the weight of the fetus during the last trimester of pregnancy. This is reflected in the figures: the net change in weight for infants in Rotterdam and The Hague was about 240 grams, or 8–9 per cent of the weight in normal times. A decline in birth length was also observed but was less apparent than the change in

---

[42] See also: Smith, 'Effects of Maternal Undernutrition', 234; Stein and Susser, 'Fertility, Fecundity, Famine', 135–138.

[43] Ó Gráda, *Famine*, 106. See also: Van den Brink, 'Birth Rate Trends', 318–323.

[44] Ó Gráda, *Eating People Is Wrong*, 164; Hionidou, *Famine and Death in Occupied Greece*, 178–189.

weight.[45] Based on the birthweights and lengths of 1,345 infants born in the University Maternity Clinic in Amsterdam, I. S. Sindram demonstrated in 1953 that, at the lowest point in April 1945, the average birth weight was 340 grams below normal. From this, he concluded that there was a two-month lag after official rations started deteriorating as well as a three-month recovery period after liberation.[46] The seminal work by Stein et al. has also confirmed that prenatal exposure to the Dutch famine during the third trimester of gestation reduced birth weight by about 300 grams (−9 per cent) and length at birth (−2.5 per cent), as well as reduced postpartum maternal weight (−4.3 per cent), placental weight (−15 per cent), and head circumference (−2.7 per cent).[47] The study also asserted that – as was the case with fertility – all these effects were only apparent below a threshold value of official food rations of 1,500 kcal.

In his study, Smith also found that the percentage of stillborn infants after the fifth month of gestation reduced during the famine, which is counterintuitive to what one might expect during famines.[48] These findings were confirmed by Stein et al., who discovered that perinatal losses in the famine-struck west had, paradoxically, remained below even those in non-famine areas.[49] Nicky Hart later explained this paradoxical trend by emphasising the importance of regional inequalities in maternal health status. She ascribed the comparatively favourable stillbirth rates in the famine region to advantageous socio-economic factors before the war, or, what she refers to as the 'successive intergenerational improvements in maternal health status' in the highly developed and urbanised western Netherlands.[50]

Long-Term Consequences

By the summer of 1945, famine mortality and morbidity had disappeared, and their effects on fertility were reversed even sooner. Yet, some

---

[45] Smith, 'Effects of Maternal Undernutrition'.

[46] I. S. Sindram, 'De Invloed van Ondervoeding op de Groei van de Vrucht', *Nederlands Tijdschrift voor Verloskundige Gynaecologie* 53 (1953): 30–48.

[47] Stein and Susser, 'The Dutch Famine, 1944–1945, and the Reproductive Process. I. Effects on Six Indices at Birth', *Pediatric Research* 9 (1975): 70–75. See also: Sindram, 'De Invloed van Ondervoeding'; Stein et al., 'Intrauterine Famine Exposure and Body Proportions at Birth: The Dutch Hunger Winter', *International Journal of Epidemiology* 33 (2004): 831–836.

[48] Smith, 'Effects of Maternal Undernutrition', 236–239. See also: Neurdenburg, 'Algemeene Statistiek der Mortaliteit en der Morbiditeit', 355.

[49] Stein et al., *Famine and Human Development*, 151–153.

[50] Nicky Hart, 'Famine, Maternal Nutrition and Infant Mortality: A Re-Examination of the Dutch Hunger Winter', *Population Studies* 47 (1993): 27–46.

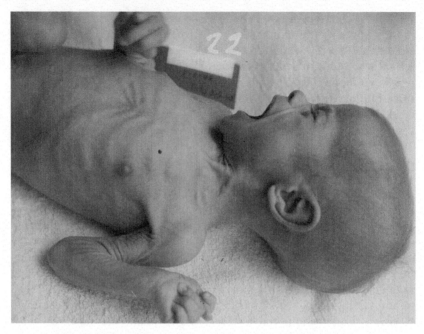

Illustration 8 Malnourished infant in Burgerweeshuis
Amsterdam, 1945.

biological effects of the famine lasted much longer: some even have an
impact today. Studies of men and women exposed to the Dutch famine
have provided a rare opportunity for epidemiologists to look at these
long-term effects of malnutrition in the early-life environment. Indeed,
the Hunger Winter has become the classic case for studies on the link
between in-utero exposure to malnutrition and health in later life. Lumey
and Van Poppel explain the investigative uniqueness of the Dutch case:
'For ethical and practical reasons, such studies could not otherwise be
carried out in humans.'[51] In order to investigate associations between
prenatal conditions and adult health, individuals exposed to the Dutch
famine in specific times of gestation have been compared with those born
in the same city or region, but before or after the famine, as well as being
compared to outcomes in the unexposed north and south of the country,
or to same-sex siblings.

---

[51] Lumey and Van Poppel, 'The Dutch Famine of 1944–45 As a Human Laboratory', 60.
For another overview, see: Wheatcroft and Ó Gráda, 'The European Famines of World
Wars I and II', 263–268.

Pioneering studies in this field commenced in the mid-1960s and have their origins in the study of mental development. Stein et al. were interested in the possible effects of prenatal (under)nutrition on the development of the brain and subsequent mental competence. Smith's 1947 study had demonstrated that prenatal exposure to the Dutch famine was linked to reduced birth weights, which indicated that the Hunger Winter might form a good case to examine the association between prenatal undernutrition and mental state in adulthood. The research group obtained access to major data sources of the CBS and the Ministry of Defence, which held records of over 400,000 men aged 18 who were examined at conscription for military service. In the end, their study could show no association between prenatal nutrition and the available measures of mental competence.[52] Nonetheless, the collected data were used for a variety of other studies, which suggested that famine exposure was associated with being in the highest weight for height category and with an affected central nervous system development in men who had been exposed during early gestation.[53] As the data on the recruits were limited to men and did not include birth records, the researchers additionally analysed data on pregnancies from 12 hospitals as well as the births and deaths from over 300 population registers across the country, thereby exploring the environmental conditions during gestation and confirming the above-mentioned effects on births detected by Smith.[54]

The results from Stein et al. encouraged epidemiologists to follow up on these original findings on mental health, obesity, and the central nervous system, and to explore different questions concerning the relationship between prenatal undernutrition and health in later life. A second series of studies, which commenced in the 1990s, used data from Dutch psychiatric registries to examine psychiatric conditions in adults who had been exposed in utero to famine conditions. Following up on the observed increase in stillbirth related to congenital nervous system anomalies described by Stein et al., these studies found a twofold increased risk of schizophrenia as well as schizoid personality disorder in men exposed during early gestation.[55] This same twofold increase in

[52] Stein et al., 'Nutrition and Mental Performance: Prenatal Exposure to the Dutch Famine of 1944–1945 Seems Not Related to Mental Performance at Age 19', *Science* 178 (1972): 708–713.

[53] G. P. Ravelli et al., 'Obesity in Young Men after Famine Exposure in Utero and Early Infancy', *New England Journal of Medicine* 295 (1976): 349–353; Stein et al., *Famine and Human Development.*

[54] Stein et al., *Famine and Human Development.*

[55] Susser and Lin, 'Schizophrenia after Prenatal Exposure to the Dutch Hunger Winter of 1944–1945', *Archives of General Psychiatry* 49 (1992): 938–939; Susser et al., 'Schizophrenia after Prenatal Famine: Further Evidence', *Archives of General Psychiatry*

schizophrenia among men and women exposed in early pregnancy has been described in later studies on the Chinese Great Leap Forward famine of 1958–1962.[56] Prenatal exposure to famine has also been associated with other psychiatric conditions such as antisocial personality disorder and mood affective disorders, but these findings were less consistent.[57]

In the same period that this study on psychiatric outcomes started, a third approach was developed through a series of studies based on infants identified from hospital records in the famine-affected areas. These were the first prospective studies on the Hunger Winter, which examined and followed up on a female population that had been prenatally exposed to famine from 0–50 years. These studies, also conducted in the early 1990s, included 1,108 singleton girls born between August 1944 and April 1946 in the former Wilhelmina Gasthuis hospital in Amsterdam. Based on these data and combined with over 700 interviews, Lumey et al. found a clear increase in birth weight following first-trimester exposure and a decline in birth weight after third-trimester exposure.[58] The study also found that indicators of reproductive performance (e.g., age at first birth, family size, birth spacing, and probability of not having children) were not related to famine exposure.[59]

A fourth approach added the data from male births from the same hospital, examining 2,414 singleton births in total at age 50, focusing on the glucose and insulin profile, blood pressure, and body mass index (BMI) in particular. The study found elevated 2hr glucose levels among men and

---

53 (1996): 25–31; Hoek et al., 'Schizoid Personality Disorder after Prenatal Exposure to Famine', *American Journal of Psychiatry* 153 (1996): 1637–1639.

[56] D. St. Clair et al., 'Rates of Adult Schizophrenia Following Prenatal Exposure to the Chinese Famine of 1959–1961', *JAMA* 294 (2005): 557–562; M. Q. Xu et al., 'Prenatal Malnutrition and Adult Schizophrenia: Further Evidence from the 1959–1961 Chinese Famine', *Schizophrenia Bulletin* 35 (2009): 557–576. See also: Lumey, Stein, and Susser, 'Prenatal Famine and Adult Health', *Annual Review of Public Health* 32 (2011): 250–251.

[57] Neugebauer et al., 'Prenatal Exposure to Wartime Famine and Development of Antisocial Personality Disorder in Early Adulthood', *JAMA* 282 (1999): 455–462; Brown et al., 'Further Evidence of Relation between Prenatal Famine and Major Affective Disorder', *American Journal of Psychiatry* 157 (2000): 190–195.

[58] Lumey et al., 'The Dutch Famine Cohort Study: Design, Validation of Exposure, and Selected Characteristics of Subjects after 43 Years Follow-up', *Paediatric and Perinatal Epidemiology* 7 (1993): 54–67. Lumey and Stein, 'Offspring Birth Weights after Maternal Intrauterine Undernutrition: A Comparison within Siblings', *American Journal of Epidemiology* 146 (1997): 810–819.

[59] Lumey and Stein, 'In Utero Exposure to Famine and Subsequent Fertility: The Dutch Famine Birth Cohort Study', *American Journal of Public Health* 87 (1997): 1962–1966; For an overview of these studies, see: Lumey, 'Reproductive Outcomes in Women Prenatally Exposed to Undernutrition: A Review of Findings from the Dutch Famine Birth Cohort', *Proceedings of the Nutrition Society* 57 (1998): 129–135.

women exposed to famine in late gestation.[60] There was no association detected between exposure to undernutrition and blood pressure in adult life.[61] The most consistent outcome of this series of studies was that famine exposure was linked to an increase in body weight, BMI, and waist circumference, especially in women exposed during early gestation.[62] Their follow-up study at age 58 confirmed most of the initial findings.[63]

A fifth series of studies on the 'Dutch Hunger Winter Families' included a wider sample of 3,307 births in three clinics in the famine-affected cities, which now also included siblings. These studies, conducted parallel to the fourth series, aimed to examine some of the above-mentioned associations and added measures of cardiovascular disease risk and hand morphology. Significantly, these studies confirmed that there was indeed an association of prenatal famine exposure and a higher prevalence of type 2 diabetes in any trimester during pregnancy.[64] In later studies, this same association with type 2 diabetes was detected in men and women exposed to the Chinese famine and the Ukrainian famine of 1932–1933.[65] This fifth series of studies also confirmed the increase in body weight, BMI, and waist circumference in women exposed to famine in utero, but not in men.[66]

In sum, of all the examined conditions in the 'Dutch Hunger Winter Cohort', associations between prenatal famine exposure and adult body size, type 2 diabetes, and schizophrenia show the most consistent patterns. Conclusions on the long-term impact of prenatal exposure to the

---

[60] Anita C. J. Ravelli et al., 'Glucose Tolerance in Adults after Prenatal Exposure to Famine', *Lancet* 351 (1998): 173–177.

[61] Tessa J. Roseboom et al., 'Blood Pressure in Adults after Prenatal Exposure to Famine', *Journal of Hypertension* 17 (1999): 325–330.

[62] Ravelli et al., 'Obesity at the Age of 50 Y in Men and Women Exposed to Famine Prenatally', *American Journal of Clinical Nutrition* 70 (1999): 811–816.

[63] Rebecca C. Painter et al., 'Blood Pressure Response to Psychological Stressors in Adults after Prenatal Exposure to the Dutch Famine', *Hypertension* 24 (2006): 1771–1778; Susanne R. de Rooij et al., 'Glucose Tolerance at Age 58 and the Decline of Glucose Tolerance in Comparison with Age 50 in People Prenatally Exposed to the Dutch Famine', *Diabetologia* 49 (2006): 637–643.

[64] Lumey et al., 'Cohort Profile: The Dutch Hunger Winter Family Studies', *International Journal of Epidemiology* 36 (2007): 1196–1204; Lumey et al., 'Food Restriction during Gestation and Impaired Fasting Glucose or Glucose Tolerance and Type 2 Diabetes Mellitus in Adulthood: Evidence from the Dutch Hunger Winter Families Study', *Journal of Developmental Origins of Health and Disease* 1 (2009): S164.

[65] Lumey et al., 'Prenatal Famine and Adult Health', 247; Lumey, M. D. Khalangot, and Vaiserman, 'Association between Type 2 Diabetes and Prenatal Exposure to the Ukraine Famine of 1932–33: A Retrospective Cohort Study', *The Lancet Diabetes & Endocrinology* 3 (2015): 787–794.

[66] Stein et al., 'Anthropometric Measures in Middle Age after Exposure to Famine during Gestation: Evidence from the Dutch Famine', *American Journal of Clinical Nutrition* 85 (2007): 869–876.

Dutch famine on mental health in later life have recently also been drawn, with women in particular having poorer mental health in later midlife than men.[67] Other associations have been suggested as well, for example, with the level of cholesterol, coronary artery disease, kidney disease, lung disease, depression, and breast cancer; however, these patterns were more variable or inconsistent and would require a larger sample.[68]

Following up on the detected health impairments in later life, in recent studies Ekamper et al. have used the national military conscription records and linked death files to examine adult mortality after age 18 at the individual level, revealing that the Dutch Hunger Winter Cohort died at a higher rate than people born before or after the famine. Studying the relation between prenatal famine and survival through to age 63, they found a 12 per cent increase in mortality after famine exposure in early gestation but not after exposure in late gestation, as well as an 8 per cent increase after early postnatal famine exposure. These outcomes were independent of intermediary life conditions, including education and BMI.[69] In other cases as well, an association has been suggested between prenatal famine exposure and mortality in middle-age men and women; for example, following the Finnish famine of 1866–1868 and the Chinese Great Leap Forward famine. The Hunger Winter study – examining mortality at individual levels – has, however, been much more refined.[70]

The exact mechanisms behind these outcomes are not yet known, but the latest research suggests that famine exposure 'silences' certain genes in unborn children that underlie the relationship between prenatal adversities and adult health. Indeed, the latest series of studies on the Dutch

---

[67] Thijs van der Broek and Maria Fleischmann, 'Prenatal Famine Exposure and Mental Health in Later Midlife', *Aging and Mental Health* 21 (2017): 166–170. For this study, data were used from the Netherlands Kinship Panel Study.

[68] See, for example: Roseboom, *Prenatal Exposure to the Dutch Famine and Health in Later Life* (Enschede: Ipskamp Printing Partners, 2000); Painter, *The Pathophysiology of Cardiovascular Disease after Prenatal Exposure to Maternal Undernutrition during the Dutch Famine* (Amsterdam: Buijten en Schipperheijn, 2006); Lumey and Van Poppel, 'The Dutch Hunger Winter of 1944–45', 59; De Rooij et al., 'Prenatal Undernutrition and Cognitive Function in Late Adulthood', *Proceedings of the National Academy of Sciences of the United States of America* 107 (2010): 16881; Renate H. M. de Groot et al., 'Prenatal Famine Exposure and Cognition at Age 59 Years', *International Journal of Epidemiology* 40 (2011): 327–337; Lumey et al., 'No Relation between Coronary Artery Disease or Electrocardiographic Markers of Disease in Middle Age and Prenatal Exposure to the Dutch Famine of 1944–5', *Heart* 98 (2012): 1653–1659.

[69] Ekamper et al., 'Independent and Additive Association of Prenatal Famine Exposure and Intermediary Life Conditions with Adult Mortality between Age 18–63 Years', *Social Science & Medicine* 119 (2014): 232–239.

[70] Lumey et al., 'Prenatal Famine and Adult Health', 251–252. They also found this in the case of Bangladesh, based on data from Matlab region births in the hungry versus the harvest season in the period 1974–2000.

Hunger Winter Cohort focuses on epigenetics and hypothesise that the previously investigated associations may even be transgenerational. Changes in DNA methylation (the process by which methyl groups are added to the DNA molecule) seem to be responsible for the adverse outcomes in later life. Studying the difference in DNA methylation between men and women with famine exposure and an unexposed same-sex sibling suggests that nutrition in early pregnancy may trigger widespread and persistent epigenetic changes.[71] The association of DNA methylation with prenatal conditions seems to depend on timing and sex, which matches the specificity in phenotypic outcomes described above, including the timing- and sex-specific neonatal outcomes and psychiatric and metabolic conditions in later life.[72] The most recent study by Tobi et al. indicates that epigenetic mechanisms may indeed mediate the influence of adverse environmental conditions during gestation on long-term metabolic health, which is a vital understanding for all future studies on this subject.[73]

Conclusion

The new demographic evidence presented in this chapter has revealed much about the chronology and geography of the Dutch famine, including the groups of people most and least affected by the food shortage. During the crisis months of September 1944–July 1945, the number of estimated war-related excess deaths among civilians was 35,000 in the three famine-exposed western provinces, of which an estimated over 20,000 were related to the famine. Deaths in these provinces began to rise sharply after December 1944 and were at their worst in March 1945. While deaths quickly declined after May 1945, it took until the summer of that year to reach normal patterns again, which reiterates the fact that the liberation should not be taken as a demarcation line in investigating

---

[71] Bastiaan T. Heijmans et al., 'Persistent Epigenetic Differences Associated with Prenatal Exposure to Famine in Humans', *Proceedings of the National Academy of Sciences of the United States of America* 105 (2008): 17046–17049; Marjolein V. E. Veenendaal et al., 'Transgenerational Effects of Prenatal Exposure to the 1944–45 Dutch Famine', *BJOG* 120 (2013): 548–554; Elmar W. Tobi et al., 'DNA Methylation Signatures Link Prenatal Famine Exposure to Growth and Metabolism', *Nature Communications* 5 (2014): 1–13; Lumey and Van Poppel, 'The Dutch Famine of 1944–45', 68.

[72] Heijmans et al., 'The Epigenome: Archive of the Prenatal Environment', *Epigenetics* 4 (2009): 526–531; Tobi et al., 'DNA Methylation Differences after Exposure to Prenatal Famine Are Common in Timing- and Sex- Specific', *Human Molecular Genetics* 18 (2009): 4046–4053.

[73] Tobi et al., 'DNA Methylation As a Mediator of the Association between Prenatal Adversity and Risk Factors for Metabolic Disease in Adulthood', *Science Advances* 4 (2018): 1–10.

the effects of the famine. In the famine's wake, fertility followed similar patterns with birth rates in the urban west two to three times lower, although these births can be considered delayed rather than lost.

This chapter has also demonstrated that the age-, sex- and cause-specific mortality patterns of the Dutch famine showed major similarities to other 'modern' famines; most notably, those experienced elsewhere in occupied Europe during the Second World War. The patterns described in this chapter are all indicative of an early-stage famine, which serves as a vital framework for examining and understanding socio-political responses to the Dutch famine. If the Hunger Winter was not an extreme and long-lasting famine, then community efforts to fight these conditions are highly likely to have emerged alongside state and individual responses. Interestingly, in the Dutch case, the age-specific mortality patterns deviate from most of these other famines when investigating child mortality. While children are vulnerable to famine, Dutch children in the age group 5–14 years seemed hardly affected by the famine conditions. These new demographic findings suggest that children's resilience to the famine conditions was the result of policy or socio-cultural factors rather than physiological ones – a hypothesis that is further explored in the following chapters.

4   Central Government and Food Administration

'This was probably one of the most exciting days so far', Secretary General of Economic Affairs Hans Max Hirschfeld noted in his diary on 17 September 1944.[1] While the Allied Operation Market Garden was in full swing, Hirschfeld had spent the afternoon drinking coffee at an informal gathering that included Director General of Food Supply Stephanus Louwes and Chairman of the business sector Herman Woltersom. The reason for this 'exciting' get-together had been a rather urgent one. From the beginning of that month, all preconditions for a functioning rationing system had gradually eroded. The country's infra-structure had been heavily damaged by Allied bombings and, in the days leading up to the invasion, the German *Wehrmacht* and *Kriegsmarine* had been confiscating all kinds of transportation and heavy machinery.[2] The problems with the food supply quite effectively called into question the legitimacy of the Dutch food officials, who had been working with the occupier for over four years. Hirschfeld and Louwes knew that, whatever the outcome of the battle, their role in maintaining the central rationing system would be simultaneously more difficult and more important than ever before.

Louwes and Hirschfeld had anticipated the Allied invasion for quite some time. As early as January 1944, they had drawn up an economic emergency plan, which predicted that rations would immediately be lowered in the case of an invasion. In addition, municipalities, industries, and companies would have to cultivate land themselves, thereby replacing the national food system in favour of local autarky. Consider-able threats to the food supply were also expected from the expansion of clandestine trade and because of transportation problems. Louwes envi-sioned three possible scenarios: the first, an end to the war – not by invasion – but by other 'acts of war' in the west; the second involved an

---

[1] NIOD, 212a, inv.no. 167, Diary Hirschfeld, 17 September 1944.
[2] NIOD, 216h, inv.no. 87, Minutes RBVVO, 9–11 September 1944; De Jong, *Het Koninkrijk* 10b, 1–2.

invasion of Belgium, the north of France, and part of the southern Netherlands: 'the periphery'; and the third, an Allied invasion in the western Netherlands. The second and third scenarios were considered the most dangerous since they would most likely interfere with civilian food transports. In their plan, Louwes warned that 'if the more or less stabilized (war) situation would take longer than eight weeks, [this] will have devastating consequences'.[3] Essentially, the west would simply be unable to provide enough food for all its 4.3 million inhabitants. Yet Louwes and Hirschfeld sounded positive in their overall assessment: 'The organisation for coping with these various possible events has been prepared. Even the smallest units, the distribution circles, would be able to act independently, whilst maintaining good cooperation with the invading army (allies). Interruption of transportation will not lead to chaos.'[4]

This chapter seeks to unravel the various strategies the Dutch food officials pursued after they realised that the second scenario had become reality. In their review of state responses to the famine, previous studies have traditionally focused on centralising attempts or the adverse effects of individual coping strategies on the administrators' policies.[5] This chapter demonstrates that the crisis also instigated the Dutch food officials to act in defiance of their usually centrally minded policies, by decentralising and delegating tasks related to food provisioning and allowing certain forms of self-help, which methods are actually considered by famine scholars to be common government responses to the threat of famine.[6] By examining the choices these food administrators made in terms of centralising or decentralising, the following sections reveal the controversies that were inherent in their responses. In this regard, we follow the Dutch food officials' trajectory, the legitimacy issues underlying their responses, as well as the outcomes of their decisions. As all decisions concerning the food supply were necessarily executed in conjunction with the German civil authorities, this chapter builds on both Dutch and German sources. Their perspectives on the specific challenges posed by the food shortage elucidate the new

---

[3] NIOD, 212a, inv.no. 102, Note Louwes to Hirschfeld on food position in the Netherlands after possible invasion, 11 January 1944. See also: inv.no. 103, Note Louwes to PFCs and representatives of cities on delegation of responsibilities after resumption war activities on Dutch soil, 12 May 1944.

[4] NIOD, 212a, inv.no. 102, Note Louwes.

[5] De Jong, *Het Koninkrijk* 10b, 163–173; Van der Zee, *De Hongerwinter*, 156–157; Trienekens, *Tussen ons Volk en de Honger*, 373–385; Barnouw, *De Hongerwinter*, 37–45, 59–62; Klemann, *Nederland 1938–1948*, 464–467.

[6] Ó Gráda, *Famine*, 210–216, 240–241; Ó Gráda, *Black '47 and Beyond*, 49–50.

discourse that emerged amongst Dutch and German officials to uncover a different side to the role of German civil authorities.

Regaining Centralised Control

During the first two months of the food crisis, from early September to November 1944, it was hard for Dutch food officials to regain any form of control over the rationing system. With war conditions continuously in flux, planning for the food supply proved extremely difficult. Regular communications with German food and transportation officials discontinued after September 1944 and ceased almost completely in the following months.[7] In addition, direct contact with the *Reichskommissar* for the occupied Netherlands, Arthur Seyss-Inquart, had not yet been established. The main obstacle for the food administration was coping with actions from the German civil and military authorities that directly affected the central rationing system; in particular, the demolition of harbours and waterways and large-scale requisitioning of anything that could be appropriated for the German war effort. Needless to say, the railway strike on 17 September and the subsequent German embargo on shipping traffic ten days later severely disrupted the state-organised food system, which in the previous four years of occupation had managed to avert a serious shortage of food.

Both the Dutch and German central administrations were severely affected by the changing war circumstances. In early September 1944, after rumours of Allied forces rapidly marching into the country, about 65,000 members of the Dutch NSB fled to the east of the country and Germany, leaving the party disintegrated. A large part of the German and Dutch employees of the Reich Commissariat also fled eastwards, decreasing its number of personnel to a mere 420. Other Dutch senior civil servants left their posts as well, including several NSB mayors. That same month, the Dutch Secretary General of Internal Affairs Karel J. Frederiks went into hiding, leaving Hirschfeld as the only secretary general to stay in office throughout the occupation period. The loss of the secretary general reduced the already weak grip the department had on central governance. While steering and coordination of local governance did not completely disappear in the final phase of the occupation, there was hardly any central leadership left. Most of this steering came from the level of the provinces (or parts thereof), with governance practices

---

[7] NA, 2.21.238, inv.no. 117, Report Louwes, 16.

thus becoming increasingly characterised by personal regimes, based on the capacities and drive of those left in prominent positions.[8]

Hirschfeld and Louwes were two of those prominent administrators. Due to the severe transportation difficulties, securing a regular food supply proved harder for them than anticipated. The Directorate of Food Supply (RBVVO) led by Louwes had been preparing stockpiles for emergency situations such as the Allied invasion since the beginning of September 1944, resulting in secret food reserves greatly exceeding the two to three week supplies officially allowed by the occupying authorities. In addition, 25,000 tons of rye had just been imported from Germany, which should have been traded for potatoes.[9] These reserves could not, however, make up for the fact that the railway strike and the embargo fully coincided with the potato-harvesting period in the Netherlands. About 70 per cent of all potatoes in the province of Drenthe had already been harvested that month but now could not be transported. An attempt to transport foodstuffs from the southern provinces, now an active battlefield, resulted in the killing of four carriers and the confiscation of supplies by the *Wehrmacht*. The only option was renegotiating food transports from the northeast as, without cooperation of the German authorities, the harvest there would be left to rot, making famine in the west inevitable.[10]

The dialogue between Dutch and German administrators was reopened after Seyss-Inquart agreed to partially lift the shipping embargo on 16 October 1944. Due to the changed German military interests that dictated the avoidance of hunger riots at all costs, both parties suddenly converged in their desire to salvage the potato harvest. This remarkable switch in attitude is exemplified by the German decision to release Dutchmen who had been working on German fortifying projects to help with the harvesting, even though this decision meant potentially slowing down these projects in the east of the country. Their release was granted on the condition that the rest of the 20,000 men needed would be recruited from the west. For good reasons, Dutch industrialists and mayors mistrusted German motives in these negotiations, fearing the potato campaign would be exploited by the occupier to lure industrial workers into forced labour. But Head of the German *Hauptabteilung Ernährung und Landwirtschaft* Von der Wense promised that the men

---

[8] Hirschfeld, *Bezetting en Collaboratie*, 27; Romijn, *Burgemeesters in Oorlogstijd*, 571–579.

[9] NA, 2.21.238, inv.no. 117, Report Louwes, appendix K. See also: NA, 2.11.30.05, inv. no. 2, Week report 4–11 September 1944; Trienekens, *Tussen ons Volk en de Honger*, 375–376.

[10] NIOD, 212a, inv.no. 117, Circular Letter RBVVO, October 1944; NA, 2.11.30.05, inv. no. 2, Week report 9–16 October 1944; NA, 2.21.238, inv.no. 117, Report Louwes, 18.

would work in food supply only and in return would receive an administrative leave from work, as well as food, housing, salary, and extra coupons: they were also allowed to send these back home. Because Von der Wense had been on good terms with Dutch officials throughout the occupation, the Dutch delegation was convinced it was in the country's best interest to cooperate.[11] On 18 October, the official call for adult men to enlist for the potato campaign was published. The promises of extra rations and a paid leave of absence proved effective: two days after the call, about 800 men from the city of Rotterdam had sent in their applications and were scheduled to leave for Drenthe three days later. That same morning, the first 700 men left by boat from Amsterdam.[12]

Despite this promising beginning, the responses from the Dutch government-in-exile and the organised resistance illustrate the difficult manoeuvring position of the Dutch food officials. London asserted that, after the German embargo and destruction of land- and waterways, it was impossible to cooperate with the occupier ever again. On 19 October, the government proclaimed its fears via Radio Orange – the Dutch broadcast of the BBC's European Service – stating that the men would be used for forced labour and that this was all just a trick to break the railway strike.[13] Infuriated with London, Hirschfeld wrote in his diary: 'We all know that within six weeks it will be clear who was right, we or London.'[14] Hirschfeld urged the pro-German press to remain irresponsive as this would further disrupt the campaign, but his suggestions were ignored. Combined with the effects of widely spread resistance posters and leaflets, applications dropped to almost zero. When Radio Orange repeated the warnings two days later, two thirds of those who had already applied had withdrawn as well. The net result was that, in late October, 2,240 instead of the needed 20,000 men worked the potato fields. German authorities released 7,000 'Organisation Todt' labourers from their duties, but still this did not suffice.[15] With food shortages growing rapidly, some resistance groups acknowledged that they might have misjudged the situation. The illegal newspaper Trouw, for example, stated: 'We are talking about the certainty of famine against a chance of, let's say, one

---

[11] NIOD, 212a, inv.no. 117, Circular Letter RBVVO, October 1944; inv.no. 167, Diary Hirschfeld, 18 October 1944; Hirschfeld, Herinneringen uit de Bezettingstijd (Amsterdam: Elsevier, 1960), 150–151.
[12] NIOD, 212a, inv.no. 117, Message to Hirschfeld, 20 October 1944.
[13] NIOD, 212a, inv.no. 117, Government message, 19 October 1944.
[14] NIOD, 212a, inv.no. 167, Diary Hirschfeld, 19 October 1944. It should be mentioned that Hirschfeld finished this part of his diary on 4 February 1945, meaning that he already knew the answer to his question.
[15] NIOD, 212a, inv.no. 119, Report on potato harvest 17 October–20 November 1944.

in ten, of partly averting this. We consider the evil of hunger threatening the major population centres such a disaster that we do not feel the courage to stop people from harvesting.'[16] The campaign resumed; however, it had clearly lost its momentum.

In addition to government opposition and resistance groups, two other factors made it especially difficult for the Dutch food administration to regain centralised control. Firstly, large-scale German raids on adult men in the western provinces disrupted the organisation of the food supply, which also fuelled distrust among the population towards the Dutch authorities.[17] On 22 November, when there was only bread left for one day in The Hague, Louwes and Hirschfeld met with *Wehrmacht* Commander Modrow and other German officers at Seyss-Inquart's *Beauftragte* for The Hague and the province of South Holland, Ernst Schwebel's house. The Dutch officials asserted that they had reached a stalemate and that the only solution to avert famine was to exempt the tens of thousands of men who had gone into hiding from persecution. The *Wehrmacht* officials found this difficult to accept, but Schwebel and Modrow recognised that the rationing system was on the brink of collapsing and grudgingly agreed.[18]

This agreement between Dutch and German officials caused another big clash with London in the following month. Just before Christmas, the German authorities published a decree ordering all Dutchmen between the ages of 16 and 40 to register for work in return for extra rations from reserved stockpiles. With famine striking the west, London and the Dutch resistance considered the so-called *Liese Aktion* a 'legalised raid'. Hirschfeld and Louwes, on the other hand, wanted to comply to protect the fragile food system. By mid-January it became clear that, with less than 10,000 applications, the German action had failed; the German *Wehrmacht* responded with more raids.[19] These raids seriously damaged the status of the Dutch food administration. Transporters went into hiding and farmers withheld supplies, choosing instead to sell their produce illegally on black markets or to people who travelled to the countryside in search for food.

Interlinked with this legitimacy issue was the exponential growth of clandestine trade. Although an integral part of the economics of daily

---

[16] NIOD, 212a, inv.no. 117, 'Aardappelrooien', *Trouw*, October 1944.
[17] NA, 2.11.30.05, inv.no. 2, Week report 20–25 November 1944.
[18] NIOD, 212a, inv.no. 167, Diary Hirschfeld 22 November 1944.
[19] NA, 2.21.238, inv.no. 117, Report Louwes, 11; Hirschfeld, *Herinneringen uit de Bezettingstijd*, 173–175. Maass, *The Netherlands at War*, 211–212; De Jong, *Het Koninkrijk* 10b, 123–141; Meindert Fennema and John Rhijnsburger, *Dr Hans Max Hirschfeld: Man van het Grote Geld* (Amsterdam: Bakker, 2007), 125–126.

life during the occupation, black-market trade did not play a prominent role in the Netherlands until the food crisis. Before the autumn of 1944, about 20–25 per cent of the agrarian production ended up in black markets, or 10 per cent of the entire economic production. In almost every other occupied country in Europe, this percentage was much higher.[20] Historians have argued that the reason clandestine trade was kept under control was the legitimacy of the pre-war government that had implemented the market regulations, not to mention the legitimacy of these same officials who executed the policies during the war. Crucially, the Dutch food authorities had been able to organise central rationing efficiently before the Allied invasion, making it nearly possible to live on official rations alone; an unthinkable circumstance for the people of occupied France and Belgium, who had been suffering from severe shortages ever since the winter of 1940–1941.[21] During the crisis, however, black-market trade became a huge problem for the authorities. Thus, the task for the Dutch food authorities was twofold: devising a new centralised rationing system in collaboration with the German authorities and seeking the trust and commitment of all those involved in the production and transportation of foodstuffs.

Mobilising transportation was key to restoring the rationing system, but it turned out to be exceedingly difficult with ongoing German requisitioning, food transporters in hiding, and growing fuel shortages. In their efforts to find a solution, in mid-November 1944, the RBVVO arranged the so-called fifty-fifty deal, which encouraged companies to gather and transport potatoes from the northeast themselves, keeping half of the cargo plus 50 kilograms per family member – provided they handed over the other half to the Dutch Potato Trade Association (*Vereniging ter Behartiging van de Nederlandsche Aardappelhandel*: VBNA) for central rationing. Later, the RBVVO readjusted this to 50 per cent for the VBNA, 15 per cent for social institutions and 35 per cent for personal use, as well as 35 kilograms per family member. When the arrangement ended on 9 December, it comprised some 208,000 people. Most of their vessels arrived late December or early January, thereby disrupting the central food supply. On 3 January, the RBVVO admitted that they could not live up to its promises and confiscated most of the supplies for central

---

[20] Klemann and Kudryashov, *Occupied Economies*, 269; Klemann, *Nederland 1938–1948*, 211–217, 548–553; Klemann, 'De Zwarte Markt', 534–535, 560.
[21] Klemann and Kudryashov, *Occupied Economies*, 279–80; Kenneth Mouré, 'Réalités Cruelles: State Controls and the Black Market for Food in Occupied France', in *Food and War in Twentieth Century Europe*, 169–182.

rationing, promising that they would be delivered back to the families in better times.[22]

This initiative tentatively kick-started food transports; however, dividing the cargo was as difficult as finding transportation. For example, when the first potato transports arrived in Amsterdam, pro-German mayor Edward Voûte surreptitiously reserved extra supplies for his city. The disruptive local food politics urged Hirschfeld to consult with *Beauftragte* Schwebel. On 1 December, the two had a prolonged meeting during which they discussed the failing of the Department of Water Management, which was officially responsible for food transports. Schwebel subsequently put the matter before Seyss-Inquart, who agreed to install a new committee responsible for all transports over inland waters. On 5 December, Hirschfeld met with Louwes, the mayors of Amsterdam and Rotterdam Voûte and Frederik Müller, and representatives from Water Management. The outcome of this meeting was the establishment of the Central Shipping Company for the Food Supply (CRV), which would become the core of the central rationing system.[23]

The CRV was established to encompass all inland shipping within the occupied Netherlands. Hirschfeld, Louwes, Müller, and Voûte formed the board of the company, with Hirschfeld functioning as its highest authority. Hirschfeld placed executive authority of the CRV with the RBVVO's Department of Transportation, while the central office took a seat in Amsterdam under Director H. Ivens, functioning as a joint body of the Departments of Agriculture and Fisheries and Water Management. To ensure cooperation, owners of ships, vessels, and tugboats received official assurances from both Dutch and German sides.[24] The German authorities issued the so-called *Bolle-Scheine*, signed by *Schiffahrtbevolmächtigte* A. H. C. Bolle, to assure that the ship owners would be free from German requisitioning measures.[25] Despite this somewhat promising outlook, the RBVVO held realistic expectations about the CRV's capabilities and German promises. They also fearfully anticipated the winter months: 'If frost sets in, we will be hopelessly

---

[22] NIOD, 212a, inv.no. 118, Report on potato deliveries, VBNA Head Office, 1 March 1945; Louwes, 'De Voedselvoorziening', 640; Hirschfeld, 'De Centrale Reederij', 5. See also: Trienekens, *Tussen ons Volk en de Honger*, 376.

[23] NIOD, 212a, inv.no. 167, Diary Hirschfeld, 29 November, 1, 5 December 1944; Hirschfeld, *Herinneringen uit de Bezettingstijd*, 154–155; Hirschfeld, 'De Centrale Reederij', 5–7; De Jong, *Het Koninkrijk* 10b, 177–181.

[24] NIOD, 216h, inv.no. 88, Insurances for inland shipping, 22 December 1944.

[25] The German *Wehrmacht* initially demanded that empty vessels would transport machines and other confiscated materials to the east but abandoned this demand later on. NIOD, 216h, inv.no. 319, Correspondence *Hauptabteilung Verkehr Generalkommissariat für Finanz und Wirtschaft* on allowing food transports, 27 December 1945. See also: Klemann, *Nederland 1938–1948*, 464–465.

lost .... If war activities resume north of the rivers, we need to rely on caritas and divide amongst ourselves whatever there is left.'[26]

Seyss-Inquart officially approved the establishment of the CRV on 11 December, followed three days later by the first private meeting between Hirschfeld and the *Reichskommissar*. Up till then, the *Reichskommissar* had avoided a private get-together with the secretary general, which historians have attributed to Hirschfeld having a Jewish father, making him a *Mischling* (mixed-blood) according to Nazi racial doctrine.[27] The meeting on 14 December was a turning point in the food crisis as this was the first clear indication that the German civil authorities had shifted their policies in favour of food supply: this gesture confirmed their feelings of responsibility in averting famine. Significantly, it was during this meeting that Seyss-Inquart first suggested the possibility of 'neutralising' the western Netherlands, inferring that this region would be designated as an area where no fighting needed to take place.

The day after the meeting, Hirschfeld publicly declared the constitution of the CRV.[28] The announcement was followed by a special call from Louwes to shipmen, explaining the need for centralisation and the importance of cooperation: 'People are, simply said, starving in the full meaning of the word .... Our water transportation, your job, is the decisive element in the food shortage of these days.'[29] Because the difficulties with the Department of Water Management persisted, on 28 December Seyss-Inquart authorised Hirschfeld to take over its transportation department entirely, appointing J. J. Oyevaar as his representative. According to Oyevaar, the CRV had three defining characteristics: a business-like and reasonable relationship with the occupation authorities, a strict demarcation of responsibilities of the RBVVO and the transportation department, and a constant aim towards a greater mobilisation of domestic materials and supplies.[30]

The efforts of the CRV had considerable success. Over a period of 25 weeks, the company transported over 170,000 tons of food (excluding

[26] NA, 2.11.30.05, inv.no. 65, Report RBVVO, 19 December 1944. See also: NIOD, 0876b Voedselvoorziening, inv.no. 57.

[27] Fennema and Rhijnsburger, *Dr Hans Max Hirschfeld*, 128–129.

[28] NIOD, 216h, Press release constitution CRV, 15 December 1944 (published in legal, pro-German newspapers on 18 December 1944); Press release Hirschfeld, 16 December 1944.

[29] NIOD, 216h, inv.no. 77, Call Louwes to shipmen, December 1944.

[30] NIOD, 212a, inv.no 98, Report Transport department of Department of Water Management by J. J. Oyevaar, 20 April 1945; inv.no. 100, Letter of mandate regarding the Department of Transport from Seyss-Inquart to Hirschfeld, 28 January 1945; inv. no. 37, Post-war report Hirschfeld on policy during the occupation, 22 October 1945; inv.no. 98, Report J. J. Oyevaar.

the Red Cross shipments to be discussed later), of which four fifths comprised consumption potatoes, which constituted about 1.3 kilograms of weekly potatoes per head of the population in the west.[31] While the CRV became of foremost importance for the central rationing system, adverse war circumstances made it impossible for the company to function at its full potential. First of all, requisitioning by the German *Wehrmacht* and *Kriegsmarine* continued throughout the famine and encompassed more than simply taking Dutch transportation. Even though shortages grew larger by the day, between 30 October and 14 December 1944 1,931 wagons carrying 28,216 tons of potatoes from the provinces of Drenthe and Groningen were sent across the border to western Germany; almost 50,000 tons followed in the crucial famine months January–February 1945. Officially, however, the Germans might have been 'entitled' to part of the cargo because of the German rye that had been imported just before the Allied invasion.[32]

The ever increasingly strict German regulations and surveillance also did their part to slow the food transports down.[33] Secondly, Allied air raids on vessels not only instilled fear among the transporters, but also damaged a great number of ships.[34] A third factor was the winter frost and its lagged effects on transportation. The frost slowed down imports between late December 1944 and mid-February 1945, which by the last week of January had come almost to a complete standstill. Finally, and perhaps most importantly of all, the growing fuel shortage put great strain on food transports. By March, there was hardly enough fuel to keep vital services such as pumping stations and soup kitchens running, let alone to allow food transports to continue.[35] As part of the final struggle, the RBVVO offered its last transporters part of their cargo in return for their labour. CRV Director Ivens even proposed a tow plan, envisioning civilian volunteers towing boats carrying foodstuffs by hand.[36] The last

---

[31] Hirschfeld, 'De Centrale Reederij', 10; Population on 31 December 1944. CBS, *Jaarcijfers voor Nederland 1943–1946*, 14.

[32] NIOD, 039 *Generalkommissariat für Finanz und Wirtschaft*, Note *Hauptabteiling Ernährung und Landwirtschaft* on consumption potatoes, 16 December 1944; Note *Geschäftsabteilung der Hauptvereinigung der deutschen Kartoffelwirtschaft*, 19 Feburary 1945.

[33] NIOD, 216h, inv.no. 312, Report CRV, 12 January 1945.

[34] NIOD, 216h, inv.no. 313, Week report CRV 18–24 March 1945.

[35] See, for instance: NIOD, 216h, inv.no. 313, Report meeting CRV, 15 February 1945; NIOD, 212a, inv.no. 167, Diary Hirschfeld, 5 February and 19 March 1945.

[36] NIOD, 216h, inv.no. 77, Letter E. C. Teunissen, Transportation representative RBVVO in the West, 10 March 1945; NIOD, 212a, inv.no. 107, Letter Hirschfeld to Müller on tow plan, 12 March 1945; See also: NIOD, 216h, inv.no. 312, Report CRV, 14 March 1945; inv.no. 325, Personal notes Ivens, 28 March 1945.

Illustration 9 Arrival of shipment of sugar beets, 1945.

German coal trains arrived in the west by late March; by mid-April, the food transports had ended.

During the first months of 1945, centralisation became a top priority for the German civil administration. In their private meeting on 7 January, Seyss-Inquart promised Hirschfeld to prioritise the recovery of Dutch authority in the west and again affirmed that neutralising the west might be a solution to the various political and military difficulties. Prevention of disorder and chaos was also still considered a priority among German administrations. To combat administrative disintegration, Seyss-Inquart granted Hirschfeld full executive powers over the Department of Transportation, appointed the National Socialist mayor of Rotterdam Müller as Head of Internal Affairs in the three western provinces, and authorised Woltersom as the formal representative for the organised industries. No hierarchy existed among these three, and rather remarkably, developments in the war were left out of their meetings. 'Leader of the Dutch people' Mussert was denied a position in the governance reforms, as Seyss-Inquart refused to assign the role of internal affairs to the NSB. From January onwards, Seyss-Inquart and Hirschfeld met weekly in The Hague to discuss urgent matters, which the *Reichskommissar* preferred to his own headquarters in Apeldoorn because it was 'a better environment to talk'.[37]

Seyss-Inquart also further centralised his own administration by giving authority over the German civil administrations in the three western provinces to his *Beauftragte* for South Holland and The Hague: Schwebel.[38] Seyss-Inquart's *Beauftragten* continued to closely supervise the mayors in their regions during the final months of occupation, including firing several of them and assigning new 'reliable' men to take over their posts. Despite the poor prospects for Nazi Germany, considerable numbers of National Socialists still applied for the position of mayor because they held the job in high regard and were willing to take on its difficult tasks. The governance changes also meant that business-like deliberations on urgent governance issues took priority over political steering. For some NSB mayors, this choice for a more technocratic crisis management and 'good' governance came a as relief, not in the least because they knew they would be held accountable for collaborating with the enemy after the war.[39]

Following his meeting with Seyss-Inquart on 7 January in which the controversial subject of neutralising the west was raised, Hirschfeld went on to consult with several other high-placed Dutch officials. Together, these men decided to inform the Council of Trusted Representatives (*College van Vertrouwensmannen*), the secret representatives of the exiled Dutch government in the occupied territory, who would then pass on the information about the developments to London. However, in their telegram to London, former Secretary Generals Leonardus J. A. Trip and Aarnout M. Snouck Hurgronje failed to mention Seyss-Inquart's proposition but, instead, stated that 'these gentlemen [Hirscheld and others]

---

[37] BA, R70NL-60, Message *SS-Sturmbannführer* Wölk, 29 January 1945; NIOD, 212a, inv. no. 167, Diary Hirschfeld, 7, 16 January 1945; inv.no. 114, Secret letter agreements Hirschfeld, Müller, and Woltersom with Seyss-Inquart after meeting 12 January 1945. See also: Romijn, *Burgemeesters in Oorlogstijd*, 596–600.

[38] NIOD, 216h, inv.no. 89, Letter Seyss-Inquart on position of Schwebel to Secretary Generals of Dutch Departments, 23 February 1945.

[39] Romijn, *Burgemeesters in Oorlogstijd*, 577– 579.

with regard to the famine in Netherlands are willing, if needed in consultation with the occupier, to prepare the constitution of a relief committee under auspices of neutral powers'.[40] Admitting after the war that this was a 'colossal policy mistake', the council neglected the opportunity presented by Seyss-Inquart, which for him was a sign that the Dutch and the Allies were not willing to negotiate.

Official Rations

Dealing with an irregular and highly insufficient food supply during the crisis period, one of the most important issues the food officials faced was how to divide available foodstuffs. After the Allied invasion in September 1944, the country was split into three rationing areas: the southern Netherlands (provinces of Zeeland, North Brabant, Limburg), the western Netherlands (provinces of North Holland, South Holland, Utrecht), and the northeastern Netherlands (provinces of Groningen, Friesland, Drenthe, Overijssel, Gelderland).[41] All three areas maintained different rations throughout the crisis period with the two occupied areas directed by the RBVVO in The Hague; as for the south, it was initially directed locally during the first weeks after liberation and, after 23 December 1944, by the new Central Rationing Office established in Vught (North Brabant).[42] Among these three rationing areas from 1 October 1944 onwards there were considerable differences. Official rations reached famine proportions in the western provinces only.

It should be noted, however, that the food situation in the liberated south also reached critical levels after Operation Market Garden. In the autumn of 1944, the average adult consumer was entitled to less than 1,250 kcal per day; nowhere near the Allies' desired target of providing 1,600 kcal to Europe's liberated people. Local shortages were even more severe as official rations in the province of North Brabant dropped to 600–800 kcal. The brief food crisis in the south was relieved in late November when the first Allied supplies arrived from Brussels and Antwerp, and it was after this point that rations slowly improved.[43]

---

[40] Cited in De Jong, *Het Koninkrijk* 10b, 1281.
[41] Until 9 June 1945, 'south' did not include South Limburg.
[42] Directorate of Food Supply, Overview official rations in West, East and South Holland over the period 1 October 1944–8 January 1946. The official rations were documented throughout the crisis.
[43] NIOD, 233b, inv.no. 33, Circular letter SHAEF, December 1944; inv.no. 27, 'Food position in the Netherlands', 16 December 1944; inv.no. 33, Letter Bedell Smith to Prime Minister Gerbrandy, 23 December 1944; Message General Clark to Gerbrandy, 22 March 1945; BHIC, 127.04, inv.no. 428, 'Food Rations 5', 17 March 1945; Telegram Manufacturers Union and Trade Union Eindhoven to Queen Wilhelmina,

Being home to the country's largest agricultural areas, the northeast proved capable of producing enough food to support itself throughout the crisis. While the province of Friesland, for example, lowered its weekly bread rations from 1,800 grams to 1,400 in February 1945, the city of Amsterdam – only 150 kilometers away – was entitled to a mere 500 grams per week.[44] This was indeed an advantagous position for the people in the northeast, who also had more opportunities than urban dwellers in the west to complement their official entitlements with extra-legal food supplies from nearby farms. Nevertheless, the food supply requirement of the tens of thousands of evacuees who also now resided in the northeast (and mostly relied on the official 1,300 kcal per day) meant that the hardship of the food crisis was still a very real experience in this region.[45] The inability of the RBVVO to divide the available supplies in the occupied areas more equally should be considered as a firm confirmation that the famine was essentially a transportation problem.

As shown in Figure 4.1, following Operation Market Garden official rations decreased immediately, dropping below a meagre 750 kcal for adults after 26 November 1944. With regard to these adult rations, food authorities chose to make food entitlements irrespective of profession or labour intensity. This was contrary to the pre-crisis situation and most likely done because many workplaces had cut hours or closed during the crisis. Figure 4.1 shows that the period of winter frost brought about the first low point in January. The small peaks in February, March, and April correlate to the extra rations provided by the Red Cross. The absolute bottom was reached in May 1945 when the west was isolated from the rest of the country and supplies were completely exhausted. In the last week before liberation, official rations contained only 364 kcal: there was nothing left to look forward to if the German surrender had taken longer.

Figure 4.1 also reveals the considerable differences between the official rations children and adults were entitled to. While adults

---

11 November 1944; Jan A. van Oudheusden, Marian Omtzigt, and Ria van den Heuvel-Habraken, 'Feest en Frustratie: Het Leven achter het Front', in *Tussen Vrijheid en Vrede: Het Bevrijde Zuiden, September 1944–Mei 1945*, eds. Oudheusen and Henk Termeer (Zwolle: Waanders, 1994), 78–79. See also: De Zwarte, 'Voedsel, Spoedig en Radicaal! Voedseldistributie en Hulpverlening in Amsterdam, Eindhoven en Groningen tijdens de Hongerwinter, 1944–1945', MA Thesis University of Amsterdam (2013).

[44] NIOD, 0332, inv.no. M4, Report Food Commissioner Friesland, 5 February 1945; Directorate of Food Supply, Overview weekly rations in Western Netherlands per product, 1 October 1944–5 January 1946.

[45] Groninger Archieven [GA], 1841 Gemeentebestuur Groningen 1916-1965, inv.no. 194, Letter Provincial Food Commissioner to mayor about the declaration of the state of emergency, 19 February 1945; GA, 63, inv.no. 157, Correspondence on distribution and food supply, 1945.

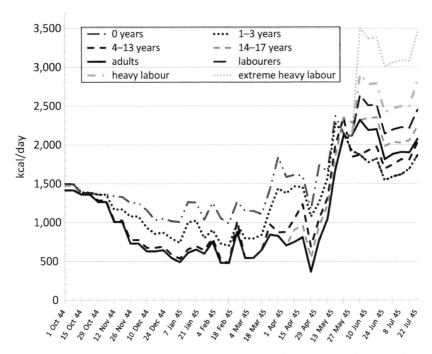

Figure 4.1 Weekly rations in kcal per day in the western Netherlands for different age groups and professions, 1 October 1944–29 July 1945.
Source: NA, 2.11.23.02, inv.no. 192, Reports on rationing in the Netherlands, 1946

generally require a higher calorific intake, from October 1944 to June 1945, infants and toddlers received far superior rations, showing the deliberate choice made by the food authorities to focus on the vulnerable youngsters. In April 1945, the official rations for infants even went so high as 1,800 kcal: more than the rations had been for both children and adults before the crisis. By contrast, children above four years of age received no such privileges and were entitled to the same poor rations as the adults, rising only a little after mid-March 1945 thanks to the Red Cross allocations. While this conscious choice by the Dutch food administration might seem odd considering the vulnerability of young children to food deprivation, these children's diets were, in fact, largely compensated by non-governmental food allocations, as will be explained later. All authorities, including the German occupier, approved and stimulated this redistribution of food.

The composition of the rations differentiated by age group also reflects certain choices. Adult rations (including children above 4 years) consisted largely of carbohydrates: mainly potatoes, bread, and sugar beets (7 times 3 kilograms). Indeed, for several weeks in 1945, adults were entitled to hardly any fats in their diets. In early February, for example, adults were entitled to 1 kilogram of potatoes, 500 grams of bread, 250 grams of peas, and 50 grams of cheese per week.[46] Young children, on the other hand, were entitled to all remaining supplies of (skimmed) milk and other products rich in protein and fat, which was not only considered healthier, but also indispensable for their growth and development. These fat and protein entitlements were the main element responsible for their superior calorific intake. Infants, the most defenceless of all, received the highest calorific rations from the RBVVO. Fat and protein levels in the rations of children of 1–3 years of age deviated from infant rations from respectively November and January onwards. The rations of these two groups merged again after the war. In a similar way, it took until the last week of May before adult rations rose above those of their offspring.

In practice, of course, these official rations can hardly be considered individual, as intra-household allocation ultimately determined individual consumption. For example, Dutch doctors were well aware that older family members benefited from the relatively favourable infant and young children rations, thereby offsetting the intended effects.[47] Nor did the buying entitlements necessarily mean that the products were actually available for purchase; more often than not, products were unobtainable due to a permanent backlog in food deliveries.

In addition to official rations, the RBVVO gave extra entitlements to certain vulnerable groups. Hospitals had to divide the sick into two urgency groups with only the most urgent cases (e.g., chew and swallowing disorders, diabetes, tuberculosis, severe gastrointestinal illnesses) entitled to extra rations. While extra rations had initially also been made available for people who were more than 20 per cent underweight for their height, over the course of the famine, the threshold was raised to 33 per cent and later even to 40 per cent underweight.[48] On 7 March 1945, Head of Public Health Banning sent a circular letter to medical

[46] NIOD, 244, inv.no. 1141, Diary C. S., 10 February 1945.
[47] J. Van Lookeren Campagne and H. F. Wiers, 'Kinderziekten in Bezettingstijd', in *Medische Ervaringen*, 294; Van Lookeren Campagne and Wiers, 'De Voedselrantsoenen voor Kinderen in den Bezettingstijd', in *Medische Ervaringen*, 303.
[48] The Food Council had already made preparations for special hospital nutrition in case of emergency in June 1944. The state of emergency was announced in November 1944 and lasted until 15 June 1945. Bok, *De Kliniek der Hongerziekte*, 24–25.

Table 4.1 *Official rations of adults in four cities during four selected periods*

Period	Amsterdam	Rotterdam	Utrecht	Delft
October 1944	1,283	910	1,090	1,010
February 1945	479	550	466	390
April 1945	659	690	620	730
May/June 1945[a]	2,045	2,400	2,007	1,800

[a] Amsterdam 28 May–2 June; Rotterdam 3–9 June; Utrecht 6–11 June; Delft 19–26 May.
Source: Burger et al., *Malnutrition and Starvation* II, 126–127, 153, 186, 210

inspectors in the west to include all cases of hunger oedema and cachexia in these relief schemes, which comprised an extra 2 kilograms of potatoes, 500 grams of peas, and 800 grams of bread per week: quite a considerable amount.[49] The state supplied young and expecting mothers with extra rations of oatmeal and milk powder whenever possible, which in practice was only after Red Cross shipments arrived. Their official rations dropped from 2,099 kcal in October 1944 to 1,144 kcal at its low point in January 1945. The reality, however, was much different. According to a survey from SHAEF, in February 1945 the nutrition available for pregnant women only consisted of 731 kcal: it was this deficit that was responsible for the long-term effects on their offspring that we saw in Chapter 3.[50]

Within the three western provinces, official rations could still differ considerably (Table 4.1). One the one hand, these differences were the outcome of municipal authorities prioritising their own local supply. Towns enjoying waterway access, such as Amsterdam, or situated close to food-producing areas, such as Utrecht, were able to turn the bureaucratic disintegration at central level to their own benefit. On the other hand, these local differences also resulted from state policies that had been planned and carried out since mid-1943. These dictated that local autarky, and its implied efficient use of local supplies and materials, was preferred in the case of an emergency. Therefore, as transportation difficulties during the crisis made it impossible to approximate official rations throughout the western provinces, and the RBVVO reckoned it

---

[49] Banning, 'Voeding en Voedingstoestand', 22–24. In Amsterdam, applications for special diets for people suffering from oedema started in February 1945. SA, 5257 Distributiedienst, inv.no. 233, Report municipal distribution office 1945, 103. See also: Bonzon and Davies, 'Feeding the Cities', 320.
[50] NIOD, 212a, inv.no 116, Documents on Red Cross relief, 1945; Evaluation by H. M. Sinclair from the Oxford Nutrition Survey for SHAEF, as published in: Smith, 'Effects of Maternal Undernutrition', 234.

was more important to avoid wasting food than having equal rations, these directives meant that smaller villages situated within or near food-producing areas were often much less affected by the crisis than the larger cities only a few kilometres away.[51] Yet certainly, not all smaller cities and villages fared better than the large conurbations, as exemplified by the dire situation in Delft (population: 55,000) (see Table 4.1), which was located in between the large cities of Rotterdam and The Hague but had much less resources of its own. The food authorities constantly had to decide on who to prioritise in the food allocations, even when external relief finally reached the occupied areas in late February 1945. The RBVVO later admitted that they had made a mistake by excluding certain smaller towns from these first Red Cross distributions, as by March, the situation had become so deplorable that 'even the villages' were suffering from hunger.[52]

Soup Kitchens

The provision of food via soup kitchens was one of the most important forms of state-organised relief during the Hunger Winter. The RBVVO had established a soup kitchen system as early as 1940 for those not able to cook their own meals as well as for groups entitled to extra rations, such as schoolchildren and labourers: these were the aptly named Communal Kitchens (CK). Involvement of the National Socialist NVD made participation extremely unpopular, and so the kitchens switched their main task to providing coupon-free meals for factory workers.[53] This all drastically changed after the Allied invasion. After gas and electricity were cut by the authorities in October–November 1944 to save fuel for vital economic services, the CK was suddenly required to provide for most of the population in the occupied areas. Additionally, because many of the NVD officials had fled the country in September 1944, the RBVVO managed to take full control and eliminate the undesirable National Socialist involvement that had previously hindered the CK's popularity.[54] In a short time, the RBBVO had adjoined all existing soup

[51] NIOD, 0332, inv.no. C3, Report food supply Vianen, 11 December 1944; WA, 0056, inv.no. 130, Letter on situation in municipality of Purmerend from acting mayor of Purmerend to Commissionar of the Queen in the province of North Holland, 14 May 1945.

[52] NA, Louwes, inv.no. 117, Report Louwes, Appendix K.

[53] Dols et al., 'De Centrale Keukens', 67–75; Dols and Van Arcken, 'Food Supply and Nutrition', 327–328.

[54] The NVD maintained responsibility for the so-called German kitchens, which provided meals to *Wehrmacht* soldiers, *Volksdeutsche* and families of SS soldiers. NIOD, 179 Winterhulp/NVD, inv.no. 529, Month report NVD Amsterdam, February–March 1945.

kitchens, including those for factory workers and schoolchildren, and erected new emergency kitchens throughout the country.[55]

The 'state of emergency' within the CK system became effective on 26 October 1944, setting in motion a strong decentralisation. Every two distribution circles (the units in which local food rationing was organised) were appointed a regional leader, whom the RBVVO provided with regulations and rationing schemes from The Hague, which in practice were difficult to streamline due to a lack of communication and unequal division of means of transportation. RBVVO's Department of Mass Feeding was responsible for coordinating the kitchens and meals; the regional leaders were then responsible for allocating food, collecting ration stamps, transporting the food from the kitchens to the distribution posts, and distributing the food.[56] This division of labour was similar throughout the occupied area, including the northeast, where the population also suffered from gas and coal shortages and was simultaneously burdened with the care for tens of thousands of evacuees from the south.[57]

The number of CK participants rose exponentially after gas and electricity were cut. In The Hague, for example, the CK needed to adapt from serving 3,700 people on 1 September 1944 to a staggering 209,400 on 1 December that same year.[58] For smaller cities and towns without any existing soup kitchens, this task was nearly impossible.[59] Because numbers kept rising while shortages grew, the individual meals reduced in size from one litre in September 1944, to three-quarter litre in the fall and finally to one-half litre from the winter onwards: hardly enough to satisfy. As one Amsterdam municipal official succinctly described the situation: 'The overall complaint is that half a litre per day is too little to live on and too much to die from.'[60]

---

[55] Dols et al., 'De Centrale Keukens', 67–75.
[56] Dols et al., 'De Centrale Keukens', 103; NA, 2.11.30.06, inv.no. 133, Circular letter Head inspector Mass Feeding, J.R. Hoekstra, 22 March 1945; inv.no. 241, Letter J. P. van Loon to Louwes, June 1945.
[57] GA, 1841, inv.no. 194, Letter P. V. C. Ebels to mayor of Groningen, 8 November 1944; Letter mayor of Groningen to municipal services, 4 December 1944. The emergency situation in the city of Groningen was announced on 26 February 1945. GA, 1841, inv. no. 194, Letter Ebels to mayor, 19 February 1945. See also: NIOD, 244, Diary J. E., 10 February 1945.
[58] Haags Gemeentearchief [HGA], 0610–01 Gemeentebestuur Den Haag, inv.no. 337, Municipal report over 1944.
[59] For example: WA, 0056, inv.no. 1482, Minutes municipal meeting, 1 November 1944; Gemeente Archief Schiedam [GAS], 346 Gemeentebestuur Schiedam, inv.no. 4246, Municipal report over 1944. On their first day of food distribution, the CK in Schiedam immediately needed to provide for over 14,000 persons.
[60] NIOD, 244, inv.no. 1129, Diary H. H., 14 January 1945.

Table 4.2 *Number of participants in Communal Kitchens in seven western cities, March 1945*

City	Number of participants	Population[a]	Percentage
Amsterdam	250,000	772,824	32.3
Rotterdam	220,000	610,385	36.0
The Hague	220,000	450,949	48.8
Utrecht	80,000	173,328	46.2
Haarlem	30,000	149,862	20.0
Leiden	60,000	83,467	71.9
Delft	28,000	59,282	47.2

[a] Population on 31 December 1944
Source: NIOD, 212a, inv.no. 108, Weekly report Department Food Issues RBVVO, 11–17 March 1945; CBS, *Jaarcijfers Nederland 1943–1946*, 14

Table 4.2 shows how severely the population in the urban areas depended on CK during the famine. In fact, this dependence was even more crucial as these numbers were documented before the actual height of the crisis: in April 1945 over 400,000 people, or more than half of Amsterdam's population, participated in the meal system. That same month, the kitchens cooked 1,800,000 hot meals per day in the west plus almost 200,000 in the other occupied areas, covering 183 municipalities.[61]

For the food administration, problems with the over-exhausted CK were considerable. Again, there was first the dreaded question of who to prioritise in state relief. After September 1944, the RBVVO ordered that coupon-free meals for the less fortunate had to be cancelled in favour of fair allocation; this halt on coupon-free meals also included those for schoolchildren and labourers. Yet, while the Dutch food authorities officially argued that school kitchens had to close in preference for central control, sources reveal another important reason: to exclude the NVD from this part of the rationing system as well.[62] When state relief to schoolchildren was unavoidably terminated as part of this plan, the Dutch authorities knew very well that this left a vulnerable group exposed to food deprivation – and it was for this reason that they allowed and

[61] NA, 2.11.30.06, inv.no. 241, Letter Van Loon to Louwes, June 1945; Dols et al., 'De Centrale Keukens', 75, 100–101.
[62] SA, 5258 Gemeentelijke Dienst Kinderkleding en –Voeding, inv.no. 3, Report October 1943–July 1946. See also: NA, 2.19.070.01, inv.no. 199, Report NVD office Utrecht on September 1944–February 1945.

encouraged grassroots initiatives to fill this gap. Another vulnerable group left out of state relief were the elderly who, according to Louwes, were not allowed to receive anything extra from the German occupier because they supposedly had little meaning for the future of society.[63]

On the other hand, other specific groups were entitled to extra meals from the CK. At the behest of Seyss-Inquart and in consultancy with Berlin, the *Wehrmacht*, families of Dutch SS Eastern Front volunteers, and *Volksdeutsche* continued to receive extra meals. These groups were entitled to two ration cards instead of one from January 1945 onwards, with extra rations of meat and butter made available for their children.[64] People working in '*lebenswichtige*' services (e.g., food supply, gas and electricity, water supply, garbage collection, transportation services, police, undertakers, CK, health services, postal services) also remained entitled to extra rations. This was not simple preferential treatment but a conscious strategy to prevent society from total collapse.[65] In general, during the food crisis the German authorities only interfered in the food supply for those groups that, according to them, deserved extra rations and left the overall allocation of the scarce food supplies in the hands of the Dutch food authorities.

With the establishment of special 'diet kitchens' for those suffering from stomach and intestinal troubles, diabetes, and tuberculosis, the RBVVO was also responsible for feeding society's most vulnerable groups.[66] From November 1944 onwards, they also took care of infant nutrition; in particular, babies who could not be breastfed.[67] A final group that posed specific challenges concerned the Chinese and Dutch East Indies communities in the cities, as they were accustomed to and preferred different staple foods. On the initiative of Hirschfeld, who had lived in the Dutch East Indies himself, the CK integrated Chinese

---

[63] Louwes, 'De Voedselvoorziening', 622.

[64] BA, NS19/2429, Telegram Rauter to Berlin on emergency situation in the Netherlands, 10 January 1945; BA, R70NL-41, Circular letter Rauter to Kommandeur des SS-Ersatzkommandos, 13 February 1945; NA, 2.11.30.06, inv.no. 4, Week report 19–31 March 1945; inv.no. 155, Correspondence RBVVO with Hauptabteilung Ernährung und Landwirtschaft, March–April 1945.

[65] NA, 2.11.30.05, inv.no.2, Week report 27 November–3 December 1944, 19–25 February 1945; inv.no. 68, Report meeting Louwes and Von der Wense, 22 March 1945.

[66] Zoethout, 'De Dieetkeukens in de Jaren 1944–1945', *Voeding* 8 (1947): 237–240. There were similar diet kitchens in the Northeast: GA, 1841, inv.no. 194, Notes from GGD, 15 February and 23 March 1945.

[67] NA, 2.11.30.05, inv.no. 2, Week report 9–16, 16–23, 23–30 October, 30 October–6 November, 6–13 November 1944; NA, 2.11.30.06, inv.no. 148, Correspondence on infant nutrition, 1944–1945.

restaurant holders into their kitchens, ensuring that many of the 'Orientals' were allocated rice instead of potatoes during the crisis.[68]

The quantity and quality of mass feeding also posed a continuous issue. New products and famine foods made their way into the diets although authorities still had only limited knowledge about their nutritional value. At the same time, it was their task to advise the public on their usage.[69] The first state trials with sugar beets in the CK started in November 1944, followed by tulip bulb trials in December, which according to a CK report 'worked out very well, although they need a long preparation time before they become palatable'.[70] This solution, however, did not prevent further downfall. In Leiden, the nutritional value per meal dropped from 483 kcal in October 1944 to 335 kcal in December with a final drop to 268 kcal in April 1945.[71] And, overall, the menus were sombre and repetitive. People in Rotterdam gave all sorts of inventive and creative names to reflect what was obviously a poor-tasting soup, calling it 'cement soup, dirty socks soup, mouse tails soup' and even 'dirty laundry water'.[72] The 1945 municipal report of Schiedam summarised the dismal situation with the statement that 'it was the biggest depression in the history of the food supply when we prepared fodder for human consumption'.[73]

Finally, the kitchens also had to cope with severe organisational problems, such as the lack of materials and hygiene measures. For the Department of Mass Feeding under J. P. van Loon, it was impossible to exercise centralised control over all CKs in the west. Some of these organisational issues, such as corrupt staff, were also a product of gender imbalances, as it was mostly men who ran the CK.[74] As we will discover

[68] NA, 2.11.30.05, inv.no. 2, Week report 2–9 October 1944, 15–22 January, 29 January–5 February, 26 March–2 April 1945.
[69] Ideas on preparing sugar beets for civilian nutrition were first formulated in early 1944. NA, 2.11.30.06, inv.no. 181, Report on cooking techniques CK, January 1944; Rigter, 'De Gezondheids- en Voedingsraad in Oorlogstijd', 237.
[70] NA, 2.11.30.06, inv.no. 181, Report CK Zwijndrecht, December 1944.
[71] Erfgoed Leiden en Omstreken [ELO], 0257, inv.no. 52, Concept report on mass feeding in Leiden, 1945. To improve the meals, from March 1945 onwards, the kitchens even added casein powder to the meals. NA, 2.11.30.06, inv.no. 194, Circular letter on use of casein, 6 March 1945.
[72] Stadsarchief Rotterdam [SR], 273 Verzameling WOII, inv.no. 1501, Diary H. v.d. W., 7 February 1945; GAS, 460 Collectie Tweede Wereldoorlog, inv.no. 19, Correspondence CK Schiedam, March–May 1945.
[73] GAS, 346, inv.no. 4247, Municipal report on 1945.
[74] NA, 2.11.30.06, inv.no. 61, Circular letter PVC Groningen to Kitchen Staff, 11 April 1945; inv.no. 78, Correspondence 14 November–3 December 1944; Report on post inspection, 20 December 1944; inv.no. 176, Report District Leader CK in Rotterdam, 5 April 1945; HGA, 0655-01 Centrale Keukens van de Gemeente 's-Gravenhage, inv. no. 19, Annual report 1945. See also: De Jong, Het Koninkrijk 10b, 165–166.

Illustration 10 Children scraping out the bins outside a soup kitchen.

Illustration 11 Women preparing tulip bulbs for consumption in
Rotterdam soup kitchen, 1945.

later, the desperate food conditions combined with malpractices in the
male-dominated CK drove women to gather in large public protests on
the streets. While gatherings of more than five people were strictly
forbidden by the occupier around this time, the fact that Dutch and
German police perceived them as 'innocent housewives' fighting for their
families precluded any forceful intervention. Eventually, in most large
cities, women managed to form female supervisory boards to oversee the
CK, which was a clear confirmation that public kitchens and communal
feeding belonged to their domain, not to those of men. By giving in to the
women's demands, local authorities alleviated part of the growing social
tensions and protests surrounding the food supply.[75] Yet, despite all of
these measures, the exhaustion of all supplies by the end of April could

---

[75] E.g., Regionaal Archief Dordrecht [RAD], 260 Distributiedienst van de Gemeente
Dordrecht, inv.no. 310, Correspondence Director CK and mayor, February–April
1945; inv.no. 466, January–March 1945; ELO, 0046 Rijksbureau voor de
Voedselvoorziening in Oorlogstijd, afdeling Massavoeding, inv.no. 213, Letter to Van
Loon, 18 April 1945. See Chapter 7.

not prevented. Consequently, the RBVVO failed to meet its main priority, which was keeping the CK open to feed the people until liberation.[76]

Decentralisation and Delegation

As the crisis-time organisation of the CK already shows, the food administrators not only focused on centralisation but also introduced decentralising measures. These measures derived from the fact that, in addition to restoring the central rationing system, Hirschfeld and Louwes were confronted with the challenge of identifying the most vulnerable while making the most of local supplies and transportation. In compliance with the German occupying authorities, new directives also had to be issued on how to deal with individual coping strategies, such as food expeditions and the growing black-market trade. In this respect, the German authorities proved remarkably lenient on multiple occasions, due to the military instructions to avoid popular unrest. *Marinebefehlshaber* Stange reveals this conciliating stance in his war journal entry for January 1945: 'A solution to the nutritional problem (in addition to the human side) is of fundamental importance for the German occupation, as starving and freezing masses in the large cities are breeding ground[s] for Bolshevism.'[77] However, the CRV and CK were not enough to mitigate the famine conditions in the west. Therefore, other solutions had to be considered.

As we have seen in the introduction to this chapter, decentralisation had been part of the Dutch food officials' plans all along. One of the envisioned emergency measures in the plan of January 1944 was that Provincial Food Commissioners (PVCs), as administrative heads of provinces and rationing districts, would be authorised to act autonomously to enable efficient use of local supplies and transportation.[78] Thanks to these instructions, after the loss of communication with the Central Rationing Office (CDK) in Zwolle in September 1944, local authorities were able to issue emergency ration cards independently. Municipalities were additionally granted permission to cultivate non-agricultural land and to

[76] NA, 2.11.30.05, inv.no. 2, Week report 23–31 April 1945; *Jaarverslag van Amsterdam 1945: Het Jaar der Bevrijding* II (Amsterdam: Stadsdrukkerij, 1946), 31.
[77] NIOD, 001, inv.no. 656, *Kriegestagebuch Marinebefehlshaber Vizeadmiral* Stange, January 1945.
[78] NIOD, 212a, inv.no. 102. This decree was issued by Hirschfeld in October 1943 and circulated to PVCs and representatives for large urban areas in the spring of 1944; inv. no. 103, Note Louwes to PVCs, 12 May 1944. See also: inv.no. 31, Letter Hirschfeld to Directors of trade organisations, 9 March 1945; NA, 2.21.238, inv.no. 117, Report Louwes, 17.

redistribute the harvest among local social institutions, schools, elderly homes, and the poor. For the ploughing up of pastureland, the PVCs provided special permits and subsidies and an extra 20 million Reichsmark released by the Department of Finance for the municipal purchase of foodstuffs and accompanying costs.[79] What the authorities had not envisioned in their plan, was that communications with the central authorities in The Hague would remain largely intact, which led to much confusion about the reach and limits of local autarky. More significantly, the decentralising measures resulted in considerable local differences in official rations. These unsatisfactory results eventually led the RBVVO to constitute a new CDK in The Hague for the three western provinces. Eventually, in March 1945, Louwes admitted to Von der Wense that the intended decentralisation of authority from national to provincial levels had been unsuccessful.[80]

While decentralisation of the rationing system had more or less failed, delegation of food provisioning tasks – which had not been planned – was quite successful. The food officials were divided over this issue: Hirschfeld firmly believed in centralisation only; however, Louwes did recognise the benefits of delegating relief tasks.[81] The inability to identify those in need at the individual level was the main reason the RBVVO allowed newly emerging self-help entities to take over relief responsibilities. One such example of state responses to self-organisation was intra-company aid, which played an important role during the crisis. Many of these companies, in addition to travelling to the northeast to buy food supplies to redistribute among staff members, had already started allotment gardens in urban parks and wastelands. Dutch food authorities initially promoted such actions but, when shortages grew over the course of the winter, the Directorate of Agriculture took measures to limit the allotments in favour of a more equal distribution of food. After lengthy debates, the food officials and representatives from the business sector came to an agreement that comprised strict regulations and new legislation but allowed companies to grow and harvest their own food supplies – even at the height of the crisis.[82]

[79] NIOD, 216h, inv.no. 20, Circular letter Hirschfeld to mayors in the western Netherlands, 29 January 1945; BA, R83 Niederlande, inv.no. 62, Letter Secretary General Rost van Tonningen to Fischböck, 24 January 1945.

[80] NA, 2.11.30.05, inv.no. 68, Report meeting Louwes and Von der Wense, 22 March 1945.

[81] NIOD, 212a, inv.no. 167, Diary Hirschfeld, 7 and 11 January 1945.

[82] NIOD, 212a, inv.no. 62, Letter Chamber of Commerce and Factories of the province North-Holland to Hirschfeld, 13 February 1945; inv.no. 107, Note Hirschfeld to Director of Agriculture on company allotments, 9 February 1945; Letter Director of Horticulture to Hirschfeld, 21 March 1945. See also: NIOD, 216h, inv.no. 166, Circular Letter PVC South Holland, 27 February and 15 March 1945.

The most important delegating measure was to allow a new, NGO body to take over relief responsibilities. Louwes had already acknowledged that neither he nor the RBVVO was capable of making a distinction between those in need and those who were not at the individual level and was therefore the driving force behind this new body.[83] As Chapters 7 and 8 reveal, grassroots relief organisations mushroomed throughout the occupied areas in the autumn of 1944. Louwes aspired to coordinate these local efforts in order to retain some level of control, but also to receive official approval from Seyss-Inquart. In early December 1944, meetings were held between Louwes and representatives of the Interdenominational Counsel of the Churches (*Interkerkelijk Overleg*: IKO). Louwes acknowledged the IKO's strong position in taking on relief responsibilities: city dwellers trusted the churches because of their critical stance towards the occupier, and the organisation also provided a link with food-producing communities in the northeast of the country. Moreover, the IKO could embody the 'apolitical' organisation, which the occupier would require for this job. On 11 December, a meeting was arranged via Schwebel between an IKO representative – the Finnish Consul General A. J. Th. van der Vlugt, who also had connections with the resistance – and Seyss-Inquart, who agreed with the initiative on the condition that there would be just one body for both emergency relief and the evacuation of children. His approval led to the establishment of the Interdenominational Bureau for Emergency Nutrition (*Interkerkelijk Bureau voor Noodvoedselvoorziening*: IKB), which became the only organisation officially allowed to gather food alongside the rationing system.[84]

The German civil authorities adopted a dualistic attitude towards the IKB and NGO relief in general. At first, Seyss-Inquart openly praised the efforts of the cooperating churches in providing relief to the west: he even commended the famous appeal by religious leaders in late December 1944, who called upon their communities during the Sunday mass to cooperate with the food authorities and condemn black marketeering. The *Reichskommissar* also agreed that the IKB could redistribute leftover supplies from the Red Cross shipments as long as this did not interfere with central rationing.[85] In addition, German *Wehrmacht* and *Kriegsmarine* aided in the child evacuations by offering empty space in

---

[83] NA, 2.11.30.05, inv.no. 68, Meeting Louwes and Von der Wense, 22 March 1945.

[84] NIOD, 1076, inv.no. 23, Report meeting IKO and Louwes, s.n.; Ravesloot, *De Houding van de Kerk*. Van Rossem, *Inter Kerkelijk Bureau*, 10.

[85] BA, R70NL-60, Note on pulpit letter churches, 7 January 1945; Message *Sonderkommando Frank to Befehlshaber Sipo und SD*, 5 January 1945; NIOD, 212a, inv. no. 167, Diary Hirschfeld, 7 January 1945; NA, 2.11.30.05, inv.no. 25, Report meeting Louwes, Rohde and Schwebel, 21 March 1945.

trains and vessels. Seyss-Inquart further proposed some of the decentralised relief plans himself. For example, during a conversation with Hirschfeld in mid-March 1945, he offered to retrieve foodstuffs to feed children
from the northeast in wagons hooked on to *Wehrmacht* trains.[86] Despite
these mutual efforts, Louwes had to continuously negotiate on behalf of
the IKB with the occupying authorities about NGO relief, which he
called the 'secondary rationing system', as Seyss-Inquart was never
wholly convinced about the nature and objectives of this organisation.

Seyss-Inquart's attitude towards the IKB changed around the middle of
February 1945, most likely because CRV shipping traffic had resumed by
that time. On 16 February, the *Reichskommissar* instructed his representatives that, because of the appalling food situation, stricter measures and
surveillance was needed and that only one single body could be responsible
for the food supply – the RBVVO. All other relief efforts, 'special actions'
(*Sonderaktionen*), could only be successful if they concerned the surplus of
farmers who had already delivered their quota to central rationing. As no
farmer was in a position to do both, this precondition could never be met
and, as Seyss-Inquart asserted, these special actions only disturbed and
endangered the general food supply. From that date, all *Sonderaktionen* by
private initiatives, including the churches, were officially forbidden. About
a month later, the *Reichskommissar* also forbade military units to assist with
child evacuations, even if they had space available for civilian transport.[87]
Von der Wense raised similar objections to the IKB. But Louwes, fearing
troubles with the Red Cross shipments if no NGO was involved in redis-
tributing the food supplies to the needy, continued – successfully – to
defend the stance that no other body but the IKB was able to organise
relief, thereby avoiding a premature halt to the IKB's work.[88]

The German civil and military authorities did not stop there with their
limitations and increasingly restricted other forms of food transports as
well. They became extremely apprehensive regarding the involvement of
resistance groups in food transports, which was happening throughout
the occupied areas on a large scale. This, for example, led them to
search all Red Cross transports from November 1944 onward.[89] The

---

[86] NIOD, 212a, 167, Diary Hirschfeld, 12 March 1945. There are no sources available that
reveal the *Wehrmacht*'s response to Seyss-Inquarts plans.

[87] BA, R70NL-60, Circular letter *Befehlshaber Sipo und SD*, 16 February 1945; Circular
letter Deppner to BdS 17 February 1945; NIOD, 212a, inv.no. 106, Letter Wimmer and
Schwebel to Hirschfeld on *Sonderaktione*, 12 February 1945; NIOD, 001, *Tagesbefehl* 10/
45, 16 March 1945.

[88] NA, 2.11.30.05, inv.no. 68, Meeting Louwes and Von der Wense, 22 March 1945.

[89] BA, R70NL-41, Note Rauter, 2 January 1945; R70NL-54, Letter gez. Deppner *SS
Sturmbannführer* to all *Einsaitz und Aussenkommandos*, and border police, 20 November
1944.

combination of 'corruption' and the dwindling food supplies incited Seyss-Inquart to impose a product ban in late January 1945, which dictated that no cereal products, pulses, oil, cheese, or butter could cross the IJssel line from east to west. The ban followed a decree issued on 6 December 1944, which prohibited men between the ages of 17 to 40 from crossing the IJssel. The inspections were carried out by German border police, who were even authorised to search *Wehrmacht* vehicles for illegal goods.[90] On grounds of 'the emergency situation in the western provinces and the subsequent black hoarding in the eastern provinces', the decree also stipulated that only four harbours (i.e., Harlingen, Stavoren, Lemmer, and Zwartsluis) were allowed to remain open for food transports. Private packages with foodstuffs meant for family or friends in the west of maximum of 2 kilograms were still allowed to pass in vehicles belonging to the RBVVO, in total 100 kilograms per truck.[91]

Yet, border officers were not authorised to confiscate foodstuffs not meant for the black market, as this fell under the authority of the Dutch Crisis Control Service (*Crisis Controle Dienst*: CCD), which rerouted confiscated foodstuffs back into the rationing system. In a circular letter, *Höhere SS und Polizeiführer* Rauter explained: 'This will avoid the impression that the German occupying troops take advantage of the hardship of the western provinces.'[92] Shortly after, the *Reichskommissar* proposed a general ban on food transports not belonging to the RBVVO. While Hirschfeld was hesitant about a total ban, he agreed that uncontrolled, or 'wild', transports needed to end. On 1 March 1945, all bridges across the IJssel were closed for civilian crossings and food transports except those belonging to the RBVVO.[93]

The closing of the IJssel bridges resulted in serious difficulties for urban dwellers who had been travelling to the northeastern provinces in search for food. These food expeditions are popularly known in the Netherlands as '*hongertochten*' (hunger journeys: see Chapter 6) and are central to the Dutch collective memory of the Hunger Winter. Indeed, the closing of the IJssel line for hunger journeys is exemplary of the dualistic attitude Dutch and German authorities adopted towards these individual coping strategies. To begin with, the instructions given to police and military units indicate that, during the famine, a clear distinction was made between extra-legal food gathering meant for private use

---

[90] BA, R70NL-41, Letter gez. Hofmann to *Oberkommando der Heeresgrupphe* H, 31 January 1945.
[91] NIOD, 216h, Decision Hirschfeld on transport of foodstuffs across the IJsselline, 29 January 1945.
[92] BA, R70NL-41, Circular letter Rauter, 8 February 1945.
[93] BA, R70NL-41, 1 March 1945; NIOD, 216h, Decision Hirschfeld, 29 January 1945.

and food gathering for black-market trade. In light of maintaining social order, German repressive measures against black-market trade and looting sharpened during the crisis: punishment by execution was not uncommon.[94] Food expeditions, on the other hand, were tolerated by the Dutch and German authorities, despite the obvious adverse effects on central rationing. In March 1945, Seyss-Inquart even suggested to move all potatoes to a small town close to the IJssel line for the public to gather themselves – an idea that was deemed 'uneconomical' by Hirschfeld and never made public.[95] While popular and scholarly narratives maintain that hunger travellers often returned empty-handed from their journeys, the instructions of the Germans and CCD clearly state that only professional black marketeers would be apprehended. In February 1945, the Director of the CCD sent out the following guidelines:

The work by the CCD is portrayed as if surveillance on black marketeers does not exist, while the officials are trying their very best to apprehend those poor people, who with great effort obtained some foodstuffs, and then seize everything that they have obtained. Preferably, it is added that the controller then keeps the confiscated goods for himself .... The above-mentioned dictates that in these times, in which the needs are extremely high, inspection of individual persons, private individuals, who are forced by the dire situation to travel to the countryside in an attempt to purchase food, will not take place.[96]

Similarly, *Wehrmacht* soldiers were told that Dutch authorities had explicitly ordered civilians to retrieve foodstuffs from the countryside and that unauthorised requisition would be punished.[97] The change in attitude over the course of the crisis is further exemplified by the requisitioning of bicycles – a sensitive subject in Dutch popular memory. While on 16 October 1944 a direct order was given to *Wehrmacht* soldiers to confiscate all usable men's bicycles, an order from 15 January 1945 dictated that individual requisitioning of bicycles was now strictly forbidden.[98] That same month, the German *Merkblatt für die Truppe* explained that individual requisitioning sabotaged the systematic use of land while also harming the *Wehrmacht*'s reputation and was, therefore,

[94] BA, R70NL-41, inv.no. 73, Note *Befehlshaber Sipo und SD* in The Hague, 22 November 1944.

[95] NIOD, 216h, inv.no. 312, Report CRV, 28 March 1945; NIOD, 212a, inv.no. 167, Diary Hirschfeld, 3 March 1945.

[96] NIOD, 216h, inv.no.100, Circular letter Director CCD G. Diepenheim, 22 February 1945. See also: Tresoar, 350, inv.no. 231.

[97] NIOD, 001, inv.no. 656, *Kriegestagebuch Vizeadmiral* Stange, November 1944; BA, R70NL-60, Message *Einsatzkommando* Rotterdam to *Wehrmachtkommandantur*, 21 February 1945.

[98] BA, R70NL-54, Letter Rauter on bicycle confiscations, 16 October 1944; NIOD, 001, *Besondere Anordnungen*, 15 January 1945.

punishable by imprisonment or even death.[99] This is not to say that individual soldiers or other German officials never requisitioned food-stuffs from civilians for personal use. Yet these harsh, punishing measures and regulations allowing individual food expeditions shed a new light on individual coping strategies and, as they clearly distinguished food expeditions from black-market trade, thus reveal these expeditions as a grey area of trade and consumption.

Restoration

After the liberation in May 1945, there was time to take stock of the situation and it became clear how severely the war had disrupted the Dutch food system. In the final struggle, the occupier had taken away factory installations, heavy machines, and most of the available transport means. What they did not confiscate, they often destroyed: railroads, ports, bridges, and power stations all needed reparation work, which added further difficulties to the resumption of food transports. In addition, the cattle stock had diminished by 25 per cent, pigs by over 50 per cent, and poultry by an incredible 80 per cent. This meant that livestock farming would take a considerable time to recover. This damage was accompanied by wide-scale inundations, covering about 8.5 per cent of Dutch cultivated soil (538,670 acres). Yet the most serious problem facing the liberated Netherlands was probably still the coal shortage. Therefore, even though imports of foodstuffs, raw materials, and machines resumed shortly after liberation, the combination of these factors meant longer recovery times.[100] Turning back to the official rations shown in Figure 4.1, by the end of May 1945, Allied relief supplies managed to raise official rations to an ample 2,000 kcal. However, these rations declined again over the summer once the initial Allied relief supplies had been allocated. This period of recovery and restoration was marked by the continuation of the food supply organisation that had gone on before the liberation, demonstrating that the food crisis was indeed not solved with German unconditional surrender.

As is usual during periods of political transition following crisis, societal relations and political regimes became fluid after the war with

---

[99] BA, R70NL-54, inv.no. 522, *Merkblatt für die Truppe*, 10 January 1945. It is unclear whether the *Wehrmacht* actually enforced these policies.

[100] United Nations Archives and Records Centre [UN], AG 18-004 Bureau of Areas, S-1245-0000-0364, Reconstruction plans, 23 May 1945; S-1209-0000-0394, Survey of first year of Liberation, 29 August 1946.

continuities in the food supply prevailing over abrupt change.[101] Driving this continuity were the Dutch food authorities, who already during the occupation had drawn up plans for the post-war food supply, envisioning a swift but complex recovery and reconstruction period.[102] Under supervision of the Allied interim military administration and the Netherlands Military Authority (NMA), the RBVVO was able to resume its work with rapidity. New emergency entities such as the IKB had proven their effectiveness and continued to function during the immediate post-war period, providing coupon-free meals for people suffering from hunger oedema and cachexia. As the food situation improved over the summer and most malnutrition cases had been cured, the IKB discharged its emergency relief on 1 August 1945.[103]

The summer presented a transition period from decentralised elements to centralisation of the food supply in other aspects as well. Because of the major transportation problems, it took the RBVVO three weeks to regulate a normal food supply again, which necessitated the continuation of the CRV until the end of June 1945.[104] Moreover, the decentralised CK system was in desperate need of uniformity and equality but, instead of downsizing, the CK initially grew larger because of the many repatriates depending on soup kitchens. After gas and electricity became available again in June 1945 and the provision of coupon-free meals stopped, participation quickly declined and the CK organisation was reduced to one main office in The Hague and 25 district leaders across the country: these replaced all the regional leaders and inspection services. Most CK, however, terminated in June.[105]

---

[101] Romijn, 'Liberators and Patriots: Military Interim Rule and the Politics of Transition in the Netherlands, 1944–1945', in *Seeking Peace in the Wake of War: Europe, 1943–1947*, NIOD Studies on War, Holocaust and Genocide, eds. Stefan-Ludwig Hoffmann et al. (Amsterdam: Amsterdam University Press, 2015), 117–144.

[102] See, for instance: NIOD, 212a, inv.no. 31, Letter Hirschfeld to Directors of trade organisations, 31 March 1945; Note F. Houtgraaf to Hirschfeld on transportation after war, 13 April 1945.

[103] NA, 2.11.30.05, inv.no. 10, Report dr G. C. E. Burger, Leader Medical Feeding teams to IKB, 2 June 1945; Letter Central IKB to local IKB offices, 16 July 1945.

[104] NIOD, 216h, inv.no. 326, Letter Major J. J. Eshuis, Section VI, Subsection Food and Agriculture Staff Breda to Netherlands Military Administration, 10 May 1945; inv. no. 324, Letter Ministry of Agriculture, Fisheries and Food Supply to Director Ivens, 29 August 1945; Hirschfeld, 'De Centrale Reederij', 14; Louwes, 'De Voedselvoorziening', 646.

[105] For example, in Amsterdam in the first weeks of June, the CK grew to 604,000 participants, almost 80 per cent of the population. *Jaarverslag van Amsterdam 1945*, 32; NA, 2.11.30.06, inv.no. 241, Letter J. P. van Loon to Louwes, June 1945; inv. no. 57, Report from Acting Director of CK Tilburg over 1945, May 1946; inv.no. 241, Letter J. P. van Loon to Louwes, June 1945; inv.no. 106, Circular letter Van Loon, 8 December 1945.

This transition period demonstrates how the problems with food supply were far from over after liberation. A radio message from Louwes on 5 October 1945 further illustrates that, even during the autumn of 1945, the Netherlands was still recovering:

Nutrition cannot be brought to pre-war levels, nor can we abolish rationing measures and open free market again .... Nobody wants to prolong rationing longer than needed, but from my outline it has become evident that the food position is not ready for regular, free channels. As long as scarcity prevails, it will be the task of the government to ensure that there are no shortages and that there is a rightful allocation of supplies.[106]

Due to the above-mentioned destruction of economy and agriculture, the harvest of 1945 was smaller than usual but in 1946, both agricultural production and rations more or less stabilised. In December 1945, official rations for manual workers were still set at a modest 2,230 kcal per day compared to the 3,290 kcal they consumed on average back in 1930. In fact, it took the Dutch food administration until the spring of 1946 to return rations to pre-war levels again.[107] Dutch livestock was reduced to such an extent that animal products remained scarce until the late 1940s. Because of this prolonged scarcity of meat and other products, clandestine production and trade continued to be an issue for national authorities. Illegal production had risen up to 40 per cent in 1945 and continued to flourish after liberation. It was only after the Marshall Plan took effect in the Netherlands in 1948–1952 that the Dutch economy equalled pre-war levels and food scarcity was effectively abolished in all parts of the country.[108]

In addition to the continuity of crisis-time organisations, the post-war assessment of the Dutch and German officials involved in the food supply also tells us something about government responses to the famine or, at least, how they have been judged. The post-war assessment of Dutch food officials largely revolved around the question of whether they had made the right decision to remain in their position during the war, and whether they had collaborated with the German occupier in that function. Being the only secretary general that stayed at his post throughout the occupation, Hirschfeld continues to be a controversial subject

---

[106] NA, 2.21.238, inv.no. 64, Radio speech Louwes 'Perspectives on the Food Supply', 5 October 1945.

[107] Banning, 'Voeding en Voedingstoestand', 32; Klemann, *Nederland 1938–1948*, 202–211; Futselaar, *Lard, Lice and Longevity*, 79.

[108] Blom, 'De Tweede Wereldoorlog en de Nederlandse Samenleving: Continuïteit en Verandering', in *Crisis, Bezetting en Herstel: Tien Studies over Nederland, 1940–1950*, ed. Blom (The Hague: Nijgh & Van Ditmar, 1989), 170; Klemann, *Nederland 1938–1948*, 202–207, 211–213, 546–547; Klemann and Kudryashov, *Occupied Economies*, 325–335.

among Dutch historians, in which debates judgements of his moral and the ethics of his policies play an important role.[109] Hirschfeld had been the recipient of much animosity from the government-in-exile and resistance groups and, as expected, faced severe criticism after the war.[110] Indeed, he was never modest about his own role: 'The overall command rested with me, and the battle, which mostly had to be fought with the occupier, was my fight.'[111] A committee of inquiry that investigated the behaviours of civil servants during the war assessed Hirschfeld's activities in two categories: government policies and policies aimed at helping the resistance. For the first category, he was pardoned with the conclusion that his great skills and conscious policies had provided a great service to the Dutch people; however, for the second charge he was found guilty. Despite this verdict, in September 1946, Hirschfeld's forced resignation was annulled on appeal to the highest administrative court. He continued to be involved in domestic economic affairs until the late 1940s, working on the preparation and coordination of the Marshall Plan in the Netherlands. After Hirschfeld resigned from office in 1952, he remained a member of numerous commissions in the business sector, reflecting the high esteem the sector had for him after the war.[112]

The post-war evaluation of Louwes' occupation policies was much more favourable. The committee of inquiry concluded that he had continuously pursued food policies that were in the Netherlands' best interest and, by doing so, had managed to steer the country away from catastrophe. Although they disapproved of some of his measures, which mainly related to re-issuing ration cards connected to personal identity, the committee absolved him from any blame.[113] After the war, Louwes continued his career in food politics in the international arena. He became the special advisor to the Food and Agriculture Organisation (FAO) and, in 1947, he was designated as the first director of the FAO's European department. Louwes died on 25 January 1953, decorated as

---

[109] For an excellent exposé on this entire debate, see: Madelon de Keizer, 'Hans Max Hirschfeld: De Juiste Man op de Juiste Plaats ...?', *BMGN-Low Countries Historical Review* 123 (2008): 423–432.

[110] NIOD, 212a, inv.no 37, Report 'Stakingsbevel', 1 October 1945; Report 'Mijn Beleid als Secretaris-generaal en mijn standpunt ten aanzien van de "illegaliteit"', 22 October 1945.

[111] NIOD, 212a, inv.no 37, Report 'Mijn Beleid'.

[112] NIOD, 212a, inv.no 37, Letter Hirschfeld to Minister of Trade and Industry, 4 March 1946; Romijn, *Snel, Streng en Rechtvaardig: De Afrekening met 'Foute' Nederlanders 1945–1955*, 2nd ed. (Amsterdam: Olympus, 2002), 136–140; Joggli Meihuizen, *Noodzakelijk Kwaad: De Bestraffing van Economische Collaboratie in Nederland Na de Tweede Wereldoorlog* (Amsterdam: Boom, 2003), 284–291; Fennema and Rhijnsburger, *Dr Hans Max Hirschfeld*, 137–270.

[113] NA, 2.21.238, inv.no. 117, Report Committee Fentener van Vlissingen, 1946.

Grand Cross Knight in the Order of the Dutch Lion, and with the media celebrating him as the 'great agricultural engineer' who had 'saved the Dutch from starvation'.[114]

These accolades were reserved for the winners of the war and, as could be expected, the German authorities faced very different fates. The most important contact persons for the Dutch food administration, Schwebel and Von der Wense, were interned in Allied POW camps for several years after the war and, together with Hirschfeld, had to testify in Nuremberg against their former *Reichskommissar*. The fact that Von der Wense and Louwes remained in contact during the first post-war years reinforces the already strong notion that their cooperation had indeed been pleasant, considering the boundaries of war and occupation.[115] For Seyss-Inquart, the famine played an important role in his Nuremberg trial: 'Because on the occasion of the shipping and railroad strike, he [Seyss-Inquart] prohibited the import of food .... That is one of the most serious charges made against him.'[116] The official complaint stated in great detail that, as *Reichskommissar*, Seyss-Inquart was responsible for famine in the Netherlands and for the subsequent great mortality – which was initially estimated at 50,000 deaths, and later changed to 25,000 – many of these deaths, they (incorrectly) alleged, were presumably children. When asked about what he had done to alleviate conditions, Seyss-Inquart answered:

I gave Secretary Hirschfeld all authority, including transportation, and this man, although hesitantly and reluctantly, re-established traffic – and he will confirm that I supported him in every possible way. Food supplies were brought into Holland. But many weeks had passed in vain. Then, in my sector of influence, I provided additional allotments, about which witness Von der Wense and, I believe, the witness Schwebel can give you information in their interrogations.[117]

Seyss-Inquart also asserted that 'the food question in the Netherlands was doubtless the most difficult question of the whole administration, and I believe, from the special aspects of this case, it was the most difficult in all the occupied territories'.[118] In the end, the Nuremberg judges dropped the charges against Seyss-Inquart for his alleged responsibility for the famine in the western Netherlands. Seyss-Inquart's appeal

---

[114] NA, 2.21.238, inv.no. 181, Newspaper clippings on Louwes's death, January 1953.
[115] NA, 2.21.238, inv.no. 110, Correspondence between Louwes and Von der Wense family, 1946–1947.
[116] NIOD, 458, inv.no. 24, Nuremberg Trial Seyss-Inquart, 11 June 1946, 11430.
[117] NIOD, 458, inv.no. 24, Nuremberg Trial Seyss-Inquart, 11 June 1946, 11432.
[118] NIOD, 458, inv.no. 24, Nuremberg Trial Seyss-Inquart, 11 June 1946, 11428.

to the Dutch Queen Wilhelmina for a Royal Pardon based on his 'efforts to protect the Dutch from disaster in the period December 1944 to April 1945' was, however, not answered. For all other atrocities that he committed during the occupation of the Netherlands, among them his responsibility for the death of three quarters of the 140,000 Jewish civilians, Seyss-Inquart was hanged.[119]

Conclusion

Throughout the food crisis, food authorities were continually occupied with the balancing act of keeping the rationing system centralised as it was or allowing decentralised elements to filter in. Within the context of these Dutch-German food politics, two important choices need to be emphasised. Firstly, the allocation of food via official rations and soup kitchens establishes that priority was given to keeping socio-economic vital services running and to protect certain vulnerable groups from starvation; most notably, infants, young children, and the sick. Offering no extra rations to children above four years old, the RBVVO reckoned that older children could be sufficiently supplemented by the new relief entities. The fact that official rations dropped below 750 kcal after November 1944 – reaching 400 kcal at the height of the famine – is a clear sign that the population depended on entitlements other than official rations to survive the famine. The second choice was very much interlinked with the first; namely, that the authorities preferred maximising consumption over maintaining the integrity of the rationing system. This is exemplified by their decision to allow and stimulate self-organisation and local relief efforts. Furthermore, this decision enabled them to differentiate between self-help and profiteering: a resolution reflected in the instructions to allow food expeditions despite the knowledge that they could adversely affect the central rationing system. How all these individual and communal coping strategies emerged and played out is the focus of the following chapters. But first, Chapter 5 turns to another vital aspect of state intervention during the Hunger Winter, revealing how food at this tense point of the war became yet another weapon in the arsenal of battle – the negotiations on food relief at the international level.

---

[119] Seyss-Inquart was hanged on 16 October 1946, together with nine other Nuremberg defendants. Henk J. Neuman, *Arthur Seyss-Inquart: Het Leven van een Duits Onderkoning in Nederland* (Utrecht: Ambo, 1967), 352–353; Koll, *Arthur Seyss-Inquart*, 611–613.

5   The Politics and Practices of Allied Relief

The food drops in late April and early May 1945 are probably the ultimate symbol of the Allied liberation of the Netherlands. For 10 consecutive days, Allied heavy bombers dropped supplies at an extremely low altitude onto designated zones in the densely populated western provinces, undisturbed by the German occupying forces. The British called it 'Operation Manna': the Americans – a somewhat unseemly choice – 'Operation Chowhound'. People in the streets and up on rooftops welcomed their liberators with flags and other national symbols, not knowing that the actual German unconditional surrender would take another week. To this day, eye witnesses remember these joyous moments vividly. In the memories of some, the dropped food parcels have transformed into Swedish white bread, literally falling as manna from heaven.[1]

However important the food drops may have been symbolically, the actual contribution of the parcels to relieving the famine was rather limited. Not only were the quantities of food relatively small but, quite significantly, this emergency aid arrived only a few days before liberation. Why did it take the Allies this long to relieve the starving Dutch? This question seems especially pertinent when considering the willingness of the German civil authorities to cooperate with relief plans from December 1944 onwards, as Chapter 4 has demonstrated. Apparently, factors other than German animosity must have played a role in the prolonged absence of immediate food relief.

This chapter investigates the question of relief from the perspectives of the people and institutions responsible for organising emergency food aid at the international level. What steps could be and were taken by the Allies to alleviate hunger in the occupied Netherlands?[2] We will see that

---

[1] Nico Scheepmaker, *Het Zweedse Wittebrood* (Baarn: Erven Thomas Rap, 1979), 5–7; Klemann, 'De Hongerwinter', 264.

[2] To some extent, the sources and approach utilised in this chapter reflect Bob Moore's pioneering study 'The Western Allies and Food Relief to the Occupied Netherlands,

relief planning and military strategies proved inevitably to be in conflict with each other, just as they had been elsewhere in food-deprived occupied Europe. Throughout the war, the British government's approach to relief was characterised by its determination to stick to their blockade policy ('economic warfare') and to avoid any international competition over food. This meant that food aid was never to be given priority over the supreme goal of an Allied military victory.[3] In the end, this made relief intervention in the occupied Netherlands heavily politicised: even the small amounts of supposedly 'neutral' food relief reaching the western provinces in early 1945 can be regarded as part of this political power struggle. The aim of this chapter is to investigate when and how Allied relief contributed to fighting the famine conditions and, in a broader sense, to provide an interpretation of Allied emergency aid within the complex process of reordering Dutch society and reshaping the future of post-war Europe.

Relief or the Liberation of Corpses

On 26 October 1943, the Allied governments adopted a proposal from US President Franklin D. Roosevelt, placing overall responsibility for relief of Europe's liberated populations in the hands of the interim military authorities. This decision was incorporated in the Civil Affair Agreement between the US, British, and Dutch governments in May 1944, which assigned responsibility for the welfare of the Dutch people to SHAEF, led by Supreme Commander General Dwight D. Eisenhower.[4] In the period of Allied military rule following liberation, SHAEF would prevent 'disease and unrest' under the instruction to provide 'minimum relief' only. A 'SHAEF Mission to the Netherlands' would be accredited for all civil affairs activities – including relief – in areas not affected by military operations while the Netherlands Military Authority (NMA) would become the implementing body. Together, these military

1944–45' (1992). This chapter advances his approach by not only examining the relief negotiations, but also the results of international emergency food aid both during and directly after the liberation. Moore, 'The Western Allies'. See also: De Zwarte, 'De Voedseldroppings van 1945: Waarom duurde het zo Lang?' *Geschiedenis Magazine* 3 (2017): 26–29.

[3] Joan Beaumont, 'Starving for Democracy: Britain's Blockade of and Relief for Occupied Europe, 1939–1945', *War & Society* 8 (1990): 57–82; Ben Shephard, 'Becoming Planning Minded: The Theory and Practice of Relief 1940–1945', *Journal of Contemporary History* 43 (2008): 405–419; Hionidou, *Famine and Death in Occupied Greece*, 16; Zweig, 'Feeding the Camps', 825–851.

[4] 'Directive to Supreme Commander Allied Expeditionary Force', 12 February 1944, published in: Eisenhower, *Eisenhower's Own Story of the War*, iv.

authorities would assist the Dutch government in the recovery process until the political situation was judged to be sufficiently stabilised for democratic elections to be held. As already outlined out in 1943, the United Nations Relief and Rehabilitation Administration (UNRRA) would aid them by taking over relief responsibilities.[5] Internal messages and reports indicated that SHAEF expected a swift liberation of the Netherlands – the assumed 'zero date' was 1 October 1944.[6]

The failure of Operation Market Garden left SHAEF with the unexpected and complex task of providing relief to a country that was only half liberated. No longer willing to await Allied approval, some of the Dutch ministers grew anxious about establishing advanced elements of their government administrations on Dutch territory, fearing that every day the government remained in London would lead to loss of prestige and legitimacy.[7] But SHAEF and the NMA deemed the arrival of the Dutch ministers inopportune, believing the government was not fully aware of the existing military conditions and difficulties under which it would have to carry out its duties.[8] Furthermore, the NMA's headquarters in liberated Brussels had just been established, and its chief, Major General Hendrik J. Kruls, was in no need of help and considered to be fully competent to deal with such difficulties himself. As chief of the SHAEF Mission to the Netherlands, Major General J. K. Edwards bluntly stated: 'I am convinced that the presence of ministers will prove to be an embarrassment rather than be of assistance to him at this time.'[9]

---

[5] The NMA would, in the first stages, be placed at the disposal of the supreme commander and later assume temporary governmental responsibility until the Dutch government itself was able to do so. 'Memorandum of Agreement Regarding Civil Administration and Jurisdiction in Netherlands Territory Liberated by an Allied Expeditionary Force', published in: Gerbrandy, *Eenige Hoofdpunten van het Regeeringsbeleid in Londen Gedurende de Oorlogsjaren 1940–1945* (The Hague: Rijksuitgeverij, 1946), 130–133; NARA, 331, Entry 2, Box 117, Letter on Civil Affairs Directives from Eisenhower to commander in chief 21st Army Group, 14 August 1944; Frank S. V. Donnison, *Civil Affairs and Military Government North-West Europe 1944–1946* (London: Her Majesty's Stationery Office, 1961), 129; Dick C. L. Schoonoord, *Het 'Circus Kruls': Militair Gezag in Nederland, 1944–1946* (Amsterdam: NIOD, 2011), 10–14; Patricia Clavin, *Securing the World Economy: The Reinvention of the League of Nations, 1920–1946* (Oxford: Oxford University Press, 2013), 297–304; Romijn, 'Liberators and Patriots', 120–122; Shephard, 'Becoming Planning Minded', 410–412.

[6] NARA, 331, Entry 40, Box 276, Report Requirements the Netherlands, Six Months, 31 August 1944.

[7] NARA, 331, Entry 152, Box 264, Fortnightly report SHAEF Mission Netherlands, 13 October 1944.

[8] Romijn, 'Liberators and Patriots', 130–131; Fasseur, *Eigen Meester, Niemands Knecht*, 416.

[9] NARA, 331, Entry 152, Box 264, Fortnightly report SHAEF Mission Netherlands, 1 October 1944.

Tensions between the Dutch government and the NMA increased further over the food situation in the liberated south. While official daily adult rations during the occupation comprised approximately 1,600 kcal, under military responsibility, these dropped below 1,000 kcal. A police report from Eindhoven concluded mid-November 1944 that 'the food problem has now, and this applies to all circles of our city, become so urgent, that it not only overshadows all other problems, but entirely controls everything.'[10] The NMA struggled with poor transportation and communication possibilities; meanwhile, its employees did not show themselves to be quick improvisers.[11] In pressing letters to General Eisenhower, Prince Bernhard – husband of Crown Princess Juliana and commander-in-chief of the Dutch Forces of the Interior – stressed the popular dissatisfaction with the treatment of evacuated Germans, who were being fed full army rations, whilst the Dutch received about half the quantity of food they had consumed during the occupation.[12]

Unfortunately, feeding the liberated people was not the only problem. As it became evident that the German forces would not surrender soon, plans had to be revised for relieving the occupied areas as well. Without a doubt, the main civil affairs task facing SHAEF would lay in the densely populated provinces of North and South Holland and the western part of Utrecht – the so-called B2 area. On the very day Montgomery lost the battle of Arnhem, Queen Wilhelmina summoned Gerbrandy to approach the British Prime Minister Winston Churchill to discuss relief for those who remained under German control.[13] After numerous requests, on 5 October 1944, the prime ministers finally met in London. Given the current estimations of the food supply, Gerbrandy warned that the western population could survive only until 1 December of that year: a paltry two months. But Churchill was undeterred: while sympathetic to the Dutch suffering, he responded that any food admitted would directly or indirectly nourish the Germans, who were also out of food. He also believed that there was a good chance that the Netherlands would be liberated before 1 December.[14] Although Gerbrandy was bitterly disappointed by Churchill's response, it probably did not come to him as a

[10] NARA, 331, inv.no. 414, Police report on mood among citizens of Eindhoven, 15 November 1945.
[11] NARA, 331, Entry 153, Microfilm box 1, Message Edwards to De Guingaud, 7 December 1944. Donnison, *Civil Affairs and Military Government*, 138–140.
[12] NARA, 331, Entry 2, Box 117, Message SHAEF Main signed Eisenhower to 21 Army Group, 12th Army Group, 7 November 1944.
[13] De Jong, *Het Koninkrijk* 10b, 1083; Moore, 'The Western Allies', 96.
[14] TNA, PREM 3/221/11, Minutes interview Churchill and Gerbrandy, 5 October 1944; NARA, 331, Entry 2, Box 117, Letter Morton to Bedell Smith, 12 October 1944.

surprise. The British War Cabinet had been exploiting every weapon at its disposal to bring the war to a speedy end, and any decision infringing on their policy of economic warfare was to be overruled immediately.

Not easily discouraged, the Dutch government decided to take the case to the people. Gerbrandy held a press conference in front of the Ministry of Information, while Queen Wilhelmina reached out via the Home Service of the BBC. Their pleas led to international public support for the Dutch situation and even to the organisation of a day of prayer.[15] In support of their desperate plight, Gerbrandy and Queen Wilhelmina wrote several pressing letters to world leaders. Queen Wilhelmina herself alerted President Roosevelt: 'The suffering [in western Holland] is no less than frightful and it is no exaggeration to say that famine is imminent.'[16] In the meantime, the Dutch cabinet had already approached the neutral Swedish and Swiss governments to inquire about relief opportunities from their countries and, as early as 2 October, Sweden declared to be perfectly agreeable to this idea.[17]

The Dutch government was unaware that the Allies had already been discussing plans about neutral relief as well. Provided that the Dutch government made full arrangements with the Swedes, the British War Cabinet saw no objections from the blockade point of view. Since 1941 they had allowed foreign exchange within the blockade area that enabled occupied territories to purchase food from neutral countries.[18] Eisenhower also approved of the plan, being apprehensive that serious food shortages would steadily increase until the moment of liberation, a date that was impossible for him to predict. Sometime in late October, the supreme commander stated: 'I recognize [that] part of relief supplies will fall into German hands, but I accept this risk. Any assistance to the Dutch civil population that can be provided before liberation will ease the relief problem subsequent to liberation.'[19] President Roosevelt responded likewise to the Queen's letter by stating that the United States

---

[15] De Jong, *Het Koninkrijk* 10b, 184; Van der Zee, *The Hunger Winter*, 97; Moore, 'The Western Allies', 97.

[16] NARA, 331, Entry 2, Box 117, Message from Joint Chiefs of Staff to Eisenhower, 26 October 1944.

[17] NARA, 331, Entry 2, Box 117, Letter Foreign Office to Chiefs of Staff, 5 October 1944; NIOD, 233b, inv.no 28, Telegram Van Kleffens to Bern, 11 October 1944; Letter C. H. C. Flugi van Aspermont Genève to Dutch government, 19 October 1944. See also: Gerbrandy, *Eenige Hoofdpunten*, 128–129.

[18] TNA, WO 220/668, AMSSO to SHAEF Forward, 6 October 1944; FO 238/303, Telegram FO to Stockholm, 19 October 1944; Beamont, 'Starving for Democracy', 65–66.

[19] NARA, 331, Entry 2, Box 117, Letter SHEAF Main signed Eisenhower to British Chiefs of Staff, 29 October 1944. Also cited in: Moore, 'The Western Allies', 98.

'is most anxious that such assistance be provided as quickly as practicable consistent with achieving the complete defeat of Germany', thereby agreeing to any plan for food relief from Sweden as long as it did not interfere with military interests.[20]

These considerations left the British Chiefs of Staff with four possible relief schemes that were discussed in London on 6 November 1944: (1) a Swedish ship would bring relief supplies from Gothenburg to a Dutch port, most likely Amsterdam; (2) an ICRC ship would bring cargo from Lisbon; (3) supplies would be dropped by air onto three principle towns in the western Netherlands; (4) a Red Cross barge would take supplies from Basel down via the Rhine.[21] In the following negotiations between the Allies and Germans, military considerations became of prime importance to all parties. Germany quite clearly favoured the last plan: according to SHAEF, this was only because they wanted the Rhine navigable for their own benefit. The Allied Headquarters dismissed the idea of airdrops, since there was no guarantee that the supplies would actually reach the civil population. The Allies did, however, regard an initial symbolic airdrop of supplies after liberation to be 'essential' in terms of psychological warfare, indicating that, for them, the symbolic value of airdrops was always motive rather than outcome.[22] The first two plans seemed agreeable, but the British War Cabinet considered Red Cross shipments from Lisbon less desirable in view of the many requests from other Nazi-occupied countries.[23] Thus, the only proposition left at this point to consider seriously was relief from neutral Sweden. Eisenhower assured Gerbrandy that SHAEF saw no objection from a military point of view: 'It appears most desirable that these relief ships move as soon as possible.'[24]

Despite the promising outlook, no progress was made in the following weeks. As Van der Zee has put it, 'nothing but reassuring promises and soothing noises had come from the Allies, and little help had been

---

[20] NARA, 331, Entry 2, Box 117, Message Joint Chiefs of Staff to Eisenhower, 26 October 1944.

[21] NARA, 331, Entry 2, Box 117, Message SHAEF Main signed Eisenhower to British Chiefs of Staff, 6 November 1944.

[22] NARA, 331, Entry 2, Box 117, Message SHAEF Main G-5 signed Eisenhower to War Office, 15 November 1944.

[23] TNA, FO 238/303, Message FO signed W. G. Hayter to Ambassador Sir Neville Bland, 9 November 1944; CAB 119/140, COS meeting 27 October–7 November 1944; Letter Foreign Office to Secretary Chiefs of Staff Committee, 30 October 1944; WO 220/668, Admiralty to FO, 26 October 1944; PREM 3/221/11, AMSSO to SHAEF Main, 3 November 1944.

[24] NARA, 331, Entry 2, Box 117, Letter SHAEF Main signed Eisenhower to Combined Chiefs of Staff and British Chiefs of Staff, 15 November 1944. See also: TNA, WO 219/1325.

given'.[25] Shortly after SHAEF refused to open the Rhine for transportation, the Germans denied observers from the ICRC to distribute the Swedish supplies on grounds that the Netherlands was now a combat zone and any relief permitted needed to be distributed by the German and Dutch Red Cross. Although this would mean an enormous concession from the Allied side, Secretary of State for Foreign Office Anthony Eden initially endorsed this change of plans. However, soon after, a secret report from the Netherlands was received that stated that all lorries and petrol belonging to the Dutch Red Cross had been confiscated and its officers were resigning as a protest against the forcible appointment of a Dutch 'Germanic SS official', Carel Piek, as its new chief.[26] While food relief ships in Sweden and Lisbon lay ready with German approval, the Allies immediately put the plans for Swedish relief on hold until further notice: relief would not be allowed until satisfactory arrangements for distribution could be made.[27]

By December 1944, the fear had become a reality and the food shortage had turned into famine. In spite of continuous pleas from the Dutch government – which had now moved part of its administration to the liberated part of the Netherlands – negotiations seemed stranded. On 16 December, Gerbrandy wrote to Eisenhower: 'Relief for the occupied Netherlands at the time of the liberation must have priority above everything, even above the slogan: first of all, defeat of Germany. The Netherlands government cannot accept the liberation of corpses.'[28] The supreme commander himself also grew anxious to get supplies into the Netherlands, being fully aware that western Holland presented a much more serious problem than France or Belgium. Eisenhower argued that 'a ton sent before starvation is worth five sent too late'.[29] But Churchill was still not convinced about the severity of the situation and delayed approval of new relief plans. Indeed, the prime minister needed a great deal of persuasion to believe even that the famine was a real problem: 'Before the liberation of Western Europe, we used to be told that most of the inhabitants would be starving. When we got to France and found the

---

[25] Van der Zee, *The Hunger Winter*, 170.

[26] TNA, FO 238/303, Letter R. A. Gallop to Sir Nevil Bland, 7 December 1944; Aart W. Wassenaar, *Van Winterhulp via Oost-Compagnie en Marseille naar Rode Kruis: De Loopbaan van Carel Piek Voor, Tijdens, en Na de Bezettingstijd 1940–1945. Een Geschiedenis van Idealisme en Collaboratie* (Soesterberg: Aspekt, 2016), 139–145.

[27] BA, NS19/3403, Telegram Rauter to Berlin, 14 December 1944.

[28] Cited in: De Jong, *Het Koninkrijk* 10b, 1115.

[29] TNA, PREM 3/221/11, Message Eden to Churchill, 17 December 1944. See also: TNA, CAB 66/57, Report War Cabinet on the position with regard to food, agriculture and nutrition in France, Belgium, and Holland, 4 November 1944; Van der Zee, *The Hunger Winter*, 170–172.

inhabitants alive, we were told that it was the Belgians who were short of food, and now that we are in Belgium, the Dutch are proclaimed as the principal sufferers. Where will it stop?'[30]

A crucial clue to Churchill's seemingly indifferent behaviour in this discussion is that he was convinced that relief shipments would compromise economic warfare. According to the principles of economic warfare, no foodstuffs were allowed to pass the blockade to enemy-occupied territories (either directly or indirectly), except for the benefit of POWs.[31] The blockade had been a key military strategy of the Allies ever since the First World War, most infamously the blockade of Germany, which lasted well beyond surrender, until 1919.[32] During the Second World War, the War Cabinet made only two major concessions: early 1941 in Vichy France and in Greece in 1942.[33] 'The best way to end the famine is speedy victory and, however hard the decision, food ships must come second to victory ships', Churchill had infamously argued during the Bengal famine in 1943.[34] Evidently, the Dutch were not the only (indirect) victims of the blockade policy. During the last months of war, the possibilities for sending relief supplies to German concentration camps had dramatically expanded as well but, again, the rigid Allied blockade policy made it impossible to fully exploit these opportunities.[35]

Other considerations also played a role. During the war, the question of food aid became intertwined with the British import programme, as diverting shipping and food supplies meant less capacity for domestic imports. Food imports in Britain had halved from an average of 22 million tons before the war to between 10.6 and 11.5 million tons in the years 1942–1944. Although, generally speaking, the British diet was much better compared to that in most of occupied Europe as well as in Germany and Austria, the British sacrifice in food consumption during

---

[30]   TNA, PREM 4/29/12, Cherwell to Churchill, without date.

[31]   TNA, FO 837/1223, Camps to Markbreiter, 20 January 1942. According to Minister of Economic Warfare Hugh Dalton, POW's were 'a single exception, which is of course enjoyed by Allied as well as British prisoners, [and] is made possible by the special conditions under which POWs are detained and by the sanction afforded by the presence of prisoners on both sides'. TNA, FO 837/1232, Letter Dalton to Maitland, 8 October 1941.

[32]   Mary E. Cox, 'Hunger Games: Or How the Allied Blockade in the First World War Deprived German Children of Nutrition, and Allied Food Aid Subsequently Saved Them', *The Economic History Review* 68 (2014): 600–631; C. P. Vincent, *The Politics of Hunger: The Allied Blockade of Germany, 1915–1919* (Ohio: Ohio University Press, 1985).

[33]   Beaumont, 'Starving for Democracy'; Hionidou, *Famine and Death in Occupied Greece*, 15–19, 231–236.

[34]   'Food for India', *Economist*, 30 January 1943. Cited in: Ó Gráda, *Famine*, 185.

[35]   Zweig, 'Feeding the Camps'.

the war was well in excess of her allies: the United States and Canada. Especially middle-class food consumption standards deteriorated considerably. The poorer section of the working class, on the other hand, were the main beneficiaries of the rationing control, similar to the situation in the Netherlands before the food crisis. The British government had to account for the declining food supplies, and allocating shipping for food aid thus came with significant risks, including popular discontent and loss of British support for the war effort.[36]

There was also the domestic aspect of the Channel Islands, which had been occupied by the Germans since June 1940. Living standards had already deteriorated considerably on the islands but, following the blockade by the British Royal Navy after the invasion of Normandy, food shortages in the autumn of 1944 also evolved into a severe food crisis. Similar to the situation in the Netherlands, in September–October 1944, Churchill maintained that the Germans were solely accountable for feeding the population on the islands and that sending food aid would only prolong their resistance. As the Germans refused to discuss surrender, on 7 November the prime minister finally overcame these objections, although it would take until December 1944 before the first Red Cross ships bringing food and medical aid arrived. The Channel Island's last winter also became known as the 'hunger winter', and naturally diverted the UK's attention from the pleas from the Dutch and many other occupied countries in this same period.[37]

Even though immediate relief proved extremely difficult to achieve due to these other wartime considerations, the increasing pressure exerted by the Dutch government did contribute to relief planning for the post-war B2 area. On 8 November 1944, the Committee for Relief Supply in Western Holland, under the auspices of the War Cabinet in London, convened for the first time, with the intention of coordinating all relief bodies after the war. When, in December, they concluded that overseas aid would remain a serious obstacle, SHAEF transferred relief responsibility to Montgomery's 21st Army Group. This decision was not welcomed by the Dutch government, which had lost its faith in the army's ability to take care of the civil population as it had failed to do so in the south.[38] By January 1945, the problem of preparing relief seemed so complex that the Allies decided that a special group was required to concentrate on stockpiles and prepare plans for utilising all forms of

---

[36] Zweiniger-Bargielowska, *Austerity in Britain*, 32–44.
[37] Charles Cruickshank, *The German Occupation of the Channel Islands* (London: Oxford University Press, 1975), 259–286.
[38] De Jong, *Het Koninkrijk* 10b, 1104–1108.

transport. This communication body was named 'Commando Western Holland District' and was placed under command of the senior British Army Officer General Alexander Galloway. However, just as the Dutch had feared, no directive was given to these headquarters until February 1945, and no planning began until that March.[39]

Finally, on 19 January 1945 – over three months after the initial Swedish promise – an agreement was reached between the German and Swedish governments. Two Swedish ships would sail under safe passage from Gothenburg to the important Dutch harbour in Delfzijl with 5,000 tons of relief supplies, after which the distribution was to be arranged by two Swedish representatives residing in the Netherlands. Meanwhile, an ICRC ship loaded with relief supplies at Lisbon was also ready to set sail to Gothenburg. This cargo would be withheld until the Allies received reports of the satisfactory distribution of the Swedish cargoes.[40] For the Allies, this was a highly attractive proposition, made even more so since one of the Swedish representatives had been doing valuable intelligence work for them for the last couple of years. Concluding an agreement was in the best interest of the German occupier as well. Not only did they want to prevent popular unrest and rioting in the short term, but, as we saw in Chapter 4, misguided fear of those conditions becoming a breeding ground for Bolshevism was also expressed among German high-ranked officials.[41]

Neutral Bread

The route for the two Swedish ships – the *Dagmar Bratt* and the *Noreg* – was proposed by the Germans. The ships would sail through Swedish territorial waters to a suitable position off the coast of Malmo and, from there, proceed with German escort through the Kiel Canal to Delfzijl. This route was not considered at all ideal for the Allies as the Kiel Canal was of great military importance to Nazi Germany. Since the alternative route around the north of Denmark would not have inconvenienced Germany either, the proposition quite clearly seemed an attempt to get as much operational advantage from the passage of these ships as possible.[42] The Swedes, in turn, asked the British Chiefs of Staff if a port

---

[39] Donnison, *Civil Affairs and Military Government*, 142; Moore, 'The Western Allies', 102–103.
[40] NARA, 331, Entry 2, Box 118, Letter Chiefs of Staff to SHAEF Main, 19 January 1945 (ref 499).
[41] NIOD, 001, inv.no. 656, *Kriegestagebuch Marinebefehlshaber Vizeadmiral* Stange, January 1945.
[42] TNA, FO 371/42378, Correspondence Netherlands Embassy and Mr Steward, 22 and 28 December 1944.

other than Delfzijl could be made available, since the winter frost would thwart the unloading of the supplies and transporting them to the distribution centres. But the Admiralty assured them that no other port could be given a limited safe-conduct without upsetting Allied military operations.[43] Once again, all decisions for enabling 'neutral' aid were driven by military considerations.

On 28 January, the *Dagmar Bratt* and the *Noreg* finally moored at the port of Delfzijl, bringing the Dutch a cargo containing just over 3,700 tons of high-quality food supplies.[44] The Swedish Red Cross delegates had hoped to begin distribution immediately, but transportation needed to be suspended because of the ice situation and administrative delays. It took until 5 February before the first barges – painted with large Red Cross marks to prevent Allied shootings – were dispatched to Amsterdam. Distribution of the supplies began on 26 February and was handled by the Directorate of Food Supply under supervision of Swedish Red Cross delegate Walter Ekman. In Delfzijl as well as in the west, other 'neutral' Swedish representatives were assigned, approved by both the Allies and Germans.[45] By this time, it had taken five months for relief to reach the public.

The Swedish supplies managed to raise rations for one week only but, nevertheless, it made a profound impact. Adult rations in the western Netherlands increased from 476 kcal in the week of 18 February to 878 kcal in the week following 25 February. For children aged 4–13 years, who were entitled to a larger portion of Swedish white bread and vegetables, rations even temporarily increased to 1,009 kcal. Condensed milk and cod-liver oil were reserved for the younger children and infants, who enjoyed the highest rations of all. Unfortunately, in the week after the Red Cross distribution, official rations fell again to a mere 544 kcal.[46] More supplies were desperately needed.

Getting more emergency food aid into the occupied Netherlands was, however, not so easy. Gerbrandy tried to convince the Allies that a regular relief scheme was necessary, arguing that the Dutch could not possibly wait for relief until after liberation. Some Dutch ministers went

---

[43] TNA, ADM 116/5350, Report Admiralty, 5 February 1945.
[44] This cargo consisted of 2,250 tons of flour, 534 tons of peas, 513 tons of margarine, 280 tons of oatmeal, 75 tons of dried vegetables, 57 tons of condensed milk, and 10 tons of cod-liver oil. 'Hulp van Zweden', *Lichtflits: Dagelijksch Nieuwsblad*, 16 February 1945; NIOD, 212a, inv.no. 116, Press release 29 January 1945; Report Count Morner, 3 March 1945.
[45] TNA, ADM 116/5350, Report Swedish Red Cross, 9 February 1945; BA, R70NL-59, Telegram 24 February 1945; Letter *SS Sturmbahnnführer* Deppner to BdS Zwolle, 11 February 1945.
[46] NA, 2.11.23.02, inv.no. 192, Report on official rations October 1944–July 1945.

Illustration 12 Swedish Red Cross ship *Hallaren*, 1945.

even further by articulating that the situation had become so desperate that relief measures needed to be prioritised over all other considerations, even military ones.[47] But the British War Cabinet was dealing with several serious obstacles; the most urgent of these was the fact that the Swedish government had only limited supplies at its disposal, certainly not the requested 5,000 tons per week. Bringing supplies from England was also out of question as this would interfere with the economic blockade.[48] Furthermore, the US government was not particularly helpful in providing aid, owing to Roosevelt's view that shipping from the US was not desirable until the war was over.[49]

In a meeting held at the British Ministry of Food in mid-February, the implications of the famine conditions were discussed extensively, including what special action could be taken, which supplies could be provided, and how they could be distributed. British nutritional experts were invited to this meeting with the aim of working towards an international relief system necessary for the reconstruction of post-war Europe.[50]

---

[47] NARA, 331, Entry 2, Box 118, Letter Wilhelmina to King George, Roosevelt, and Churchill, 15 January 1945; Entry 152, Box 264, Fortnightly report SHAEF Mission Netherlands, 16 January 1945.

[48] TNA, PREM 3/221/12, Letter R. A. Gallop to Desmond Morton, 2 February 1945.

[49] TNA, PREM 4/29/12, FO to Washington, 8 December 1944.

[50] NARA, 331, Entry 2, Box 118, Message Troopers to SHAEF Main G-5, 18 February 1945; James Vernon, *Hunger: A Modern History* (Cambridge, MA: The Belknap Press of Harvard University Press, 2007), 150–151.

Among them was Sir Jack Drummond of the Ministry of Food, who stated that, in his view, the Allies were 'faced by a position in which it was quite impossible for the Germans to bring in sufficient food to feed the population of the large towns in the west and northwest reasonably well, even if they wished to do it, and an extremely serious situation might be expected when this area was liberated'.[51] For these experts, relief from neutral resources appeared vital to safeguard Europe's post-war future.

Burdened with this task, the British War Cabinet continuously weighed the implications of additional shipments and instituting a regular relief scheme against the potential damage this might cause to their military efforts. On 5 February 1945, the green light was given to send the Swiss ship *Henri Dunant* to Delfzijl with the understanding that this was an interim measure and no further consignments would be approved until reports about the distribution of the first ships had been received. But since distribution had been postponed, no such reports were available.[52] After careful deliberation, sanction was given for additional shipments from Sweden. In late March, the War Cabinet agreed that a regular relief scheme of 5,000 tons per week was to be instituted under the aegis of the Swedish government or the ICRC, but this time the Admiralty objected. A regular supply would increase the German capacity to resist, while also becoming an embarrassment to Allied operations in the Kiel Canal. Nevertheless, the safe-conduct agreement, which had expired on 15 March, was extended to 1 April to cover the voyage of the third Swedish ship *Hallaren*.[53] From the German side, Seyss-Inquart appeared willing to provide his full cooperation, as long as no organisation emerged 'which could gain a position similar to the Hoover Committee in 1914–18 Belgium'.[54]

In the months from February to April 1945, a total of five Red Cross shipments – three from Sweden, one from Switzerland, and one from the ICRC – arrived in the occupied Netherlands, bringing a total of approximately 14,000 tons of quality products into the country. In addition, an ICRC train with Romanian cereals designated for the Netherlands was stranded in Germany, after which the German government approved of

---

[51] TNA, PREM 4/29/12, Minutes War Cabinet Meeting, 5 February 1945.
[52] TNA, CAB 119/140, COS Meeting 5–12 February 1945. Only a preliminary report from one of the leaders of the Dutch resistance movement dating 4 March indicated transportation and distribution were carried out 'in a manner which even in normal times would be considered good'. TNA, PREM 3/221/12, Memorandum War Cabinet by Eden, 14 March 1945.
[53] TNA, ADM 116/5350, Report Admiralty C. H. M. Waldock, 18 March 1945; CAB 122/993, Message War Office to Washington, 23 March 1945.
[54] NIOD, 212a, inv.no. 167, Diary Hirschfeld, 3 March 1945.

an alternative transport of 2,600 tons of rye from Westphalia.[55] The costs of these shipments could not be recouped from the Allies, since they had to be entirely 'neutral'. The Swiss supplies were paid for by the ICRC and other relief committees while the Swedish gifts were in part a gift from the Swedish government and, for one-seventh, granted by the Dutch Aid Committee in Sweden. The remaining six-sevenths was funded by the Dutch government itself.[56] The greater part of the parcels consisted of cereal products, dried vegetables, rice, and milk; however, the ships also brought much-needed medicines such as insulin, anti-diphtheria serum, sulfathiazole, cod-liver oil, vitamin B1 and C, and scabies pesticide as well as boxes with children's clothing.[57] A final Swedish ship moored in the port of Delfzijl on 12 April, but was ordered to sail out again by the Germans without unloading to await the impending battle for Groningen offshore.[58]

In terms of measurable effects, the supplies meant eight weeks of daily rations increased by 200–400 kcal with greater allowances for the specific needs of different age groups; for infants, their rations reached almost pre-crisis standards. Perhaps most important of all, relief arrived during the height of the famine (at least in terms of mortality) and certainly mitigated famine conditions after March 1945. Notably, the Directorate of Food Supply used the Red Cross supplies for coupon-free distribution of bread (400 grams) every fortnight, as well as three separate handouts of margarine (125 grams). Part of the supplies were designated for the soup kitchens, where every third day a 'Swedish' or 'Swiss meal' could be distributed, enabling the CK to save up food for an additional quarter litre the remaining two days.[59] Initially, only the larger towns were included in the Red Cross distributions but, in late March, when the food officials found that hunger had reached the countryside as well – especially villages with large numbers of factory workers – the

---

[55] The second Swedish shipment was ensured by the *Hallaren* (4,100 tons) and the third by a second voyage of the *Dagmar Bratt* and the *Noreg* (3,237 tons). The Swiss *Henry Dunant* arrived in Delfzijl on 8 March, bringing 3,287 tons of supplies. UN, AG 18-004 Bureau of Services, S-1245-0000-0769, Statement on the Don Suisse, 19 March 1945; TNA, ADM 116/5350, Message Norton Berne to Foreign Office, 27 March 1945; WO 220/668, Admiralty to C-in-C's, s.a.; NIOD, 216h, inv.no. 312, Minutes CRV 15, 28 February 1945; NIOD, 233b, inv.no. 18, Report by S. (underground movement) to Dutch government, 15 April 1945; Hirschfeld, 'De Centrale Reederij', 10; De Jong, *Het Koninkrijk* 10b, 1085–1087, 1096.

[56] De Jong, *Het Koninkrijk* 10b, 1098.

[57] NIOD, 212a, inv.no. 116, Protocol Red Cross Germany, 9 March 1945; Huizinga, 'Geneesmiddelen-verzorging', 191–192.

[58] TNA, WO 220/668, Message Stockholm to Admiralty, 4 April 1945.

[59] NIOD, 212a, inv.no. 116, Report Count Morner, 3 March 1945.

distribution was expanded to the entire western provinces.[60] Despite the impressive nature of these figures and food relief supplies, they were just a drop in the ocean, especially when we consider that, in total, the people in the occupied west received less than 5 kg of food relief per capita over a period of two and a half months. In comparison, during the same period the still occupied Channel Islands received 70 kg per capita from neutral sources.[61]

Manna from Heaven

Meanwhile, negotiations about Allied relief had resumed, in particular talks concerning the possibility of deploying aircrafts to drop food supplies onto the principle urban areas. While the Allies acknowledged this tactic mostly for its symbolic value, the Dutch government had been proposing the implementation of air supply by using transport aircrafts as early as the autumn of 1944. On 13 November, the American authorities had welcomed this idea but, almost immediately, the British Air Ministry communicated their desire to first examine the military implications. Their official report, two weeks later, concluded that the use of Dutch aircrafts would only be allowed if they were to be incorporated into the transport command of the Royal Air Force (RAF) and thus become subordinate to their commands. When the focus shifted towards the occupied areas, the Combined Chiefs of Staff dismissed airdrops entirely. The airplanes would have to be diverted from combat operations; moreover, relieving the Dutch also conflicted with planned assistance for Allied POWs, 'which project has been accorded a priority second only to requirements for defeat of Germany'.[62] In addition to these military objections, negotiations stalled after approval was given for the Red Cross shipments because a preliminary investigation demonstrated that the 21st Army Group could not possibly execute such an operation with airplanes from their Second Tactical Air Force – allegedly, only heavy bombers could.[63]

Nevertheless, by March 1945, new political considerations had led the Allies to re-examine the contribution airplanes could make to the introduction of relief supplies. One major incentive was that estimations of the Dutch food supply indicated that it would be completely exhausted by 28 April: after this point, deaths through famine would occur 'on a

---

[60] NA, 2.21.238., inv.no. 117, Report Louwes.   [61] De Jong, *Het Koninkrijk* 10b, 1103.
[62] NARA, 331, Entry 2, Box 118, HQ USSTAF to Eisenhower, 27 March 1945.
[63] NIOD, 233b, inv.no. 33, Letter Albarda to Queen Wilhelmina, 16 January 1945; De Jong, *Het Koninkrijk* 10b, 1344.

considerable scale'.[64] In addition, the Commando Western District had calculated that there would be an approximate two to three weeks' delay prior to the delivery of food and medical supplies via any method of surface transportation, which would evidently lead to more victims; however, these would now fall under Allied responsibility.[65] What also played a central role was the psychological value of relief via air, which had increased considerably. Regular reports from the occupied areas stated that virtually nobody believed that liberation was technically 'impossible' and that the Dutch felt they were being sacrificed because the Allies saw no strategic advantage in saving them.[66] Even if Gerbrandy's desperate appeals – to act now or face the consequences after liberation – contributed to this shift in attitude cannot be validated, it is certain that the Dutch government ensured that immediate relief remained firmly on the Allies' agenda.

In light of these considerations, the possibility of liberating the western Netherlands at the earliest possible moment was also reconsidered. On 27 March, SHAEF circulated a report stating that it was unlikely that the enemy would withdraw from the Netherlands by itself and that the best practical approach would be to advance east-west across the IJssel, via Utrecht to Leiden. These operations would inevitably involve heavy casualties. Moreover, a large operation in the Netherlands necessitated a serious weakening of the main armies in Germany, which Eisenhower rejected: at that time, military presence was imperative for the final collapse of Nazi Germany.[67] SHAEF thus concluded that, from a military standpoint, it was far from advisable to undertake operations in the western Netherlands and that all possible preparations should be made to enable relief via air supply as proposed.[68]

The SHAEF report advising against the military operations in the west coincided with the advance of the 1st Canadian Army and Second British Army in a northwesterly direction, successfully liberating a great part of the northeastern provinces. According to the SHAEF Mission Netherlands, the condition of the liberated provinces turned out to be

---

[64] NARA, 331, Entry 2, Box 118, SHAEF Forward signed Eisenhower to AGWAR and AMSSO; Message to Blaskowitz, 23 March 1945. See also: TNA, PREM 3/221/12.

[65] NARA, 331, Entry 152, Box 264, Fortnightly report SHAEF Mission Netherlands, 31 March 1945.

[66] NARA, 331, Entry 2, Box 118, Report 'The Occupied Netherlands To-day and To-morrow', 17 March; NARA, 331, Entry 2, Box 118, Report KWD Strong et al. on conditions in Holland, 20 March 1945.

[67] Eisenhower, *Eisenhower's own Story of the War*, 114.

[68] NARA, 331, Entry 2, Box 118, Report SHAEF FWD to AGWAR and AMSSO, 27 March 1945; Eisenhower, *Crusade in Europe* (London: William Heinemann Limited, 1948), 449.

comparatively good. While food was in short supply in the provinces of Gelderland and Overijssel, health conditions were actually more favourable than they had expected. In Groningen, Friesland, and Drenthe, food was still plentiful, although the coal shortage there appeared to be the main problem. In addition to nutritional surveys from the territories, a nutritional laboratory was set up in Oss (North Brabant) and Red Cross relief teams were deployed to Enschede (Overijssel) and Assen (Drenthe). Self-contained medical teams stood by in the east, ready to enter the B2 area when needed.[69]

Evidently quite aware of their precarious position, the German civil authorities in the occupied Netherlands indicated their willingness to negotiate. On 2 April 1945, Hirschfeld met in private with Seyss-Inquart to discuss the possibility of abandoning Hitler's 'scorched earth' order as well as to neutralise part of western Holland from military activities. As outlined in Chapter 4, neutralisation had already been proposed by the *Reichskommissar* in December 1944 and January 1945 but, due to miscommunication from the Council of Trusted Representatives, these plans had failed to reach London. Prior to the meeting, Seyss-Inquart had conferred with the German Minister for Armament Albert Speer about disobeying the *Führer*'s order, who agreed that total destruction was to be avoided. Speer had been opposing 'scorched earth' policies ever since Hitler gave the first orders to this end in late July 1944, including the infamous 'Nero Decree' of March 1945, which called for the destruction of Germany's own infrastructure.[70] Following this understanding and on his own initiative, the *Reichskommissar* expressed interest in contacting the Council of Trusted Representatives. In fact, Seyss-Inquart startled Hirschfeld by informing him that he and the German intelligence service had known about their existence since the summer of 1944.[71]

The rapprochement initiated by Seyss-Inquart should not be understood as unique to the Dutch case. In fact, several high-ranking Nazi leaders acted in similar ways. For example, during the final weeks before the impending German defeat, the Third Reich's Plenipotentiary

[69] NARA, 331, Entry 152, Box 264, Fortnightly report SHAEF Mission Netherlands, 15 April 1945 and 30 April 1945.
[70] Gitta Sereny, *Albert Speer: His Battle with the Truth* (London and Basingstoke: Macmillan, 1995), 456–487; Joachim Fest, *Speer: Eine Biographie* (Berlin: Alexander Fest, 1999), 255–257, 264–278; Ian Kershaw, *Hitler: Vergelding 1936–1945* (Utrecht: Het Spektrum, 2000), 1029–1030.
[71] NIOD, 458, inv.no. 27, Hearing Hirschfeld, 14 June 1946, 11686; NIOD, 212a, Diary Hirschfeld, 2 April 1945; Fennema and Rhijnsburger, *Dr Hans Max Hirschfeld*, 129–130; Stephen Dando-Collins, *Operation Chowhound: The Most Risky, Most Glorious US Bomber Mission of WWII* (New York: Palgrave Macmillan, 2015), 65–70.

(*Reichsbevollmächtigter*) for occupied Denmark Werner Best similarly fought implementation of the scorched earth order.[72] At an even higher level, Himmler himself had defied Hitler's orders about scorched earth and fighting the war until the bitter end through his attempts to negotiate a truce with the Allies. Knowing there was little hope for winning the war, in early 1945, Himmler made use of his contacts in neutral Sweden to connect with the vice president of the Swedish Red Cross, Count Folke Bernadotte. The *Reichsführer SS* presented himself to the Swedes as a reasonable politician, offering to let 10,000 Scandinavian-Jewish prisoners go and to refrain from demolishing concentration camps and killing prisoners during the Allied advance. Himmler did not keep his word but, thanks to Bernadotte, the agreement saved the lives of over 20,000 prisoners. In the end, the proposed truce never took place as Churchill and Eisenhower refused to talk with Himmler. Infuriated with these actions, on 29 April – one day before he killed himself – Hitler stripped Himmler of all his party and state services.[73] The actions of Best and Himmler show that it was not uncommon during the final phase of the Third Reich for high-placed Nazis to present themselves as conciliatory and independent negotiators; it is perhaps within this context that we should view the actions and attitude of Seyss-Inquart as well.

On the evening of 12 April, a meeting took place between Seyss-Inquart, Schwebel, P. J. Six (Forces of the Interior) and Van der Vlugt (IKO), which had been preceded by a number of conversations of an exploratory character between Van der Vlugt and Schwebel.[74] The *Reichskommissar* gave his full support to relief work – military situation permitting. The Dutchmen raised the matter of abandoning further destructive measures, now that Germany had inevitably lost the war, and they even quoted Hitler's *Mein Kampf* and Clausewitz's *Vom Kriege* to push home their obligation to discontinue fighting under these circumstances. Seyss-Inquart informed the resistance leaders that the original directive to destroy all non-military capital goods during retreat had been withdrawn at his special request after an interview with Speer. He asserted that there existed only one order to carry out under all circumstances; namely, to hold the Dutch coastal region as long as a state of war continued in Germany. The meeting concluded with the understanding that if the Allied troops halted before the Grebbe line and committed no further

---

[72] Ulrich Herbert, *Best: Biographische Studien über Radikalismus, Weltanschauung und Vernunft 1903–1989*, 5th ed. (Bonn: Dietz, 2011), 398–400.

[73] Peter Longerich, *Heinrich Himmler: Biographie* (Munich: Siedler, 2008), 740–752.

[74] Gerbrandy, *Eenige Hoofdpunten*, 167–177; De Jong, *Het Koninkrijk* 10b, 1287–1293; Romijn, *Burgemeesters in Oorlogstijd*, 598–599; Koll, *Arthur Seyss-Inquart*, 556–558.

acts of war against the coastal zone, the German military command would be prepared to forgo inundation or to destroy further areas and goods as well as give full support to relief work. Both sides agreed that an eventual arrangement amounting to an unofficial truce '*mit Gewehr bei Fuβ*' should be carried out as inconspicuously as possible.[75] Seyss-Inquart discussed these events during his Nuremberg trial:

I made the decision to end the occupation of the Dutch territories and not carry out my duties to the Reich. I went to General Secretary Hirschfeld and we discussed this problem. We arrived at the decision to get in touch with our confidential agents in The Hague – which was illegal for us to do. We tried to negotiate with them on the basis that the Allied troops should not advance against Holland, so that any further destruction would not come about; that the Allies would take over the feeding of the Dutch population and that we would wait for the end of the war.[76]

Seyss-Inquart also agreed for two other representatives to cross the lines into liberated territories and convince the Dutch government to open into negotiations with him. He criticised the Allies for not taking care of the civilian population and failing to send more relief supplies, despite his rapprochement in December. Clearly, there was a change in attitude for Seyss-Inquart, who after December 1944, became actively involved in food politics in the occupied areas: however, now he placed all responsibility for the famine with the Allies. After learning the details, Gerbrandy flew to London to brief Churchill about the meeting with Seyss-Inquart; meanwhile, Prince Bernhard travelled to SHAEF Head-quarters in Reims to brief Eisenhower.[77] Churchill responded hesitantly by saying that the Russians had already harboured certain suspicions that the US and UK would arrive at some secret arrangement with Germany, thereby allowing their forces an easy march into Germany. Even an agreement with the Germans just on the issue of food aid for the occupied territories could potentially upset Anglo-Soviet relations, which the UK and US not only feared from the perspective of post-war power relations, but also with regard to the release of their respective POWs in the Red Army's hands.[78] Churchill thus concluded that Stalin would

---

[75] TNA, PREM 3/221/12, Report meeting 12 April, Churchill to Eden, 16 April 1945; NARA, 331, Entry 2, Box 118, Message Netherlands Interior Forces to SHAEF, 14 April 1945; NIOD, 458, inv.no. 27, Hearing Schwebel, 14 June 1946, 11704; Dando-Collins, *Operation Chowhound*, 72–74.

[76] NIOD, 458, inv.no. 24, Nuremberg Trial Seyss-Inquart, 11 June 1946, 11433.

[77] NARA, 331, Entry 2, Box 118, Message Netherlands Interior Forces to SHAEF, 14 April 1945; De Jong, *Het Koninkrijk* 10b, 1294–1299.

[78] Moore, 'The Western Allies'; Rüdiger Overmans, 'The Repatriation of Prisoners of War Once Hostilities Are Over: A Matter of Course?' in *Prisoners of War, Prisoners of Peace:*

not be inclined to concur. He would, however, place the proposal before the War Cabinet, discuss it with Roosevelt and Eisenhower, and communicate with Eden in Washington to discuss the matter with Molotov.[79]

The Dutch ministers also remained hesitant. Gerbrandy remarked that Seyss-Inquart, with talks about an informal truce, would still hold the means of blackmail against them 'with the knowledge of Hitler, Himmler, or whoever rules in Germany with some tortuous ulterior motive, such as causing trouble between ourselves and the Russians'. Minister of Transport and Water Management, Theodoor P. Tromp, was entirely against talking to the enemy on the grounds that 'any proposal from a Nazi must automatically be mistrusted'.[80]

Yet the British War Cabinet considered the Dutch proposal together with SHAEF's relief plans very seriously, a shift in mindset that was surely related to the imminent Allied invasion of Nazi Germany and the risks of liberating a half-starved country. As mentioned, only twice before had a relaxation of the blockade been approved – both times as a result of political and military considerations, not just for humanitarian reasons. The British Chiefs of Staff agreed with Eisenhower that an immediate attempt to drop suitable supplies ought to be made, in spite of the risk that these supplies might fall into German hands. They also conceded that the proposal for an informal truce should be accepted, provided that adequate assurances were obtained that E-boats (*Schnellboot*) and U-boats near Dutch ports would remain inactive.[81] Yet this time it was the US Joint Chiefs of Staff who delayed the initiative, remaining adamant about not sending supplies through the blockade.[82] Churchill asked Roosevelt to help withdraw this opposition, now seemingly convinced that 'the plight of the civil population in Occupied Holland is desperate'.[83] Roosevelt also seemed willing, but in his reply he stated that Stalin should approve of the plans as well, in order to

Captivity, Homecoming, and Memory in World War II, eds. Moore and Barbara Hately-Broad (Oxford: Berg, 2005), 11–22.
[79] TNA, PREM 3/221/12, Note on discussion between Churchill and Gerbrandy, 15 April 1945; Gerbrandy, *Eenige Hoofdpunten*, 147–148.
[80] TNA, PREM 3/221/12, Note Desmond Morton to Churchill, 16 April 1945.
[81] TNA, CAB 119/140, COS meeting 9 and 16 April 1945; CAB 122/993, Memorandum British Chiefs of Staff, 10 April 1945; Meeting Chiefs of Staff Committee, 16 April 1945.
[82] TNA, WO 220/668, JSM Washington to AMSSO, 7 April 1945.
[83] TNA, 3/221/12, Churchill to Roosevelt, 10 April 1945; Eden to Churchill, 11 April 1945; Winston S. Churchill, *The Second World War: VI Triumph and Tragedy* (London: Cassell & Col. Ltd, 1954), 410. See also: Letter C-939 in: Warren F. Kimball, ed., *Churchill & Roosevelt: The Complete Correspondence, III Alliance Declining, February 1944–April 1945* (Princeton: Princeton University Press, 1984), 623–624.

prevent misunderstanding or animosities.[84] However, the unfortunate and unexpected death of the president on 12 April made this matter an ambiguous point of discussion, delaying the plans for several crucial days.

When Seyss-Inquart received inquiries from London about whether he would be willing to work with Eisenhower on further arrangements, he responded positively. Churchill had informed the supreme commander about the possibility of 'neutralising the occupied west', as Seyss-Inquart also called it, and Eisenhower agreed that this seemed a very good option, provided that it would not contravene with the principle of unconditional surrender. Eisenhower knew that living conditions in the west had been steadily deteriorating and that the situation had become almost intolerable, as he wrote in his memoirs: 'Judging from the infor-mation available to me, I feared that wholesale starvation would take place and decided to take positive steps to prevent it.'[85] He urged Churchill to push the matter through on the lines he suggested with all possible speed. Again, the military benefits played an important role – if an informal truce could be accomplished, SHAEF would only have to set up a small force on the Dutch frontier, leaving a much larger force available for Eisenhower's decisive move on to Lubeck.[86]

The decision to enter into formal negotiations came about under highly adverse circumstances. The German *Wehrmacht* continued to inundate swathes of land, lay minefields, and charge dykes; meanwhile, the SS continued to execute Dutchmen and -women who were allegedly working for the enemy. Prince Bernhard quite rightfully feared that 'destruction will be carried out by desperados notwithstanding German High Command orders to the contrary'.[87] On 17 April, the fragile trust established between the German occupier and the Allies suffered a major blow when General Blaskowitz, anticipating Allied aerial landings, ordered the inundation of the Wieringermeer – a large polder and important agricultural area in the east of North Holland. Churchill responded with equal ferocity and told Gerbrandy that he 'ought to tell the authorities with whom he was negotiating that he (Mr Winston Churchill) had said that if any dykes were blown while negotiations were still proceeding then those responsible would be branded as war crim-inals'.[88] Bedell Smith concluded that this devastating act could be

[84] Letter R-743 in: Kimball, ed., *Churchill & Roosevelt*, 631.
[85] Eisenhower, *Crusade in Europe*, 454.
[86] TNA, PREM 3/221/12, Office Ministry of Defence Isman to Churchill, 19 April 1945.
[87] NARA, 331, Entry 2, Box 118, Message Prince Bernhard to Bedell Smith, 2 May 1945.
[88] TNA, PREM 3/221/12, COS Staff conference 18 April 1945.

justified on the basis of military necessity but that no further destructions would be tolerated. That same day 'Beetle' summoned Air Commodore Andrew Geddes, mastermind behind Operation Overlord and Operation Market Garden, to commence planning for an air operation with heavy bombers that would provide relief to the Dutch, despite the still considerable opposition at the highest levels.[89]

On 23 April, the Combined Chiefs of Staff formally authorised Eisenhower to negotiate a truce that enabled the introduction of relief on the condition that it did not prejudice the principle of unconditional surrender. There was, however, still disagreement on how to proceed. While the British preferred to go straight for a truce, the Americans proposed that the matter should be left to Eisenhower's discretion entirely. In the end, the elaborate unconditional surrender policy initially agreed upon was reduced to a mere set of guidelines for the supreme commander.[90] Although they were still apprehensive about upsetting Anglo-Soviet relations over the question of food aid, both sides did concede that the Russians should simply be informed and not consulted, as Roosevelt had proposed. Churchill warned: 'I have already made it clear ... that I am not prepared to let the Russians veto the plan.'[91] The Soviet command was, however, invited to be present at all discussions with German representatives. In response, Soviet Liaison Officer General Antonov added one more condition to the list; namely, that the local German command was obliged not to transfer its troops to other parts of the front during the armistice period, including the eastern Soviet-German front.[92]

Expecting a crucial delay in finalising road transportation for relief, Eisenhower immediately pushed for the implementation of an adequate air supply. He assigned two strategic bomber forces – the RAF Bomber Command and the Eighth US Air Force – which, as a test run, would drop the first supplies during the night of 25–26 April.[93] In order for aid

[89] NIOD, 458, inv.no. 27, Hearing Schwebel, 14 June 1946, 11708–11709; Dando-Collins, *Operation Chowhound*, 89–94.

[90] TNA, PREM 3/221/12, Telegram from Washington to Foreign Office, 22 April 1945; CAB 122/993, Message Combined Chiefs of Staff to SHAEF, 23 April 1945; PREM 3/221/12, Message AMSSO to JSM Washington, 21 April 1945; Donnison, *Civil Affairs and Military Government*, 144. For all articles of agreement, see: NARA, 331, Entry 2, Box 118, Articles of Agreement SHAEF, without date.

[91] TNA, CAB 122/993, Telegram Churchill to British Chiefs of Staff, 21 April 1945.

[92] TNA, CAB 122/993, Message SHAEF Forward to War Department, 24 April 1945; NARA, 331, Entry 2, Box 118, Message Military Mission Moscow to Combined Chiefs of Staff and Eisenhower, 27 April 1945.

[93] NARA, 331, Entry 2, Box 118, Message Air Staff SHAEF to USSTAF Main, 24 April 1945.

to be distributed quickly, SHAEF broadcasted radio announcements explaining the operation to the public on 24 April. The Germans were instructed not to fire at the aircrafts; the Dutch were instructed to collect and distribute the supplies. Allied airplanes also dropped leaflets addressed to German soldiers, warning them to refrain from immoral conduct: 'After defeat, you will be searched out, tried, and punished.'[94] A message was simultaneously despatched through the underground to Seyss-Inquart, requesting an immediate meeting between him and representatives of Eisenhower.[95]

Seyss-Inquart and Blaskowitz replied by stating that they agreed as a matter of principle to the introduction of food relief but rejected airdrops for reasons of defence. In addition, airdrops would make only a minimal contribution to solving the food problem; moreover, distribution could not be sufficiently controlled. As an alternative, Seyss-Inquart proposed food supplies be brought in by ship and train with distribution executed by the Dutch food administration. Schwebel simultaneously assured resistance leader Van der Vlugt in a secret message that they were doing everything to help the Dutch, even against their own interests of defence.[96] As a result of the German attitude, SHAEF immediately called back the bombers, postponing the airdrops until further notice.[97] Although neither of them was convinced by the concept of airdrops, Louwes and Hirschfeld advised Seyss-Inquart to accept the airdrops but only in four designated zones under their direction: the airfields Schiphol, Ypenburg, and Waalhaven, and the racecourse Duindigt. At the beginning of their meeting, Seyss-Inquart was said to have sarcastically introduced the subject with words from Friedrich Schiller's *Lied von der Glocke*: '*Doch der Segen kommt von oben*' (though the blessing comes from higher).[98] On 26 April, the German authorities agreed to the airdrops and one day later they accepted the invitation to meet with Allied representatives. The RBVVO was formally instructed to organise the collection and distribution of the food supplies.[99]

---

[94] NARA, 331, Entry 2, Box 118, Leaflet to German Soldiers, without date.

[95] NARA, 331, Entry 2, Box 118, CBS message MUS 384, 25 April 1945. See also: NIOD, 0867 Voedseldroppings, inv.no. 2, Report on air drops over Holland.

[96] NIOD, 086 Beauftragte des Reichskommissars, inv.no. 439, Correspondence Schwebel and Van der Vlugt, 25 April 1945.

[97] NARA, 331, Entry 2, Box 118, Message SHAEF Forward signed Eisenhower to AGWAR and AMSSO, 27 April 1945. See also: TNA, CAB 119/140; PREM 3/221/12.

[98] NARA, 331, Entry 2, Box 118, CBS Message 384, 25 April 1945; NIOD, 212a, inv. no. 160, Notes on meetings Hirschfeld with Schwebel and Seyss-Inquart, 25 April 1945; inv.no. 162, Diary Hirschfeld, 25 April 1945.

[99] TNA, PREM 3/221/12, Minister of Defence to Churchill, 27 April 1945; NIOD, 216h, inv.no. 93, Report on dropping of food supplies by Allied airplanes, Directorate of Food Supply, Chr. M. Pool, 12 May 1945; inv.no. 93, Message Seyss-Inquart to Allied

That following day, Schwebel and one of Blaskowitz's representatives crossed the front line at Amersfoort and briefly spoke with Major General Sir Francis de Guingand, Montgomery's Chief of Staff, and other Allied representatives in a Catholic school building in the small village of Achterveld. This first meeting was exploratory in nature and limited to matters directly connected with the introduction of food supplies into western Holland. As such, it was a direct continuation of Schwebel's contacts (from early April onward) with Hirschfeld and Van der Vlugt. Another meeting within Allied lines was arranged to take place in two days.[100] De Guingand later wrote about this day: 'There was an atmosphere of subdued excitement around us, for it was obvious to everyone that something of great moment was taking place.'[101] It had been Eisenhower's intention to commence the food drops immediately following this meeting, but his plan was thwarted by storm and fog ravaging northwestern Europe. After the weather had cleared overnight, on Sunday morning 29 April, the first Lancaster heavy bombers were able to take off from the Ludford Magna airfield in the East Midlands. The first RAF mission comprised 500 tons, dropped onto four zones following routes and other arrangements that were designated by Seyss-Inquart himself.[102]

On Monday 30 April, a second meeting was held at St. Joseph's school in Achterveld. This time, Seyss-Inquart was present to talk with Eisenhower's deputy Bedell Smith personally about the airdrop operation and other aspects of the Allied relief plans. The Allied delegation was formed by Major General Strong, De Guingand, and Galloway. *Reichskommissar* Seyss-Inquart was accompanied by Schwebel, as well as high-ranked Navy, Army and Airforce officers. Representing the Dutch interests were Prince Bernhard and a delegation of food and transportation experts from the occupied areas, including Louwes and nutrition experts Dols and Banning, as the negotiations formally concerned food politics only. To the surprise of many, Major General Ivan Susloparov had been

Headquarters, 25 April 1945; Telegram Seyss-Inquart, 27 April 1945; NIOD, 212a, inv.no. 147, Note Seyss-Inquart to Louwes, 27 April 1945. NIOD, 086, inv.no. 439, Correspondence Van der Vlugt and Schwebel, April–May 1945.

[100] NIOD, 212a, inv.no. 162, Diary Hirschfeld, 28 April 1945; NIOD, 458, inv.no. 27, Hearing Schwebel at Nuremberg Trial Seyss-Inquart, 14 June 1946, 11704.

[101] Francis de Guingand, *Operation Victory* (London: Hodder and Stoughton, 1947), 446.

[102] NIOD, 216h, inv.no. 93, Message Seyss-Inquart to Allied Headquarters, 26 April 1945; Report on dropping of food supplies for the population of Utrecht, North and South Holland by Allied airplanes, Directorate of Food Supply, Chr. M. Pool, 12 May 1945; Dando-Collins, *Operation Chowhound*, 119. For more on this mission, see: Hans Onderwater, *Operatie 'Manna': De Geallieerde Voedseldroppings April/Mei 1945* (Weesp: Romen Luchtvaart, 1985), 30–33.

assigned at the very last minute to attend the meeting as the Soviet representative.

It soon became clear that the German delegates had not been authorised to negotiate on the military clauses of the truce, restricted from doing so while the German commander in the western Netherlands was still in touch with his superiors. The conference thus only dealt with the provision of relief. During the first part of the proceedings, Bedell Smith read out the broad general proposals for feeding the Dutch, after which he obtained German agreement to these in principle.[103] The meeting then split up into various syndicates of Allied, Dutch, and German representatives to deal with the details in separate gatherings. It was agreed that the aerial supply would increase as rapidly as possible to 1,550 tons daily, with a regular supply by land commencing on 2 May and the first relief ships to arrive in Rotterdam two days later.[104] Seyss-Inquart showed himself to be fully aware of his responsibility in easing the burden of the Dutch; the Dutch representatives even unanimously agreed that the *Reichskommissar* had behaved in a dignified manner.[105] Bedell Smith, who had spoken with Seyss-Inquart in small chambers while enjoying a stiff glass of gin together, wrote to Eisenhower:

The arguments regarding the hopelessness of the German position and the futility of further loss of life visibly made a deep impression on the *Reichskommissar*, who, towards the end of the conversation, hardly spoke above a whisper, but nothing would shake his conviction that the Germans in Holland must continue the struggle so long as a government of any kind existed in Germany.[106]

In his turn, on 2 May, Seyss-Inquart wrote to Hitler's successor as *Führer* and Reich Chancellor Grand Admiral Karl Dönitz about the meeting with equal optimism, requesting either personal directions or full executive power: 'From the seriousness of the offer and the attitude adopted towards me, I got the impression that serious negotiations about general questions in the interest of the Reich are possible as well.'[107] On that same day, however, Blaskowitz had written to OKW, stating that Eisenhower had

---

[103] NARA, 331, Entry 2, Box 118, Message SHAEF signed Eisenhower to Combined Chiefs of Staff, 1 May 1945; NIOD, 212a, inv.no. 162, Diary Hirschfeld, 1 May 1945. See also: TNA, PREM 3/221/12; Dando-Collins, *Operation Chowhound*, 135–144; Eisenhower, *Eisenhower's own Story of the War*, 115.

[104] NARA, 331, Entry 2, Box 118, Memorandum for Eisenhower from Bedell Smith, 1 May 1945; De Guingand, *Operation Victory*, 450–451.

[105] NIOD, 212a, inv.no. 162, Diary Hirschfeld, 1 May 1945.

[106] NARA, 331, Entry 2, Box 118, Memorandum for Eisenhower from Bedell Smith, 1 May 1945. For more on Bedell Smith's view on this meeting, see: Walter Bedell Smith, *Eisenhower's Six Great Decisions* (New York: Longmans, Green and Co., 1956), 197–199.

[107] BA, R3/1625, Letter Seyss-Inquart to Dönitz, 2 May 1945.

requested more food drops but that he rejected this for reasons of military objectives: 'My battle assignment remains unchanged.'[108]

Eventually, the Germans and Allies agreed to expand the air supply operation to ten dropping zones, which would be approached from 7:00 a.m. to 3:00 p.m. daily.[109] Similar to the initial four designated zones, most areas were airfields, but also other open areas convenient for dropping and gathering supplies without unnecessary losses, all marked with a white cross to pinpoint the centre. Green lights were fired to inform the pilots that they were in the correct area, while red lights warned them from entering a restricted zone.[110] The operation was unique, as it marked the first time that supplies were dropped at a low altitude without the use of special parachute containers. Each aircraft carried sufficient rations to feed about 3,280 people for one day. These rations, among other things, consisted of flour, dehydrated meat, potato mash powder, dehydrated vegetables, bacon, egg powder, cheese, milk powder, margarine, sugar, tea, salt, pepper, mustard, dried peas, lentils and beans, and chocolate. On the British side, eight million rations were packed and ready to be flown in; another six million were ordered to be packed and flown in by the US.[111]

For ten consecutive days, RAF Lancasters and USAAF B-17 heavy bombers dropped food onto the western Netherlands.[112] Due to adverse weather conditions, the British Operation Manna started two days before the American Chowhound bombers arrived, which also meant that the RAF struggled more with start-up problems. The first food drops in Rotterdam, for instance, were bungled because part of the payload fell into the harbour and another part ended up in a mine field. What was left of the parcels was, according to SHAEF, plundered by starving civilians. Out of a total of 5,294 flights, only two US bombers were lost: fortunately, without any casualties.[113] Former USAAF navigator Richard C. Hall stated about his experiences with the food drops:

---

[108] BA, R3/1625, Letter Blaskowitz to OKW, 2 May 1945.
[109] These dropping zones were: Valkenburg, Ypenburg, Duindigt, Waalhaven (later Terbregge), Gouda, Schiphol, Vogelensang, Bergen/Alkmaar, Hilversum, Utrecht. Seyss-Inquart requested that Waalhaven airport be changed for Kralingsche plas, because of the adverse waterlogged condition and land mines, one of which even exploded during the first drops. NIOD, 086, inv.no. 439, Letter Schwebel to Van der Vlugt, 29 April 1945.
[110] NARA, 331, Entry 2, Box 118, Air plan, 30 April 1945.
[111] UN, AG 18-004, S-1245-0000-0365, Netherlands Information Bureau, 29 April 1945; NARA, 331, Entry 2, Box 118, Message General Dyxhoorn to Gerbrandy, 29 April 1945. See also: Scheepmaker, *Het Zweedse Wittebrood*, 124–126.
[112] On two days, the RAF and USAAF had to cancel one of their missions due to bad weather. For more on these missions, see also: Onderwater, *Operatie 'Manna'*, 60–85; 128–130; De Jong, *Het Koninkrijk* 10b, 1344–1351.
[113] TNA, WO 29/2268, Message SHAEF G-3 to Air Staff, 1 May 1945; ELO, 0257, inv. no. 51, Final report on food drops by Directorate of Food Supply, 1945; NIOD, 086, inv.no. 439, Correspondence Schwebel and Van der Vlugt, 29 April 1945.

An arrangement was worked out by which the Germans allowed the RAF and the Eighth Air Force to fly in at low altitude over a very carefully specified route and drop food parcels. If we got off course, they would fire a red flare to warn us, but they would not shoot .... On the 6th of May, I was the navigator on a pathfinding crew, leading a large group of B-17s. But instead of going in a formation, we went single file. To the best of my recollection, I did not know until early that morning, when they woke us up for the briefing and instructions, that we would be dropping food supplies. It was a little different flying a B-17 over continental Europe and feeling you were actually doing something good .... I remember scaring the life out of a cow, who was trying to gallop ahead of the bomber, very clumsily, and ended up in the canal. I also remember that people spelled out 'thank you' in blooming tulips, so I know when the tulips bloom in Holland. I am delighted to have been part of the operation; I felt good about it at the time and I still do.[114]

Although initially suspicious of the Allied operations, the German forces soon cooperated with the mission. After the first flights, the *Wehrmacht* removed its troops and artillery from the dropping zones. Help even came from unexpected places and in unexpected numbers; in some areas, German soldiers volunteered to help retrieve packages from mine fields, leaving at least one soldier critically wounded. The Dutch also offered their services to such an extent that many of them had to be turned away.[115]

The results of Operation Manna/Chowhound are shown in Table 5.1. While the entire operation was impressive in terms of effort and negotiations to say the least, the outcome for the population was somewhat less extraordinary: the total amount of the drops (7.8 million kilograms) equalled a mere 3 kilograms of food per person in the starving urban west. The psychological value of the food drops for the starving Dutch can, however, hardly be overestimated. In line with the hopes and aspirations of the Allies, the society 'For Women by Women' (*Voor Vrouwen door Vrouwen*) wrote in its minutes on 7 May 1945: 'The arrival of the Allied airplanes dropping packages with food supplies was an unforgettable moment. For many of us, their help came just in time.'[116] Even nutrition expert Dols wrote about the events:

I can be brief about the food drops: it was for everybody in the western Netherlands one of the greatest moments in their lives, when on that Sunday morning allied bombers flew over the city and dropped food instead of bombs on marked airfields. Together with Mr Louwes I stood on the rooftop of the home of Mr A. Th. L. van der Vlugt, member of the Interdenominational Council, watching our salvation emotionally, but also filled with gratitude to all, who had enabled this through courage and sacrifice.[117]

---

[114] Interview author with former USAAF navigator Richard C. Hall, Baltimore, 9 November 2016.

[115] NIOD, 216h, inv.no. 93, Report on food drops.

[116] SR, 124 Genootschap Voor Vrouwen Door Vrouwen, 1809–1977, inv.no. 6, minutes 7 May 1945.

[117] Dols, 'Enkele Persoonlijke Herinneringen aan het Einde van de Hongerwinter, 1945', *Voeding* 16 (1955): 408.

Illustration 13 Operation Manna/Chowhound, food drops onto airfield Valkenburg by USAAF B-17 bomber.

Illustration 14 Food drops at Terbregge, Rotterdam.

Table 5.1 *Number of airplanes and packages delivered to different municipalities from 29 April to 8 May 1945*

City	Number of flights	Number of bags/ packages	Total in kilograms	Central distribution	Soup kitchens, IKB, hospitals, etc.[a]
Alkmaar	88	15,438	130,123	105,012	25,111
Amsterdam	1,179	183,819	1,421,149	1,116,293	304,856
Delft	–	19,849	150,449	104,552	45,897
Dordrecht	–	23,974	179,806	132,843	46,963
Gouda	53	20,818	154,937	113,374	41,563
Den Haag	1,303	236,976	1,876,383	1,435,049	441,334
Haarlem	186	29,248	245,209	177,690	67,519
Hilversum	84	14,748	113,323	92,174	21,149
Leiden	418	85,688	644,681	494,028	150,653
Rotterdam	1,750	334,540	2,416,525	1,701,134	715,391
Utrecht	233	55,721	507,570	401,202	106,368
Total	5,294	1,020,819	7,840,155	5,873,351	1,966,804

[a] Divided as follows: soup kitchens 1,213 tons; hospitals 215 tons; IKB 207 tons; other (e.g., NMA, Forces of the Interior, children's parties) 332 tons.
Source: ELO, 0257, inv.no. 51, Final report on food drops by Directorate of Food Supply, 1945[118]

The airdrops covered a period of time in which the Netherlands was facing the complex transition from war to peace.[119] Following the meeting on 30 April, Seyss-Inquart was summoned to Flensburg by Dönitz;

[118] According to the sum of daily reports on the missions sent to SHAEF, 5,086 airplanes were used, bringing a total of 10,035 tons of supplies, plus an unknown amount on 8 May. Onderwater has calculated that 10,913 tons were dropped from 5,626 airplanes, of which 5,554 were successful flights. However, another Allied report from 8 May indicates that the total amount of food supplies delivered up till then was 5,927 tons. This number corresponds with the total tonnage mentioned in a CBS publication. The final report from Pool also indicates 5,294 airplanes, but calculates of 7,458 tons dropped. The differences are likely a result from the total tons dropped (over 10,000 tons) and usable supplies transported after loss and damage (7,800 tons). The lowest number (5,900) seems to correspond with the total amount ending up in central rationing. Table 5.1 seems thus a reliable representation of the results of the food drops. NARA, 331, Entry 2, Box 118, reports SHAEF from General Dyxhoorn, signed Eisenhower to Dutch government in London, 30 April–8 May 1945. See also: WO 219/20; NIOD, 216h, inv.no. 93. Report on food drops; NIOD, 249-0867, inv. no. 2; Onderwater, *Operatie 'Manna'*, 140–141; CBS, *Economische en Sociale Kroniek der Oorlogsjaren* (Utrecht: W. De Haan, 1947), 216.

[119] Romijn, 'Liberators and Patriots'. An excellent account of the dynamics of political normalisation and reconstruction in neighbouring Belgium is given in: Conway, *The Sorrows of Belgium: Liberation and Political Reconstruction, 1944–1947* (Oxford: Oxford University Press, 2012).

shortly after, he was arrested by the Allied forces occupying Hamburg. The former *Reichskommissar* stated during his Nuremberg trial that he had always felt responsible for finishing the tasks of his administration and had tried everything within his power to return to the Netherlands: 'I was of the opinion that we were in the first row in the hours of triumph and we can lay claim to be in the first row in the time of misery and disaster as well.'[120] On 4 May, Montgomery accepted the unconditional surrender of all German armed forces in northwestern Europe. The following day, Lieutenant General Charles Foulkes of the 1st Canadian Corps summoned General Blaskowitz to Hotel de Wereld in the city of Wageningen to sign a separate document for the implementation of the Instrument of Surrender. After a 24-hour consultation period, Blaskowitz returned to discuss the technical execution of the surrender of his armed forces. The German occupation had officially ended, and relief could now finally pour in.

The Greatest Stockpile in Europe

The transition from occupation to liberation began with a period of interim rule by the Allied military command. In late February 1945, General Edwards had been replaced by Major General John G. W. Clark as chief of the SHAEF Mission Netherlands, and the latter finally pushed for the preparation of relief. The constant pressure from the Dutch government had revealed a lack of long-term planning. In addition, it had become clear that, as a result of the Ardennes offensive, the 21st Army Group had diverted stockpiles meant for the B2 area (i.e., the western provinces) to the urgent needs of Belgium. Furthermore, after appointing Galloway as head of the West Holland District, Montgomery burdened the commander with his own army division, making his civilian responsibilities subordinate to his military position. Towards the end of March, Galloway's West Holland District was renamed the Netherlands District and, with Clark's support, commenced making detailed plans: first, to replenish the stockpiles to the original 30,000 tons and then to steadily increase these supplies until a sufficient quantity was reached for the relief of all people still living under occupation.[121]

Awaiting the day of liberation with great anxiety, Allied Civil Affairs and NMA officers in the south began working on 'the greatest grocery

---

[120] NIOD, 458, inv.no. 24, Nuremberg Trial Seyss-Inquart, 11 June 1946, 11434.
[121] Gerbrandy, *Eenige Hoofdpunten*, 147; Donnison, *Civil Affairs and Military Government*, 143; De Jong, *Het Koninkrijk* 10b, 1109–1110; Moore, 'The Western Allies', 105–106.

stockpile in Europe'. An agreement between SHAEF and the Dutch government dictated that the latter was responsible for the reception of supplies, adequate distribution, as well as for taking all reasonable steps to make use of local resources.[122] In the early stages, military assistance would be given for guarding and handling the supplies, but the NMA was to assume responsibility for transportation and distribution as soon as possible. The NMA's Emergency Supply Commission (*Commissariaat Noodvoorziening*), in collaboration with the regular Dutch food administration, would play a central role in these executive relief tasks.[123] In order to honour the Allied relief responsibilities, the 21st Army Group approved of meeting the bill of 18,000 personnel – men and women – requested by the Netherlands District to carry out its duties.[124]

Following the Achterveld Agreement, on 2 May 1945, the first Canadian-built Dodge trucks as part of Operation Faust, filled with food supplies, drove from liberated Rhenen towards the occupied city of Utrecht. Once in enemy territory, the trucks were handed over to Dutch drivers, who were given a half hour's crash course in handling them, as they had not driven gasoline-powered vehicles for a long time. In total, the trucks brought 5,200 tons of food supplies through enemy lines: among other things, these supplies contained lard, canned meat, biscuits, and sugar – all high-density foodstuffs high in calorific value.[125] One of the drivers explained to a local journalist that it felt extremely strange to be transporting food into German-occupied territory. The German police present avoided discussing the current military situation but expressed that they had enough of war and that 'this food business was very nice' but that 'the main thing for America and Great Britain to do would be to fight Bolshevism and save Europe'.[126] On 5 May, Allied relief was strengthened by the first two relief coasters arriving in Rotterdam, followed by a steady supply of food and coal by sea every three days. The B2 stockpiles by that time comprised 32,162 tons on the ground in Belgium and South Holland, 11,300 tons in barges and coasters in harbours, 71,831 tons in the UK, and 53,000 tons in the US. Together, the Allied supplies aimed to, at the very least,

[122] NARA, 331, Entry 2, Box 118, Instructions for Civil Affairs Supplies SHAEF signed Newman, 10 March 1945.
[123] De Guingand, *Operation Victory*, 438–439; Gerbrandy, *Eenige Hoofdpunten*, 146–147; Van Baarle, *Slag om B2*, 13–20.
[124] NARA, 331, Entry 152, Box 264, Fortnightly report SHAEF Mission Netherlands, 15 March 1945.
[125] Van Baarle, *De Slag om B2*, 59; UN, AG 18-004, S-1245-0000-0365, 'The Blessings of Food', 4 May 1945.
[126] UN, AG 18-004, S-1245-0000-0365, 'Food Supply Continues', 5 May 1945.

help cover the agreed sixty days' maintenance period in May and June 1945.[127]

Relief was now pouring in via air, road, and sea; yet, the scarcity of transportation and the deplorable state of the country's infrastructure seriously delayed internal distribution. As explained in Chapter 4, inundations, German requisitioning, fuel scarcity, and destroyed harbours and waterways had disrupted the food system to such an extent that the food supply could not resume immediately. The food crisis that prevailed after the liberation was thus, again, a transportation rather than a supply problem. It was not until 10 May before Allied relief began reaching the public in significant amounts.

And even then, with only 3 kilograms of food per urban dweller, the food parcels collected from the airdrops seemed painfully insufficient to feed people outside the principal towns in the west. Moreover, the variety of the products made sorting and distributing a difficult task. For example, 5 grams of dried meat was equalised to 10 grams of boneless meat, while 10 grams of potato puree was equal to 50 grams of potatoes.[128] In the week after liberation the free distribution in Red Cross stores raised rations to 773 kcal for adults, 1,048 kcal for children aged 4–13 years, and even 1,763 kcal for infants. Again, this emphasis on infant rations seems remarkable. The following week, when more Allied supplies from land and sea began reaching the large towns and the Emergency Supply Commission started its distribution, rations increased by an additional 300 kcal. During the second half of May, relief distribution began to run more smoothly and, in the week of 27 May, adult rations exceeded the magical 2,000 kcal, all thanks to the Allied relief supplies.

In addition to food supplies, another major Allied contribution to relieving the Dutch was made by the so-called Medical Feeding Teams. Before the liberation, SHAEF had appointed a nutrition committee consisting of Dutch, Belgian, and British experts, who were assigned the task of devising plans for dealing with cases of acute starvation. Further to this plan, the NMA recruited volunteers from the liberated areas, who were subsequently trained in a special school set up by the Red Cross under supervision of Dr G. C. E. Burger, the general director of Section VIII of Public Health. Several days before the Armistice, the German authorities had admitted a special mission of these Allied

---

[127] NARA, 331, Entry 2, Box 118, Message SHAEF signed Eisenhower to Dutch Government, 4 May 1945; Report 7 May 1945.
[128] NIOD, 216h, inv.no. 91, Circular letter Dols to soup kitchens, 3 May 1945; ELO, 0257, inv.no. 51, Final report on food drops; Van Baarle, *De Slag om B2*, 75–76.

nutritionists, headed by Drummond, permitting them to connect with Dutch public health authorities in order to prepare a medical mission. After the unconditional surrender, 51 Medical Feeding Teams – formed by one physician, one head nurse, five nurses, five social workers, two drivers and one administrator – under command of Lieutenant Colonel Laman Trip were rushed into the western provinces. Another 61 relief teams were deployed to provide social aid to various categories of displaced persons.[129] Along with the Medical Feeding Teams, nutritional survey teams proceeded with rapid clinical and dietary surveys in the recently liberated areas, the main results of which have been discussed in Chapters 3 and 4.

First appearances of the people's condition had proven most deceptive, SHAEF concluded several days after the liberation. On the advent of the Allied troops, the soldiers were greeted with cheers and bunting; but it was an enthusiasm that concealed the suffering that was still going on behind closed doors. General Clark stressed the reality in his report: 'It is an empty country, inhabited by the hungry, and in the towns, a semi-starved population .... It is no exaggeration to state that, had liberation been delayed for another 10 days or so, many thousands of people would surely have died of hunger.'[130] The Allies also arrived at this valid conclusion after receiving the first reports from the Medical Feeding Teams, which went door-to-door and consulted local physicians to find malnourished people. The teams had divided the affected population into three groups eligible for aid: 'normal underfed' people (25 per cent body weight loss), actual starvation (e.g., cachexia, pronounced oedema), and those with medical complications. Emergency hospitals became swamped with emaciated patients, many of them moribund or in an otherwise critical condition. In all, the teams treated about 28,000 patients in cooperation with municipalities and IKB polyclinics. Of these people, 3,000 were treated in hospital. Emergency food aid was distributed to almost 190,000 people.[131]

After providing initial emergency aid to those most in need, the Allied military administrators worked with local and national relief authorities

---

[129] NARA, 331, Entry 152, Box 264, Fortnightly report SHAEF Mission Netherlands, 15 April 1945; UN, AG 18-004, S-1245-0000-0769, Welfare notes, 30 June 1945; Banning, 'Occupied Holland', 540; Burger et al., *Malnutrition and Starvation*, vol. 1, 34–35; Donnison, *Civil Affairs and Military Government*, 143–144; De Jong, *Het Koninkrijk* 10b, 1113.

[130] NARA, 331, Entry 2, Box 118, Message SHAEF Mission NL Clark to SHAEF Mission NL Rear, 10 May 1945; Entry 152, Box 264, Fortnightly report SHAEF Mission Netherlands, 15 May 1945.

[131] Burger et al., *Malnutrition and Starvation*, vol. 1, 48–57.

towards restoration of the centralised state. Most of these bodies had roots in resistance groups and civil society. Significantly, in all relief agencies, women occupied central positions, which was much less the case in the pre-war Netherlands and thus demonstrates Dutch women's enhanced public roles during the war and in the direct post-war period.[132] In February 1945, the NMA authorised Relief Aid Red Cross (*Hulpactie Rode Kruis*: HARK) to coordinate all charitable initiatives in the south, functioning as a federation of voluntary agencies closely linked to the actual Red Cross.[133] Several other important relief funds and committees collected supplies abroad. In another example, in March and April 1945, the campaign 'South Helps North' managed to collect 90,000 food parcels in addition to clothes, shoes, and furniture.[134] Ironically, only a few weeks after liberation, when the west managed to recover due to the Allied relief supplies, an opposite campaign 'North helps South' was established, to aid the war-stricken part of the country.

Much earlier, in late October 1944, the Dutch government in London had enforced the constitution of the Dutch People's Reconstruction Movement (*Nederlands Volksherstel*: NVH) to coordinate the collection of supplies for purposes of relief from all parties that desired to be involved.[135] Working closely together with the NVH, another important role was assumed by the Union for Female Volunteers (*Unie voor Vrouwelijke Vrijwilligers*: UVV), who had local departments spread throughout the country. Established in 1938, the UVV managed to occupy a central role in the overall relief movement, respected and consulted upon by the generally male-dominated post-war institutions.[136]

The influence of military interim rule on relief practices was thus limited to matters of provision and supervision. Contrary to relief practices in other European countries, UNRRA only played a minor role. In early 1945, the Dutch government became increasingly sceptical about the utility of UNRRA and Gerbrandy even pressed for complete

---

[132] NARA, 331, Entry 2, Box 118, Letter Central Committee Netherlands Red Cross Eindhoven to Eisenhower, 29 April 1945; Hoffmann et al., 'Introduction', 9–14; Romijn, 'Liberators and Patriots', 127–130.

[133] See, for example, Utrechts Archief [UA], 831-9 Nederlandse Rode Kruis Hulpkorps, Sociale Verbindingsgroep S-1, inv.no. 4, 6; Ed de Neve (pseud. Willem J. M. Lenglet), *Nederlandsch Roode Kruis Hulpkorps: Zijn Ontstaan en Zijn Arbeid* (The Hague: Van Stockum, 1945).

[134] De Jong, *Het Koninkrijk* 10b, 1114–1115; GA, 63, inv.no. 179, Newsletter HARK 1944, 15 March 1945.

[135] GA, 63, inv.no. 179, Bulletin American Council of Voluntary Agencies for Foreign Service, Sub-Committee on the Netherlands, 1 October 1945.

[136] UA, 756 Stichting Nederlands Volksherstel, afdeling Utrecht, inv.no. 123, Report on activities UVV, June 1945.

withdrawal. Supposedly, the UNRRA machinery was too cumbersome and formalistic, with no special benefits for its contributing countries. But UNRRA's European supply responsibility was to begin six months after liberation, so they were reluctant to authorise procurements in advance of liberation. Eventually, by the time UNRRA's responsibilities in the Netherlands should have commenced, there was no need for permanent representation anymore, as the military authorities had already arranged all relief in light of the envisioned political transition.[137] This distinguished the Netherlands from Greece, among other countries, which received massive aid and relied predominantly on UNRRA to meet the most immediate needs.[138] In the Netherlands, UNRRA did secure supplies of agricultural machinery, seeds, clothing, textiles, as well as medical and sanitation supplies, which were all also desperately needed for the social and economic reconstruction of the country.[139]

The Allied relief responsibility was never meant to last long beyond liberation. Thus, shortly after military operations in Europe had ceased, SHAEF decided that its civilian responsibility needed to be terminated at the earliest possible date.[140] With the return of the government, on 31 May 1945, the SHAEF Mission Netherlands was formally accredited to Queen Wilhelmina and moved to The Hague. The Netherlands District handed over its responsibility for the civilian supply to the NMA and Dutch civil authorities on 1 July when mobility and the food supply had more or less resumed.[141] At that time, Eisenhower had also instructed that the first or 'military phase' of the operation in the Netherlands had ended. Now, in accordance with the Agreement of 16 May 1944, full responsibility for the civil administration in the Netherlands would be resumed by the government.[142] On 14 July, SHAEF dissolved, and the SHAEF Mission to the Netherlands ceased to exist.[143]

---

[137] TNA, FO 37/-41163, Correspondence Sir G. Rendel and Mr Hall, 17, 22, 23, 28 November 1944; UN, AG 18-003, S-1209-0000-0406, Minutes of meeting of Administrative Council, 5 March 1945.

[138] Voglis, 'The Politics of Reconstruction: Foreign Aid and State Authority in Greece, 1945–1947', in *Seeking Peace*, 277–284.

[139] UN, AG 18-003, S-1228-0000-0076, Analysis of the Lamping memorandum, 3 February 1945.

[140] NARA, 331, Entry 2, Box 118, Letter SHAEF Main signed Eisenhower to 21st Army Group and SHAEF Missions NL and B, 12 May 1945.

[141] NARA, 331, Entry 2, Box 41, Letter Bedell Smith to Clark, 20 May 1945; Romijn, 'Liberators and Patriots', 140.

[142] NARA, 331, Entry 2, Box 118, Letter Clark to Netherlands Government, 4 July 1945.

[143] The SHAEF Mission Netherlands was actually split into an American and British element, working as integrated headquarters until all major tasks were completed or could be terminated. NARA, 331, Entry 152, Box 264, Fortnightly report SHAEF Mission Netherlands, 30 June 1945; Entry 1, Box 41, Letter Colonel Jones on

However, because of the continuing transportation and subsequent distribution problems, the 1st Canadian Army remained in the Netherlands for a longer period and in greater strength than originally planned. Aid at this stage was mainly offered in the form of harvesting, clearance of debris in war-damaged cities, and bulk transports.[144] The Allies certainly could not bring instant relief to all troubles – extreme shortages of clothing and textiles, not to mention the lack of fuel and raw materials, continued to persist. Nevertheless, by the end of July, the food supply was relatively regular and adequate, which was largely thanks to the achievements of the Civil Affairs mission and the B2 stockpiles, which by October had imported nearly 840,000 tons of food. In addition, government imports of food and the 1945 harvest of grains, pulses, oil seeds, and root crops especially contributed to the country's recovery.[145] By the second half of 1945, the average national level of consumption was estimated at 2,600 kcal per daily capita, ranking the Netherlands once again among the highest levels of Western Europe.[146]

Conclusion

The politics and practices of Allied relief during the Dutch food crisis were characterised by continuous tensions between military strategies and humanitarian concerns. Despite the lengthy and detailed negotiation process, the main impact of the Allied contribution to relieving the famine took place only after the war had ended. Throughout the famine, the terms of humanitarian aid were always determined by the political and military situation. Ultimately, the severe restrictions imposed on the Red Cross shipments thwarted the institution of a regular relief scheme, subsequently preventing the shipments from achieving their full potential to alleviate the crisis. The contribution of the famous airdrops was mostly symbolic, which was exactly what the Allies had wanted. For them, the food drops were a political instrument, important for their legitimacy and post-war power relations as it contributed to verifying an end to the war in a visible and spectacular fashion. Because of the continuing transportation and distribution problems, it was not until the end of May

termination duties of HQ Netherlands District, 30 June 1945; Donnison, *Civil Affairs and Military Government,* 150–151.

[144] NARA, 331, Entry 152, Box 264, Fortnightly report SHAEF Mission Netherlands, 15 July 1945.

[145] *Final Report of the Supply and Economics Branch, G-5/CA of the British and USFET Military Mission to the Netherlands* (formerly SHAEF mission to the Netherlands) (S.l.: s.n., 1945).

[146] Lindberg, *Food, Famine, Relief,* 83–84.

1945 that the military authorities managed to establish a regular food supply. Nevertheless, the Allied provision of post-war relief, both nutritionally and medically, ensured that famine conditions ended not long after liberation. In July 1945, the Allied military relief responsibility in the Netherlands seemed completed and civil authority was assumed by the interim Dutch government. In this respect, the Allies not only played a prominent role in the economic and social recovery of the famine-affected areas, but, more broadly, had a significant influence in the restructuring of the post-war Netherlands. Significantly, the meagre contribution that Allied relief made to the people's diets during the war certainly indicates that most Dutch people survived the famine conditions through resources other than official rations and state-provided relief; an argument that will be further explored in the following chapters.

6   Coping at Household and Individual Levels

In March 1945, an intelligence agent in the occupied Netherlands wrote to the government in London: 'Starvation is an experience that cannot be compared with anything else: he who has no experience with it himself will always remain like a person born blind to whom one tries to describe colour ... with my own eyes I saw a man, between Schiedam and Rotterdam, scraping horse-dung together to pick out the grains of oats.'[1] The informant's account is telling of the ways in which the struggle for food and fuel dominated daily life during the last months of occupation. 'Everything is about food and fire', as one man wrote in his diary.[2] Hunger incited people to consume food substitutes such as tulip bulbs, sugar beets, and beech nuts; some even resorted to eating cats, dogs, pigeons, or seagulls to battle their hunger.[3]

The overall deprivation changed cityscapes drastically as well. A female office clerk observed: 'Compared to the once so vibrant city, where you could "eat from the street" Amsterdam has turned into a ruin, treeless and disgusting.'[4] Standards of hygiene declined dramatically as a consequence of the famine. A combined lack of soap and hot water and an explosion of fleas, lice, and nits haunted most city households.[5] To make matters worse, infrequent garbage collection due to a lack of transportation, manpower, and fuel resulted in landfill sites in parks and on city fringes while overflowing sewage systems filled the air with

---

[1] NARA, 331, Entry 2, Box 118, Report 'The Occupied Netherlands To-day and To-morrow', 17 March 1945.

[2] J. L. van Riemsdijk, *Hongerwinter: Dagboek* (S.l.: s.n., s.a.), 5 January 1945. See also: Kees Slager, Nienke Feis, and Paul van der Graag, *Hongerwinter: Verhalen om te Onthouden* (Amsterdam: Link, 1985), 84–92. Names of the interviewees in this book are fictitious.

[3] Slager et al., *Hongerwinter*, 82; Van der Zee, *De Hongerwinter*, 116–117; Voglis, 'Surviving Hunger', 27.

[4] NIOD, 244, inv.no. 1520, Diary M. T. (30-year-old female office clerk in Amsterdam), 7 February 1945.

[5] De Jong, *Het Koninkrijk* 10b, 195–196, 209–210; Slager et al., *Verhalen om te Onthouden*, 55–58.

nauseating smells.[6] The end of German rule might have been in sight, but for most city dwellers in the western Netherlands it was impossible to see beyond the parasites, refuse, and their ever-present hunger.

Yet, despite the horrific circumstances posed by the food and fuel shortage, the Dutch did not fall into apathy. As Chapter 4 has already suggested, many urbanites were able to fend for themselves to some extent, finding ways to acquire food and fuel outside legal channels. As historian Jan Romein put it shortly after the war: 'After September 1944 … every buyer and seller became a black marketeer, for otherwise both the one and the other would have perished from hunger.'[7] Scholars have stressed that wartime black markets were always contradictory in this respect, functioning as a means of survival but, at the same time, draining those economic resources that could actually battle inequalities.[8] This chapter investigates these often clandestine responses to the famine at individual and household levels, at the intersection of competing senses of entitlement, legitimacy, justice, and power that were all bound up with the daily struggle to meet individual supply needs. As strategies commonly deployed in times of famine, this chapter focuses on crime, black-market trade, food expeditions, and fuel gathering. Indeed, these coping strategies showed major similarities to comparable modern famines and food crises in German-occupied Europe.[9]

Crime and Impunity

During the German occupation, crime rates in the Netherlands grew well above pre-war levels. With foodstuffs, fuel, household items, textiles, and shoes becoming increasingly more scarce, people turned to clandestine ways of obtaining these items, outside legal channels. A shift in the nature of reported crime reflects this development. Economic criminal offenses rose while violent and sexual offenses declined – a trend that was also seen in the rest of occupied Europe as well as in Great Britain.

---

[6] *Jaarverslag van Amsterdam 1945*, 2; Dienstverslagen 1944 Gemeente Amsterdam, Dienst Stadsreiniging, 5; Dienstverslagen 1944 Gemeente Amsterdam, Schoonmaakdienst en Gemeentewasserij, 5–6; Van der Pauw, *Rotterdam in de Tweede Wereldoorlog*, 638–639; Van der Boom, *Den Haag in de Tweede Wereldoorlog*, 232.

[7] Romein, 'The Spirit of the Dutch People', 177.

[8] Mark Roodhouse, 'Popular Morality and the Black Market in Britain, 1939–1945', in *Food and Conflict in Europe*, 243–265; Voglis, 'Surviving Hunger', 25; Klemann and Kudryashov, *Occupied Economies*, 387.

[9] Ó Gráda, *Famine*, 52–54; Ó Gráda, *Black '47 and Beyond*, 104–114; Arnold, *Famine*, 91; Hionidou, *Famine and Death in Occupied Greece*, 35, 87–104; Paul Steege, *Black Market, Cold War: Everyday Life in Berlin, 1946–1949* (Cambridge: Cambridge University Press, 2007), 14. See also: Tönsmeyer et al. *Coping with Hunger and Shortage under German Occupation* Part II.

Throughout the country, crime rates reached a peak in 1942. From that year onward, economic crime – for the largest part theft – comprised over 90 per cent of all reported criminal offenses. This partly resulted from the criminalisation of economic offenses instigated by the occupier, which after 1941 placed economic courts under strict German supervision. In June 1942, *Arbeitseinsatzlager* Erika in Ommen was designated to punish war-related economic violations such as black-market trade, thereby 'relieving' the overburdened prisons.[10] Although the source materials on the Hunger Winter period are extremely fragmentary and sometimes contradictory, they all allude to the increase of criminal activity; after September 1944, crime in the urban west reached new heights.

As one of the prime examples of famine-specific criminality, looting increased exponentially. In the early autumn of 1944, women and children in Amsterdam, Rotterdam, and The Hague began collectively plundering bakery carts; their bold actions triggered by increasing shortages combined with growing German repression. The large-scale raids on adult men had torn families apart, leaving the burden of the crisis to fall on women with exceptional severity. In Rotterdam, by 24 November 1944, 24 bakery carts had already been robbed by the public. On one single day in January in Amsterdam, a mob of women stole 80 loaves of bread from a cart in the city centre, another mob looted a bakery in the east of the city, while yet another stole a cart with 20 hl (one hl equals about 70 kilograms) of potatoes designated for the soup kitchens. One driver was beaten to death while trying to protect his cargo, although sources remain unclear whether women and children were responsible for this act. In The Hague, looting was at an all-time high when the Nazi hunt on adult men was in full force and people were forbidden to go out into the streets. Women at this point were infuriated with the authorities and defied these orders without precedent.[11] As a warning, German authorities put up pamphlets stating that looters would be executed and immediately put these words into action. An eyewitness wrote: 'On

---

[10] J. C. Hudig, 'De Criminaliteit in Rotterdam tijdens den Oorlog', *Mensch en Maatschappij* 21 (1946): 343; Rijk Rijksen, *Criminaliteit en Bezetting* (Assen: Van Gorcum, 1956), 53–54; Peter Hoving, 'Oorlog en Kriminaliteit', MA thesis, Vrije Universiteit Amsterdam (1985), 34–60; Futselaar, *Gevangenissen in Oorlogstijd 1940–1945* (Amsterdam: Boom, 2015), 95–103. For political offences, the Germans also opened concentration camps in Amersfoort and Vught.

[11] NIOD, 244, inv.no. 1023, Diary M. S. (male town clerk Rotterdam), 24 November 1944; NIOD, 244, inv.no. 1129, Diary H. H. (senior official municipality of Amsterdam), 4 January and 2 February 1945; SR, 273, inv.no. 119, Diary N. D. (female teacher HBS Rotterdam), 13 December 1944, 21 April 1945. See also: Van der Pauw, *Rotterdam in de Tweede Wereldoorlog*, 598, 608–609; Slager et al., *Verhalen om te Onthouden*, 147–150.

Spui Square, a 16-year-old boy tried to plunder Hus' bakery. He then had to write on a large sign "I am a looter", was shot by the Germans forthwith, and lay publicly on the street for 24 hours for everyone to see.'[12] Two women were shot for theft in other parts of the city that same day. Rumours about these events spread throughout the country, leading some to believe that the Germans quelled the lootings in The Hague with no less than 30 deaths.[13] By contrast, looting seems not to have played a significant role in Utrecht. Crime expert Rijk Rijksen explains this by emphasising the 'calm and individualistic nature' of the urban population, as well as the absence of large raids and demolitions.[14]

Petty crime and thieving became widespread during the famine as well. In the Zuider hospital in Rotterdam everything edible had to be locked away because it would otherwise be stolen by patients and staff alike.[15] A large number of these petty criminals were children, many of them acting on instructions from their parents. During the famine, hordes of children roamed the streets, knocking on doors to beg for food. In former shopping streets, women and children sang for food scraps instead of coins. Others were involved in illegal street trade, petty theft, and demolishing empty houses, parks, and streets to retrieve firewood.[16] 'Basically, you did nothing else than gather food and fuel all day. That was it', recalled Koos, a young boy at the time, from Amsterdam.[17]

Schools closed for prolonged periods or otherwise followed adjusted schedules due to the fuel shortage. And even when they were open, many children did not attend. In Amsterdam, in the autumn of 1944, about 20 per cent of the schoolchildren were absent; in February 1945, this number rose as high as 40 per cent.[18] Disintegrated family life due to the occupier's repressive measures, a malfunctioning juvenile police force, over-burdened juvenile court system, and the shutdown of youth

---

[12] NIOD, 0332, inv.no. L11, letter W. M. to family in Amsterdam, 24 November 1944. See also: 26 January 1945; NIOD, 244, inv.no. 2805, Diary S. P.-B. (female nurse in The Hague), 22 November 1944; Slager et al., *Verhalen om te Onthouden*, 149–150; Koster, *Honger in Rotterdam*, 14–15; Frank A. M. van Riet, *Handhaven onder de Nieuwe Orde: De Politieke Geschiedenis van de Rotterdamse Politie tijdens de Tweede Wereldoorlog* (Zaltbommel: April, 2008), 611–612.

[13] NIOD, 0332, inv.no. 25, Letter Nunspeet to Groningen, 14 December 1944.

[14] Rijksen, *Criminaliteit en Bezetting*, 46. See also: De Jong, *Het Koninkrijk* 10b, 191–192; Arnold, *Famine*, 86–91.

[15] Bok, *De Kliniek der Hongerziekte*, 32–33.

[16] SA, 5225, inv.no. 7284, Report on City Brigade Amsterdam, February–December 1944; NIOD, 244, inv.no. 1129, 2 March 1945; *Jaarverslag van Amsterdam 1944*, 138; *Jaarverslag van Amsterdam 1945*, 150; *Jaarverslag van Amsterdam 1945*, II, 1–2; Slager et al., *Verhalen om te Onthouden*, 105–114; Van Riet, *Handhaven onder de Nieuwe Orde*, 618.

[17] Slager et al., *Verhalen om te Onthouden*, 84.   [18] *Jaarverslag van Amsterdam*, II, 2–3.

associations contributed to youth criminality as well. Moreover, the disorganisation of the legal system in the occupied areas meant that petty offenders who were somehow arrested were rarely prosecuted.[19]

Yet not all criminality during the famine was petty or individual by nature. A strong increase in organised crime was recorded in both the cities and the countryside.[20] Broadly speaking, two groups can be distinguished: one appealing to the authority of the German occupier and the other to that of the resistance. Men, dressed in German *Wehrmacht* or SS uniforms and often in the presence of Dutchmen, robbed people in the city streets on a daily basis.[21] The same was true for the countryside, farms in particular were target of German-Dutch robberies. Their pickings were symptomatic of the widespread deprivation: where once money and valuables were the main objective, now the loot mostly comprised more essential items: foodstuffs, clothes, and other textiles, shoes, and bicycles.[22]

Resistance groups also often appropriated German uniforms to further their own plans; for example, while robbing distribution offices for the purpose of stealing identity cards and ration carts, just like before the crisis.[23] But as the value of coupons decreased and became localised, more foodstuffs-in-kind were needed to feed people in hiding, whose numbers had swelled after the railway strike. Disguised in German or Dutch police uniforms, they made it clear to their victims they were on the 'good side' and that the products they stole were designated for their patriotic struggle, although, death threats were not uncommon.[24] In some cases, the legitimacy of the resistance was plainly abused. In Rotterdam, a gang of about 50 men under the leadership of Jan Steketee had infiltrated the anti-German *Ordedienst*. In the name of the resistance, they confiscated goods on a daily basis, selling them to the Germans or trading them on the black market until Steketee was eliminated and the rest of his gang arrested.[25]

---

[19] Hudig, 'De Criminaliteit in Rotterdam', 348.

[20] Van der Pauw, *Rotterdam in de Tweede Wereldoorlog*, 641.

[21] NIOD, 244, inv.no. 1121, 4 January 1945; inv.no. 1520, 27 January 1945; Van Riet, *Handhaven onder de Nieuwe Orde*, 621–623.

[22] NIOD, 0331, inv.no. C8, Report Feldgendarmerie The Hague, December 1944.

[23] NIOD, 0331, 216K Departement van Justitie, inv.no. 314, Police reports on investigations into armed robberies banks and population registers. Between October 1942 and August 1944, the CDK recorded over 180 of these robberies across the country, some involving thousands of cards. NA, 2.06.037 Centraal Distributiekantoor, inv.no. 278, Documents on robberies of distribution offices, 1942–1944.

[24] NIOD, 216K, inv.no. 301, Police Reports on muggings, armed robberies, theft, and fire in several municipalities in District Arnhem, 1944–1945.

[25] Van der Pauw, *Rotterdam in de Tweede Wereldoorlog*, 644–645.

Most reported crimes during the famine were thus connected to the food system. For instance, in 1945, multiple large burglaries took place at RBVVO warehouses and abattoirs, where food supplies were stored for central rationing and soup kitchens. In these cases, the German authorities were usually notified with additional punitive interference by the Dutch *Landwacht*, a group of armed members of the National Socialist Movement (NSB) who had received police tasks on the initiative of Rauter from March 1945 onward.[26] At a local level, theft and corruption at distribution offices and soup kitchens also became problematic. According to the chief of the Central Rationing Office, officials who were caught usually stated that they had acted on the orders of resistance groups.[27] In a more extreme yet less harmful example, during the height of the famine, some hard-up families hid the corpses of their deceased family members so they could collect their rations.[28] In addition to these offences, black marketeering and crimes against price regulations also increased. As mentioned, the German authorities took extreme measures to combat professional black marketeering. On 19 February 1945, for example, German soldiers carried out a raid against black marketeers near Rotterdam's Noordplein, killing two people and injuring six.[29]

Based on the accounts from qualitative sources, one would expect reported crime rates to have risen exponentially during the winter of 1944–1945. However, crime statistics from the largest and most affected cities show quite the opposite. Indeed, official police reports on criminal offenses and violations reached an absolute low during 1944–1945, even compared to pre- and post-war crime rates. Rotterdam was a perfect example of this phenomenon, where total violations and offenses actually halved in 1944 compared to the previous years (from 29,138 to 15,086) and halved again in 1945 (8,721).[30] In Amsterdam, The Hague, and Utrecht, crime statistics in the years 1944–1945 show a similar pattern although less pronounced. Violent crimes and sexual offenses barely

---

[26] NIOD, 086, inv.no. 81, Reports The Hague police to Beauftragte des Reichskommissars, 1945; NA, 2.11.30.06, inv.no. 155, Correspondence Hauptabteiling E und L and RBVVO The Hague, March-April 1945; inv.no. 164, Letter CK Dordrecht to Chief of Mass Feeding greater Dordrecht and Zwijndrecht District, 2 March 1945.

[27] SR, 444-02 Gemeentesecretarie Rotterdam, Afdeling Algemene Zaken, inv.no. 364, Municipal report over 1945; NIOD, 212a, inv.no. 167, Diary Hirschfeld, 9 April 1945.

[28] Feltkamp, *De Begrafenismoeilijkheden in 1945 te Amsterdam*, 47–50. These acts were seen in besieged Leningrad and occupied Greece as well. Mazower, *Inside Hitler's Greece: The Experience of Occupation 1941–1944* (New Haven: Yale University Press, 1993), 38–41; Hionidou, *Famine and Death in Occupied Greece*, 28; Ó Gráda, *Famine*, 54.

[29] Van Riet, *Handhaven onder de Nieuwe Orde*, 606–607.

[30] *Jaarcijfers der Gemeente Rotterdam 1942–1947*, 84.

featured during the last months of war, which might be explained by the fact that food deprivation weakened people and reduced their libido. The additional facts that alcohol was hardly obtainable during the crisis and that theatres and dance halls were closed might have played a role here too; although, it is impossible to make any affirmative statements about this.[31]

Other studies, however, have demonstrated that reported crimes and violations were much higher than these official police reports let on. J. C. Hudig has shown that, of all crimes reported in Rotterdam, theft and burglary featured most prominently. The number of reported burglaries in 1945 was even twice as high as in 1942. The record was set in February 1945 with 1,101 reported break-ins in one month: over 4 times the total number in 1939. Rotterdam police records state that from all reported thefts, on average only one out of seven investigated cases was solved.[32]

For Amsterdam, monthly statistics are available, which are shown in Figure 6.1. Examining the number of reported thefts in correspondence with overall reported criminal offenses and violations clearly demonstrates how theft dominated during the crisis, outlining a distinct pattern compared to pre- and post-crisis criminality. As per Figure 6.1, the lowest number of reports is seen for September 1944, which was likely connected to the expectation that the Netherlands would soon be liberated. In October, reported crime began rising again, reaching a peak in March 1945 – it was not by chance that this peak coincided with the height of the famine. Theft, as an economic crime, declined after the war, although overall reported crimes rose. This seems to indicate that the proportionally high economic crime levels were indeed a distinct famine trait.

Comparing these official reports to personal statements and witnesses, these statistics hardly seem a reliable indicator of criminal activity. The 'dark figure' of unrecorded crime makes these figures a reflection of enforcement and reporting activity rather than of the extent of illegal behaviour. First of all, victims were less likely to report a crime if the perpetrator was not expected to be found, if there was only a small chance of getting stolen goods back, or if authorities punished too

---

[31] Gemeentelijk Bureau voor de Statistiek Rotterdam, *Jaarcijfers der Gemeente Rotterdam 1942–1947* (Rotterdam: Gemeentelijk Bureau voor de Statistiek, 1949), 84; *Maandberichten Amsterdam*, 1938–1946; Bureau voor de Statistiek en Voorlichting Gemeente's Gravenhage, *Statistisch Jaarboek 1946* (The Hague: Trio, 1948), 39; *Statistische Berichten 1946 der Gemeente Utrecht*, 17; Hudig, 'De Criminaliteit in Rotterdam', 245–246, 343.
[32] Hudig, 'De Criminaliteit in Rotterdam', 346–347.

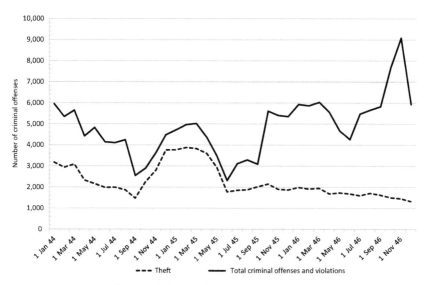

Figure 6.1 Reported theft and total reported criminal offenses and violations in Amsterdam, 1944–1946.
Source: Maandberichten Amsterdam, 1944–1946

harshly.[33] Secondly, prosecution of offenses suffered a severe setback because of the transportation difficulties and other circumstances of war. In cities such as Rotterdam, Schiedam, and The Hague, the civil service had been decimated because of the raids on adult men. In anticipation of one such raid, on 8 November, German authorities in Rotterdam even took away the police's firearms, returning only a small number more than a month later.[34] Thirdly, policemen also struggled with the overall deprivation, slowed down by the cold and hunger.[35] One additional explanation is that it was common knowledge that the German occupation was coming to an end and that, for many individual policemen still on duty, the boundaries between illegal and legal behaviour blurred in

---

[33] Hudig, 'De Criminaliteit in Rotterdam', 341–342.

[34] NA, 2.06.082, inv.no. 2, Report November–December 1944. Even without raids on adult men, in early 1945 only 1,200 policemen worked in Amsterdam, compared to their pre-war strength of 2,200. Hoving, 'Oorlog en Kriminaliteit', 57; Van der Pauw, *Rotterdam in de Tweede Wereldoorlog*, 598, 607; Geraldien von Frijtag Drabbe Künzel, *Het Recht van de Sterkste: Duitse Strafrechtspleging in Bezet Nederland* (Amsterdam: Bert Bakker, 1999), 220–227; Futselaar, *Gevangenissen in Oorlogstijd*, 169–175.

[35] Hudig, 'De Criminaliteit in Rotterdam', 342; Guus J. J. Meershoek, *Dienaren van het Gezag: De Amsterdamse Politie tijdens de Bezetting* (Amsterdam: Van Gennep 1999), 335–337.

the face of deprivation and extreme repression, which led them to look the other way when witnessing such activities.

The Urban Black Market

Black markets became an integral part of daily life during the food crisis. Before 1944, about 20–25 per cent of the agrarian production had flowed into black markets, which was relatively low compared to the degree of illegal production and consumption in almost every other occupied country in Europe.[36] But, with the disintegration of the central rationing system in the autumn of 1944 and the subsequent decreasing rations, black-market consumption changed from a welcome dietary addition into an absolute necessity for survival. Clandestine agricultural production rose to 43 per cent in 1944 and stayed at this level in the following year.[37] Instead of qualifying as a form of resistance against the German occupier, black-market trade was now portrayed and seen by state authorities and resistance groups alike as a 'crime against society'.[38]

During the food crisis, black markets underwent three fundamental changes: (1) prices rose exponentially; (2) monetary transactions diminished and barter became dominant; and (3) the black market became more than ever a plurality of local markets, differing greatly in supply and prices. In all conurbations in the western Netherlands, black-market prices for foodstuffs, fuel, and textiles soared. The Directorate for Prices noted that this exorbitant price rise was not only an expression of an out-of-control price level, but also the result of a strong reduction of the amount of illegally available goods.[39] Table 6.1 demonstrates average black-market prices recorded by the Dutch food and price authorities in several large towns in the western Netherlands before and during the famine, including the official retail prices for each product.

[36] Klemann and Kudryashov, *Occupied Economies*, 269–272.
[37] Klemann, 'De Legale en Illegale Productie in de Landbouw, 1938–1948', *Neha Jaarboek* 60 (1997): 307–338; Klemann, 'De Zwarte Markt', 537; Klemann, *Nederland 1938–1948*, 212.
[38] NIOD, 0332, inv.no. j1, Anonymous letter from Joint Amsterdam Resistance Group to Amsterdam greengrocers, s.a.; Antonius J. A. C. van Delft, *Zwarte Handel: Uit de Bezettingstijd 1940–1945* (Amsterdam: Uitgevers-Maatschappij Holland, 1946), 35–36; L. G. Kortenhorst, 'Het Economische Leven', in *Onderdrukking en Verzet* II, 281; Klemann, 'De Zwarte Markt', 533–535; Futselaar, *Lard, Lice and Longevity*, 66–168; De Zwarte, 'Grenzen Vervagen: Economische Criminaliteit in Amsterdam, 1940–1945', *Ons Amsterdam* 63 (2011): 202–207.
[39] NA, 2.06.082 Ministerie van Economische Zaken: Directoraat-Generaal voor Prijzen en Voorgangers, inv.no. 2, Report from the Representative for the Prices over November–December 1944. See also: *Jaarverslag van Amsterdam 1944*, 1.

Table 6.1 *Black-market prices compared to official prices 1942–1945*

Product	Unit	Official prices 1944	Black-market prices			Index Off. 1944=100
			1942	1943	Winter 1944–1945	
Potatoes	Kg.	0.10	0.40	0.40	7–	7,000
Bread	800 gr.	0.19	0.98	1.18	40–	21,053
Butter	Kg.	2.60	25–	45–	150–	5,769
Cheese (full-fat)	Kg.	1.75	5.50	14–	60–	3,429
Milk (stand.)	L.	0.17	0.80	1–	10–	5,882
Beef	Kg.	0.60	6–	15–	60–	10,000
Sugar	Kg.	0.55	4–	14–	80–	14,545
Salt	Kg.	0.17	–	–	10–	5,882
Eggs	Pc.	0.10	0.85	1.25	7–	7,000
Kidney beans	Kg.	0.50	2.75	3–	40–	8,000
Wheat flour	Kg.	0.26	3.50	5–	60–	23,076
Oatmeal	Kg.	0.34	7.50	8–	55–	16,176
Cognac	L.	4–	25–	70–	150–	3,750
Cigarettes	20 pc.	0.90	2.50	6–	60–	6,667
Matches	Package	0.15	–	3.50	10–	6,667
Shoes (men)	Pair	7.90	40–	65–	150–	1,899
Bicycle tire	Pc.	3.55	40–	150–	400–	11,268
Anthracite	Hl.	3–	16–	17.50	160–	5,333

Source: Table based on *Economische en Sociale Kroniek der Oorlogsjaren*, 266

Table 6.1 shows that black-market prices had been steadily increasing throughout the occupation period but reached an absolute peak in the winter of 1944–1945. Astronomical prices were recorded in all categories; notably, prices increased most rapidly in bulk foods such as bread, wheat flour, oatmeal, potatoes, and pulses. The Department of Economic Affairs attributed this distinct price increase to the relatively unfavourable ratio of the weight, volume, and nutritional value of these products. In other words, potatoes and bread were more adversely affected by the transport difficulties than 'luxury' products such as butter, cheese, or liquor.[40] The price increase of bread is the most marked with an average of 40 guilders per loaf (800 gr) calculated by the CBS and even 80 guilders per kg documented by the food authorities in The Hague.[41] These prices are even more exorbitant when one

---

[40] NA, 2.06.082, inv.no. 2, Report August-October 1944. See also: J.H. van Stuijvenberg and C. Van den Berg, 'Zwarte Prijzen van Consumptiegoederen gedurende de Bezettingsjaren', *Economisch-Statistisch Kwartaalbericht* I (1947): 27.
[41] Calculations by Food Council in: *Voeding* 6, 110–111.

considers that the average manufactural worker earned about 25–35 guilders per week at the time and that the annual wage of 75 per cent of Dutch workers was below 2,000 guilders.[42]

The example of bread prices also accentuates how black-market prices could differ greatly. While before the crisis many products had a relatively stable street value, from late 1944 onward, prices varied literally per hour. The drastic decrease in transportation and movement opportunities was key to this development as well as the introduction of emergency ration cards in September 1944 with strictly localised stamps.[43] Rotterdam illustrates this complicated set of events, where prices on black markets in Rotterdam North and South varied notoriously because of control posts at both sides of the bridges across the Meuse.[44]

This price discrimination can be explored further when investigating prices paid for specific commodities in one locality in the same time period. While black markets pose specific difficulties for criminologists and historians alike, in the Dutch case, there is a unique source allowing for this kind of close examination. The NIOD archives contain thousands of letters from Dutchmen and -women, assembled after a 1946 radio call by NIOD Director Loe de Jong asking people to send in prices paid during the war.[45] In Figures 6.2a–c, Amsterdam has been chosen to demonstrate the various prices paid for bread, butter, and potatoes. From the hundreds of letters from Amsterdam, only those prices seemingly reliable (e.g., with precise price and date of purchase) have been selected. Prices paid outside the city are also not taken into account.

The price discrimination displayed in Figures 6.2a–c highlights the problem with average black-market prices, such as those in Table 6.1 and general historiography, which suggest that the products were part of a homogenous market, at which price levels approached uniformity.[46] Figures 6.2a–c, however, show just how misleading the term 'market' is. In February–March 1945, when the famine was at its worst, people

[42] Average wages in September/October 1942: *Economische en Sociale Kroniek der Oorlogsjaren*, 293. See also: Van Delft, *Zwarte Handel*, 10; Klemann, 'De Zwarte Markt', 535.

[43] NA, 2.06.082, inv.no. 2, Report November–December 1944; Christensen and Futselaar, 'Zwarte Markten', 105.

[44] Kortenhorst, 'Het Economische Leven', 284.

[45] NIOD, 932a Zwarte handel. Klemann has impressively analysed all of these letters, putting together a price index for no less than 96 products based on 25,000 entries. His focus, however, was on price development in legal and illegal markets for each consecutive year of the occupation and not on price discrimination. Klemann, 'De Zwarte Markt', 543–544.

[46] For example, Van Delft stated that during the famine period one hl of wheat cost 4,000 guilders. Van Delft, *Zwarte Handel*, 11. See also: Klemann, 'De Zwarte Markt', 544; Futselaar, *Lard, Lice and Longevity*, 160–161.

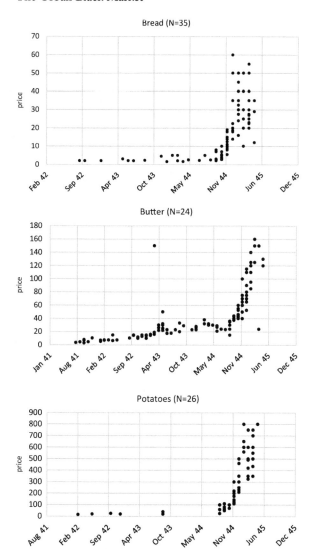

Figure 6.2 Self-reported black-market prices by different individuals (N) for bread (pc), butter (pound), and potatoes (hl) in Amsterdam, 1941–1945.
Source: NIOD, 932a Zwarte handel, File A+B

paid anything between 10 and 50 guilders for a loaf of bread; 85–160 guilders for a pound of butter; and 325 and 800 guilders for a hl (about 70 kilograms) of potatoes. Most likely, these differences would be even greater if the sample was more diverse: the socio-economic profile of the writers consists mostly of middle- and upper-class professions. There is every reason to assume that these urban, middle-class consumers were at a disadvantage at these black markets, where sellers were predominantly working-class citizens who could easily mislead these uninformed and inexperienced buyers. Generally, people paid lower prices when they were acquainted with the seller. The price discrimination also results from the lack of information necessary for price mechanisms to function. In all cities, consumers had to deal with this problem of imperfect information.[47] Likewise, these urban consumers were often not even in a position to bargain as the overall scarcity never left black marketeers without buyers.

The prices that urban dwellers paid within the city differed significantly from those paid in the countryside. Previous studies have calculated urban prices at 172 per cent of those paid in the countryside in 1944 and 211 per cent in 1945.[48] Other authors have put forward slightly lower numbers, ranging from 24 per cent difference for butter to as much as 167 per cent for meat.[49] Yet these indexes, again, do not fully take into account price discrimination, which was actually greater in the countryside than in the cities. In the letters with self-recorded prices, many people stated that it was common to pay about ten times less at farms than in the city. As some farmers often still sold at 'old', pre-crisis prices, the lowest prices paid in the countryside were indeed much lower than those at urban black markets. Excesses were common as well, as many farmers only sold their produce for extreme prices. This happened even in the northeastern provinces, where black-market prices had remained fairly constant up till then.[50] For example, in December 1944 one man bought a hl of potatoes in Amsterdam for 150 guilders and, in the rural area of West Friesland (North Holland), approximately 40 kilometres away, the same amount for 7.50–15 guilders. Similarly, one single onion was sold in the city for 50 cents while fetching only 5 cents in the countryside.[51] Perhaps the most extreme example of black-market price variations was that a pound of tulip bulbs for human consumption in Amsterdam in February 1945 cost 18 guilders; meanwhile, in Groningen people still bought tulips – as decoration – for 0.75 guilders per piece in March 1945.[52]

---

[47] Futselaar, 'Incomes, Class, and Coupons', 180–181; Albert K. Das Gupta, *Planning and Economic Growth* (London: Allen & Unwin, 1965). See also: Roodhouse, 'Popular Morality and the Black Market in Britain', 250–252.

[48] Klemann, 'De Zwarte Markt', 548.

[49] Christensen and Futselaar, 'Zwarte Markten', 106.

[50] *Jaarverslag van Amsterdam 1944*, 1.   [51] NIOD, 932a, Zwarte handel.

[52] NIOD, 932a, Anonymous letter 31 February 1946 Amsterdam; NIOD, 244, inv. no. 1331, Diary J. E. (male journalist and NSB member Groningen), 9 March 1945.

For most people, the inflated urban black-market prices were impossible to pay. From late November onward, monetary transactions markedly diminished and barter or exchange prevailed, as was the case elsewhere in occupied Europe.[53] This demonetisation trend started as money began rapidly losing value, mainly because hardly anything was still available to buy but also because people (correctly) expected that the postwar government would target those who had enriched themselves during the war, either by monetary reform or via prosecution. In addition, after the Allied invasion the Dutch Bank froze all bank accounts, allowing individuals to withdraw a maximum of only 100 guilders per week.[54]

The stories of extreme bartering practices are countless; for example, in Amsterdam, January 1945, a golden ring could buy you 20 pounds of wheat.[55] That same month, a bank employee traded his beloved piano accordion for 1 hl of potatoes and 1 hl of onions.[56] For a family in The Hague, two sets of new underwear bought 100 kg of potatoes.[57] Some trading commodities were especially in high demand. Cigarettes, for instance, became of high value as tobacco sales terminated in November 1944. The same was true for shoes and textiles. The textile production and distribution had already started to deteriorate since late 1943. In 1944, items could only be bought licensed, and even then, not much was available.[58] As a result, illegal trade fairs in which extreme barter was practised thrived during the famine, thereby fostering price inflation on the black market.[59]

Now that we know more about what was paid at black markets, it is possible to turn to the people themselves who were involved. While it is most likely that almost everybody in the occupied areas was involved in illegal selling or buying during the famine, the exorbitant prices suggest

---

[53] Futselaar, *Lard, Lice and Longevity*, 184–185; Klemann and Kudryashov, *Occupied Economies*, 286–87; Hionidou, *Famine and Death in Occupied Greece*, 44–45.

[54] At the same time, real wages had been steadily decreasing, while circulating money had increased due to higher expenditures from Dutch administrations and the German occupier. In December 1944, up to 5.3 billion guilders in coins and bank notes circulated. De Jong, *Het Koninkrijk* 10b, 223.

[55] NIOD, 244, inv.no. 1129, 14 January 1945.   [56] NIOD, 932a.

[57] NIOD, 0332, inv.no. 46, Letter Hendrik from The Hague to family in Breda, 3 May 1945.

[58] In early 1944, adults – men only – had been entitled to two coupons every fortnight for 20 cigarettes, 5 cigars, 10 cigarillos, or 40 grams of tobacco. Only a few exceptions with regard to textiles were made for evacuees, war victims, and expecting mothers. *Jaarverslag van Amsterdam 1944*, 21–22; *Jaarverslag van Amsterdam 1945*, 35.

[59] Hirschfeld himself had approved of municipal trade fairs in early 1944, following the first example in Rotterdam but, during the crisis, many were established by individuals outside of municipal control. NIOD, 212a, inv.no. 63, Circular letter Hirschfeld to Chambers of Trade and Industry, 3 April 1945; *Jaarverslag van Amsterdam 1944*, 74–75.

that urban black markets remained rather confined. Comparing the Dutch case to the Greek black market, the latter was far bigger and 'blacker' because there was much less food available and also because the Greek crisis lasted much longer. Furthermore, the worst of the black market in Greece was not seen in the first famine year, which leads one to assume that the Dutch black market would have been more comprehensive as well, had the famine (like its Greek counterpart) lasted longer.[60]

Broadly speaking, seven factors can be identified that played a determining role in access to black markets: means, mobility, contacts, knowledge, skills, willingness, and solidarity. The reasons for buying at urban black markets were very much interlinked to these factors; generally speaking, the black market served those who could afford it and those with not many other options. Looking for relatively affordable products that were high in nutritional value, most lower-income families could only buy or exchange occasionally at urban black markets. According to post-war surveys, 51 per cent of the interviewed working-class families in Amsterdam did not have the means to buy at the black market, compared to 21 per cent from the richer 'south' quarter of the city.[61] A woman from Amsterdam explained:

The black marketeers would stand on the corner of the Rozendwarsstraat. They sold these pies made out of wheat, asking seven guilders per slice. That was extremely expensive, as I only made 22 guilders per week. We would buy a slice now and then, to have something extra. Besides that, we hardly bought anything from black marketeers. I did clandestinely buy a bread coupon once, which was hardly affordable: 60 guilders that thing cost me.[62]

Others were forced to buy on the black market more regularly; for example, women with young children whose husbands had been taken away, ill and elderly people, and people in hiding from the occupier. The crisis thus forced many law-abiding people to act in illegal ways. For Jewish people in hiding, the famine brought more misery to their already dangerous situation. A young Jewish couple in hiding in Amsterdam recalled that, in January 1945, they had to sell their last jewellery in exchange for one loaf of bread at 40 guilders. They also paid 30 guilders for a kilogram of peas, which they ended up eating raw: 'The costs were enormous. We are financially ruined, but … we made it out alive.'[63]

---

[60] Hionidou, *Famine and Death in Occupied Greece*, 108, 148–157.
[61] By contrast, Kruijer also concluded that working-class citizens had more opportunities to buy at black markets than wealthier families (89 against 80 per cent). Kruijer, *Sociale Desorganisatie*, 112.
[62] Slager et al., *Verhalen om te Onthouden*, 71–72.
[63] NIOD, 932a, Letter S. A., 28 January 1945.

Just like its consumers, black marketeers came in many shapes and sizes. Of course, a clear difference existed between professional black marketeers and people who sold food or ration stamps illegally. During the crisis, networks of black marketeers stretched throughout the occupied areas. Travelling from the cities with barter goods such as coal and textiles, professional black marketeers traded for large quantities of foodstuffs in the countryside at low prices, selling them again for extreme prices in the cities. Sometimes, criminals stole and slaughtered cattle and other livestock to sell on urban black markets.[64] People who profited from the desperation were unanimously condemned by the population, who viewed such acts as a 'crime against society'.[65] In attempts to exercise their authority among the population, resistance groups intervened by putting up posters and distributing pamphlets that denounced black marketeering. Sometimes they even intervened directly, such as in Barneveld (Gelderland), where resistance fighters chained a 34-year-old farmer to a signpost with a placard on his chest stating: '… is selling rye for the price of f850 per hl; eggs for the price of f1.65 per piece and meat for the price of f40 per pound'.[66]

As opposed to professional black marketeers, many individuals became involved in black-market trade because of the hardship of their circumstances. Inexperienced with these activities, they hardly made the best profit, especially since they were in a hurry to sell goods and coupons as everything soon lost value. Afterwards, more experienced black marketeers would sometimes resell the coupons for more profit, right before they became exchangable in the retail shops. One woman from Rotterdam explained in a post-war interview:

I will tell you honestly, I have sold many ration cards. I would go to a corner of the street where more people were standing. Among other places on Noordplein. That was the largest black market in Rotterdam. I would get twenty guilders for such a ration card. But those people buying the cards, would wait until the coupons were made available and then sold them separately. That way, they could make one hundred and fifty guilders out of it: one sugar coupon, one butter coupon, one bread coupon, and so on.[67]

As for the background of these individuals, both the professional black marketeers and the people incidentally selling were mostly working-class

---

[64] NIOD, 216K, inv.no. 301, Police reports; inv.no. 659, Military constabulary Department Geldermalsen to headquarters in Arnhem, 10 March 1945; NIOD, 932a Zwarte handel.
[65] De Zwarte, 'Grenzen Vervagen'.
[66] NIOD, 216K, inv.no. 301, Police report 1 March 1945.
[67] Slager et al., *Verhalen om te Onthouden*, 69–70.

citizens. Similarly, the principle sites of black-market trade were working-class neighbourhoods. Children were often involved in street trade as they were less likely to be caught and prosecuted.[68] Another infamous figure on the black market was the so-called broker, who carried no commodities and was thus impossible to arrest. The broker's motto was: 'I am not involved in black-market trade, but if there is anything I can help you with, please let me know!'[69]

Hotels and restaurants also took part in the earnings. While most restaurants were closed, clandestine places remained open to serve the wealthiest. For example, a hotel manager in The Hague was caught buying 30 portions a day from a soup kitchen for 20 cents per meal, selling them again for 5 guilders per plate after adding small pieces of meat and bread.[70] It was well-known that many Chinese restaurants also profited from black marketeering, asking about 15 guilders for a plate of noodles.[71] Licensed street vendors also often crossed the line from legal to illegal sales. During the winter, vendors started selling alternative whipped cream made out of sugar beet foam (slagcreme), which was not illegal to do, if it complied with price regulations. However, in Amsterdam several men were caught earning up to 1,200 guilders per week with this famine treat.[72]

Even though prices decreased considerably, black-market trade continued for quite some time after the liberation. In June 1945, on average 10 people a day were arrested in Amsterdam for black marketeering and, during one raid alone in Rotterdam, over 70 people were arrested. To a lesser extent, similar activities also continued in The Hague and Utrecht, which corresponds with the lower crime rates in these cities during the Hunger Winter. The nature of black-market trade and consumption shifted after the war from staple goods and fuel to luxury products such as cigarettes, liquor, and chocolate: this is illustrative of the recovery of the food crisis over the summer of 1945.[73] A significant change occurred

---

[68] NIOD, 932a; SA, 5225, inv.no. 7284, Report on City Brigade Amsterdam; *Jaarverslag van Amsterdam 1944*, 143; Slager et al., *Verhalen om te Onthouden*, 69–73.

[69] Koster, *Honger in Rotterdam*, 22–23.

[70] NA, 2.06.082, inv.no. 2, Report November–December 1944. See also: NARA, 331, Entry 2, Box 118, Report 'The Occupied Netherlands To-day and To-morrow', 17 March 1945; Buck Goudriaan, *Leiden in de Tweede Wereldoorlog Van Dag tot Dag: Een Kroniek van 10 Mei 1940 tot 15 Augustus 1945* (Leiden: F. G. W. Goudriaan, 1995), 224.

[71] NIOD, 0332, L13, Report Cannegieter, May 1945.

[72] SA, 5225a, inv.no. 8389, Police reports 4 January, 5 March 1945.

[73] NARA, 331, Entry 152, Box 264, Fortnightly report SHAEF Mission Netherlands, 15 June 1945; NA 2.06.082, inv.no. 2, Report on investigation into size and means of fighting black-market trade and illegal production of consumption goods, December

in the autumn of 1945, when Minister of Finance Piet Lieftinck introduced a nationwide monetary reform aimed to tackle black-market money,
which included an exchange of bank notes and freezing all bank accounts
until an investigative committee gave clearance. To document the effects
of the monetary reform, authorities in Amsterdam recorded the daily rate
of several products sold on an infamous 'black' street between 12 September and 10 October 1945. On 12 September, a pound of butter sold for 34
guilders: the following day for 100 guilders. Similarly, a bar of chocolate
could cost anything between 4 and 12.50 guilders. After the reform in
early October that reduced the amount of liquids by 60 per cent, the same
pound of butter was sold at a much lower 16 guilders, while bars of
chocolate were sold for 2.50 guilders.[74] Still, it was not until economic
controls were dismantled in the course of the late 1940s and early 1950s
that the greater part of black-market trade finally disappeared.

Hunger Journeys

Food poverty not only dominated daily activities in the cities, but also
drove people out of town in search for food. The short-lived character of
the German blockade made the Dutch case very different from besieged
Leningrad, for example, where during the first winter people mostly had
to survive on resources from within the blockade area.[75] During the
Dutch famine, thousands of urban dwellers embarked on food expeditions each day to nearby rural areas to buy or exchange goods for
foodstuffs. Visiting farms for food had been common in earlier years as
well, just as elsewhere in occupied Europe, but the nature and scale of
the expeditions in 1944–1945 were not comparable to anything witnessed before. Hirschfeld said that these 'hunger travellers' (*hongertrek-
kers*) were one of the clearest images of the prevailing famine he had
seen.[76] As the main alternative for buying on urban black markets, food
expeditions became essential for many households to survive. In collective memory, the hunger journeys feature prominently as courageous
endeavours by starving urbanites – women especially – who travelled
under extreme circumstances with bicycles, pushcarts, and strollers in

---

1946; SA, 5225, inv.no. 7284, Reports week 20–27 January 1945 and 15 May–1 July
from the State Police in Amsterdam, Bureau of Economic Affairs.
[74] NA, 2.06.087, Ministerie van Economische Zaken: Centraal Archief, inv.no. 443, Black-
market prices in Tweede Rozendwarsstraat in Amsterdam, 12 September–10
October 1945.
[75] Reid, *Leningrad*, 158–173.
[76] NIOD, 212a, inv.no. 167, Diary Hirschfeld, 25 January 1945. Part of diary finished on
18 February.

search for food. During their trips, they not only had to endure harsh weather conditions, but also exposed themselves to repressive measures by the German occupying authorities.[77]

Historians have generally viewed food expeditions as part of black-market consumption, which impaired central food rationing and created growing inequalities.[78] Yet at the time, these expeditions were not considered to be so harmful as scholars have, in hindsight, assumed. On the contrary, Dutch and German authorities not only turned a blind eye to the hunger travellers, but even encouraged their actions. If we recall, the transportation difficulties forced national authorities to allow individuals to take matters into their own hands, preferring to maximise consumption (and thus avoiding wasted food) over maintaining the integrity of the rationing system. This policy was maintained up until the Central Shipping Company was able to resume its activities. On 1 March 1945, the food authorities closed the IJssel bridges for all individual travellers with the idea that this would support the central rationing system; nevertheless, thereafter food expeditions were still tolerated in the western provinces. Indeed, the CCD was instructed only to apprehend professional black marketeers. Likewise, the German *Wehrmacht* had orders not to confiscate foodstuffs from hunger travellers or to act against them in any way that might harm the *Wehrmacht*'s image.[79] In light of the substantial latitude that the hunger travellers were given, it is thus worthwhile to also examine these food expeditions as valuable coping strategies, and not just as elements obstructing central rationing.

Investigating these food expeditions starts with G. J. Kruijer's study from 1951, published under the title 'Social Desorganisation' (*Sociale Desorganisatie*). Shortly after the liberation, Kruijer interviewed people from Amsterdam and the countryside and recorded their experiences with food expeditions. His findings revealed much about its scale: an astonishing 62 per cent of the surveyed families in Amsterdam had embarked on food expeditions. They did this an average of 13.7 times per family, with each trip resulting in about 42 kg of food acquired.[80]

---

[77] NIOD, 0331, inv.no. D, Essays Mulo-exam Dutch on 'hongertochten', 1946; Banning, 'Voeding en Voedingstoestand', 26. The NIOD library contains dozens of personal testimonies and semi-fictional accounts in which this image of the hunger journeys is reaffirmed.

[78] Trienekens, *Tussen ons Volk en de Honger*, 381; Klemann, 'De Zwarte Markt', 544, 560; Klemann, *Nederland 1939-1948*, 466; Christensen and Futselaar, 'Zwarte Markten', 105; Futselaar, 'Incomes, Class, and Coupons', 195–196; Klemann and Kudryashov, *Occupied Economies*, 289.

[79] NIOD, 216h, inv.no. 100, Circular letter Director CCD G. Diepenheim, 22 February 1945; NIOD, 001, inv.no. 522, *Merkblatt für die Truppe*, 10 January 1945.

[80] Kruijer, *Sociale Desorganisatie*, passim.

Unfortunately, the materials from his extensive research have not been well preserved and therefore do not permit a full re-examination of his analysis. The exceptions are one survey from Amsterdam and a questionnaire from the municipality of Nieuwer-Amstel (nowadays Amstelveen). The survey in Amsterdam was conducted in the Kerkstraat where mostly skilled craftsmen, civil servants, and other lower middle-class families lived. All 196 surveys include the profession of the head of the household, family composition, denomination, number of rooms, and whether they had embarked on day journeys or longer expeditions (i.e., spending one or more nights away from home).

Analysis of this sample largely corresponds with the general conclusions made by Kruijer with the main deviation that only 42.9 per cent of the surveyed families had gone on food expeditions, compared to the average of 62 per cent of all 1,600 interviewees in Kruijer's study. Again, these figures highlight that all percentages should be viewed as rough estimates. Of the people that embarked on food expeditions, 54.8 per cent undertook day journeys, all in the province of North Holland and within a range of 20–25 kilometres. Approximately 66.7 per cent went on longer journeys, of which only 12 per cent travelled to the northeastern provinces, indicating that most people could still obtain food from the western provinces during the famine. Of the 57.1 per cent who stayed at home, 42 per cent did so because they were not physically able to travel, 17.9 per cent because they received food supplies from outside the city, and 12.5 per cent because they still had enough money to buy or exchange at the urban black markets.[81] This last percentage reiterates to us that black-market trade was indeed subordinate to these food expeditions as a strategy to obtain extra-legal food supplies.

The questionnaire from Nieuwer-Amstel uncovers the perspective of the direct peripheral region. Nieuwer-Amstel was a municipality comprising a town, some smaller villages, and a large countryside area bordering the south of Amsterdam. The survey was completed and sent back by a special committee formed by the mayor, chief clerk, police officer, advertising consultant, and a farmer.[82] They stated that the townspeople had played little role in helping the travellers as they suffered from deprivation themselves. About 90–95 per cent of the hunger travellers came from Amsterdam who, because of their proximity to Nieuwer-Amstel, never stayed the night.

---

[81] NIOD, 0331, inv.no. C, Surveys Kerkstraat.
[82] SA, 30355 Archief van de Gemeente Amstelveen: Secretarie, inv.no. 4285, Questionnaire University of Amsterdam and corresponding answers by municipality of Nieuwer-Amstel, 7 August 1946.

Table 6.2 *Prices asked in Nieuwer-Amstel for different foodstuffs, in guilders per kg, 1944–1945*

	Spring 1944	September 1944	1 January 1945	1 May 1945
Potatoes	0.10	0.15	0.15	0.15
Butter	3.00	3.50	8.00	10.00
Grains	0.20	0.25	0.25	0.25
Pulses	0.30	0.35	0.35	0.35

Source: SA, 30355, inv.no. 4285, Questionnaire Nieuwer-Amstel, August 1946

In order to ascertain the extraordinary nature of these expeditions, one need only look to the sources; according to the survey, the crowd on the by-roads was comparable to one on a busy day in the capital's main shopping street. The Nieuwer-Amstel committee confirmed that there was no surveillance on these roads and the German *Wehrmacht* did not pay attention to individuals. Based on police arrests in the area, they estimated that about 90 per cent of the visitors bought foodstuffs for private use and 10 per cent ended up in the black market: individual buyers usually did not barter, as was the case in most other rural areas. Table 6.2 shows the average prices farmers asked for various foodstuffs before and during the famine. Although these numbers were likely on the lower side and excesses probably occurred in this town as in any other, the differences one observes between these figures and the urban black-market prices in the previous section are striking. It is important to note here that these figures confirm that food expeditions were much more advantageous for urban dwellers – that is, for those mobile enough to leave the city.

In addition to Kruijer's surveys, notebooks kept by farmers during the famine period provide an insight into the socio-economic profile of the hunger travellers. As a safety measure, a farmer in Sijbekarspel (North Holland) recorded the name, age, sex, profession, and address of all visitors who stayed the night at 'De Grenshoeve' between 20 November 1944 and 18 April 1945. The farmer and his wife had four children and were described by one of their sons as 'socially engaged people with broad political and cultural interests'. Already by 1943 onwards, urban dwellers had travelled to their farm to buy food; however, during the crisis the influx of people grew so rapidly that they were not able to sell food to anyone other than their regular customers. Nevertheless, all travellers were offered a meal and a place to sleep. Upon arrival, the farmer's wife prepared a few sandwiches and a bowl of milk, and in the morning the guests were given a bowl of wheat porridge. They were also given fresh milk upon departure, and most usually continued their march further into the Wieringermeer. The example of De Grenshoeve shows how very local and how very urban the famine actually was; once past the city limits, the sources often reveal many such farmers, even in the western provinces, with enough extra supplies to aid hunger travellers from the larger towns.[83]

Over a period of five months, 392 individuals visited De Grenshoeve, adding up to a total of 672 nights. The highest number of lodgers was recorded on 23 March 1945 when twelve visitors stayed the night, showing that many people returned to the farm after their first stopover. One 15-year-old boy from Amsterdam even stayed a staggering 30 nights with the family. The short time-span between his visits suggests that he did not return home at all but rather wandered between different places. Several other young visitors did the same. Of the 392 visitors, 73 per cent came from Amsterdam, followed by only 4.8 per cent from Haarlem and 3.6 per cent from The Hague. The remainder came from other towns in North Holland. Only two people travelled from Rotterdam and one from Leiden: 21 people arrived without identification. Two hundred and seventy-six visitors were recorded as having a profession; not surprisingly, most of these were workers, with a scattering of civil servants.

Illustration 15 Hunger journeys.

[83] NIOD, 0332, inv.no. 44, List of names visitors 'De Grenshoeve', 20 November 1944–18 April 1945.

Illustration 16 People waiting to buy food outside a farm in
Wieringerwaard.

The gender division of the group, however, is something of a surprise.
While the popular narrative of the food expeditions has often asserted
that it was mostly women who were involved in these journeys, the record
of lodgers at De Grenshoeve shows otherwise. For this particular farm,
67.9 per cent of the visitors were male – a healthy majority – and only
23.2 per cent of the visitors were female (8.9 per cent unknown). Moreover, of these men, 48.1 per cent belonged to the 'dangerous age group'
17–40 years: dangerous because they were the target of German raids in
connection to their forced labour programme.[84] On average, male visitors were 32.7 years old and females 27.3 years. These numbers about the
gender composition thus contradict the popular image of women as the
predominant travellers in these food expeditions. Kruijer himself had
also pointed out this contradiction by stating that, of his surveyed people,
58 per cent believed that there had been more women on the roads, while
in practice his surveys indicated that women accounted for 42 per cent of
the hunger travellers.[85] Apparently, in collective memory women have
become much more connected to the hunger journeys than men, while

[84] Of the visitors, 9.2 per cent were younger than 17 years; 27.1 per cent older than 40 years
and, for 15.4 per cent, age remains unknown. The oldest man to visit the farm was 66
years old.
[85] Kruijer, *Sociale Desorganisatie*, 129–134.

evidence tells us we should be cautious when focusing on female participation only. The idea that these journeys were illegal and obstructed by the occupier has likely contributed to the misconception that food expeditions belonged mostly to the female spectrum of famine responses.

Another notebook, kept by a farmer in the northernmost part of North Holland province, portrays a similar image. The owner of the 'Martini-heerd' farm in the Wieringermeer registered his visitors from 8 February until 12 April 1945. As in De Grenshoeve, people would knock on their door and ask for shelter from the late afternoon until the evening. They were all given a bowl of pea soup before going to sleep in the hay barn, but not before being asked to hand in their identification cards and matches. In two months, 155 individuals stayed a total of 170 times at the farm. Before February, the family had already hosted about 300 people. For these lodgers, Amsterdam was yet again the main point of departure (54.9 per cent), followed by Haarlem (10.3 per cent) and The Hague (9 per cent). Additionally, these visitors comprised mostly men – 68.4 per cent against 31.6 per cent women – a similar ratio to De Grenshoeve. The age difference is also comparable to the previous example: male visitors were on average 37.8 years old against the female 26.9 years.[86] The relatively younger age of the women here suggests that it was mostly women without children who embarked on these expeditions. Having to take care of children is likely also the reason that far fewer women than men in general left the city in search for food, despite the popular image of the food expeditions suggesting otherwise.

Three general observations can be made from these sources. Firstly, the purpose of the food expeditions was not just to obtain large quantities of food, as previous studies have suggested. Some people travelled for days or even weeks, while others did not return home at all, especially those people with relatives or acquaintances in the countryside.[87] Days spent at farms meant days being reasonably well fed. In other words, food expeditions were an objective in themselves and not just a means to an end.[88] This was also the reason why many travellers took their children along or returned with them several days after an initial visit. For

[86] NIOD, 0332, inv.no. 45, List of names visitors 'Martiniheerd', 8 February 1945–12 April 1945. This pattern was also confirmed by other sources: Personal archive Van Diepen family, Notebook with visitors during the Hunger Winter.

[87] For example: A. Boekschoten-Van Pesch, 'Dagboek van een Hongerwinter', in *Hilversum in de Tweede Wereldoorlog*, ed. Ed van Mensch (Hilversum: Albertus Perk, 2010), 48–50.

[88] See also: Banning, 'Voeding en Voedingstoestand', 26; Report on journey by son Reijer, 12 December 1944 in: *Twee Werelden een Hongerwinter: Utrechtse Dagboeken van een Vader en Zoon, 1944–1945*, ed. George Bootsma (Hilversum: Verloren, 2010), 105–115.

example, a 40-year-old railway official, his wife, and 14-year-old son from Utrecht travelled from 8 to 18 January 1945 to Nijkerk and Wezep (Gelderland) and from there across the IJssel to Ommen. After a total of 250 kilometres, their total yield was a mere 3.5 hl potatoes, 30 pounds of rye and 10 eggs. But during this trip, they mostly stayed with farmers who fed them nutritious meals, which clearly was just as valuable.[89]

Secondly, men played a much bigger role in the food expeditions than has been commonly assumed. As we have seen in Amsterdam at least, men still had plenty of opportunity to travel. However, the fact that more men than women stayed overnight does not necessarily mean that fewer women travelled to the countryside to obtain food. One cannot rule out the possibility that women chose not to stay the night for reasons of safety or impropriety, which would oblige women to make shorter day trips. Thirdly, even during the height of the famine, the food expeditions remained a predominantly working-class and lower middle-class undertaking. Shame most likely played an important role in the absence of higher middle-class and upper-class families, nor does this distinct socio-economic profile seem to have shifted a great deal over the course of the famine.[90]

The small numbers from Rotterdam, The Hague, and other towns written down in these notebooks are by no means a reflection of a more forgiving food situation. The predominance of Amsterdam travellers in the above-mentioned documents is purely a matter of location. As the north of the province of North Holland became flooded with Amsterdammers, urban dwellers from other localities sought their respective havens. From Rotterdam, most people migrated to southern rural areas (e.g., Zuidelijke Eilanden, Westland), and later to more distant farmlands eastwards in the Veluwe and the provinces of Gelderland and Overijssel.[91] People from The Hague and Leiden did not have such hinterland close by and were forced to travel farther at a much earlier stage.[92] For all individuals and households involved, however, mobility was always key.

---

[89] NIOD, 0331, inv.no. A1, Letter J. Boom to RvO on hunger journeys, 16 February 1946.
[90] Klemann and Kudryashov have stated that when hunger became widespread, bourgeois men and women forgot their pride and went to forage the countryside as well. Klemann and Kudryashov, *Occupied Economies*, 288.
[91] NIOD, 244, inv.no. 324, 1319, 187, 1805. NIOD, 212a, inv.no. 167, Diary Hirschfeld, 30 March 1945; Slager et al., *Verhalen om te Onthouden*, 119–120; Van der Pauw, *Rotterdam in de Tweede Wereldoorlog*, 608.
[92] Marcus G. Verwey, *Leiden in Bezettingstijd: Herinneringen van een Gemeentebestuurder* (Leiden: A. W. Sijthoff's Uitgeversmij NV, 1946), 123–125; Hendrik M. van Randwijk, 'Hongertochten tijdens de Hongerwinter', in *Onderdrukking en Verzet* II, 655. Goudriaan, *Leiden in de Tweede Wereldoorlog*, 213; Van der Zee, *De Hongerwinter*, 53.

For smaller towns, this disadvantage could be even greater. For example, people from Voorschoten struggled with access to food because they lived in the vicinity of Leiden and The Hague, first having to pass these cities during their food expeditions before reaching more abundant farmland to the north or south.[93] In this respect, Utrecht was much better located, as these residents could travel relatively smaller distances to visit farms nearby and eastwards to Salland and Twente (Overijssel).[94] In general, the hunger travellers worked in concentric circles. At first people travelled to nearby farms but, as supplies became exhausted, they were pushed further into the eastern provinces or sometimes even Friesland and Groningen.[95] In addition to these overland routes, the ferries between Amsterdam and Friesland were widely used by hunger travellers (as well as for sending parcels to the western provinces). In the night of 8–9 January 1945 a disaster occurred when two ferries collided, killing 13 people, which shows the many dangers of these long journeys.[96]

Irrespective of the distance, experiences on the road were quite similar. Roads and bridges were crowded with hunger travellers, who became inherently part of the land- and cityscapes during the famine. A traffic count on the Deventer bridge on Monday 25 February 1945 recorded a total of 1,489 pedestrians, 4,205 cyclists, 115 horse and wagons, and 97 handcars and tricycles, against only 11 trucks, 20 cars, and 62 *Wehrmacht* vehicles that day.[97] To aid the hungry passers-by, Red Cross posts opened along the busy roads and in main stopover towns. Travellers could stay the night or find treatment in improvised sleeping halls.[98] But the dangers of the journey did not only involve exhaustion. On 24 February 1945, an Allied bomber shelled the busy road between Nunspeet and Hulshorst (G), killing 2 travellers and leaving 14 critically

---

[93] NIOD, 0332, inv.no. K1, Christmas recollections December 1944, W. F. A., 1954.

[94] Ton H. M. van Schaik, 'Zo Moe van te lang Wachten', in *Twee Werelden Een Hongerwinter*, 28; Dairy Dorus Bootsma and Reijer Bootsma, in *Twee Werelden Een Hongerwinter*; Dolly Verhoeven, '"Verder hebben we Heel Gewoon Geleefd": Dagelijks Leven in Utrecht tijdens de Bezetting', in *Een Gewone Stad in een Bijzondere Tijd: Utrecht 1940–1945*, ed. Johannes van Miert (Utrecht: Het Spectrum BV, 1995), 191.

[95] *Jaarverslag van Amsterdam 1944*, 1; J. Groesbeek, P. van Roggen, and D. N. de Weerd, *Duizend Wonden Bloeden: Episodes uit het Werk der EHBO-ers Gedurende de Jaren 1940–'45 in Apeldoorn* (Apeldoorn: Nederlandse Vereniging Eerste Hulp bij Ongelukken, 1946), 34–36.

[96] Sieneke de Rooij, *De Boot naar Lemmer: Een Verhaal uit de Hongerwinter* (Leiden: De Witte Uitgeverij, 2009), 117–126.

[97] NIOD, 0331, inv.no. a5, Traffic count IJssel bridge Deventer, 25 February 1945.

[98] NIOD, 244, inv.no. 1348, Diary J. L., (21-year-old man from Tuindorp Oostzaan), December 1944.

injured.[99] According to post-war interviews, these shootings occurred on a daily basis: 'The English probably did not see that they were all starving people, trying to gather food for their families. Maybe they thought they were troop transports. I don't know.'[100]

The food expeditions also provoked sharp antagonism between city and countryside. While urban dwellers were starving, their compatriots in nearby rural areas still enjoyed surplus food, which caused a significant transfer of wealth from the cities to the countryside. Not unusually, farmers misused their dominant position over urban residents and, aside from asking exorbitant prices, some demanded exorbitant barter exchanges. Particular regions in North and South Holland, such as the Wieringermeer and Barendrecht district, gained an especially bad reputation because of these farmers. One woman recalled:

My linen, all my table silverware, my rug, a Smyrna stair-carpet, I traded everything for food. But always with farmers here in the west. Because when we went to Friesland, there we could still buy food. But here in the west ... after a while they also rejected linen. It was gold they were after. Some even had a sign on their lawn: 'No more linen'. So, you did not even have to knock on their doors .... My red coral necklace, which my mother had given to me, they did want. I got potatoes in return.[101]

Some farmers went even further. Several women stated after the war that farmers had asked for sexual favours in return for food, which was one of the main reasons women rarely travelled alone. 'Hunger prostitution' was the term commonly used, and it was not judged harshly: everyone knew the appalling circumstances in which women had to take care of their families. One woman remembers a 60-year-old farmer, who told her she would get potatoes in return for sexual intercourse: 'I thought about it and thought about it .... Look, I would have done it. I really mean that. But the fear of getting pregnant was too big. So I didn't. But otherwise, I would have. You were that desperate, that you would have done anything for food.'[102] Although little is known of its facts and figures, hunger prostitution was also documented by Dutch doctors, who had observed that the introduction of this behaviour had caused the epidemiological situation in

[99] NIOD, 216K, inv.no. 301, Police report, 24 February 1945.
[100] Slager et al., *Verhalen om te Onthouden*, 127. See also: 126–128.
[101] Slager et al., *Verhalen om te Onthouden*, 118. See also: 140–146.
[102] Slager et al., *Verhalen om te Onthouden*, 144. See also: J. J. Zoon, 'De Huid- en Geslachtsziekten in Oorlogstijd', in *Medische Ervaringen*, 474; Slager et al., *Verhalen om te Onthouden*, 144–146. In occupied Greece, sexual intercourse was also exchanged for food during the famine. Hionidou, *Famine and Death in Occupied Greece*, 98.

the western Netherlands to change and venereal disease to spread among new groups of people.[103]

Although tensions between city and countryside heightened during the famine, it should be mentioned that pleasant experiences were also plentiful. Some people never came into contact with heartless farmers and later held fond memories of the rural population sharing their homes and food.[104] Essays written by Dutch high school students in 1946 on the food expeditions exemplify these dualistic experiences. One girl wrote about a night spent in a school building in Ermelo (Gelderland): 'Many people say that it is such an awful thing. But actually, you may not sleep well, but it is a lot of fun. The women had to sleep on the stage and the men in the auditorium. It became a large party room. Us women, or whatever you want to call it, of course chatted hectically. That made a lot of noise on the stage. You could hear the men yell: "If you do not keep quiet, I will toss a chair on the stage."'[105] Consistent with other sources, the essays underpin the great variety of attitudes by farmers and hunger travellers alike.

From the agrarians' perspective, the influx of urbanites brought both opportunities and difficulties. The food crisis generally offered agrarians the opportunity to sell their surplus at high profits. In addition, as the authorities allowed the food expeditions, helping urban dwellers did not involve much personal danger. Simultaneously, the hunger journeys posed major challenges that urban dwellers hardly understood. Post-war interviews with agrarians emphasise that it was nerve-racking for the farmers to have people knocking on their door and ring their bell from early in the morning until late at night, never contemplating the pressure it put them under. An agrarian from the Wieringermeer (North Holland) explained: 'The attitude of the travellers was unfair. The demander was perhaps number 2,000 and did not even consider that the farmer's supplies might be depleted but just called us "miserable farmer".'[106] Moreover, the agrarians were not providing food for the hunger travellers alone but also needed to satisfy the needs of many people in hiding – resistance groups, relief organisations, as well as their own family and acquaintances.[107] A farmer from Olst (Overijssel) could initially aid hunger travellers with lard and bacon but soon ran out of produce to sell. By February, over 600 people from all large towns in the west had visited his farm. Because he had not harvested his grain yet, the

---

[103] Zoon, 'De Huid- en Geslachtsziekten in Oorlogstijd', 474.
[104] Slager et al., *Verhalen om te Onthouden*, 115–146.
[105] NIOD, 0331, inv.no. D, Essays Mulo-exam Dutch, 1946.
[106] Kruijer, *Sociale Desintegratie*, 246   [107] Kruijer, *Sociale Desintegratie*, 243–249.

farmer eventually had to borrow from neighbours and a local miller to feed his guests. When the authorities closed the IJssel bridges on 1 March 1945, the family felt something close to relief – hosting 20 unfamiliar faces a day in addition to 14 family members and friends staying over had been exhausting.[108]

Another common complaint was that city dwellers showed little respect for the agrarians' position and lifestyle. The attitude of the travellers annoyed them, especially when they considered the farms to be an inexhaustible source of food and harboured suspicion when denied supplies or shelter. They unanimously characterised most city dwellers as rude, ungrateful, and disrespectful, which also derived from the widespread feeling that city people felt superior to them.[109] A farmer in Heiloo (North Holland), who hosted city folk from late September 1944 onward, recalled that people from Amsterdam were the most demanding and anti-social: they urinated in the barn, lit matches in the hay, and hardly showed any sign of gratitude for the food and shelter provided.[110] Another farmer, from Haarlemmermeer (North Holland), stated: 'The greater part was ungrateful, 50 per cent simply assumed we would help them ... now that their troubles are over, they walk past farmers with contempt again.'[111]

The lack of understanding from the hunger travellers was also most commonly mentioned when asked about the profits farmers made during the Hunger Winter. A teacher from the rural district North Hollandse Grasland stated: 'Yes, now the "city folk" need us, and later they won't even look at us. Let them trade and pay. Profit from it!'[112] Other farmers explained that they were not simply profiting from the situation but compensating for the hardship they had endured in the 1930s. They also mentioned that barter indeed became dominant: not because they wanted to fill their wardrobe, but because they needed to provide the basic needs for their family, other people living in the countryside, as well as their staff. The black sales were necessary to cover the expenses of clandestine food supply and the costs were higher because everything else needed to keep their businesses functioning likewise became more expensive.[113] Kruijer concluded that livelihood security was a major determining factor in the attitude of the farmers during the Hunger

[108] NIOD, 0332, inv.no. J7, Post-war report 'Oorlogswinter 1944–1945', A. Santink, Olst.
[109] Kruijer, Sociale Desintegratie, 248–250.
[110] NIOD, 0332, inv.no. K20, Letter C. de Graaf farmer Heiloo to RvO, 27 March 1946.
[111] Kruijer, Sociale Desintegratie, 249.   [112] Kruijer, Sociale Desintegratie, 243–244.
[113] Kruijer, Sociale Desintegratie, 243–245.

Winter, fearing return of the pre-war situation would occur after the liberation.[114]

What were the effects of food expeditions on consumption levels? Kruijer's research has calculated that the 62 per cent of the families participating in the scavenging trips took home on average 42 kg of food each trip. This section has added the important nuance that for many travellers, the meals obtained during their overnight trips were at least as valuable as the final yield. This successful infrastructure for obtaining food brings an important nuance to the scholarly view of food expeditions as counter-productive.[115] Even though it can be concluded in hindsight that the food expeditions were detrimental to central rationing at the national level, one cannot say that food would have been more equally divided otherwise. On the contrary, it is likely that, without the food expeditions, more supplies would have ended up in urban black markets, which were – due to the prohibitive prices – beyond the reach of most working- and lower middle-class families.

In their nutritional surveys, the Medical Feeding Teams asked families from Amsterdam, Rotterdam, Utrecht, and Delft about the extra-legal food they had obtained during the famine.[116] Table 6.3 shows that, in all these towns during the height of the famine in February 1945, food outside of legal channels became more important for household consumption than official rations. Unfortunately, Table 6.3 does not differentiate between food obtained via black markets, food expeditions, or household stocks. Urban gardening, wild picking, and fishing contributed to the extra-legal consumption levels as well. Moreover, during the winter the vegetable consumption played a vital role, as vegetables (cabbage, carrots, and onions in particular) were widely available in the western Netherlands, albeit more to fill their stomachs and for vitamin intake than to increase the calorific intake.[117]

Table 6.3 also shows the considerable local differences in food availability, placing Utrecht in a much more favourable position than the other three towns. The significance of the food expeditions was also confirmed by Hirschfeld himself. On 30 March 1945, he wrote: 'Finally,

---

[114] Kruijer, *Sociale Desintegratie*, 252–253.

[115] See, for example: Trienekens, *Tussen ons Volk en de Honger*, 381.

[116] Burger et al., *Malnutrition and Starvation*, 62. For Amsterdam, 139 families (689 persons) in 10 districts; Rotterdam, 88 families (457 persons) in 10 districts; Utrecht, 62 families (288 persons) in 4 districts; Delft, 37 families (179 persons) in 9 districts.

[117] Trienekens, *Voedsel en Honger in Oorlogstijd*, 88–89; Tom Vorstenbosch et al., 'Famine Food of Vegetal Origin Consumed in the Netherlands during World War II', *Journal of Ethnobiology and Ethnomedicine* 13 (2017): 1–15; See also: Th. Van Schaik, 'Voedingsmiddelen door den Mensch tijdens de Oorlogsjaren 1940–1945 Gebruikt, die Voordien in Nederland Vrijwel Onbekend Waren', *Voeding* 6 (1946): 93–109.

Table 6.3 *Estimated calorific intake outside legal channels and official rations*[a] *for adults in four cities during four selected periods*

	Amsterdam	Rotterdam	Utrecht	Delft
October 1944	564	725	648	370
	1,283	*910*	*1,090*	*1,010*
February 1945	724	770	938	870
	479	*550*	*620*	*390*
April 1945	446	580	713	450
	659	*690*	*620*	*730*
May/June 1945	408	320	128	360
	2,045	*2,400*	*2,007*	*1,800*

[a] Official rations in italics (see Chapter 4, Table 4.1).
Source: Burger et al., *Malnutrition and Starvation* II, 126–127, 153, 186, 210

the sugar beet from the west and the food expeditions contributed to the people's nutrition. The fact that the population is able to survive at these low levels is partly the result of companies suspending their activities, thereby enabling the workers to scavenge. Death by starvation has been largely averted because of the people's own efforts to obtain food.'[118] This statement by the secretary general is of enormous significance as the highest food official was not at all in favour of such decentralisation and private initiatives.

The Hunt for Fuel

For most people, the struggle for fuel was almost as desperate as the struggle for food. Following the military activities in the south, in September 1944 households were put on short gas and electricity rations, while the fuel distribution stopped altogether. In the summer of 1944, households had been allocated four units of fuel for the winter, but not all families had collected these units and now some received none at all.[119] To make matters worse, due to the deteriorating coal situation in early October 1944, electricity was cut off in the western provinces, followed by gas in the course of late October and early November. In the case of lighting, people were very resourceful: lighting candles and oil lamps but also making batteries or even driving bicycles in their living rooms to

[118] NIOD, 212a, inv.no. 167, Diary Hirschfeld, 30 March 1945.
[119] *Jaarverslag van Amsterdam 1944*, 21; Koster, *Honger in Rotterdam*, 18.

generate power.[120] Nevertheless, enjoying the pleasure of light was not their main concern during the final months of war. No gas also meant no heat and no means to cook food, both of which were indispensable during the wet autumn and cold winter months of 1944–1945.

As the fuel shortage affected all households, the hunt for fuel became an all-encompassing obsession throughout the occupied west. Instead of preparing meals at home, an ever-increasing group of people became entirely dependent on the state-run soup kitchens for their meals. Even so, while soup kitchens could give out meals, they could not solve the lack of heating and for most households, scavenging for fuel was the only alternative to buying cokes or anthracites for exorbitant prices at urban black markets. People started to crowd at sites where coal was previously used, such as marshalling yards and industrial areas, searching desperately for leftovers. Besides coal and cokes, people also tried to obtain turf from peatlands, even digging through shell paths, football fields, and waste piles to look for flammable materials.[121] These poor yields quickly disappeared in home-made emergency stoves ('*majo-kacheltjes*'), which were basically pipes with a hole in it. One man recalled: 'You would put all sort of things in it. Tram blocks, but also old shoes, waste, rags, everything to get you warm and enable you to cook. We were already wearing our coats indoors, of course.'[122]

Illegal logging was one of the main fuel-driven activities during the famine.[123] Already in mid-October 1944, people in Amsterdam and The Hague were seen chopping down trees and dragging firewood through the cities, especially after dark but also before the 8:00 P.M. evening curfew. In Rotterdam, logging activities started just a little later, as the city's gas delivery was only cut off in late November. By December, the cold had made people bolder in their approach, sawing trees in broad daylight in parks, squares, and along street lanes.[124] All sorts of people

---

[120] NIOD, 244, inv.no. 187, Diary P. G. -H., Rotterdam, September–November 1944; inv.no. 1805, Diary S. P. -B. (female nurse in The Hague), The Hague, October 1944. *Jaarverslag van Amsterdam 1944*, 2, 18; Slager et al., *Verhalen om te Onthouden*, 80–81; Van der Zee, *De Hongerwinter*, 120.

[121] *Jaarverslag van Amsterdam 1945*, 1–2; Dienstverslagen 1944 Gemeente Amsterdam, Dienst Stadsreiniging, 1; Van Miert, '"En Toen kwam het er Eigenlijk op aan": September 1944–September 1945', in *Een Gewone Stad in een Bijzondere Tijd*, 202; Koster, *Honger in Rotterdam*, 18–19; Barnouw, *De Hongerwinter*, 33–34. Slager et al., *Verhalen om te Onthouden*, 48–50; De Jong, *Het Koninkrijk* 10b, 182.

[122] Slager et al., *Verhalen om te Onthouden*, 47.

[123] Illegal logging had occurred earlier during the occupation as well, especially in winter time. Initially, municipalities would give licenses to gather firewood, but already in 1942, it was forbidden. NA, 2.06.076.08 Rijksbureau voor Hout, inv.no. 106, Circular letter Directorate for Wood, October 1943.

[124] NIOD, 244, inv.no. 1230, Diary C. J. v. B. (male office clerk Amsterdam), 15 October 1944; inv.no. 2805, 18 October 1944; NIOD, 244, inv.no. 187, Diary C. G. -H.

were involved in these practices, but in many cities, women and especially children participated most actively. This was partly due to the absence of men in South Holland, but perhaps more so because women and children were less likely to be arrested. According to a woman from The Hague: 'Even proper ladies and gentlemen are walking around with rucksacks, bags, and carts with wood.'[125] The fuel scarcity drove people in the northeast to scavenge for firewood as well; although, this was not on the same scale, as gas was still available there every other day.[126]

The hunt for firewood proved disastrous for cityscapes. In most towns, local authorities closed off some parks entirely, but these measures were of little help. In Amsterdam, 14 parks were entirely or partially demolished, adding up to a total surface of 75 ha. In addition, 23,130 meters of wooden garden fence, 27,919 trees (36.1/1,000 population) and about 3,000 tree poles were stolen.[127] In The Hague, the situation was quite similar. The fuel shortage had driven the population to fell their beloved 'ornaments of The Hague' – its avenue trees – but also parks and a large part of the Scheveningse Bosjes. Despite vigilante groups trying protect the urban green, about 20,000 trees fell to the axe (44.4/1,000) and 400 ha of forest, park, and gardens were demolished.[128] Vigilantes out to save the trees in Rotterdam did not help much either. Within days, the Oude Plantage in the Kralingen quarter was robbed completely bare. The same fate awaited the Sterrebos in Schiedam.[129]

The situation was even worse in the poorer city of Leiden where, by January, almost all trees had been chopped down. At the time of liberation, only 390 of the former 5,330 trees were still standing (59.2/1,000).[130] Haarlem witnessed a similar destruction of city parks and

(young woman Rotterdam), 28 October 1944; NIOD, 244, inv.no. 1843, Diary J. K. (male teacher Amsterdam), December 1944; GAR, 273, inv.no. 119, Diary N. D. (female teacher HBS Rotterdam), 13 December 1944.

[125] NIOD, 0332, L13, Report Cannegieter. See also: Slager et al., *Verhalen om te Onthouden*, 100–103.

[126] J. J. Leeninga and E. J. Westra, *En tóch Staat de Martini: Groningen onder Duitsch Schrikbewind* (Groningen: Niemeyer, 1945), 122; Pim Kooij, 'Geregelde Schaarste: Economische Aspecten van Groningen in Oorlogstijd', in *Groningen in Oorlogstijd: Aspecten van de Bezettingsjaren 1940–1945*, ed. Elisabeth A. J. Boiten (Haren: Knoop & Niemeijer, 1980), 163, 171.

[127] Population on 31 December 1944. CBS, *Bevolking der Gemeenten van Nederland op 1 Januari 1944, 1945 en 1946* (Utrecht: W. De Haan, 1947), 37–63.

[128] In total from all causes, 188 ha forest and parks, 33.5 ha terraced gardens, and 50,000 trees. Abraham Schierbeek, *Den Haag 1945: Een Documentatie over de Jaren 1940–1945* (The Hague: De Hofstad, 1945); De Jong, *Het Koninkrijk* 10b, 183; Van der Boom, *Den Haag in de Tweede Wereldoorlog*, 232.

[129] Koster, *Honger in Rotterdam*, 18–19.

[130] Goudriaan, *Leiden in de Tweede Wereldoorlog*, 219–220. De Jong, *Het Koninkrijk* 10b, 183.

gardens. At the end of the occupation, the city counted 10,000 fewer trees than in 1940 (66.7/1,000).[131] In the province of Utrecht, the most severe losses were located in the areas close to major population centres such as Zeist, Driebergen, Rhenen, Leusden, and Baarn.[132] Despite reasonably well-functioning vigilante groups called 'tree patrols', the city of Utrecht lost about 5,000 trees (28.8/1,000), in addition to many garden fences and shrubberies.[133] And Hilversum, even though located in the wooded area Het Gooi, lost an astonishing 13,000 trees (165.3/1,000).[134] These numbers clearly, and with emphatic imagery, point to the sheer scale of the hunt for fuel, not to mention the large numbers of people involved.

The fuel shortage affected not just the city's greenery, but almost everything made out of wood that was accessible to the public. In order to prevent total urban demolition, the municipality of Utrecht removed all wooden benches from its parks.[135] To avert theft of benches and boards from public schools they also appointed special night guards. This was a worthwhile job, as the guards were given a small stove to keep warm, which provided cooking heat as well. The situation was so grave that the population even began removing wooden blocks from the tram rails, leading to road blockages and accidents. Several streets in the Amsterdam city centre and nineteenth-century quarters became completely inaccessible as a result of these sabotaging forages. The speed of demolition was impressive. For example, the tram track on the Koninginneweg in Amsterdam, numbering 275,000 small wooden street blocks (4,500 m^2), was completely taken apart within only a few hours. In The Hague, about 14,000 m^2 of wooden paving was removed by both the public and the authorities: the latter used the paving to fuel soup kitchens.[136]

Empty houses also fell victim to the demolition rage, especially in the former Jewish quarters. One man remembers in a post-war interview:

[131] G. M. Nieuwenhuis, *Vijf Jaren Oorlog over Haarlem: Verslag van de Gemeentelijke Bemoeiingen van 1940–1945* (Haarlem: Gemeente Haarlem, 1947), 106–110; Peter Hammann et al., *Lizzy: 126 Dagen Tulpentaart en Appelschilletjesthee* (Weesp: In Blijde Druk, 2015), 14.

[132] Staatsbosbeheer, afdeling Bosstatistiek, 'Verliezen aan onze Houtopstanden, Hoofdzakelijk toegebracht gedurende de Oorlogsjaren', *Nederlandsch Boschbouw Tijdschrift* 22 (1950): 358–367.

[133] Verhoeven, 'Dagelijks Leven in Utrecht', 193.

[134] Gemeente Hilversum, *Verslag over de Jaren 1939–1949* (Hilversum: Gemeente Hilversum, 1951), 64–71.

[135] Verhoeven, 'Dagelijks Leven in Utrecht', 193.

[136] NIOD, 244, inv.no. 1129, Diary H. H., 9 March 1945; Dienstverslagen 1945 Gemeente Amsterdam, Dienst Publieke Werken, 5–6, 37–46; *Jaarverslag van Amsterdam 1945*, II, 1.

At a certain point, me and my father went into the Jewish quarter, where all the houses stood empty. Then we went into those houses and kicked the doors in and removed everything made of wood. You were really scavenging the city. Everywhere you saw groups of people. Huge numbers stole wood. Everything was nicking, and it was tolerated by everyone, at all levels. Your parents made you do it as a kid, and there was nothing bad about it.[137]

The Amsterdam authorities called them 'beam squads', because they mostly acted in groups to remove the larger wooden constructions, such as supporting beams and staircases, often selling the wood on the black market. Individuals scavenging the sites collected the remaining pieces, during which dozens were injured from the now structurally weakened buildings, several fatally.[138] Empty houses throughout the urban west were destroyed in a similar manner, and not just by men – women participated just as fervently: 'For example, they demolished these large warehouses from Van Gend & Loos, on the Parallelweg in Rotterdam. Those were quite some beams: they were about half a square metre and ten to twelve metres long .... Where they found the strength .... It is incomprehensible.'[139] Urban dwellers living close to coastal areas also broke into houses that had been evacuated and closed off by the Germans as part of the Atlantikwall.[140] In The Hague, about 1,800 empty buildings were completely demolished; in Amsterdam, the number of houses was approximately 1,500, about half of which were located in the former Jewish quarters.[141]

By March, most 'public resources' had been depleted and people, especially those from the working-class neighbourhoods, turned to burning their own homes. Doors, wooden floors, and even staircases were fed to the stoves, which temporarily brought some warmth but in the end made their houses even colder because it ruined the insulation. Stories about these demolitions are as abundant as they are heart-wrenching: 'My mother started to burn our own home. We lived in the sort of house where you live downstairs and sleep upstairs, you know. Well, my mother burned the entire staircase to the bedrooms. We could only enter upstairs from the side.'[142] In another example, a mother recalled: 'I demolished

---

[137] Slager et al., *Verhalen om te Onthouden*, 41.
[138] NIOD, 244, inv.no. 1141, Diary C. A. L. S. (Chief municipal department Amsterdam), 20 November 1944; Dienstverslagen 1944 Gemeente Amsterdam, Opruimingsdienst, 7–8; *Jaarverslag van Amsterdam 1945*, 2. Barnouw, *De Hongerwinter*, 34–35. Hinke Piersma and Kemperman, *Openstaande Rekeningen: De Gemeente Amsterdam en de Gevolgen van Roof en Rechtsherstel, 1940–1950* (Amsterdam: Boom, 2015), 120–125.
[139] Slager et al., *Verhalen om te Onthouden*, 103.
[140] Goudriaan, *Leiden in de Tweede Wereldoorlog*, 219–220; Van der Boom, *Den Haag in de Tweede Wereldoorlog*, 232.
[141] De Jong, *Het Koninkrijk* 10b, 184.   [142] Slager et al., *Verhalen om te Onthouden*, 52.

Illustration 17 People demolishing empty houses for firewood in The Hague.

everything in our home made of wood … cots, picture frames, sewing kit … even the doors disappeared into the stove … cupboards, stair steps … not all, but every other. That way, you could still get upstairs.'[143] According to a post-war survey by the NMA, in Amsterdam, about 15 per cent of all households had burned their interior in part or entirely; in smaller towns investigated in South Holland, this was about 12 per cent, but in Rotterdam, it was 45 per cent.[144] For many people, the only alternative during the cold winter months was to stay in bed all day and sleep as much as possible.

The police proved utterly powerless when it came to preventing the demolition of public spaces and private dwellings. In fact, most sources indicate that poor police surveillance was the main cause for the attack on urban greenery and empty houses.[145] The police force had been woefully understaffed because of the German raids and was dealing with the same

[143] Slager et al., *Verhalen om te Onthouden*, 54.
[144] The survey was based on approximately 2,500 households, and should thus be considered a very rough estimate. De Jong, *Het Koninkrijk* 10b, 186. The much higher rates for Rotterdam most likely also resulted from unequally sized groups. In Rotterdam, three-fifths of the interviewees had an annual wage below 1,400 guilders; in Amsterdam only a third.
[145] Schierbeek, *Den Haag 1945*.

scarcity of supplies and transportation as everybody else. On 13 February 1945, Seyss-Inquart pressed for more strict surveillance and one week later *Höhere SS und Polizeiführer* Rauter officially prohibited tree felling; nonetheless, for local police it was impossible to follow through on all incidents.[146] In Amsterdam, the municipality had walled off the empty houses, but this had the opposite effect and encouraged the astute scavengers, who chopped away parts of the wall and left the remainder standing as a handy shield to steal away undisturbed.[147] In Noordwijk, police confiscated over 2,000 axes and saws from residents to try and thwart wood theft. About 100 of the worst offenders were punished by the mayor, who made them chop and saw wood for local soup kitchens.[148]

In practice, most people who were arrested were released shortly after, as the individual nature of most activities likely appealed to the authorities' conscience in these difficult times.[149] A 24-year-old office clerk from Amsterdam, suspected of stealing scaffolding poles on Christmas day, for example, explained 'that he lived without fuel entirely and that his wife was due to be released from hospital'. [150] A man from The Hague who had been at the police station twice for wood theft wrote to his family: 'It was simply an emergency situation, and the police knew very well that people were not doing this for the fun of it.'[151] Generally, the Germans authorities did not do much to intervene; *Wehrmacht* regulations stated that tree-felling would only be constrained if it endangered flight coverage or military installations.[152] Nevertheless, most likely some people were shot by the Germans if caught stealing fuel.

The fact that liberation would not solve the fuel problem was something the people in the south had learned the hard way. Similar to the activities described above, during the winter months, people in the liberated areas scavenged for wood in parks, gardens, and forests as well. In response, on 25 January 1945 the Dutch Military Commissioner of liberated North Brabant implemented regulations to protect the forestry; henceforth, a permit was required for carrying saws, axes, or other tools

---

[146] NIOD, 216K, inv.no. 333, Documents on tree felling in several municipalities, November 1944–March 1945; 'Bekendmaking: Streng Verbod van Kappen van Bomen', *Dagblad voor het Noorden*, 20 February 1945.
[147] Dienstverslagen 1944 Gemeente Amsterdam, Opruimingsdienst, 7–8.
[148] De Jong, *Het Koninkrijk* 10b, 183–184.
[149] SA, 5225a Gemeentepolitie Amsterdam, inv.no. 8387, 8389, Police reports November 1944–April 1945.
[150] SA, 5225a. inv.no. 8389, Police report 25 December 1944.
[151] NIOD, 0332, inv.no. k24. See also: SA, 5225a, inv.no. 8389, Police report 29 December 1944; Slager et al., *Verhalen om te Onthouden*, 42.
[152] NIOD, 001, inv.no. 656, *Kriegestagebuch Vizeadmiral* Stange, November 1944.

used for felling trees. Violation of these regulations was punishable with a maximum of one year in prison or a 2,000-guilder fine.[153] After the west had been liberated, the State Forestry Commission notified the Director General of Wood that the felling of trees still did not seem to be slowing down. Mayors in forest-rich municipalities in close proximity to urban areas requested a ban on the transportation of wood, since surveillance and inspection of all who owned saws or axes was impossible. This ban was implemented in late July 1945.[154] By that time, the hunt for fuel had left physical scars on cityscapes that would be visible for years to come.

Conclusion

The severe food and fuel deprivation during the final months of war prompted urban dwellers in the occupied west to take matters into their own hands. Yet not everybody resorted to the same means of resisting the famine conditions. Due to the transportation difficulties, black-market prices rose to astronomical levels. Since most households did not have the means to purchase or barter at the black markets regularly, any man or woman socially and physically capable to do so ventured out into the countryside in search for food. Combined with a shared moral sense of what was acceptable and rational behaviour, these factors made responses to the famine largely class-based. Working-class families were hit harder because they had less means to buy or barter food; nevertheless, they often enjoyed better contacts in the city and countryside than middle- or upper-class families. For the middle class, the famine presented particular difficulties, as although they did not have enough material means for food, bourgeois decency prevented them from acting in illegal ways or embarking on food expeditions on a large scale.

These individual and household responses to the famine also reveal much about the nature of the Dutch famine. Firstly, the strategies pursued by these individuals clearly demonstrate that the crisis was essentially a transportation problem and not the result of a food availability decline. Food was evidently to be found in the countryside. So much so that, even during the height of the famine, many farmers still had surplus food that enabled urbanites to retrieve supplies or share in home-cooked meals. Secondly, the household and individual responses reveal the Hunger Winter as an early-stage famine and not a situation of

[153] NA, 2.06.076.08 Rijksbureau voor Hout, inv.no. 106, Provincial decree protection forest, 25 January 1945.
[154] NA, 2.06.076.08, inv.no. 106, Letter Staatsbosbeheer to Director of Wood, 18 June 1945; NA, Press message, 26 July 1945.

outright starvation. Despite the fact that the fabric of daily life was torn by the material conditions and farmers often abused their privileged position, there was also much cooperation and solidarity between and among urbanites and agrarians. Most importantly, throughout the crisis, there were ample opportunities for most individuals to fight the impact of famine at household levels, and the results of their actions continued to be worthwhile. The strong and active reaction from the population demonstrates that, although hunger was severe, it was not excessive in the sense that it turned people inward. Chapters 7 and 8 demonstrate that these expressions of cooperation and solidarity during the famine reached far beyond household levels alone.

7   Community Strategies

In order to function properly, centralised rationing systems require a shared sense of social entitlements, fairness, and justice.[1] During the Dutch food crisis, this legitimacy of state authorities in the food system became highly contested amongst the people: a legitimacy crisis that was connected to a declining legal food production and associated official rations on the one hand, and rising black-market trade and other extra-legal ways to obtain food on the other. The food and fuel scarcity caused black-market prices to explode, which, as Chapter 6 has shown, only the wealthiest could afford. The astronomical black-market prices incited able-bodied urban dwellers to head out into the countryside to obtain foodstuffs at lower prices. With more than half of the urban households participating, these food expeditions were indispensable for mitigating famine conditions at the household level. Yet they also left a particularly vulnerable group behind: people who were unable to embark on food expeditions or buy regularly at the black market. These were the poor, the sick and elderly, people in hiding, and housebound single parents with young children.

Who took care of these vulnerable people during the famine? This chapter aims to answer this question by shifting the traditional focus away from governmental and external organised relief by, instead, investigating 'internal' relief operations.[2] Until now, these communal coping strategies during the Dutch famine have received little scholarly attention. Historians have asserted that people were primarily fending for themselves during the famine, while solidarity and cooperation all but disappeared.[3] That is to

---

[1] Trentmann, 'Coping with Shortage', 22; Bonzon and Davies, 'Feeding the Cities'.
[2] Part of this chapter, focusing on the case of Amsterdam, has been previously published: De Zwarte, 'Save the Children: Social Self-Organization and Relief in Amsterdam during the Dutch Hunger Winter', *Food & History* 14 (2016): 51–76. For governmental and external organised relief during the Dutch famine, see: Burger et al., *Malnutrition and Starvation*; Moore, 'The Western Allies'.
[3] Kruijer, *Sociale Desorganisatie*; Trienekens, *Tussen ons Volk en de Honger*; Klemann *Nederland 1938–1948*; Pauw, *Rotterdam in de Tweede Wereldoorlog*, 637; Futselaar, *Lard, Lice and Longevity*, 77–78.

say, while collective social responses have been recognised in studies on pre-modern and modern famines alike, the history of the Dutch wartime food system has remained largely dominated by a state-oriented outlook.[4]

By focusing on the organisation of relief in the occupied Netherlands below the level of the government but above the household level, this chapter argues that there was a societal focus on prioritising relief for school-age children. This focus on children was coherent with relief practices during other European wartime food crises, for example in occupied Belgium during World War I, post-blockade Germany, civil-war Spain, Winter War Finland, famine-struck Greece during World War II, and post-war Italy.[5] However, the difference between the above relief efforts and the Dutch case was that child relief in the Netherlands was not solely organised top-down, but rather emerged out of self-organised networks and grassroots initiatives. The collective responsibility felt to relieve children first and foremost was shared and endorsed at all levels of society, including by the German authorities. The aim of this chapter is to advance a deeper understanding of how experienced communities – those around which people constructed their daily lives[6] – and civil society institutions functioned as a third food distribution system during the Dutch famine, in addition to those supplies acquired and allocated by the state and households.

Social Self-Organisation

Fortunately for those people most prone to starvation, the crisis situation did not produce solely self-serving responses. The state's shrinking role in providing food via official rations was partially replaced by expanded

[4] E.g., Thompson, 'The Moral Economy of the English Crowd'; Scott, *The Moral Economy of the Peasant*; Arnold, *Famine*; Vanhaute and Lambrecht, 'Famine, Exchange Networks and the Village Community'; Swift, 'Understanding and Preventing Famine'; Adams, 'Food Insecurity in Mali'.

[5] E.g., Richard L. Cary, 'Child-Feeding Work in Germany', *Annals of the American Academy of Political and Social Science* 92 (1920): 157–162; Felix M. Gentile, 'U.N.R.R.A. Child-Feeding in Italy', *Social Service Review* 20 (1946): 502–522; Farah J. Mendleschn, 'The Ethics of Friends' Relief Work in Republican Spain', *Quaker History* 88 (1999): 1–23; Helene Laurent, 'War and the Emerging Social State: Social Policy, Public Health and Citizenship in Wartime Finland', in *Finland in World War II: History, Memory, Interpretations*, eds. Tiine Kinnunen and Villa Kivimäki (Leiden; Brill, 2012), 315–354; Hionidou, *Famine and Death in Occupied Greece*, 111, 118–147; Hionidou, '"Choosing" between Children and the Elderly in the Greek Famine (1941–1944)', in *Coping with Hunger and Shortage under German Occupation*, 203–222; Nath, *Brood Willen We Hebben!*, 45–107, 228; Davies and Wheatcroft, *The Years of Hunger*, 221–222, 425–425; Cox, 'Hunger Games', 623–629.

[6] See also: Winter, 'Paris, London, Berlin 1914–1919: Capital Cities at War', in *Capital Cities at War*, 4.

public participation and communal efforts to relieve food deprivation. From the autumn of 1944 onward, local self-help entities and relief committees emerged in all towns and cities in the western Netherlands, mostly comprising people living in the same street or neighbourhood or belonging to the same religious denomination. According to block captains from the Air Raid Protection in Heemstede, this communal relief was much better organised within working-class neighbourhoods than in upper-class areas, due to the former's larger involvement in the black market, their greater awareness of the situation of neighbours, and a reduced self-centredness and 'more willingness to help one another'.[7]

The success stories of relief efforts in working-class quarters are abundant. One such effort in Amsterdam – Campaign Betondorp (*Actie Betondorp*) – initiated by Dr Wagenaar arranged the distribution of 132,000 litres of cooked meals, between early January and mid-May 1945. Under the guidance of this local physician, 500 of the 6,200 neighbours volunteered in the quarter's private food supply, emergency hospital, technical service team, security system, and even a veterinarian service. Their initial focus was feeding all children between the ages of 6 and 16, but they soon extended these requirements to 19 years: this was to discourage adolescents from working for the Germans in return for extra rations. Eventually, children between the ages of 4 and 6 were included as well. The committee also managed to occasionally intercept food that was intended for the black market with the help of local resistance groups and policemen, which was then divided equally among all neighbours: creating new networks of trust and food coalitions at the community level.[8]

A similar committee, 'Campaign on the Islands' (*Actie op de Eilanden*), focused on one of the poorest neighbourhoods in Amsterdam, where many working-class men had lost their jobs after the German harbour demolitions in September 1944. Led by secretary of the Reformed Church (*Nederduits Hervormde Kerk*) J. de Graaff and Catholic priest H. M. Finke, the interdenominational committee provided a daily

---

[7] NIOD, 0332, inv.no. E, Letter from H. C. Determeijer (Air Protection) to RvO, 18 July 1946. The Air Raid Protection was an organisation comprising volunteers and civil servants tasked with protecting civilians from air raids through education and assistance with taking precautionary measures.

[8] J. H. Wagenaar, *Een Jaar Noodcomité* (Amsterdam: Noodcomité Tuindorp Watergraafsmeer, 1946), 4–6; De Zwarte, 'Save the Children', 51–76. See also: NIOD, 0332, inv.no. B1, Van de Griek, 'De Voedselhulp'; NIOD, 0376 Kerken, inv.no. A5, Circular letter Watergraafsmeer; SR, 728 Dekenaat Rotterdam, inv.no. 104, Circular letters 'Comité Het Kralingsche Kind 1945', December 1944–February 1945; Week report IKB, 29 January 1945; HGA, 0610-01, inv.no. 999, Letter Municipal Services to mayor, 15 January 1945.

Illustration 18 People waiting for IKB food distribution in
Amsterdam, 1945.

one-litre meal from January to June 1945 to all 3,000 schoolchildren as
well as to 500 people in hiding. In addition, they served 1,250 children
aged below four years of age half a litre of porridge a day. The committee
secretly took care of 800 sick and elderly people as well, something
National Socialist authorities did not allow, since they opposed food
relief for this vulnerable group who had 'no meaning for maintaining
strength of the people'.[9] As was mostly the case with these local

---

[9] NIOD, 0332, inv.no. B1, Van de Griek, 'De Voedselhulp', 11–15; De Graaff, *De Eilanden
en de Hongersnood: Honger Winter 1944–1945* (Amsterdam: ICLEI Bureau, 1945); J. De
Graaff and H. M. Finke, *Herdenkingsalbum: Hongersnood op de Eilanden* (Amsterdam:
ICLEI Bureau, 1945).

committees, the food was supplied by informal contacts in the north-eastern provinces – 51 different municipalities in this specific case.[10]

Churches played an important role in organising food relief, albeit sometimes only for their own religious communities. For churches in the Netherlands – the Catholic church in particular – the doctrine of subsidiarity played an important role, which basically meant decentralising as much power and functions of the state as possible and taking it over themselves, not just in the political arena, but socially and economically as well. As a consequence, denominational organisations had been competing with the state for power and legitimacy in these areas. Local relief entities also fit perfectly within these principles of subsidiarity.[11] An example of a well-functioning church relief committee was the Reformed 'Help for us All' (*Hulp voor ons Allen*), established in Rotterdam in December 1944. While its name might suggest otherwise, the committee only aided the Reformed community in Rotterdam's city centre. From its creation until liberation, the all-male board of Help for us All provided relief to all 2,061 families in its parish with the help of about a hundred volunteers and support from a local abattoir. The foodstuffs they reallocated came from religious sister communities in the rural northeast of the country: this was a common occurrence with denominational relief committees. In total, Help for us All distributed over 40,000 meals, placed 36 of its children in host families to share home-cooked food, and evacuated another 200 children to the countryside.[12] While the initiative and management of denominational organisations such as Help for us All lay almost exclusively with a small group of men, the actual day-to-day execution of feeding and taking care of the children was performed by a much larger group of female volunteers, as was also the case in other relief committees. As evidenced by documents and photographs, they guided the children to the distribution points, and served and supervised the meals. Strengthened by the religious basis of many of these relief organisations, labour division in the grassroots entities thus often affirmed traditional gender roles.

The scale of local relief entities varied widely across the western Netherlands. In some cases, grassroots initiatives limited their range to include only a small circle of close neighbours. For example, a resident of the wealthy Parkweg district in Scheveningen opened a communal stove

[10] See, for instance: Tresoar, 101 Koopmans Koninklijke Meelfabrieken B. V., inv.no. 680, Documentation on the activities of the committee 'Hulp aan Holland', 1945.
[11] De Rooy, 'De Ongemakkelijke Democratie', 221–222.
[12] W. A. van Dongen, *Oorlogswinter 1944–1945: Commissie van de Gereformeerde Kerk van Rotterdam-C, 'Hulp voor ons Allen'* (Rotterdam: Meinema, 1945).

in January 1945 out of 'sincere community spirit', which sufficed in providing all 350 families in the neighbourhood with cooking heat and hot water during the crisis.[13] In Amsterdam, residents from the Laplace straat formed a mutual aid committee to share hot water and electricity as well as take care of the sick.[14]

In other towns, NGOs that emerged aspired to have a citywide impact. Citizens from Utrecht were among the first to organise relief outside of governmental structures. Already in October 1944, the local department of the Dutch Red Cross initiated a citywide organisation, incorporating municipal health services, existing local food committees, and representatives from several denominations.[15] Similarly, in Leiden the director of a bread factory set up a broad-based relief committee in collaboration with local food authorities. This 'Leiden Care Council' (*Verzorgingsraad voor Leiden*) explained: 'The food supply of the people during wartime was essentially a governmental task and not part of the competence of private individuals, yet in an emergency situation such as the one occurring in the autumn of 1944, these considerations are no reason to withhold from action.'[16] At the same time, there were at least four other relief bodies active in Leiden, all focusing on other vulnerable groups, such as children, the elderly, or the sick and hospitalised.[17] In all cases, because of their ability to identify needy or vulnerable people at the individual level, local relief committees succeeded in taking over relief responsibilities from municipal authorities.

Over the course of the crisis, these relief entities began largely to rely on the authority of two institutions – the churches and local resistance groups. While previous studies argued that even the authority of these institutions crumbled in the face of disaster,[18] the examples of local relief efforts clearly demonstrate a process in the opposite direction. Local archives reveal that, because of the social and bureaucratic chaos,

---

[13] HGA, 0610-01, inv.no. 999, Letter Municipal Services to mayor, 15 January 1945.

[14] NIOD, 0332, inv.no. L9, Letter Committee Mutual Aid Laplace straat, January 1945.

[15] Henri W. Julius, *Kinderen in Nood: De Kindervoeding in de Stad Utrecht in de Nood-Winter 1944–1945* (Utrecht: Commissie Kindervoeding voor de Stad Utrecht, 1946), 9–14; For more on Carel Piek in relation to the Dutch Red Cross, see: Wassenaar, *Van Winterhulp*, 139–157.

[16] ELO, 0257, inv.no. 8, J. Bosma and W. A. Kasteleijn, 'Overzicht van de Werkzaamheden van de Stichting Verzorgingsraad voor Leiden in de Noodwinter 1944–1945', 1950.

[17] De Jong, *Het Koninkrijk* 10b, 243; Alphons Siebelt, *'Het is een Raadsel waarvan de Bevolking heeft Geleefd' De Leidse Voedselvoorziening in de Hongerwinter* (Leiden: Primavera Pers, 2018), passim.

[18] Van der Zee, *De Hongerwinter*, 56–57; Trienekens, *Tussen ons Volk en de Honger*, 381; Van der Boom, *Den Haag tijdens de Tweede Wereldoorlog*, 231; Van der Heijden, *Grijs Verleden*, 320; Klemann, *Nederland 1939–1948*, 561; Futselaar, *Lard, Lice and Longevity*, 77–78.

resistance groups managed to become involved in most relief initiatives. Prompted by the need to feed people in hiding and their desire to control local food supply, resistance groups even came to play a central role in these relief practices.[19] This not only applied to the western Netherlands, but also for the northeast, where many local relief committees were established for the purpose of collecting supplies for the cities in the west.[20] This transfer of power and legitimacy from the state to the churches and resistance in the name of the desperate food situation was also brought to the attention of the Allies and Dutch government-in-exile. An intelligence agent in the occupied Netherlands wrote to London in March 1945:

When the farmers are urged by the 'official authorities' to give up their milk for the children in the large cities, they turn a deaf ear. But if the minister or the priest tells them to do so, they are impressed and their only question is, how about the transport? Answer: the underground movement, which sees to forged papers. The second question, however, is: how does the underground movement get hold of them? Answer: by negotiating with the Germans through third persons .... It is striking in fact how the prestige of Christianity has grown. Not only because the sermons are so often political, but especially because the clergy has shouldered such enormous social tasks. The Dutch Reformed clergyman of Slikkerveer [South Holland], told me, for example, how he and his Calvinist and liberal colleagues had taken over the entire distribution of the Swedish relief-parcels, completely circumventing the burgomaster and official distribution services.[21]

While the focus of the churches and resistance groups was on short-term relief, their involvement in food provisioning should be seen as part of the struggle for post-war power relations as well. All parties knew that the war was coming to an end and certainly the church and resistance (no less than state authorities) used these final moments to consolidate their authority and legitimacy among the population.

---

[19] NIOD, 1076 Interkerkelijk Overleg, inv.no. 24, Post-war report on relief by HOA, s.n; NIOD 189, Vrije Groepen Amsterdam, inv.no. 1, Circular letter VGA no. 1484, 16 February 1945; Centraal Bureau Kindervoeding, *Winter 1944–1945: Verslag Centraal Bureau Kindervoeding Haarlem* (Haarlem; Centraal Bureau Kindervoeding, 1946). See also: Noord-Hollands Archief [NHA], 1310 Stichting Volksherstel Haarlem, inv.no. 23, Report Volksherstel Haarlem 1945–1946; J. D. Vis, *Rapport over de Nood-Organisatie Koog-Zaandijk: Uitgebracht in de Vergadering van het Bestuur der Nood-Organisatie en het Dames-Comité, gehouden op 15 November 1945* (S.l., s.n, 1945); De Jong, *Het Koninkrijk* 10b, 244–245.

[20] For example, Tresoar, 101, inv.no. 680, Documents on aid and activities *Hulp aan Holland*, 1945.

[21] NARA, 331, Entry 2, Box 118, Report 'The Occupied Netherlands To-day and To-morrow', 17 March 1945.

In addition to local and denominational relief committees, another effective form of self-help was intra-company aid. When the food situation began deteriorating in the autumn of 1944, most companies initiated actions for gathering food and fuel for their personnel. All sorts of companies, from insurance offices and department stores to the Royal Dutch Shell and the Amsterdam Zoo, formed central procurement committees from their midst that sent out delegates to the countryside to obtain food. Usually, the obtained cargo was modest and comprised a large quantity of potatoes, legumes, firewood, or even tulip bulbs: making a small but welcome addition to the staff's meagre rations.[22] Another company response to the famine was evacuating the staff's children out of the famine-affected areas, a coping strategy that is elaborately discussed in the Chapter 8.

Organising central procurement was not easy for most companies, as transporting food supplies required approval from national or provincial food authorities, not to mention the difficult-to-obtain German 'Sonderausweis' (special permit). A collective food expedition in early 1945 by the Directorate of Wood took 26 days because of transportation difficulties, theft, confiscations, and negotiations; nevertheless, the resulting cargo of potatoes and cheese was divided equally among employees.[23] The returns of these efforts varied widely and mostly depended on whether or not the company owned transportation means and had business contacts in agricultural regions. The North and South Holland Lifeboat Company, for instance, used their own lifeboats to ship potatoes, legumes, and wheat from the province of Friesland; the board of the Steamship Company 'The Netherlands' sent a barge to the province of Gelderland to retrieve potatoes for their employees.[24]

Local and national authorities did not object to these forms of company aid, especially since it was needed for the businesses to keep functioning, or, at least to help their people through the famine. Local authorities were even willing to assist in some cases. But, for the national food authorities, the 'unfairnesses' of company self-help presented certain difficulties. As explained, the state's initial response was to force

[22] NIOD, 247 Correspondentie, inv.no. 239, Letters from R. v. G. in Amsterdam to P. v. G. in Friesland, 1944–1945; NIOD, 244, inv.no. 1129, Dairy H. H., 14 January 1945; NIOD, 0331, inv.no. A3, Report J. C. van der Leek on food expeditions and transactions Insurance office Langeveldt-Schröder Amsterdam, 24 April 1945; inv.no. A4, Report H. Cordes in Amersfoort on food transports, s.a.; NIOD, 0332, inv.no. J., Letter from Zoological Museum Artis to department store Bijenkorf, 16 February 1945; inv.no. E., Letter to UvA staff members, 28 November 1944; H. K. Choufour and W. G. N. de Keizer, *7 Magere Maanden: Ter Herinnering aan een Moeizame Doorworstelden Oorlogswinter* (Haarlem: Druk Boom-Ruygrok N. V., 1945).

[23] De Jong, *Het Koninkrijk* 10b, 236–239.   [24] De Jong, *Het Koninkrijk* 10b, 240.

companies to give up part of the cargo to central rationing. On 25 January 1945, the food authorities then closed the IJssel bridges and waterways for the transportation of cereals, legumes, butter, salad oil, and cheese to the west, thereby ending the most significant route of interregional intra-company aid. Following extensive debates between the food officials and representatives from the business sector, companies in the western Netherlands were still authorised to grow and harvest their own food supplies in allotment gardens, but the rewards for these efforts were much lower than those of company food expeditions – not in the least because it was winter.[25]

'By the Churches, for All'

While local authorities had allowed the emergence of relief and self-help entities, the Dutch and German national authorities grew concerned about the wide variety of these organisations. Director of Food Supply Louwes hoped to coordinate local efforts in order to retain some level of control, but also to receive official approval from Seyss-Inquart for non-governmental emergency aid. In early December 1944, meetings were held between Louwes and representatives of the Interdenominational Counsel of the Churches (IKO). Louwes acknowledged that the IKO was in a strong position to take on relief responsibilities, as city dwellers trusted the churches because of their critical stance towards the occupier; furthermore, the organisation also provided a link with food-producing communities in the northeast of the country. Importantly, the IKO could embody the 'apolitical' organisation the occupier would require for this job. On 11 December, a meeting was arranged via Schwebel between an IKO representative – the Finnish Consul General Van der Vlugt, who also had connections with the organised resistance – and Seyss-Inquart. The *Reichskommissar* agreed with the initiative, on the condition that there would be just one body for both emergency relief and the evacuation of children. His approval led to the establishment of the Interdenominational Bureau for Emergency Nutrition (IKB), which became the only organisation officially allowed to gather food alongside the rationing system.[26]

---

[25] NIOD, 212a, inv.no. 107, Note Hirschfeld to Director of Agriculture on company allotments, 9 February 1945; Letter Director of Horticulture to Hirschfeld, 21 March 1945. See also: NIOD, 216h, inv.no. 166, Circular Letter PVC South Holland, 27 February and 15 March 1945.

[26] NIOD, 1076, inv.no. 23, Report meeting IKO and Louwes, s.n.; Ravesloot, *De Houding van de Kerk;* Van Rossem, *Inter Kerkelijk Bureau*, 10.

On 14 December 1944, the IKB put together a board with representatives from the Reformed and Roman Catholic denominations as well as representatives from the public-school system 'to serve the emergency nourishment of ALL sections of society – even the non-religious ones [sic]'.[27] Officials from the public sector and industrial leaders joined the IKB in a special advisory committee. The Central IKB was established in The Hague, where an earlier interdenominational relief committee had already taken on child-feeding tasks.[28] The Central IKB's main task was to establish local departments throughout the occupied areas and to divide foodstuffs accordingly. The churches raised the required funds while families would pay for individual nourishment. In December 1944 and January 1945, two representatives of the IKO made trips to the northeastern provinces to talk about these plans with religious leaders, who were asked to call upon the Christian caritas of their parishes to give up food supplies and assist in the relief efforts. They also sought to connect with local relief committees, Provincial Food Commissioners, and Seyss-Inquart's provincial representatives. According to a post-war report by the IKB, it was 'due to the spontaneous collaboration of many good citizens among the authorities and private individuals that a smooth-running operation was launched'.[29] All large towns established district offices and hundreds of distribution points were opened. The IKB even set up a separate postal service for internal correspondence. Within a month, the IKB had managed to achieve the full and active cooperation of both German and Dutch officials and had attracted thousands of volunteers.[30]

The basic principle of the IKB was: 'By the churches, for all', which meant that the allocation of supplies was determined by medical or social priority, and not according to religious or political affiliation as practised earlier by denominational organisations or the National Socialist NVD. In addition to organising emergency nutrition, its second task was to evacuate malnourished children from the urban west to rural areas,

---

[27] *Charity in War-time: Final Report of the Local Interclerical Office The Hague and Its Environments* (The Hague: Interkerkelijk Bureau, 1946), 5.

[28] HGA, 0276-01 Stichting Sociale Wijkcentra, inv.no. 8, File on IKB The Hague, 1945.

[29] *Charity in War-time*, 6; NIOD, 1076, inv.no. 22, Report on journeys to northern provinces, s.n. See also: De Jong, *Het Koninkrijk* 10b, 247–249.

[30] NIOD, 182f Interkerkelijk Bureau voor Noodvoedselvoorziening, inv.no.144, Report Local IKB The Hague 'How it all started', April 1945; F. Houben, *Local Interclerical Office: Report First Quarter 1945* (The Hague: IKB, 1945). Seyss-Inquart and other high German officials did raise objections to the IKB's position later on in the crisis, as explained in Chapter 4. NIOD, 212a, inv.no. 106, Letter Wimmer and Schwebel to Hirschfeld, 12 February 1945; NA, 2.11.30.05, inv.no. 68, Meeting Louwes and Von der Wense, 22 March 1945.

which was to prove a crucial element in protecting children from starvation. For both tasks, it was imperative that the IKB established its own medical department to screen all those eligible for emergency feeding or evacuation, in cooperation with local general practitioners, paediatricians, internists, municipal health services, and the public health inspection. To ensure a fair selection, the IKB even distributed guidelines in which the chief of the medical department had meticulously explained the proper procedures and weight-for-height requirements that determined which urgency class the examined patient belonged to.[31] Contrary to the grass-roots relief organisations mentioned in the previous section, it is notable to see that, in all IKB departments, women played central roles, which might in part have to do with the absence of large numbers of men in cities such as The Hague, but also because it concerned the organisation of activities that were still considered to belong to the female domain.[32]

The IKB emergency nutrition department focused on three vulnerable groups that showed physical signs of malnourishment: toddlers (3–5 years), children (6–15 years), and adults: children, however, formed the largest group and were the first to be addressed in mid-January 1945. As the number of needy children increased so quickly, it was not possible to accept them into the feeding programmes based on doctor's notes alone. Independent medical screening ultimately determined whether children could participate in the meals six times a week (more than 20 per cent below average weight for sex, height, and age) or three times a week (15–20 per cent underweight). In The Hague, where the Central IKB was located, almost 30 per cent of the examined children fell into the highest 'urgently necessary' category.[33] Whether or not inspired by previous experiences, the IKB medical screening methods resembled the triage system that Quakers used in Germany after the blockade was lifted in 1919 to determine which children would receive extra feeding. They too had categorised children through medical examination into urgency classes according to measured nutritional deficits – without considering the child's religion or social standing – using the cut-off age of 14 years for participation.[34] The Joint Relief Committee operating in famished Greece during World War II also identified malnourished children through comparable medical examinations.[35]

[31] Herman J. Köster, *Inter Kerkelijk Bureau voor Noodvoedselvoorziening's-Gravenhage en Omstreken: Toelichting der Verstrekkingen op Medische Basis* (The Hague: IKB, 1945).
[32] HGA, 0276-01, inv.no. 8, File on IKB The Hague, 1945.
[33] NIOD, 182f, inv.no. 132, Overview of IKB work by doctor Berkhout, 1 October 1945; Köster, *Inter Kerkelijk Bureau*, 7–8.
[34] Cox, 'Hunger Games', 625–626.
[35] Hionidou, *Famine and Death in Occupied Greece*, 128.

Similar measurable criteria were applied to the other two groups, with the criteria for adults being particularly strict. Starting from 29 January, the IKB began distributing food to people over 16 years old whose lives were directly threatened by malnourishment, such as patients suffering from oedema, cachexia (>30 per cent underweight), tuberculosis, or those who had already become bedridden. The food situation was now considered to be so desperate that even the criteria for pregnant women was sharpened; not all could apply for extra food – only those who, after the correction for their pregnancy weight, were over 30 per cent under-weight. In contrast to other careful considerations by the IKB, this choice seemed based on the incorrect assumption that prenatal care was not as vital as infant relief, resulting in impairments in adult health for these as-of-yet-unborn babies. In all categories, adults who were classified as undernourished could rely on IKB relief for eight weeks, after which a new examination determined whether or not they were permitted to continue. On the advice of the Directorate of Food Supply, the IKB later also helped in preparing two kinds of infant food, one comprising milk, water, flour, and sugar (3,780 kcal/L) and the other of buttermilk, flour, and dextrin-maltose (3,584 kcal/L): both home delivered in one-litre bottles provided with full instructions.[36] In addition to these official categories, the IKB secretly cooked and delivered food to local hospitals, elderly homes, staff members of municipal emergency homes, political prisoners, and even people in hiding, thereby broadening the scope of vulnerable groups in society that benefited from IKB relief as much as possible.[37]

The supply and transportation of foodstuffs formed the most difficult tasks for the IKB. To acquire food, the IKB mostly relied on farmers from the northeastern regions who were willing to give up supplies not reserved for central rationing. Often this concerned 'secret supplies', which otherwise would likely have ended up in black markets. The IKB also received much aid from relief organisations in the northeast. During its first weeks of existence, the IKB was especially aided by the 'Professor Eerland Committee' (*Prof. Eerland Comité*), which was formed in October 1944 for the purpose of collecting supplies for hospitals in the west and resided under the Provincial Food Commissioner in Groningen, E. H. Ebels, operating with the assistance of local farmers, food industries, and private individuals. Many more local relief commit-tees contributed to the IKB's efforts: the Association for the Netherlands

---

[36] Köster, *Toelichting der Verstrekkingen op Medische Basis*, 8–13.

[37] *Charity in War-time; Hongerend Volk 1945 en Wat Deed het IKB?* (The Hague: Plaatselijk Interkerkelijk Bureau Den Haag en Omstreken, 1945).

Potato Trade (VBNA), local businesses and factories, and many others. The foodstuffs consisted mainly of potatoes, vegetables, cereals, legumes, and later on milk powder as well, brought to the west by a small group of carriers and shippers from the IKB's transport department. Their task was complicated by the need for driving documents, securities, night permits, and declarations to cross the IJssel line; in March 1945 the German authorities eliminated road transportation, allowing only minimal inland navigation until the day of liberation.[38]

After the war, an international committee inquired about the results of IKB relief through the organisation's local departments as well as via nutrition surveys conducted by the Allied Medical Feeding Teams. For the hundreds of thousands of people who received IKB relief between January and May 1945, the estimated extra 450–600 kcal consumed with these meals proved to be invaluable supplements to their meagre official rations.[39] In total, approximately half a million people – out of an urban population of 2.6 million – received IKB food relief for short or prolonged periods of time. According to estimations, the IKB delivered approximately 10,000 tons of food to the western Netherlands, or about 20 kilograms per patient.[40] This included the immediate post-war period, in which the number of IKB patients initially grew larger because Allied relief made more food supplies available, and because physicians uncovered many patients who had been in hiding or repatriated from the east. After the liberation, the increased nutritional value of official rations made food relief for most groups redundant; yet, coupon-free meals for people suffering from oedema and cachexia remained primarily IKB work.[41]

The question then arose as to whether the IKB was not essentially a 'war organisation', and whether it should delegate its tasks to regular rationing and charity organisations. Some IKB board members argued that they still had years of work left; others recognised the benefits of centralisation into a public body. When the food situation improved further over the summer and most malnutrition cases had been cured, the IKB decided to liquidate its emergency relief on 1 August 1945.[42] The IKB and IKO continued their efforts in other social welfare areas in

---

[38] *Charity in War-time; Hongerend Volk 1945 en Wat Deed het IKB?*
[39] Burger et al., *Malnutrition and Starvation.*
[40] Hendrik C. Touw, *Het Verzet der Hervormde Kerk* (The Hague: Boekencentrum, 1946), 78; De Jong, *Het Koninkrijk* 10b, 251.
[41] NA, 2.11.30.05, inv.no. 10, Report Dr G. C. E. Burger, Leader Medical Feeding teams to IKB, 2 June 1945.
[42] NIOD, 1076, inv.no. 11, Report IKB Haarlem, 15 June 1945; NA, 2.11.30.05, inv. no. 10, Letter Central IKB to local IKB offices, 16 July 1945.

close cooperation with the Emergency Supply Commission of the NMA; for instance, by taking care of the international child evacuations and by defending the rights of imprisoned National Socialists as well as their children.[43]

Child-Feeding Initiatives

The common denominator of most communal relief efforts in the western Netherlands was the aim to aid children first.[44] The focus on school-aged children reveals the inadequacies of official rationing protocols regarding their intake: this vulnerable group was allocated the same meagre rations as adults, while infants and toddlers were entitled to higher rations. On occasion, the latter were also able to obtain extra meals from state soup kitchens. It was thus assumed that younger children were less in need of extra rations – wrongfully, as it would turn out later. At the same time, the communal focus on children was coherent with the (philosophical) social position of youngsters at the time. After the Great War, the belief arose that children had a key role to play in protecting post-war society and preventing new social catastrophes.[45] Throughout the first half of the twentieth century, food relief practices in warring Europe consequently focused on children more than on any other social group.[46]

The immediate cause for civil society to step forward in defence of its children had arisen in September 1944, when the Directorate of Food Supply decided that all coupon-free meals including school meals, had to be stopped in favour of equal rationing. Since the late nineteenth century, school meals had been part of a national debate on the role of the state versus the authority of the family. In this debate, the school meal came to represent the decline of the authority of the family and the rise of state interference, as eating at school did not balance with cultural

[43] Van Baarle, *Slag om B2*; August D. Belinfante, *In Plaats van Bijltjesdag: De Geschiedenis van de Bijzondere Rechtspleging na de Tweede Wereldoorlog* (Assen: Van Gorcum, 1978), 79–80, 143; Romijn, *Snel, Streng en Rechtvaardig*, 7, 194–195.

[44] For more on these child feeding initiatives, see: De Zwarte, 'Fighting Vulnerability: Child Feeding Initiatives during the Dutch Hunger Winter', in *Coping with Hunger and Shortage under German Occupation*, 293–310.

[45] Dominique Marshall, 'Humanitarian Sympathy for Children in Times of War and the History of Children's Rights, 1919–1959', in *Children and War: An Historical Anthology*, ed. James Marten (New York: New York University Press, 2002), 184–186; Ellen Key, *The Century of the Child* (New York: G. P. Putnam's Sons, 1909).

[46] E.g., Cary, 'Child-Feeding Work in Germany'; Laurent, 'War and the Emerging Social State'; Nath, *Brood Willen We Hebben!*, 45–107, 228; Hionidou, '"Choosing" between Children and the Elderly'; Davies and Wheatcroft, *The Years of Hunger*, 221–222, 425.

patterns in the strongly family-oriented Netherlands, where the freedom of child rearing and education was highly valued.[47] School meals remained highly unpopular, with approximately 4.3 per cent (70,000) of the Dutch schoolchildren receiving meals through municipal departments in 1938.[48] Participation declined even further during the German occupation because of National Socialist involvement in the soup kitchens. In early September 1944, only 50,000 school meals per day were served.[49] Later that month, while the Dutch food authorities officially argued that school kitchens had to close in favour of central control, the actual reason was to exclude the NVD from the rationing system.[50] When state relief to schoolchildren was terminated by default, the Dutch authorities knew very well that this left a vulnerable group exposed to food deprivation – and it was for this reason that they allowed and encouraged grassroots initiatives to fill this gap.

Since the IKB was essentially an overarching institution for already-existing efforts, the nature and modus operandi of child-feeding programmes differed in each region. For instance, in Amsterdam, a child-feeding organisation called 'Mutual Aid Emergency Situation Schoolchildren' (*Onderlinge Hulp Noodtoestand Schooljeugd*: OHNS) was established by the former Head of the Municipal Department of Child Clothing and Feeding A. de Roos to aid Protestant and public schoolchildren, while the Catholics retained their own organisation. The example from Amsterdam clearly shows how the pre-war socio-relgious division or 'pillarisation' in Dutch society still played an important role during the war, even when it came to relief practices. These committees coexisted until the extreme fuel shortage around mid-February 1945 forced them to merge, with the local IKB only supplying the OHNS and soup kitchens

[47] Frans L. Ossendorp and E. J. van Det, *Kindervoeding en – kleeding in Nederland en in het Buitenland* (Amsterdam: Edelman en Barendregt, 1913), 18–19; R. Hoogland, *Kindervoeding en –kleding in Nederland: Rapport Samengesteld door het Bureau voor Kinderbescherming (Bond van Nederlandsche Onderwijzers)* (Amsterdam: s.a., 1918); L. M. Hermans and H. van Knol, *Schoolvoeding: Een Aansporing voor onze Wetgevers* (Amsterdam: s.a., 1900); H. Bijleveld and L. N. Roodenburg, '*Is het in het Algemeen Wenschelijk aan het Instituut van Schoolvoeding (Schoolkleeding) Uitbreiding te Geven?*', *Prae-Adviezen voor de Algemeene Vergadering van 1, 2, en 3 Juli 1920 te Amsterdam* (Haarlem: H. D. Tjeenk Willink & Zoon, 1920); E. C. van Leersum, *Schoolvoeding* (The Hague: Leopold, 1925), 104; Blom, 'Nederland in de Jaren Dertig: Een "Burgerlijk-Verzuilde" Maatschappij in een Crisis-Periode', in *Crisis, Bezetting, Herstel*, 1–27.
[48] NA, 3.11.30.06, inv.no. 241, Report Director of Communal Feeding L. P. van Loon to RBVVO, 20 June 1945; CBS, *Jaarcijfers voor Nederland 1943–1946*, 6–7.
[49] Dols et al., 'De Centrale Keukens', 67–75; Dols and Van Arcken, 'Food Supply and Nutrition', 327–328.
[50] NA, 3.11.30.06, inv.no. 3, Report October 1943–July 1946. See also: NA, 2.19.070.01, inv.no. 199, Report NVD office Utrecht on September 1944–February 1945.

and not interfering in the allocation of the meals.[51] In Rotterdam, many child-feeding organisations refused to merge or cooperate with the IKB because they wanted to remain independent, and a citywide relief committee such as those seen in Amsterdam or The Hague was never achieved. The local IKB in Rotterdam focused on feeding children from the poorest quarters of the city.[52] In Utrecht, as mentioned, a local department of the Dutch Red Cross started child feeding in early October 1944. Their efforts were later taken over by the cooperating churches, even though they never formally operated under the name of the IKB.[53] Similar developments took place in smaller towns throughout the occupied west, which confirms that these were indeed uncoordinated bottom-up initiatives.[54]

Illustration 19 Children receiving IKB meals in The Hague.

---

[51] NIOD, 0332, inv.no. B1, Van de Griek, 'De Voedselhulp'; *Jaarverslag van Amsterdam 1945*, 2–3.
[52] SR, 728, inv.no. 104, Weekly reports and minutes IKB, January–April 1945.
[53] Julius, *Kinderen in Nood*.
[54] E.g., NIOD, 0332, inv.no. C3; Archief Delft [AD], 8 Vereniging Armenzorg, inv.no. 17; ELO, 0257, inv.no. 1, 8; D. P. Kalkman, *Een Lichtpunt in een Donkeren Tijd: De Geschiedenis van het Noodcomité Moordrecht* (Moordrecht; Noodcomité Moordrecht, 1945).

The results of the child-feeding programmes were nothing short of impressive. The OHNS in Amsterdam grew enormously after its mandatory merger. During its start-up week in mid-February 1945, it could only provide 6,000 extra meals per day for a total of 120,000 schoolchildren; by March, this number had grown to 38,000 – feeding nearly a third of all schoolchildren.[55] When, on 10 January 1945, the Central IKB in The Hague took over from the cooperating churches, these had already been feeding some 6,000 children. Two weeks later, this number had risen to 12,000 and, between February–April 1945, it was fixed around 28,000: more than half of the children in the city.[56] In Utrecht, the Committee Child Nutrition rejected the general stance that only children who were diagnosed with malnourishment should benefit from the meals. Instead, all schoolchildren aged 6–14 years became entitled to one meal a week and those diagnosed with malnourishment could have multiple meals a week. Children aged 1–3 were only included if showing physical signs of malnourishment, as they already received extra food from the soup kitchens in Utrecht. In addition, the Committee took care of an additional 66 Jewish children in hiding by serving them porridge twice a week from an 'illegal' kitchen in Boterstraat.[57] In all cities, including smaller towns such as Delft, Zaandam, Schiedam, and Dordrecht, relief efforts resulted in the extra feeding of approximately a third to half of the neediest urban children.[58]

An additional reason why local relief efforts specifically prioritised school-age children was that younger children could not be easily fed in a school setting. But when relief organisations discovered that toddlers suffered from malnourishment just as severely – or even worse when judged by their mortality rates – by the end of February 1945 most began to include young children aged 4–5, followed by the age group of 1–3 years shortly thereafter.[59] Most of these child-feeding initiatives also

---

[55] NIOD, 0332, inv.no. B1, Van de Griek, 'De Voedselhulp.' See also: De Jong, *Het Koninkrijk* 10b, 252; De Zwarte, 'Samen tegen de Honger: Hulpverlening aan Kinderen in Amsterdam Tijdens de Hongerwinter', *Ons Amsterdam* 67 (2015): 16–21.

[56] *Charity in War-time*, 22.

[57] Julius, *Kinderen in Nood*, 17–18, 48; UA, 1364, inv.no. 318, Letter Communal Kitchens Utrecht, December 1944; UA, 1364, inv.no. 321 Letter director Communal Kitchens, 26 April 1945; De Zwarte, 'Commissie Kindervoeding hielp Utrechtse Kinderen de Hongerwinter Door', *Oud-Utrecht* 89 (2016): 32–37.

[58] AD, 217 Interkerkelijk Bureau Noodvoedselvoorziening, inv.no. 8, Reports by section child nutrition of IKB Delft, 1945; GAS, 84 Interkerkelijk Bureau Noodvoedselvoorziening, Box 1; Gemeentearchief Zaanstad (GAZ), PA-0033 Vereniging Kindervoeding Zaandam, inv.no. 18, Files on child-feeding programmes during the Hunger Winter; RAD, 154 Vereniging Kindervoeding en –Kleding, inv. no. 28, Register of number of meals provided to children, 1944–46.

[59] NIOD, 182f, inv.no. 132, Minutes meeting IKB with paediatricians, 18 April 1945; Julius, *Kinderen in Nood*, 17–18.

made efforts to place children in better-situated host families for home-cooked meals. Communal eating was generally a precondition for relief provisioning. Armed with a spoon and an enamel plate, the children walked to distribution posts that were provisionally installed in schools and church buildings throughout the cities, which were mostly run by female volunteers. A significant point regarding the strategy behind this re-distribution of food to schoolchildren was that food was always consumed collectively, mostly in classrooms, but certainly never in a household setting. Sources explain this was done to ensure that the extra ration would not be re-distributed to other household members or, quite explicitly, would not be eaten by the male head of the household.[60]

Children themselves became actively involved in their own nutrition. Following a call by the IKB in January 1945, schoolchildren in Amsterdam collected different types of food every week from friends and relatives in and outside the city, mostly peas and potatoes, which would later be added to the meals. They also helped to identify possible host families in their neighbourhoods, where the neediest children could receive a home-cooked meal once or twice a week. Children also, for example, initiated small relief actions to help classmates in dire need. The results of the participation of children were highly satisfactory, according to the IKB, especially in the poorer neighbourhoods.[61] The actual meals typically consisted of half a litre of a nutritional (if watery) mix of potatoes, vegetables, sugar beets, and sometimes tulip bulbs. On other days, it would be a plate of porridge. As one girl wrote in her diary, the food was 'not actually edible'.[62] The IKB Rotterdam calculated that the average meal comprised between 200 and 550 kcal, which was not much but still an indispensable supplement to the famine rations.[63] In Utrecht, schoolchildren ate only once a week but there the meals consisted of an ample 1,000 kcal – over two times their official daily rations.[64]

By feeding the children, civil society took over these responsibilities from the state and households to protect the future of Dutch society. But, in doing so, they inevitably established boundaries of who did or did not belong, as is exemplified by the exclusiveness of the independently operating neighbourhood and denominational committees. The Nutrition Council in Leiden explained their taking over of responsibility from parents: 'The Committee is deeply convinced that, if this plan succeeds, it will prevent a catastrophic breakdown of the health of Leiden's youth as

[60] NIOD, 0332, inv.no. B1, Van de Griek, 'De Voedselhulp'.
[61] NIOD, 0332, inv.no. B1, Van de Griek, 'De Voedselhulp', 26, 37–40.
[62] NIOD, 244, inv.no. 1430, Diary G. v. S.
[63] SR, 728, inv.no. 104, Report IKB, 28 March 1945.   [64] Julius, *Kinderen in Nood.*

well as a limitless demoralisation.'[65] This demoralisation was especially an issue when it came to religious beliefs. In Utrecht, schoolchildren were divided into three separate denominational groups and allocated two days in the schools with their own group of volunteers – women only – ensuring that 'the children were situated in the spiritual sphere that they belonged to'.[66] For toddlers, separate eating was considered less important as they were deemed too young to be influenced by alternative religious persuasions. No matter how terrible the circumstances, the future of society was thus supposedly 'better protected' when everyone kept to their own. The limits of solidarity and community of child relief during the Dutch famine were similar throughout the urban west. A woman from Rotterdam recalled the days of the Reformed relief committee in her city:

You had to be member of the church here in Rotterdam in order to receive something. Because my sister-in-law had a brother-in-law who was an elder of the Reformed church, she asked him if the church had something to eat for her children as well. And he said: 'No, because your children are not baptised'. That is just horrible ... that a brother can say something like that .... In hindsight, people have said to me: 'Members of the church pay to sustain the church, so they have certain rights'. But that a man, who is an elder, can let his own brother's children starve ... that is so harsh that it hurts.[67]

Similar painful recollections of rejection and exclusion can be found about the Catholic church. One man from Amsterdam talked about his experiences as a boy during the height of the famine:

Once I went to a church, because I had heard you could get food there. One of these men approached me, wearing a long dress: 'Hey, what are you doing here?' I said to him: 'Do you maybe have something to eat, and a place for me to stay the night?' He asked: 'Are you Catholic?' I pathetically responded: 'No, I am not Catholic' .... 'No then you cannot stay, only Catholics can stay the night'.[68]

This exclusion did not just concern individual cases and, sometimes, had far-reaching consequences. In the most extreme example, the rigid Catholic relief politics, because of their dominant pre-crisis position in Amsterdam, even resulted in all Catholic schoolchildren receiving extra meals from the OHNS, compared to only 20 per cent of Protestant and public schoolchildren.[69] Evidently, traditional cultural patterns that determined daily social life in the Netherlands before the war did not fade under the extreme circumstances but were, at least locally,

---

[65] ELO, 0257, inv.no. 27, Report Committee School Feeding, 1944.
[66] Julius, *Kinderen in Nood*, 44.   [67] Slager et al., *Verhalen om te Onthouden*, 176–177.
[68] Slager et al., *Verhalen om te Onthouden*, 177.
[69] NIOD, 0332, inv.no. B1, Van de Griek, 'De Voedselhulp'.

reaffirmed and strengthened in the face of disaster. On the other hand, the IKB demonstrated that a social move in the opposite direction was also possible. In addition, grassroots committees such as Campaign on the Islands showed that interdenominational cooperation could and did emerge during the famine. The Campaign's founders, Catholic priest Finke and Reformed pastor De Graaff explained: 'Before the war people often doubted if cooperation between people of such highly diverse spiritual mindsets was even possible, the Hunger Winter proved to us that it is possible.'[70] Evidently, the Dutch famine marked a transition period in which both progressive and conservative attitudes and actions coexisted and were institutionalised.

Because the problems with food supply were by no means resolved by the time of liberation in May 1945, most child relief committees remained active until the summer of 1945. Between May and June, the number of children participating in child-feeding programmes grew larger as relief bodies took advantage of the increased supply and transport opportunities.[71] By mid-June 1945, municipalities took over school feeding once again and participation rapidly declined, the outcome of official rations increasing to pre-war levels and the desire to normalise family life as quickly as possible. Following the declining trust in the household's authority over children's health during the famine period, collective feeding had taken away responsibility from the parents and given it to the community. After the food crisis, parents reclaimed their traditional role as caretakers, making municipal school feeding just as unpopular as it had been before the war. Apparently without much loss of legitimacy, the regular authorities resumed their social roles in the summer of 1945 as well.

The importance of the child-feeding programmes during the famine was recognised early on by post-war relief organisations as well as the interim military authorities. In July 1945, Major Miller from the Allied Relief Department in Utrecht wrote a letter stating that it had been anticipated that there would be little or no relief organisation available for children, but that they had found an excellent existing organisation capable of immediate expansion: the Committee Child Nutrition.[72] In the summer of 1945, a child-feeding committee in Gouda even concluded that, because of the local efforts in their town, not a single child had died from starvation.[73] The municipality of Amsterdam similarly

---

[70] De Graaff and Finke, *Hongersnood op de Eilanden*, 49.   [71] *Charity in War-time*, 22.

[72] Letter Major Millen, Allied Relief Province of Utrecht, 3 July 1945, in: Julius, *Kinderen in Nood*, 18.

[73] Groene Hart Archieven [GHA], 0398 Archief van het Comité voor Kinderuitzending en –Voeding Gouda, 1944–1953, inv.no. 1, Minutes 29 October 1945.

concluded that 'experts have assured that the distribution of food by the OHNS had saved hundreds of children from starving to death. It is due to the OHNS that the Amsterdam schoolchildren have surmounted the hunger period without major drawbacks'.[74]

The qualitative evidence on the impact of the child-feeding initiatives upon children's health corresponds with the mortality data presented in Chapter 3. Mortality patterns of school-age children in the urban west were hardly affected during the famine, and even remained below those in the rest of the country not exposed to famine. The Dutch case thus suggests that, while children may be physically vulnerable to food deprivation and infectious diseases, their strong social position in mid-twentieth-century society may have ensured their particular resilience to famine conditions.[75] In addition to the evacuation of 40,000 malnourished children, an endeavour discussed in Chapter 8, extensive food provisioning to Dutch children definitely affected their survival chances in a positive way. Most importantly, by targeting those children who suffered most from malnutrition during the Dutch famine, NGO relief entities were able to compensate when both the state and the family could no longer protect their children.

Women's Food Protests

A different, yet interlinked collective response to the famine concerned women's food protests, which sparked throughout the urban west in early 1945.[76] While food riots are more often associated with the early modern period, it has been demonstrated that food riots have often occurred in modern, industrialised nation-states as well, in particular during times of war and crisis. These expressions of collective action not only embodied the planned efforts of political parties or trade unions, but also emerged from the food-provisioning concerns amongst 'normal' women (i.e., those not engaged in politics). Moreover, as food riots are generally viewed as one of the common markers of an early-stage famine, they are an essential collective response to investigate.[77] For the Dutch case,

---

[74] *Jaarverslag van Amsterdam 1945*, 4.

[75] Rivers, 'The Nutritional Biology of Famine', 92–93; Kent, *The Politics of Children's Survival*, 2–3.

[76] For more on these food protests, see also: De Zwarte and Debbie Varekamp, '"Vrouwen, Eist Meer Eten!" Protest tijdens de Hongerwinter', *Historisch Nieuwsblad* 25 (2016): 78–83; Yvonne Stinnis, 'Lijfsbehoud: Vrouwen in het Verzet tegen de Honger', *Skript Historisch Tijdschrift* 10 (1988): 25–33.

[77] Lynne Taylor, 'Food Riots Revisited', *Journal of Social History* 30 (1996): 483–496. According to Ó Gráda, food riots are 'more likely to have been the product of threatened famine or the early stages of famine than of out-and-out starvation'. He

the term 'protest' seems more accurate than 'riot', as all actions in the occupied west took place in a composed and non-violent manner. The former characteristic further distinguishes these events in 1945 from the 'potato riots' in Amsterdam in 1917, where violence played an important role as part of a political power struggle and, critically, food poverty was much less severe.[78]

From the very start, the food crisis in the occupied Netherlands extended the roles of women in both the domestic and the public sphere. Women had been responsible for collecting food and preparing meals, but their role became more prominent after the German raids on adult men in the autumn of 1944. Instead of turning into passive victims, the food protests demonstrate that women used the space left open by the Nazi regime – which had a high regard for family life and motherhood in particular[79] – to their own benefit. As wives and mothers, they enjoyed more room for manoeuvring in the public sphere than men, and they appropriated their 'innocent' and 'unpolitical' social position to influence public discourse and food politics.[80] Following the decline of state legitimacy in the food system and growing feelings of inequality over food, the food protests not only situated women in the public sphere much more openly than before the crisis, it also gave them an important position in negotiations on the politics of provision, albeit one that was more complex and layered than meets the eye.

The first food protest was staged in Schiedam (South Holland), one of the towns heavily affected by the raid on adult men in November 1944. According to a post-war interview with one of the participants, Jo Vink van der Stal, a few women affiliated with the communist newspaper *De Waarheid* convened around mid-December 1944 to discuss how they could save their children from starvation, showing how politics and private life became intertwined for these women. They decided to offer their mayor a petition against the quality of Communal Kitchens (CK)

---

argues that in most historical famines, collaborative protest and resistance gives way to despair as the crisis becomes a catastrophe. Ó Gráda, *Famine*, 6–7, 55.

[78] Anne Petterson, 'Aardappelnood: Amsterdamse Arbeiders en het Socialisme tijdens het Aardappeloproer van 1917', *Tijdschrift Holland* 42 (2010): 18–39.

[79] Nicole Kramer, '*Volksgenossinnen* on the German Home Front: An Insight into Nazi Wartime Society', in *Visions of Community in Nazi Germany: Social Engineering and Private Lives*, eds. Martina Steber and Bernhard Gotto (Oxford: Oxford University Press, 2014), 171–186; Andreas Wirsching, 'Volksgemeinschaft and the Illusion of "Normality" from the 1920s to the 1940s', in *Visions of Community in Nazi Germany*, 153.

[80] See also: Victoria de Grazia, *How Fascism Ruled Women: Italy, 1922–1945* (Berkeley: University of California Press, 1992); Mareen Healy, *Vienna and the Fall of the Habsburg Empire: Total War and Everyday Life in World War I* (Cambridge: Cambridge University Press, 2004), 9, 81–86.

food and the bad organisation of local food rationing. They also demanded unspecified stricter measures against black marketeering. In January 1945, about 400 women from Schiedam, many of them accompanied by children, battled a snowstorm to hand over their demands. According to Vink van der Stal, they stood arm in arm against a cordon of German soldiers carrying machine guns. Eventually, a town clerk showed up and informed the women they could expect an answer within a few days' time. Three days later, a deputation of three women was invited into the mayor's office, while hundreds of women stood outside awaiting the news. Unfortunately, not much was achieved other than the mayor 'promising to try his best'.[81]

Yet the fight was not over, as news about the protest spread throughout the occupied areas. Just one day after the protest in Schiedam, the women of Rotterdam offered a similar petition to their National Socialist alderman of public health. According to resistance newspapers, a delegation of 40 women offered a petition signed by almost 30,000 women from all over town.[82] The province of North Holland followed suit. In Amsterdam, protests started around mid-February. To Haringa, 32 years old at the time, recollects: 'The demonstration was meant to convince the mayor [Voûte] to feel responsible for saving our children's lives.'[83] Approximately 200 women from all over Amsterdam took part in the protest, of whom five were allowed to visit the mayor. According to Haringa, the mayor brushed all responsibility aside and blamed the deteriorating food situation on the railway strike. A high-placed municipal clerk, however, reported in his diary that Mayor Voûte informed the women that he was completely aware of their situation but was unable to help, as he did not have a say in the rationing system. Interestingly, the authorities were aware of the fact that the communist resistance group behind the illegal newspaper *De Waarheid* was spreading leaflets outside that blamed the Germans for the famine: a striking detail since no arrests were made. Allegedly, after their meeting, a Dutch policeman warned the delegation about German *Wehrmacht* soldiers awaiting them outside, and he took them instead through an underground passageway towards

---

[81] 'Demonstraties van Vrouwen', *Het Parool*, 3 February 1945; 'Vrouwen eisen Maatregelen tegen de Heersende Nood!' *De Waarheid*, 10 February 1945; Tineke van de Schouw, *Opdat de Kinderen Leven* (Amsterdam: Nederlandse Vrouwen Beweging, 1957), 202–206; Secret correspondence NVB congress, 26 January 1960, www .inlichtingendiensten.nl/ambtsberichten/ 524188.pdf.

[82] Although no official sources corroborate these numbers, the fact that competing newspapers covered the story points to a certain amount of truth. 'Demonstraties van Vrouwen', *Het Parool*, 3 February 1945; 'Vrouwen eisen Maatregelen tegen de Heersende Nood!' *De Waarheid*, 10 February 1945.

[83] *Vrij Nederland*, 3 May 1980, 7.

another exit.[84] Mien de Vries, 30 years old at the time, was one of the women standing outside until she fled from the Germans: 'I still cannot understand how we found the courage, considering our responsibilities towards our children. But it was their hunger that drove us.'[85]

On 28 February 1945, the protesting women in Amsterdam descended on city hall once more, about 80 of them and, again, accompanied by their children. This time a delegation of four was allowed to enter; however, Mayor Voûte was absent. The women announced they would convene again on 1 March. The clerk's diary reveals that the situation was different this time, as the Dutch police had received German orders to immediately open fire on demonstrating women, as the city was still in a state of emergency and assemblies of more than five persons were strictly forbidden. The police lieutenant who had received the order refused these instructions, yet doubted if they could continue to ignore German orders.[86] Whether or not the women followed through with this last protest remains unclear. In any case, nobody was arrested or harmed, as it is certain that the illegal newspapers would have reported on such incidents. The example from Amsterdam demonstrates that there were limits to the leeway given to these protesting women. Yet, their achievements in negotiating with municipal authorities, especially while being visibly connected to communist resistance groups, is remarkable.

Other smaller cities witnessed similar food protests, always either urging local authorities to improve local food provisioning or demanding supervising committees in the CK. In Haarlem, for example, a food protest was sparked after news spread that a ship had arrived with food supplies designated for *Wehrmacht* soldiers. A delegation of women was led to speak with their Nazi mayor, who allegedly only promised the women that more attention would be paid to hunger patients. Not much later, the infamous *Grüne Polizei* arrived at the scene, driving women away but not yet arresting anybody.[87] In Dordrecht, a local housewives' committee asked the mayor for permission to establish supervising positions in the CK, as they had good reason to suspect the personnel – mostly

[84] NIOD, 244, inv.no. 1129, Diary H. H., 20 February 1945.
[85] *Vrij Nederland*, 3 May 1980, 7.
[86] Leaflet 'Amsterdamse Vrouwen' in: NIOD, 244, inv.no. 1129, 2 March 1945; 1 March 1945; Bert H. Voeten, *Doortocht: Een Oorlogsdagboek 1940–1945* (Amsterdam: Contact, 1946), 211.
[87] 'Demonstrerende Vrouwen Trokken Stadhuis binnen: Hongerwinter in Haarlem', *De Waarheid*, 4 May 1970; 'De Vrouwen Toonden Lef', *De Waarheid*, 14 January 1985. *Grüne Polizei* was the common name used for the German *Ordnungspolizei*, the green uniformed police force from Nazi Germany.

men – of stealing and embezzling food supplies. It took until the end of March before this women's committee officially took its post.[88] The same happened in Leiden, albeit at the very end of the occupation period.[89] Similar petitions were also delivered in smaller towns such as Purmerend and Zaandam (North Holland), the latter allegedly signed by 7,500 women.[90] The Hague and Utrecht are notably absent from these actions, which was likely related to the seats of the German administration and NSB headquarters being located in these two cities.

The examples above show that the women's food protests relied on community networks not only of local women, but also of local resistance groups and communists in particular. The sources leave no doubt that the communist resistance group behind *De Waarheid*, which comprised mostly men, was crucial in organising the protests. Well before the protests started, in late October 1944, the communist newspaper already called upon women to form committees to oversee the CK, thereby preventing corruption. However, the newspaper explicitly discouraged violent hunger riots, knowing that the occupier would answer with even more violence.[91] The communist newspaper repeated its call for 'hunger-demonstrations' in December 1944, asking for solidarity and disciplined action instead of individual looting.[92] When the desired protests did not gather pace, the journalists took a different approach, heavily criticising women for not being able to secure an adequate food supply. They affirmed that is was their responsibility, as mothers, to not let their children starve: 'As long as they only care for their own family, and wear themselves out to personally overcome this colossal crisis, there will be no way out for us.'[93] After the protests started, *De Waarheid* addressed the women in a more positive way:

Much has been said and written on the inertia of women, but now they demonstrate that they are also ready to fight. Robbed of their men, sons and fiancés, they fight against the misery and suffering that derived from measures from the hated occupier. Women, this is the way to go. Not theft and looting, but

---

[88] RAD, 260 Distributiedienst van de Gemeente Dordrecht, alsmede de Centrale Keuken, inv.no. 310, Correspondence between CK director and mayor, February–April 1945; inv.no. 466, Correspondence on situation at distribution points, January–March 1945.

[89] ELO, RBVVO, inv.no. 213.

[90] 'Zuid-Holland Strijdt voor Brood!' *De Waarheid*, 24 February 1945; 'Strijdt tegen Honger levert Succes op!' *De Waarheid*, 15 March 1945.

[91] 'De Voedselvoorziening moet Dringend Verbeterd Worden', *De Waarheid*, 30 October 1944.

[92] 'Mensenjacht en Honger in Den Haag – De Arbeidersklasse Vooraan in het Verzet', *De Waarheid*, 18 December 1944.

[93] 'Brood, Brood, Brood!' *De Waarheid*, 7 February 1945.

organised action. Women, fight for your children, demand more food. Not complaining and moping, but mass actions.[94]

The newspaper articles were supplemented with illegally created pamphlets and text murals. Again, sources state that mostly men were involved in these activities: among others, famous Dutch novelist Gerard van het Reve.[95] Many illegal photographs taken during the famine confirm these were visible all over the city. Through these actions, communists made the food problem into a women's problem, as part of a deliberate strategy to mobilise the women to fight a battle that men could not fight. Communist and social democratic newspapers also deployed the protests in heated discussions about resistance and politics in general, including discussions about the post-war order and power relations.[96]

Yet the deliberate involvement of men in these activities does not negate the role women played in organising the protests. On the contrary, women were the ones who decided to demonstrate, and they themselves handed out leaflets before and during the protests. De Vries from Amsterdam recollects: 'I don't know who organised the protest, I also did not know all the women. You were given an inside tip ... and you passed it on the women you trusted.'[97] More importantly, women took the lead during protests by demanding better food provisioning and supervising positions. In Rotterdam, Schiedam, and Dordrecht, they indeed succeeded in forming a women's committee and acquiring supervising positions.[98] In Leiden, sources do not mention communist involvement and seem solely based on community networks. The differences between the protests in, for example, Rotterdam and Leiden indicate that no central organisation was behind planning all protests, and that the women's drive for better food provisioning was the most important incentive for their actions. In other words, the women seem to have been driven by circumstances, not politics.

While, according to De Waarheid, the measurable results of the women's food protests were substantial,[99] the expansion of child-feeding

---

[94] 'Vrouwen Eisen Maatregelen tegen de Heersende Nood!' De Waarheid, 10 February 1945.

[95] Joost van Lingen and Nick Slooff, Van Verzetsstrijder tot Staatsgevaarlijk Burger: Hoe Progressieve Illegale Werkers na de Oorlog de Voet is Dwarsgezet (Baarn: Anthos, 1987), 29; Gerardus K. van het Reve, 'Haringgraten', in Tien Vrolijke Verhalen (Amsterdam: G. A. van Oorschot, 1961), 64–65.

[96] E.g., 'De Duitsche Hongerblokkade', Het Parool, 13 February 1945; 'Strijden of Hongerlijden', De Waarheid, March 1945; Stinis also refers to this policial power struggle: Stinis, 'Lijfsbehoud', 31–32.

[97] Vrij Nederland, 3 May 1980, 7.

[98] Schouw, Opdat de Kinderen Leven, 202–206; RAD, 260, inv.no. 310, 466.

[99] 'Zuid-Holland Strijdt voor Brood!' De Waarheid, 24 February 1945; 'Strijdt tegen Honger levert Succes op!' De Waarheid, 15 March 1945.

efforts in the months of February–March 1945 had more to do with previously mentioned IKB and other NGO efforts than with protesting alone. More crucial was the dialogue these women managed to establish with local authorities in times of extreme repression and the supervising positions they obtained. For the women involved, the meaning of the protests extended beyond local food provisioning. Van Ommeren-Averink stated in a post-war interview that the protests 'strengthened the confidence of the people and inspired resistance against the Nazis even further ... empowering women to act in a way men could not have done'.[100] After the war, many of these women continued to meet in separate gatherings.[101] Communist Party members, both women and men, deployed the women's food protests in their fight for equal rights among the sexes to demonstrate that women had changed during the war. Yet this battle was not easily won, as became clear soon after the war when the Netherlands largely returned to pre-war gender patterns and women's roles in the public sphere were, once again, curtailed. The food protest did, however, have an important emancipatory impact. The Dutch Women's Movement (*Nederlandse Vrouwenbeweging*: NVB), constituted in 1946, even called the role of women during the famine 'its right to existence'. NVB member Corrie Boon clarified what this new movement meant for women: 'We demanded better food for our children and more control over the local soup kitchens. We did not have good shoes, no proper clothes, no soap – it was that poor at the time. From that raw reality, the Dutch Women's Movement emerged.'[102]

Conclusion

For the occupied western Netherlands, the final months of war presented a period of declining legitimacy of state authority in the food system, which led to the rise of new types of organisations: local self-organised relief and self-help entities. Emerging from existing networks and traditional Dutch practices, these civil society organisations managed to occupy a central position between the household and state levels and, as such, effectively took over care and relief responsibilities. In doing so,

---

[100] 'Demonstrerende Vrouwen Trokken Stadhuis Binnen: Hongerwinter in Haarlem', *De Waarheid*, 4 May 1970.

[101] Hansje Galesloot and Susan Legêne, *Partij in het Verzet: De CPN in de Tweede Wereldoorlog* (Amsterdam: Pegasus, 1986), 214–217; Jolande Withuis, *Opoffering en Heroïek: De Mentale Wereld van een Communistische Vrouwenorganisatie in Naoorlogs Nederland, 1946–1976* (Meppel: Boom, 1990), 42–43.

[102] 'Uit die Rauwe Werkelijkheid Ontstond onze Organisatie', *De Waarheid*, 31 October 1986.

relief efforts mostly relied on the authority of the church and the resistance. Their strong presence turned relief provisioning into an interface through which multiple institutions and state authorities competed for control over food supply as well as legitimacy among the Dutch people. At this interface, women played a significant role, being the main group of volunteers in the male-dominated relief entities. Moreover, as 'housewives' and 'mothers', women enjoyed more freedom to negotiate with local authorities than men: an advantage that resistance fighters recognised and deployed for their political objectives.

Because local efforts were largely built on infrastructures provided by community networks and established institutions, communal relief was highly successful for the targeted groups within community boundaries; however, this particular feature also made relief practices very exclusive. Not belonging to the right neighbourhood or denomination could have a direct impact on food entitlements during the famine. Denominational boundaries were not only maintained in the crisis period, but even sometimes forcefully engaged as a result of the shared conviction among many church organisations that this was the best way to protect the future of Dutch society. This especially applied to efforts in feeding the children. These child-feeding efforts reflected a societal strategy to shift relief responsibility from the household and the state to community levels. The expectation, if not fear, of an unequal intra-household redistribution of food proved to be a major factor in deciding to feed the children collectively in school.

Overall, community efforts to take over relief from state authorities can be qualified as a great success. Most importantly, by effectively targeting society's most vulnerable groups – children, the sick and elderly, and even people in hiding – NGO relief was the main factor actively reversing the expected effects of the famine. The collective decision to help school-aged children first was supported by both the German and the Dutch authorities, and resulted in the extra feeding of approximately a third to half of the children in famine-affected areas. The fact that younger children were initially excluded from NGO relief may very well have contributed to their comparatively higher mortality rates. Those people who were left outside NGO relief and solely relied on the official rations for survival, such as the destitute, people residing in institutions, and elderly people without a social safety net, turned out to be the most vulnerable groups. Community efforts thus form a crucial part of the socio-cultural explanation as to why certain social groups fared better during the Dutch famine than others. Chapter 8 is another case in point for this argument.

8   The Evacuation of Children

Contrary to the lesser-known child-feeding initiatives, in Dutch popular culture, the evacuation of tens of thousands of Dutch children has grown into one of the canonised stories of the Hunger Winter.[1] Previous studies have attributed the success of the child evacuations largely to the IKB, thereby reaffirming the orthodox view that relief was predominantly organised top-down during the food crisis.[2] In this chapter, I challenge these assumptions by re-examining the organisation of child evacuations and assessing the backgrounds of these achievements. The main argument is that the evacuations, as part of communal efforts to fight the famine conditions, are best described as a dialogue between different individuals, social groups, and institutions, including the Dutch and German National Socialist authorities, working towards the same goal: saving the Dutch youth.[3]

The Netherlands was not unique in evacuating its children during the war. The British government organised three major evacuations of almost 3 million children and their mothers, first in September 1939, then, secondly, during the most savage period of the Blitz in August 1940, and finally, during the 'flying bomb scare' in 1944.[4] German child evacuations during the war were of similar proportions. The *Nationalsozialistische*

---

[1] Part of this Chapter has been previously published as: 'Coordinating Hunger: The Evacuation of Children during the Dutch Food Crisis, 1945', *War & Society* 35 (2016): 132–149. The most commonly used Dutch terms were *'kinderuitzending'*, followed by *'kindertransport'*.

[2] Touw, *Het Verzet der Hervormde Kerk*, 78; De Jong, *Het Koninkrijk* 10b, 252–256; Van der Boom, *Den Haag in de Tweede Wereldoorlog*, 232; Bert Willering, *Rotterdammertjes in Stadskanaal: Kinderen in de Hongerwinter 1944–1945* (Assen: Alwil, 2015), 39. Former child evacuee Frans Nieuwenhuis is the only author to elaborate on parties other than the IKB; Frans J. M. Nieuwenhuis, *Naar de Boeren! Kinderuitzendingen tijdens de Hongerwinter* (Rotterdam: Donker, 2010). Neither Trienekens, Klemann, nor Futselaar mentions the child evacuations in their works.

[3] The same has been argued for relief efforts during the Greek famine. Hionidou, '"Choosing" Between Children and the Elderly'.

[4] Ruth Inglis, *The Children's War: Evacuation 1939–1945* (London: Collins, 1989); John Welshman, *Churchill's Children: The Evacuee Experience in Wartime Britain* (Oxford: Oxford University Press, 2010).

Volkswohlfahrt (NSV) was responsible for the '*Kinderlandverschickungen*' (KLV), the aim of which was to evacuate children out of areas endangered by Allied bombings. During the years 1940–1945, the NSV relocated and took care of almost 2.5 million German boys and girls in over 9,000 KLV camps. According to their own documentation, the KLV was the '*größten soziologischen Versuch aller Zeiten*'.[5]

What sets the Dutch case apart from these examples was that child evacuations in the Netherlands were not triggered by the threat of bombings – most of the military front was stable until April 1945 – but by the immediate threat posed by hunger and starvation. The evacuations did not offer any military benefits for either side; but still, both the Dutch and German authorities became involved. No other Nazi-occupied country experienced this sort of collaboration. For example, in 1942 arrangements were made for 25,000 Greek children to be transported out of famine-affected areas to Egypt, but this scheme fell through at the last minute because the Axis governments refused to let the children go. Similarly, between 1942 and 1944 discussions were held with representatives of the Swedish government to receive a substantial number of children in Sweden from Norway, but the Quisling government refused its consent. The Swiss government also showed willingness to accept child evacuees, informing the Allies they would be prepared to take care of 50,000 foreign children; but, according to the British Foreign Office no reply was ever received from the German government. This was also the case in 1943, when the Irish Red Cross offered to receive French child evacuees in Éire.[6] The German civil authorities in the Netherlands, on the other hand – facing almost certain defeat by early 1945 – even actively collaborated with the evacuation programmes, resulting in an extraordinary cooperation between individuals and groups of all political and religious persuasions.

---

[5] Gerhard Dabel, *KLV: Die erweiterte Kinder-Land-Verschickung: KLV-Lager 1940–1945* (Freiburg: Schillinger, 1981), 14; For more on the NSV and its child evacuation programme, see: Herwart Vorländer, *Die NSV: Dastellung und Dokumentation einer nationalsozialistischen Organization* (Boppard am Rhein: Boldt, 1988); Armin Nolzen, 'The NSDAP's Operational Codes after 1933', in *Visions of Community in Nazi Germany*, 92–96; Thomas Schaarschmidt, 'Mobilizing German Society for War: The National Socialist Gaue', in *Visions of Community in Nazi Germany*, 113. In wartime Finland about 70,000 'war children' were similarly transferred to Sweden, Denmark, and Norway as part of evacuation programmes. Laurent, 'Social Policy, Public Health and Citizenship', 342; Aura Korppi-Tommola, 'War and Children in Finland during the Second World War', *Paedagogica Historica: International Journal of the History of Education* 44 (2008): 445–455.

[6] TNA, FO 837/1217, Draft statement on relief, 3 November 1944.

From Relocation to Evacuation

The Dutch child evacuations should be understood within a historical context beyond that of the German occupation. From the late nineteenth century onwards, it had become normal in the Netherlands, not unlike other European countries, to send weak and sickly working-class children to the supposedly healthier countryside. The Dutch followed the example set by Swiss theologist and social pedagogue Walter Bion (1830–1909), who had founded the first colony house for sickly ('pale-nosed') children in 1876. In 1884, the first Dutch health colonies were established, followed by the first official body, the Central Society for Child Recovery and Holiday Colonies (*Centraal Genootschap voor Kinderherstellings- en Vacantiekolonies*), in 1901. The First World War made the well-being of urban children more urgent than ever and caused exponential growth of these summer camps and health colonies in the interwar years – not just in the Netherlands, but in many other Western-European countries as well.[7]

During the occupation, it continued to be quite common for urban children to spend time in the Dutch or German countryside. Dutch and German National Socialist ideology placed youth on a pedestal as they symbolised power, energy, and fertility – three of the Nazi's key values. As mentioned in Chapter 1, following the example of the German NSV, two National Socialist welfare organisations were established in the Netherlands: Winter Aid in October 1940 and the NVD in July 1941. Both organisations aimed to coordinate all social work by local governments, churches, and private organisations, thereby endeavouring to replace the pillarised Dutch welfare system. Within this system, the NVD focused specifically on families and health care, and summer camps thus became one of their top priorities.[8] According to its own documentation, the NVD sent over 10,000 children on a 'well-deserved vacation' during its first year of existence.[9] In the years 1940–1944, thousands of Dutch children, predominantly from pro-German families, spent a summer vacation in annexed Austria as part of the '*Kinderaktion Niederlande-Ostmark*', which the Nazified Dutch newspapers gladly

---

[7] Georges G. J. Mettrop, *De Kinderuitzending in Nederland: Een Critische Studie* (Nijkerk: Callenbach, 1945), 1–3; Caroline Nieuwendijk, *De Schiedamse Bleekneusjes: Kinderuitzendingen tussen 1900 en 1979* (Schiedam: Stichting Musis, 2012), 7–11; Josep L. Barona, *The Problem of Nutrition: Experimental Science, Public Health, and Economy in Europe, 1914–1945* (Brussels: P. I. E. Peter Lang, 2010), 24.

[8] *De Nederlandsche Volksdienst*; Damsma and Schumacher, *Hier Woont een NSB'er*, 82–84; Romijn, *Burgemeesters in Oorlogstijd*, 202–216.

[9] *De Nederlandsche Volksdienst*. See also: NIOD, 179, inv.no. 310, 339, 334.

exploited for propagandistic uses. Supposedly, this was Seyss-Inquart's way of thanking the Dutch for fostering approximately 150,000 Austrian children after World War I.[10]

Illustration 20 Seyss-Inquart greets NVD children about to depart for Austria, 1941.

The NVD never succeeded in taking over Dutch social work entirely. In fact, most private and church organisations were able to continue their pre-war efforts of organising countryside summer camps for urban children until the autumn of 1944. Larger cities usually had over a dozen different councils, operating according to denomination, for these so-called *kinder-uitzendingen* (child relocations), which coexisted rather than collaborated.[11] These child welfare activities changed considerably after the Allies liberated the south of the Netherlands in the autumn of 1944. Existing

---

[10] E.g., 'Zes Duizend Kinderen naar de Gouw Opperdonau', *De Courant*, 8 July 1940; 'Nederlandsche en Duitsche Kinderen met Vacantie in Duitschland', *Het Nationale Dagblad*, 18 July 1941; 'Kinderen naar Duitschland', *Limburger Koerier*, 20 April 1943. In return, German children also visited the Netherlands: 'Duitsche Kinderen naar Nederland', *Nieuwsblad van het Noorden*, 15 March 1944; NIOD, KAII 1092, Kinderuitzendingen (NSB archive).

[11] See, for instance: UA, 816, inv.no. 834; NIOD, 182F, inv.no. 27; NIOD, 1212, inv.no. B-4.

networks of summer camps and foster parents now had to be utilised for evacuation while some of the denominationally segregated councils were eventually forced to cooperate for the first time in their history. Others continued to aid children within the pre-crisis boundaries of denomination or social class, facing the dilemma of 'fair' centralisation versus the maximum utilisation of private contacts and materials.

Many companies, municipalities, and churches in the occupied west initiated child evacuations for, and within, their own social networks. For example, the department store chain Vroom & Dreesmann, and the Bataafsche Petroleum Maatschappij (nowadays Royal Dutch Shell) arranged the evacuation of their employees' children from the west. These company evacuations were mostly small in scale but nevertheless highly effective. An Amsterdam printing company easily managed to place 20 of its children with colleagues of a sister company living in Winschoten (Groningen).[12] Together, these companies provided thousands of urban children with food and shelter.[13]

Many of the new relief entities discussed in Chapter 7 also evacuated children, albeit only those who belonged to their own neighbourhood or denomination. Help for us All, in Rotterdam, evacuated one hundred of 'their' Reformed children to the northeast, another hundred to the Wieringermeer district, and assigned several others to nearby farms.[14] Dr Wagenaar's Campaign Betondorp similarly evacuated children from its neighbourhood; 103 via the IKB, but another 55 on its own accord because it 'took the IKB too long'.[15] Again, all these local, self-initiated efforts added up to thousands of children. Later, when the IKB took over, they were called 'wild transports' of children: the famous Dutch cabaret artist Paul van Vliet was one such wildling.[16]

Other young city dwellers ended up with host families in the northeastern provinces without help from local organisations. Causing much concern to local authorities, these 'wild children' came looking for food and shelter of their own volition. Some of them hitchhiked all the way;

[12] NIOD, 1212 Kinderuitzendingen, inv.no. B9, Letter Boek- en Diepdruk Amsterdam, 12 January 1945.
[13] NIOD, 182f, inv.no. 27, Letter IKB to director of Rademaker's Cacao en Chocoladefabrieken, 30 January 1945; Letter IKB The Hague to local office Leeuwarden, 27 January 1945; NIOD, 1212, inv.no. B9, Letter Boek- en Diepdruk Amsterdam, 12 January 1945; NIOD, 179, inv.no. 529, Month report March 1945; Nieuwenhuis, *Naar de Boeren!*, 56; Van Dongen, *Oorlogswinter 1944–1945*, 17; Nieuwendijk, *De Schiedamse bleekneusjes*, 81.
[14] Van Dongen, *Oorlogswinter 1944–1945*, 17–18.
[15] Wagenaar, *Een Jaar Noodcomité*, 18–19.
[16] Van Rossem, *Tietjerksteradeel 1940–1945* (Burgum: Stichting Streekmuseum Tytsjerksteradiel, 1995), 127.

others were dropped off by their desperate parents. Some of these unorganised marches involved malnourished children walking for days or even weeks with overnight stays in improvised shelters under appalling circumstances. Without supervision or parental consent, a 14-year-old brother and sister, for example, walked an approximate 200 km from Rotterdam to a town in the province of Friesland, only because they wanted to 'unburden their parents'.[17] According to a post-war record of the children's evacuation office in the province of Friesland, several thousand children managed to find a foster home this way.[18]

The most comprehensive and successful of all evacuation initiatives was that of the IKB. Similar to the child-feeding initiatives, the IKB's success mainly resulted from its ability to function as an umbrella organisation, taking over established social networks and welfare structures of child relocation programmes. Within the first weeks after its initiation on 14 December 1944, many grassroots initiatives in the occupied west merged into the IKB, including local efforts in sending malnourished school-aged children to farms in the direct periphery and the northeastern provinces.[19] Because the IKB had the ability as well as official German approval to organise relief outside of government structures, they provided an appealing alternative to National Socialist relief work. Moreover, a public body would have probably scared off the traditional denominational institutions, which preferred to keep the religious aspect of their evacuations intact.

Due to its official status, the IKB was able to cooperate with many existing social institutions and professionals, such as local public health services and school doctors. As we saw in Chapter 7, the IKB created a medical department to examine children aged between 4 and 15 and selecting those in need of evacuation based on their weight-height ratio.[20] In contrast to the child-feeding programmes, for the evacuations they created an additional fifth class for those children that would present difficulties to their hosts on medical grounds; for instance, if they had scabies or still wet their bed. In light of the evacuations, doctors and

---

[17] Nieuwenhuis, *Naar de Boeren!*, 85–87.

[18] SR, 336 Centraal Evacuatiebureau te Rotterdam 1940–1949, inv.no. 94, Letter from Mr Nicolai in Drogeham, 1 August 1945. For more personal stories on these 'wild children', see: Elle Bosma et al., *Eastermar: De Oorlogsevacues en de Hongerkinderen in 1945* (Burgum: Streekmuseum Volkssterrenwacht Burgum, 2010).

[19] For example: GHA, CKV Gouda, inv.no. 1, Minutes December–January 1945; UA, 816, inv.no. 1651, Minutes December–January 1945.

[20] Urgency Class I meant more than 20 per cent underweight, Class II 15–20 per cent underweight, Class III 7–15 per cent underweight, Class IV <7 per cent underweight. NIOD, 182F, inv.no. 132, Overview of IKB work by Doctor Berkhout, 1 October 1945; Köster, *Toelichting der Verstrekkingen op Medische Basis*.

nurses in the large urban areas examined hundreds of children per day from January 1945 onwards with parents, churches, GPs, and schools helping to identify children in most urgent need of medical screening.[21]

The medical examination and administration of the children ran smoothly, but finding transportation proved to be far more difficult for the IKB. Dutch trains could not be used due to the railway strike and Secretary General Hirschfeld was opposed to using empty vessels from the Central Shipping Company (CRV), fearing this would interfere with central rationing.[22] As a consequence, trucks and vessels always had to be arranged last minute, and the actual journeys could take days, or even weeks, due to broken engines, lack of fuel, or German checkpoints.[23] Moreover, drivers had to navigate at night with completely darkened windows and sometimes camouflage: Allied planes fired at anything that moved. In one sad example, on 21 February 1945, an English Spitfire shot a truck evacuating 13 children from the city of Haarlem, killing 7 of them as well as their male driver and a female caretaker.[24] Fortunately, the IKB also received a great deal of assistance on their way to the northeast, with a wide range of organisations helping the children with food and shelter: the Dutch Red Cross, Communal Kitchens, local factories, churches and private committees, and many local women who brought homemade food to the overnight shelters and resting places.[25]

A report from a primary school teacher in The Hague, Mr Feenstra, exemplifies the difficulties in getting children from point A to B. Feenstra had been preparing the evacuation of some of his schoolchildren for several weeks, when, on 18 January, he received notice from a contact in the small town of Wolvega (Friesland) inviting 30 of his children to shelter there. Feenstra immediately compiled a list of those in most urgent need of evacuation, taking advice from parents and local Reformed churches. It took him and the IKB another month to arrange

[21] NIOD, 182f, inv.no. 114, Guidelines medical screening of malnourished children, January 1945; inv.no. 27, 132.

[22] NIOD, 216h, inv.no. 312, Report 14 March 1945.

[23] For extensive reports on some of these journeys, see: NIOD, 182f, inv.no. 114, 119; UA, 816, inv.no. 1658.

[24] NIOD, 1212 Kinderuitzendingen, inv.no. B4, Letter to A. Tol, 24 February 1945; Anne Wielinga and Johan Salverda, *De Lemmerboot: Levenslijn tussen Amsterdam en Lemmer* (Leeuwarden: Friese Pers, 1983), 72–73; 'Vergeten Drama bij Alkmaar Zestig Jaar Geleden: Vergissing Piloot werd 'Bleekneusjes' fataal', *Noordhollands Dagblad*, 2 March 2005.

[25] *Het Nederlandsche Roode Kruis in de Tweede Wereldoorlog* (Amsterdam: Van Ditmar, 1947), 177; Nieuwenhuis, *Naar de Boeren!*, 91; NIOD, 182f, inv.no. 114; UA, 816, inv.no. 1658; SR, 273, inv.no. 21, Report 21 March 1945.

transportation. On 14 February, the schoolchildren finally left the city by truck, accompanied by a few unfamiliar children and 'suspiciously, many adults'. The first truck broke down after only a few hundred meters of driving – an omen of the transportation difficulties yet to come. Because of the Allied air raids, most of the driving was done in the dark on smaller roads, forcing them to pull over several times. During their stops, the local population flocked towards the vehicles to offer the children sandwiches and other treats. Arriving in Wolvega, volunteering foster parents immediately took the children home with them. Feenstra went to check on the children during the following days, and was delighted to find most of them attended church on Sunday. It took the school teacher four days – by foot, train, truck, milk float, and horse-drawn carriage – to arrive back in The Hague, where he immediately began organising a second evacuation.[26]

The 'suspiciously many adults' Feenstra referred to were not uncommon during IKB evacuations. Several testimonies reveal close collaboration between local IKB offices and resistance groups to get persons in hiding into the evacuations. In Amsterdam, for example, people involved with active resistance work managed to infiltrate the local IKB office (*Hulporganisatie Amsterdam*: HOA). A circular note from the Free Groups Amsterdam (*Vrije Groepen Amsterdam*) subsequently informed its contacts that children could be enlisted for evacuation: 'We mention, for instance, children from families with people in hiding, J-children [Jewish children], children of prosecuted or executed men, children from men in forced labour, et cetera.'[27] The IKB indeed had strong connections with underground resistance groups, which is confirmed by the HOA taking care of at least 5,000 Amsterdam families in hiding due to their ethnicity or political activities against the occupier.[28] Other sources likewise indicate that the IKB evacuations were frequently used to transport members and materials of the Dutch resistance movements through the country.[29]

The results of the IKB evacuations were considerable. According to local documentation, the IKB in Amsterdam managed to evacuate most children: 6,649, followed by at least 3,720 from Utrecht,[30] 3,196 from

---

[26] NIOD, 182f, inv.no. 27, Report by Mr Feenstra, March 1945.

[27] NIOD, 189, inv.no. 1, Circular note VGA, 16 February 1945.

[28] NIOD, 1076, inv.no. 24, Post-war report on relief by HOA, s.n.

[29] See, for instance: NIOD, 182f, inv.no. 119, Report 28 March 1945.

[30] Official post-war reports from the IKB Utrecht speak of 5,600 or 6,000 evacuated children, yet 3,720 is the highest number mentioned in official IKB reports from March 1945. E. Lagerwey, *Utrechts IKO: Een Verhaal van wat de Kerken van Utrecht Deden in den Hongerwinter 1944–1945* (Utrecht: s.n., 1946).

The Hague, 1,000 from Haarlem, 626 from Schiedam, 125 from Gouda, and 120 from Delft.[31] All of these IKB evacuations took place within two and a half months' time – from mid-January until the end of March 1945. After March, the Allied advance made it too dangerous to transport children, which meant that all evacuation efforts – including those from other organisations or private initiatives – came to a halt. Together with children from villages and children sent to farms and towns within the western provinces, this brings the total of the IKB evacuations to approximately 16,000 children, and roughly 4.5 per cent of the children aged 4–15 in those seven cities.[32]

Illustration 21 Child evacuations in The Hague.

There were thus considerable local differences in the IKB's results. Because of its convenient waterway access to the IJsselmeer and ample availability of vessels, Amsterdam had the highest number of evacuated children. The success of Utrecht's IKB efforts is explained by its relatively close proximity to the outlying countryside. The IKB Utrecht even

[31] NIOD, 1427 Hulporganisatie Amsterdam, inv.no. 1; NIOD, 1076, inv.no. 24; NIOD, 182f, inv.no. 114; UA, 816, inv.no. 1651; UA, 1136, inv.no. 398; GAS, 84; GAS, 346, inv.no. 4247; GHA, 0398, inv.no. 1; Nieuwenhuis, *Naar de Boeren!*, 150.
[32] Estimated child population in these seven cities: 345,504. CBS, *Jaarcijfers voor Nederland 1943–1946*.

organised 'foot transport', comprising almost 1,000 children in total, with only a handful of female volunteers, to the nearby province of Overijssel.[33]

The city of Rotterdam is notably absent. In this city, IKB evacuations remained only marginal. The Central Evacuation Office (*Centraal Evacuatie Bureau*: CEB), an official government body, evacuated some 583 children in cooperation with both the IKB and the National Socialist NVD, but the chief of the CEB stated that 'as an official institution [the CEB] could not and would not bear this responsibility'.[34] Paradoxically, the CEB did organise the return of children who had been placed in host families and holiday camps before the Allied invasion, bringing them back to the famine-affected city in late 1944 as the CEB deemed this to be 'safer' for the children.[35] The IKB Rotterdam did make an effort but, on 20 March 1945 – due to a lack of transportation – it had still not succeeded in evacuating 'a significant number of children'.[36]

Help from the Enemy

Although the NVD child evacuations have remained largely understudied, sometimes omitted from the historical narrative entirely, the National Socialist contribution was actually considerable. Their purge from the historical narrative started almost directly after the liberation, which – considering the circumstances – was not surprising. In post-war reports, the IKB solely referred to the German occupier and the NVD alike as obstructing factors, trying to diminish the interdenominational efforts set out by their organisation. Rev. Lagerwey from the local IKB in Utrecht even asserted that 'the Kraut was averse to such an arrangement [by the IKB], which could have saved our people from starvation. His goal was to starve us to the fullest and to feed all Krauts and Kraut Jrs. from our stolen produce'.[37] Most likely, as a consequence of these post-war reports, Dutch historiography has largely adopted this narrative, in which there was no role for Dutch and German National Socialist authorities.[38]

---

[33] UA, 816, inv.no. 1651, Report, 7 March 1945.
[34] SR, 273, inv.no. 21, Report H. S. van der Waals, 'Kinderuitzending gedurende den Bezettingstijd', 1945.
[35] SR, 336, inv.no. 94, Correspondence, September–December 1944.
[36] SR, 728, inv.no. 104, Report IKB Rotterdam, 20 March 1945.
[37] Lagerwey, *Utrechts IKO*, 8.
[38] E.g., Dirk C. A. Bout and Hendrik Kraemer, *In den Strijd om ons Volksbestaan* (The Hague: Stok, 1947), 202; Touw, *Het Verzet der Hervormde Kerk*, 78; Van der Zee, *The Hunger Winter*, 196. De Jong is the only scholar who states that the NVD evacuations

As we have seen from preceding chapters, during the occupation, the NVD never managed to gain significant popularity, as the Dutch did not appreciate its attempts to replace the pre-war pillarised welfare system. The NVD's status became even more precarious when the German war expectations changed. In early September 1944, after rumours of Allied forces rapidly marching into the country, about 65,000 members of the Dutch National Socialist party NSB fled to the east of the country and Germany, leaving the party disintegrated. The NVD head office in The Hague was simultaneously cleared, with the few remaining staff members moving to a new head office in the city of Groningen.[39]

For the local NVD offices, the severe food crisis that followed the Allied invasion was considered an unexpected gift, as they reckoned that the social chaos offered them an opportunity to improve their disgraced standing among the Dutch. A report from the NVD Amsterdam in January 1945 explained to its members: 'Now that other organisations, albeit inadequately, have started to evacuate children, it is desperately necessary that the NVD transports as many candidates as possible to Groningen, Friesland, and Drenthe as well.'[40] Because the welfare organisation had gained considerable experience in sending urban children to the countryside before the crisis, they had all the contacts and organisational infrastructure necessary for a rapid start-up. Similar to the IKB system, in early 1945 the NVD medically screened thousands of children in cooperation with local health services. In February 1945, the first 612 children were evacuated from Amsterdam to small villages in the province of Drenthe, for which the NVD used German *Wehrmacht* trains.

The evacuation of children soon became a top priority for the NVD, as confirmed by their monthly report from February 1945:

One of the matters in which the NVD can work as the most competent party in the interest of the people, is the evacuation of children from Amsterdam to the north and east of the country. It is sad to see several organisations such as the IKB, the HOA, and others working independently. We believe that the situation is too severe to compete with each other over precedence.[41]

---

might have been of considerable size. De Jong, *Het Koninkrijk* 10b, 254. Nieuwenhuis and Verhagen also refer to the NVD evacuations but, similarly, without any numbers mentioned. Nieuwenhuis, *Naar de Boeren!*, 61–62; Jessica A. Verhagen, *Vergeten Kinderen: Kroniek van een Kindertransport vanuit Reeuwijk naar Drenthe tijdens de Tweede Wereldoorlog, 19 Maart–23 Juni 1945* (Soesterberg: Uitgeverij Aspekt, 2017), 21.

[39] De Jong, *Het Koninkrijk* 10a, 57, 180–204.
[40] NIOD, 179, inv.no. 529, Month report, January 1945.
[41] NIOD, 179, inv.no. 529, Month report, February 1945.

The NVD's head of office wrote with great optimism about their collaboration with the IKB and even expected them to 'be persuaded to let their children join our transports'.[42] In March, the NVD shifted to using ships of the German *Kriegsmarine* and began working in close collaboration with the CRV, aiming to take over all work from the IKB. The use of these ships meant fewer children per crossing but more frequent departures. According to their report in March, the total number of evacuated children from Amsterdam was 4,155. Amsterdam also became a gathering place for children from The Hague, Rotterdam, and Haarlem, who are included in this considerable number. Transit camps were also established in Amsterdam, Utrecht, Zwolle, and the harbour of Zwartsluis.[43] It is therefore safe to assume that these 4,155 children, either originating in Amsterdam or passers-through, can be added to the many more unregistered NVD evacuations taking a different route.

The evacuations likewise became the priority of the provincial NVD office in the city of Assen. Interim NVD Head J. Borstlap personally corresponded with every mayor in the province of Drenthe in order to obtain as many foster addresses as possible. Within less than two weeks of his request, every one of those mayors had responded. Some wrote that churches already had taken on the task, but many others stated that they expected the population to spontaneously offer full assistance to the NVD. By mid-January 1945, Borstlap had compiled a list of thousands of foster homes to send to the national NVD office in Groningen.[44] While the IKB organised the evacuations independently of local governments, NSB mayors became responsible for both collecting foster addresses and corresponding with the NVD, thereby making state involvement the main difference between the two official child evacuation organisations.

Contrary to what might be assumed from this type of organisation, National Socialist ideology proved to be of secondary importance when it came to providing these NVD children with foster homes. The initial appeal of 3 January 1945, 'Children in Dire Need', called for the same solidarity and patriotism as the IKB did that same week. Notwithstanding the National Socialist moralistic tone of the call, neither Germany

[42] NIOD, 179, inv.no. 529, Month report, February 1945

[43] NIOD, 179, inv.no. 529, Month report, March 1945; Drents Archief [DA], 0195 Provinciaal Bureau van de Nederlandsche Volksdienst te Assen, inv.no. 276, Outline child evacuations Emmen, 10 January 1945; 'Massale Kindertransporten', *De Telegraaf*, 14 March 1945.

[44] DA, 0195, inv.no. 276, Letters from mayors in Drenthe to provincial NVD office, 6–17 January 1945; inv.no. 137, Letter Borstlap to national office in Groningen, 19 January 1945.

Map 4 The Netherlands in early 1945 – main routes for child evacuations.

nor the NSB Party were mentioned.[45] The NSB mayors involved offered their active assistance with seemingly sincere concern for the well-being of the children. The evacuations offered Nazi mayors an appealing 'apolitical' opportunity to demonstrate their professional competence in the last phase of the war, as many probably already took their post-war

[45] DA, 0195, inv.no. 276, Circular letter 'Children in Dire Need', 3 January 1945. Nor were all children from NSB families.

fate into account. For example, the mayor of Westerbork, home to the country's largest transit camp for Jews, assembled a local committee within five days, found over 300 foster homes and even offered to host city hall meetings over the child evacuations.[46]

In total, the NVD evacuated an estimated 8,000 boys and girls from the famished west to the northeastern provinces. Again, it was primarily the reactivation of existing networks and contacts from the NVD that made these achievements possible. Similar to the situation with the IKB, transportation difficulties proved the most important limitation to their efforts, not unavailable foster homes or a lack of volunteers. On the busiest days in March 1945, the NVD Amsterdam received and processed over 1,500 new applications per day.[47] From the Nazified press, the NVD gained the respect they had so fiercely desired throughout the occupation: 'We need to pay homage to the diligent workers from the maligned NVD. You cannot begin to consider the effort it takes to transport so many children. It is accompanied by days and nights of non-stop labour.'[48] These last National Socialist expressions of respect towards the NVD would, however, soon disappear into oblivion.

Away from Home

The time children spent with their foster families was supposed to reflect normal family life as much as possible. In any case, this was the shared goal of all aforementioned evacuation initiatives and institutions. Consequently, this restoration of family life required selection and division of both the children and the host families along class and denominational lines. Both the IKB and the NVD put much effort into placing children from civil servants with farmers and middle-class citizens, and 'plebeians' with small farmers or working-class families.[49] The necessary registration of sex, age, class, profession of the male head of the household, and denomination was mostly done in advance by the IKB and NVD. The denominational segregation posed special problems for Catholic children, who proved difficult to place in the predominantly Protestant northeastern provinces.[50]

Foster parents could likewise apply for the 'type of child' they desired. Approximately two in three families specifically requested a girl via pre-

---

[46] DA, 0195, inv.no. 276, Letter Mayor W. M. A. Pijbes in Westerbork to the provincial office Drenthe, 8 January 1945.
[47] NIOD, 179, inv.no. 529, Month report, March 1945.
[48] 'Massale Kindertransporten', *De Telegraaf*, 14 March 1945.
[49] NIOD, 182f, inv.no. 115, Letter to IKB, 26 February 1945.
[50] NIOD, 182f, inv.no. 119, Reports 1945.

evacuation forms from the IKB and NVD, although in reality, the number of evacuated girls and boys were roughly equal. The specific preference for older girls was likely connected to their ability to assist with household chores as well as care for younger children in the family. If families did specifically request a boy, it was usually one from the youngest age group.[51] Although many children were assigned to a foster home in advance, for numerous other children their arrival was much more chaotic. Some former child evacuees even described their arrival as resembling 'slavery markets'. One woman recalled in a post-war interview: 'We were displayed in the village and the villagers could choose a child to their liking. I ended up the last one standing; I knew I was not the prettiest one. Eventually a couple took me home because I resembled their deceased daughter.'[52]

The practicalities of the ad hoc organised evacuations also presented several problems for the hosting regions and families. Often, parents did not send the mandatory ration cards with their children, causing difficulties with local food rationing. The requested cutlery or adequate clothes were, likewise, rarely provided.[53] Furthermore, since thousands of the children had not been evacuated by official organisations such as the IKB or NVD, local IKB volunteers in the northeast – men and women – not only had to find many extra foster homes on the spot, but also had to establish transit camps and care homes in schools or empty buildings at major hubs, such as in the centrally located city of Zwolle.[54] Once placed in a foster family, there were no guidelines available for the parents on how to deal with homesickness and other adjustment issues related to the new environment, including the negotiation of local dialects. Despite the IKB guidelines established for home nutrition, adjusting to the new diet posed yet other difficulties, with many children nevertheless falling ill from the heavy and greasy food they had not digested for months.[55]

The experiences of these children away from home, of course, differed from case to case. Nevertheless, of the 200 former child evacuees impressively interviewed by Frans Nieuwenhuis – a former evacuee himself – most recollect warm, hospitable, caring and loving foster families, not to

[51] See for instance: NIOD, 182f, inv.no. 114, 115, 119; NIOD, 249-1076, inv.no. 11, 24.
[52] Nieuwenhuis, *Naar de Boeren!*, 96.   [53] NIOD, 182f, inv.no. 119, Reports 1945.
[54] NIOD, 182f, inv.no. 119, Reports,1945. In the province of Zwolle, for instance, shortly after the war ended there were 12,000 children in the province of Overijssel, of whom 7,000 had been placed by IKB. Kees Ribbens, *Bewogen Jaren: Zwolle in de Tweede Wereldoorlog* (Zwolle: Waanders, 2005), 154; GAR, 336, inv.no. 94, Letter IKB Zwolle to offices in the West, 6 June 1945.
[55] Nieuwenhuis, *Naar de Boeren!*, 104–106; Willering, *Rotterdammertjes in Stadskanaal*, 51–58.

mention an abundance of food. A large number of the interviewees stayed in touch with their foster family after the war ended, and some of these connections continue even today. The dozens of former child evacuees who, in contrast to the majority, remember having a miserable time with their host families, had been forced to work as housemaids or on the farms. Some were beaten by their foster parents; others just never managed to socially engage or adjust. One interviewed woman disclosed that her foster father had sexually abused her. Contributing to these difficult relationships was the fact that certainly not all foster parents offered their home out of solidarity or Christian caritas but felt socially pressured by their church or local 'gentleman-farmers', as was common in the social hierarchies at the time.[56]

While data on the former child evacuees' memories are rich and plentiful, it is much harder to find contemporary accounts of children's experiences. A rare account of a child's experience with his evacuation can be found in the correspondence between eight-year-old Jan Spier in Spijk (Groningen) and his parents in Utrecht. Spier's letters show how normal life continued for him even under the extreme circumstances he had to endure. The letter (Illustration 22) dated 8 May 1945, provides an excellent example, as he relates the confusing days surrounding the liberation – one of the defining experiences all children shared while in foster care. In April 1945, the Allied forces finally advanced to the north, liberating the provinces of Gelderland, Overijssel, Drenthe, Groningen and Friesland in only two weeks' time. The liberation involved heavy fighting, causing the destruction of cities and towns that included many casualties amongst both military and civilians.[57] Nevertheless, Spier's letters demonstrate how acts of war were normalised and the fear surrounding the fighting was balanced by the excitement of liberation and the presence of Allied soldiers.

After the Allies had finally liberated the western provinces in May 1945, it was impossible to instantly organise the children's return home. Neither was this considered desirable. The country's destroyed infrastructure as well as communication difficulties contributed to the fact that it took the Netherlands Military Authority (NMA) months to register all evacuated children. On 1 June 1945, the IKB affirmed that 'surely there is a lot of concern for the well-being of the children, but we do not think there is much enthusiasm to receive the children back home already'.[58] As a consequence, most children stayed with their foster

---

[56] Willering, *Rotterdammertjes in Stadskanaal*, 58; Nieuwenhuis, *Naar de Boeren!*, 102–103.
[57] Klep and Schoenmaker, *De Bevrijding van Nederland 1944–1945*, 286–308.
[58] NIOD, 182f, inv.no. 87, Letter Central IKB, 1 June 1945.

Dinsdag 8 Mei

Lieve Vader en Moeder en Ria

Hoe gaat het met u en hoe gaat
het met Ria LOOPT ZIJ aL. Pa IK HeB eeN pakje
sicaReTTeN VaN de KaNadoas ge KReqeN IK HeB 2
                                                                Niet
JRooTe HDLZeN. IK HeB iN VieRdageN MiJN kleeReNHiT
Je HaT. WaT TOeN WaReN de KaNadeZeN HieRINSpyk
By onze BUURMan hebbeN WiJ 3 dagen ENdRIe
    EN een NaChTIN en Roode RY
VaChTeN IN de KELdER geweTeN TOeN viel
het het hews naast ons plaT Door een
        en
Reket bon Van Barken TOeN mijn wij naar
Roodeschool gegann U WOORT W Nog geveliciter
met de wede

                    De Hateleke gewoesen Van
                                    Jan Spier

Pa WIL U Wel even naarvan Maas gaan
even de gaeten doen van NieN Hios

DOOg   Doooooc.Macsje

                    DOch Ria

Illustration 22 Letter by Jan Spier, 8 May 1945.
Dear Father and Mother and Ria, How are you and how is Ria, is she walking yet? Dad, I got a pack of cigarettes from a Canadian. I also have two large shells. I didn't take my clothes off in four days, because then the Canadians were here in Spijk. We've spent three days and nights in our neighbour's cellar and then the house next to us was bombed by a V2. Then we went to Roodeschool. Congratulations with the peace. Greetings from Jan Spier.

parents until July 1945; some even until the end of the year. Yet even after the west had more or less recovered, not all children were wanted back home. One girl, for instance, still lived with her foster parents in September 1945, because her father wanted time to 'rebuild his flower shop' in Rotterdam.[59] For some foster families, this prolonged foster period clearly lasted too long. A telegram from Groningen to the Central IKB stated: 'In [the province of] Groningen we have noticed, especially from reports by city dwellers, that it is desirable that the children return home soon. Our bread is of poor quality and the rations are sober compared to those in the west …. The west certainly deserves the high-quality food and higher rations from the government, but a certain attitude towards the children cannot be denied.'[60] The northeast had responded rapidly and effectively to the despair in the starving west, but when tables turned over the summer of 1945, it was time for the north-east to focus on their own recovery again.

For NVD children, the return home was generally even more difficult, as many of them belonged to NSB families or had lived with pro-German foster families. In a Dutch television documentary of 2013, Coco, who was 10 years old in 1945, recalled that when the Allied forces liberated Groningen, they immediately arrested her and her foster parents – who turned out to be among the most prominent NSB families in the city of Groningen. Finally, after catching up with all the administrative work, it took the Forces of the Interior two weeks to notice that Coco did not actually belong to this family.[61] Although certainly not all NVD evacuees belonged to pro-German families or had lived with them (like Coco), the Dutch perceived collaborators with the NVD as political enemies after the war. This did not only entail trial and conviction after the war, but it was one of the main reasons for omitting the NVD from the post-war narrative on child evacuations.

Results and Post-War Continuation

On 22 June 1945, the NMA sent a circular letter with guidelines for the return of all evacuated children. The military commissar announced that it

[59] SR, 336, inv.no. 94, Correspondence, 10 September 1945.
[60] NIOD, 182f, inv.no 27, Letter from IKB Groningen to Houben, s.n.
[61] 'Hongerkinderen', *Andere Tijden*, 29 December 2013. www.anderetijden.nl/aflevering/ 95/ Hongerkinderen. Accessed 4 January 2014. Between 120,000 and 150,000 Dutch men, women, and children were held in custody on alleged charges of collaborating with the enemy after the war was over. In some cases, such as Coco's, children were interned with their parents, against direct orders from the NMA. In June 1945, the province of Drenthe alone had to take care of no less than 4,000 homeless children from collaborating NSB families as well as NVD children left without a home in the west. DA, 0196 Centrale Vereniging Opbouw Drenthe, inv.no. 221, Report activities, 11 May–20 June 1945; Romijn, *Snel, Streng en Rechtvaardig*, 7. For more on the post-war fate of NSB children, see: Ismee Tames, 'Innocence and Punishment: The War Experiences of the Children of Dutch Nazi Collaborators', in *Restaging War in the Western World: Noncombatant Experiences, 1890–Today*, eds. Maartje Abbenhuis and Sara Buttsworth (New York: Palgrave Macmillan, 2009), 87–108.

Table 8.1 *Estimated numbers of evacuated Dutch children per organisation*

Organisation	Number of children evacuated
IKB	16,000
NVD	8,000
Companies, municipalities, private initiatives	6,000
Churches (other)	2,000
'Wild' children	8,000
Total	40,000

concerned 'the return of 40,000 children, approximately 90 per cent of whom can be received back home'.[62] In another note from the same date, the military commissar of The Hague wrote that these guidelines not only applied to 'children, who have been officially evacuated by the IKB, but also to the so-called wild evacuated children and children evacuated by the NVD'.[63] To these categories, we must add church organisations operating outside of the IKB as well as companies, municipalities, and many private initiatives. Table 8.1 shows the roughly estimated numbers of evacuated children per organisation, providing insight in the orders of magnitude.

These 40,000 children represented an estimated 9 per cent of the child population between 4–15 years in the large conurbations in the west in 1945.[64] The physical removal of 9 per cent of the most affected and most severely malnourished schoolchildren, without doubt, positively affected all 40,000 lives, at least in terms of nutrition. This statement is confirmed by medical examinations of the children during and after their recovery period away from home. For example, 38 of Dr Wagenaar's evacuees from Betondorp (20 boys, 18 girls) were sent to Sneek (Friesland), where a local physician documented their weight changes. During the first two weeks, both boys and girls initially lost weight because of diarrhoea caused by the greasy food. The most significant weight gain was found in girls older than 10 and boys older than 13, demonstrating the effects of lagged puberty in males. Between their arrival on 26 March and return back to Amsterdam on 25 June 1945, two of the oldest girls (14–15 years)

---

[62] UA, 1136, inv.no. 398, Guidelines return children, 22 June 1945.

[63] UA, 1136, inv.no. 398, Note to all military commissars, 22 June 1945. See also: Schoonoord, *Militair Gezag in Nederland*, 616.

[64] Estimated child population in the 11 largest cities in the occupied western provinces (ages 4–15): 452,321 children. CBS, *Jaarcijfers voor Nederland 1943–1946*. In addition, there were also several baby and toddler transports, organised by both the IKB and via 'wild' transports. Liefke Knol, *Het Babyhuis: Kinderen en Ouders door Oorlog en Honger Gescheiden* (Amsterdam: Artemis, 2010).

had gained weight from 95 pounds to 120 pounds, while the youngest of 7 years old reported a weight gain of 5 pounds only. For boys, the oldest went up from 91 to 114 pounds and the youngest also gained 5 pounds in total.[65] In addition to the positive and rapid weight gains, the effects the child evacuations had on the health and nutrition of the remaining members of the households must also have been considerable.

Efforts in evacuating children did not end with the liberation. From the autumn of 1944, child relief practices in the liberated south fell under the influence of military interim rule. In trying to reshape the future of the post-war state and restore pre-war social relations, the military administrators in the south deemed child evacuations just as important as their northern counterparts. While the evacuations in the occupied areas remained largely fragmented, in the liberated part of the country, the NMA coordinated all efforts centrally. In December 1944, after over a year of conscientious planning, the Dutch government-in-exile and the NMA launched the National Commission for the Evacuation of Dutch Children 1945 (*Nationale Commissie tot Uitzending van Nederlandsche Kinderen 1945*; NC), which became based in liberated Den Bosch. In London, the Netherlands Government Children Committee was established to function as the British-based counterpart of the NC. The British government itself was anticipating the arrival of about 20,000 Dutch children.[66] SHAEF provided the NC with all the necessary documents and allocated transportation means.[67] The constitution of the NC thus fitted perfectly with the military administration's aspiration to restore the Dutch centralised state as soon as possible.

Similar to the child evacuations in the occupied areas, the NC initially focused on transferring malnourished children to better-situated living areas. The guidelines from December 1944 clearly outlined that the primary category comprised 'seriously malnourished children'; this was to be followed by a second category of children whose upbringing was considered in serious danger due to circumstances of war. The NC explained: 'We propose to send only severely malnourished children to England. For children coping with psychological difficulties, a quieter

[65] NIOD, 0332, B1, Van de Griek, 'De Voedselhulp', 7–8; Wagenaar, *Een Jaar Noodcomité*, 22–23.
[66] Both institutions fell under the Dutch Ministry of Social Affairs. Jan Sintemaartensdijk, *De Bleekneusjes van 1945: De Uitzending van Nederlandse Kinderen naar het Buitenland* (Amsterdam: Boom, 2002), 11–27; NIOD, 182f, inv.no. 114, Report 'Kinderuitzending', June 1945. See also: inv.no. 115; inv.no. 117; NIOD, 1076, inv.no. 11, Minutes IKB Haarlem, 15 June 1945; GHA, 0398, inv.no. 1; GAS, 500 Rode Kruis afdeling Schiedam, inv.no. 96.
[67] NARA, 331, Entry 2, Box 118, Message SHAEF Mission Netherlands to HQ, 18 December 1944.

location domestically, or possibly Belgium, is preferred.'[68] For both groups of children, malnourished or otherwise threatened by war circumstances, the NC considered it to be of highest import to evacuate children in line with pre-war denominational boundaries:

If we want the child evacuations to succeed and if we aim at drawing full support from the Dutch people, we need to ensure that the children are placed in foster families of their own religion, as well as that personnel of their own denomination will guide them there. Personalities are not fully developed until the age of 18 and prematurely placing children of different denominations together could lead to a serious flattening of society.[69]

Evidently, pillarisation was not only a factor in relief practices but even a goal, something that required active and full recovery. The restoration of pre-war social relations included reinforcing the traditional gender patterns as well. The NC's main objective for boys aged 15–18 years, for example, was physical training and 'character building' to be achieved via sports and 'proper education' in history and geography. Girls in the same age group, on the other hand, were encouraged to focus on 'simple courses in domestic sciences'.[70] More than anything, the chastity of the girls was the source of much concern as some of them had been 'engaged' during the war – meaning they had been sexually active outside marriage – which did not suit the post-war morality they envisioned.[71] In line with this reaffirmation of traditional role patterns, the NC strove to work with female volunteers and staff exclusively, 'as providing care and aid to children is pre-eminently a women's task'.[72] Evidently, the extended public role women had acquired during the crisis period diminished soon after the war, with traditional boundaries between the sexes, as well as those between denominations, being reinforced rather than blurred.

Military discipline also became an important, new factor in the post-war child evacuations. In January 1945, NMA Major Laman Trip wrote that children had to be gathered quietly from their homes and brought to one meeting point, 'in order to ensure no contact with the civil population'.[73] The city of Tilburg was selected to function as the main transit camp for all evacuations abroad, for which the NC deployed military vehicles and even airplanes. All children underwent medical examinations in Tilburg and, if

---

[68] NA, 2.13.25, inv.no. 3207, Guidelines for organisation of relief to mentally and physically suffering children in the liberated Netherlands, by psychologist P. Calon, 17 December 1944.
[69] NA, 2.13.25, inv.no. 3207.   [70] NA, 2.13.25, inv.no. 3207.
[71] NIOD, 182f, inv.no 120, Report girls' camp Barnsley, September–November 1945.
[72] NIOD, 1212, inv.no. A2, Guidelines transports abroad.
[73] NA, 2.13.25, inv.no. 3207, Letter Laman Trip (NMA) to Wijffels, Secretary National Commission for the Evacuation of Dutch Children 1945, 10 January 1945.

they were diagnosed with infectious diseases such as scabies, dusting down with DDT was obligatory. The NC further relied on a wide range of volunteers and institutions to assist them, such as public health services, the earlier-mentioned Union for Female Volunteers (UVV), paediatricians as well as pre-existing institutions for school camps and health colonies. The Social Liaison groups of the Red Cross ensured all municipalities established NC district offices. The Dutch Red Cross arranged most transports and, according to their own documentation, by the beginning of 1945 they had already transported over 70,000 persons as part of the post-war child evacuations.[74]

On 11 February 1945, the first two ships with children from the war-affected south of the Netherlands sailed to the English port of Tilbury. In the autumn of 1944, reports on the deplorable living conditions had reached the British Home Office, which then agreed to put their preparations for European child evacuations into action. The British government would cover the largest part of the costs for hosting the children, SHAEF agreed to help with transportation, and the Ministry of Food would provide food and extra rations. With the help of many hundreds of volunteers, the Women's Voluntary Serivces aided with distributing clothes. The first designated camp was a former plane factory turned hostel near Coventry, suitable to host up to 500 children, which even included an infirmary and hairdressing salon. Three months after their arrival, the first group of children was given the choice to return home or stay with foster families in the area. Most of them chose to return home, which was contrary to the decision of their peers from later groups, who for the greater part stayed with British foster families some additional weeks or months.[75]

Following an arrangement between L'Ouevre de L'Enfance and the NC, and with permission of the 21st Army Group, 300 children were shortly thereafter sent to Belgium to live with host families.[76] Over the course of the following 18 months, 30,000 Dutch children followed, first to England and Scotland, then to Belgium, Switzerland, France, Denmark, and Sweden: all countries that had fostered children from other recently liberated countries as well.[77] A Zionistic organisation in Palestine called *Irgun Olei Holland* also offered its assistance; in particular, to place Jewish children who had come out of hiding in foster care. In

[74] NIOD, 1212, inv.no A2, Instructions for establishment of local committees, z.d.; NHA, 1310, inv.no. 23, Report Volksherstel Haarlem 1945–1946; Sintemaartensdijk, *De Bleekneusjes van 1945*, 286.
[75] Sintemaartensdijk, *De Bleekneusjes van 1945*, 21–22, 26. The Queen Wilhelmina Fund also had 250,000 dollars at its disposal to help fund the evacuations.
[76] NARA, 331, Entry 152, Box 264, Fortnightly report SHAEF Mission Netherlands, 14 February 1945.
[77] Schoonoord, *Militair Gezag in Nederland*, 614; Centraal Comité Hollands-Hælpen, *De Deense Hulp aan Holland* (Copenhagen: Hollands-Hjælpen, 1946), 23–24; Sintemaartensdijk, *De Bleekneusjes van 1945*, 28–29, 265.

Table 8.2 *Evacuations abroad by National Commission for the Evacuation of Dutch Children 1945, 1945–1946*

Destination	Time period	Number of children
Great Britain	February 1945–July 1946	9,232
Belgium	March 1945–spring 1946	3,200
Switzerland	May 1945–July 1946	9,548
France	June–October 1945	350
Denmark[a]	July 1945–September 1946	5,100
Sweden	September 1945–September 1946	2,391
Total	February 1945–September 1946	29,821

[a] Excluding 500 children from the Dutch East Indies, who left for Bornholm Island in June 1947 to recover from the traumas of war and concentration camps. Sintemaartensdijk, *De Bleekneusjes van 1945*, 201–205
Source: Numbers deriving and calculated from Sintemaartensdijk, *De Bleekneusjes van 1945*, 112–119, 127–150, 169–174, 180–205, 209–230, 301–303

line with the conviction not to differentiate between 'war victims', a contested notion nowadays, the Dutch government politely refused this offer.[78] Table 8.2 differentiates the 30,000 children sent abroad to recover from the war according to destination, with most of them staying in former military and holiday camps, health colonies, or foster homes for one to several months after the war.

In addition to the evacuations abroad, the NC also placed children domestically, especially in the province of North Brabant. In total, the NC managed to place 9,500 Dutch children, most of them aged 4–12 years in foster families as part of this 'domestic family care' programme.[79] These domestic efforts had been intended as a collective measure and to instigate closer cooperation between the north and the south of the country, which had been 'so cruelly separated from each other during the winter'.[80] In addition, the NC situated another 12,000 children in Dutch holiday camps to recover from the war. As these camps were mostly in a poor state and also used by the NMA to take care of children from National Socialist families, evacuations abroad were still preferred.[81]

[78] Sintemaartensdijk, *De Bleekneusjes van 1945*, 28. There were about 3,500 of these Jewish 'war foster children' coming out of hiding after the war in the Netherlands. Martin P. Bossenbroek, *De Meelstreep* (Amsterdam: Bakker, 2001), 183, 247.
[79] NA, 2.14.08, inv.no 750, Overview domestic child evacuations, 9 August 1945; GAS, 108 Hulpactie Rode Kruis, File 1; NIOD, 182f, inv.no. 122, Letter National Commission to District Office The Hague, 17 October 1945.
[80] UA, 1136, 254, Letter Local committee Eindhoven to Utrecht, 15 July 1945.
[81] NIOD, 182f, inv.no. 122, Correspondence, August 1945.

The results of the first evacuations were deemed a great success. In April 1945, member of the UNRRA medical staff, doctor J. Trauber, reported that the Dutch children who had been brought to the Baginton camp near Coventry were steadily gaining weight and getting back to normal living. The nutrition programmes proved immediately successful for girls; boys needed more time to recover. For example, while boys 9 years of age gained only 5.3 ounces in the first week, girls of the same age put on no less than 3 pounds and 15 ounces. Yet in the second week, these same boys gained an average of 2 pounds while the girls gained only 12.7 ounces. Similar to the IKB's guidelines, the amount of food was increased each day as the children's stomachs adjusted. During their first days, many of them complained of hunger in spite of the plenitude of food available. And once the children had physically recovered, the staff encountered another obstacle, that of disobedience and misconduct; most notably, of the older boys.[82] The example of Baginton camp thus shows how nutrition was of main importance, and how (once this was resolved) social behaviour quickly became central to the recovery of the Dutch children abroad.

In connection with this shift in focus, after May 1945 the nature of child evacuations changed considerably. The IKB and other organisations involved with child evacuations were placed under the authority of the NC – much to their disappointment. The NC did copy the IKB's administrative measures and placed many of their personnel in high positions, demonstrating the high regard they had for the IKB evacuations.[83] During the transition from war to peace, the focus of the NC soon shifted from the physiologically malnourished children to the 'uprooted and psychologically malnourished' war youth.[84] A circular letter from the IKB mid-June 1945 confirmed:

The level of undernutrition, although still of importance, is no longer the decisive factor. More attention is paid to psychological abnormalities due to the war (nervousness, neuroses due to bombing, or fear of the father returning from hiding, et cetera) .... While before the capitulation physiological insufficiencies (malnutrition) was the key reason for evacuation, we now try to evacuate the children who psychologically suffered the most from war and occupation.[85]

In the NC's new guidelines for medical examinations, dating from August 1945, 'malnutrition' had now dropped from the first to the fifth

---

[82] UN, AG 18-004 Bureau of Areas, S-1245-0000-0360, Message Netherlands Information Bureau, 6 April 1945.

[83] NIOD, 182f, inv.no. 144, Report IKB inland and abroad, 1 June 1945.

[84] NIOD, 182f, inv.no. 120, Final report Scotland by doctor W. Peters, s.n.

[85] NA, 2.14.08, inv.no 755, Letter Dr Wester of the IKB to head of school doctors in The Hague, Dr Streng, 11 June 1945.

category on the priority list. Social indications henceforth came first, followed by 'TB threat', 'recovering from acute or chronical illness or surgery', and 'post-TB'.[86] Children with illnesses or respiratory problems were mostly sent to Switzerland; younger children aged 6–14 were especially welcome in Denmark and Sweden. With social criteria becoming increasingly important, 'befriended and purely democratic' England was in high demand for the older youth in particular.[87] And, because the newly targeted age group of 14–18 years was considered 'contaminated' by the war, the NC at this moment preferred collective recovery and discipline in holiday camps to individual care in foster families.[88]

With the cases of malnutrition among children dropping over the summer of 1945, by September of that year medical practitioners of the NC deemed further emergency evacuations unnecessary.[89] In November 1945, most children who had been evacuated after the liberation had returned to their homes.[90] Nevertheless, it would take until the summer of 1946 before the NC transferred all Dutch colony houses and holiday camps back to their former owners. From that point onwards, the NC carried out only a few minor tasks until it was finally liquidated in 1949. Most importantly, they arranged foster homes in the Netherlands for foreign war-affected children. This included a widely debated stay for 4,568 'Dutch' children from Dutch fathers and German mothers as well as for 850 'German' children from Dutch mothers and German fathers. In addition, the NC organised holiday camps and foster homes for 3,500 Austrian and 500 Hungarian children. On 30 April 1949, the Ministry of Social Affairs transferred the NC's authority to the newly established Central Board for Foreign Child Care.[91] In total, the NC evacuated 30,000 children abroad, placed over 20,000 children domestically, as well as hosted over 10,000 children from foreign countries.

Conclusion

The evacuation of 40,000 malnourished children during the Dutch famine illustrates the collaborative power of pre-existing social networks

---

[86] NIOD, 182f, inv.no. 122, Guidelines medical examinations, 25 August 1945.
[87] NIOD, 182f, inv.no. 114, Report IKB inland and abroad, 1 June 1945.
[88] DA, 0196, inv.no. 221, Report meeting, 18 May 1945.
[89] NIOD, 182f, inv.no. 122, Letter Houben IKB to National Commission in Amsterdam, 15 September 1945; Letter IKB to GGD The Hague, 29 September 1945. The department of Child Evacuation of the IKB was officially liquidated and fully transferred to the National Commission in early 1946.
[90] NIOD, 1212, inv.no. A2, Correspondence National Commission, November 1945.
[91] Sintemaartensdijk, *De Bleekneusjes van 1945*, 265–288.

and institutions. In the 1940s, the Netherlands enjoyed an extensive health- and family care system and had a strong civil society. These factors ensured that many networks were in place to efficiently organise relief during the crisis. Child evacuations were only one aspect of relief efforts but, similar to the child-feeding initiatives, they highlight the active role of ordinary people and grassroots initiatives in taking emergency measures. Shared ideas on the importance of continuation of family life, even in extreme circumstances, and protecting the future of Dutch society were key to this communal response to the famine conditions. Different groups and institutions found an important point of convergence by focusing on transferring children out of the famine-affected areas while trying to secure the future of Dutch society. The thousands of volunteers – mostly women – and tens of thousands of host families involved in the relief programmes make these child evacuations a paramount chapter in the history of the Hunger Winter, as well as of national and international relief practices in the twentieth century in general.

In contrast to the wartime child evacuations, their post-war counterparts can be viewed as part and parcel of larger processes of social and political transition in the Netherlands, similar to events taking place all over Western Europe. The Allied military authorities and the NMA ensured that the child evacuations would not interfere with the desired swift restoration of the centralised state. Grassroots initiatives and fragmented relief efforts were replaced by one government organisation, which was characterised not only by institutional continuity but also by an innovation in relief practices. However, the newly established NC reaffirmed pre-war moral values concerning denominational segregation and gender roles, thereby reversing some important progressive achievements in the social order during the famine period. Because the food situation significantly improved over the summer of 1945, the NC's focus soon shifted from physiologically to psychologically affected children, who were allegedly in dire need of war rehabilitation. This shift is exemplary for the quick recovery of the famine after liberation and subsequent changing priorities in post-war Dutch society.

Conclusion

In words both emotional and emphatic, Dutch historian Ernst Kossmann concluded the following about the Hunger Winter: 'Never in its history did Holland have to consider the downfall of its people and the destruction of its civilization as seriously as it had during the final months before May 1945.'[1] Over the last 75 years, both popular and scholarly discourses have cultivated powerful myths about the Hunger Winter, the most important ones being the brutal policy of starvation by the German occupier and the miraculous rescue by the Allied food drops. In literature, these myths seem informed by the assumption that the Dutch Hunger Winter is comparable to other food crises and famines caused by Nazi hunger politics. At the national level, the perseverance of these misconceptions stems from a long process of delegitimisation of the German occupier on the one hand, and the internalisation of gratitude towards the Allies on the other – processes that started right after liberation and became a central foundation for nation-building in Dutch post-war society. Through mutual influences, over time these dominant narratives have become aligned with both individual and collective memories of the German occupation in an attempt to give meaning to experiences of war, occupation, and hunger.

This book has provided a more balanced and layered view of the Dutch famine; a view that has been informed by a research strategy encompassing state, household, as well as community perspectives. We have seen that from the autumn of 1944 onwards, people living in the cities and towns of the western Netherlands battled the famine conditions in the privacy of their households but oftentimes also collectively, in self-organised networks. Emerging from existing networks and traditional Dutch practices, these community efforts managed to occupy a central position between household and state levels and, as such, effectively took over care and relief responsibilities. Most importantly, by targeting

[1] Ernst H. Kossmann, *De Lage Landen 1780–1980: Twee Eeuwen Nederland en België* II (Amsterdam: Elsevier, 1986), 204.

vulnerable groups who suffered most from malnutrition, grassroots and NGO relief entities were able to compensate when neither the state nor the family could protect its own.

While many scholarly studies still presume that the Hunger Winter was the product of the Nazi empire's exploitation and hunger politics, a closer examination of its causes has revealed that the role of the German occupier in causing and maintaining famine conditions in the western Netherlands was much more complex. Obviously, without German occupation there would not have been famine. Yet within the context of war and occupation, the famine was arguably caused and exacerbated by a culmination of various transportation and distribution problems. The Allied advance and the subsequence response by the German occupier both exerted their influence on the Dutch food system: causing the first serious food supply difficulties well before September 1944. The turning point was Operation Market Garden, with the liberation of the southern part of the Netherlands, the national railway strike, and the subsequent German embargo. However, this was just the beginning of the crisis. When the German civil authorities fully lifted the embargo in early November 1944, the circumstances had not yet produced full-blown famine.

But other factors further exacerbated the food situation. The most important one of these was the fuel shortage that followed after the liberation of coal-producing Limburg, preventing people from heating their houses and cooking food, but also restraining transportation possibilities. Another contributing issue was that a growing lack of trust in the food system contributed to a considerable growth in clandestine production and trade. Weather conditions further aggravated the situation, with a heavy frost period lasting from late December 1944 until the January 1945 that prohibited water transportation. Combined with the fuel shortages, German requisitioning of transportation, and the railway strike, this frost period accelerated famine conditions in the west. Finally, at the international level, the postponement of emergency food aid played a crucial role.

It is impossible to single out one of these factors, such as the temporary German food blockade or the continuation of the Dutch railway strike, as all of these variables were connected. Indeed, at the start of this chain of events, the German civil authorities had actively deployed the threat of famine, yet actual famine soon proved more of a menace to their own military and political position than a useful weapon of war. This German shift from withholding food to cooperation to 'avoid worse' significantly distinguishes the Dutch case from other food crises in Nazi-occupied Europe. In this context, it is impossible to refer to the German occupier as one coherent legislative or political entity. Similar to the pre-crisis situation, the German authorities in the Netherlands were internally divided, as actions from the *Wehrmacht* and *Kriegsmarine*, such as confiscations, reprisal actions, and inundations, often thwarted policies from the German civil administration. In addition to military and political motivations, it is also conceivable that German officials decided to seize the opportunity the famine presented to show good, benevolent leadership by allowing and supporting relief efforts. This German attitude is echoed by Seyss-Inquart's attempt, while standing trial at Nuremberg, to obtain a Royal Pardon based on his efforts 'to save the Dutch from starvation in the period December 1944–April 1945'.

What has usually gone unmentioned in historiography is the heavy burden the Allies placed upon the Dutch through their staunch adherence to their policy of economic warfare. Due to the Allied blockade of the German-controlled continent, during the final months of occupation only some Red Cross shipments from neutral countries were allowed into the Netherlands but only as long as they did not interfere with military strategies. Again, from political and military considerations, the Allies' reaction to the famine conditions was that relief should follow liberation and not the other way around. The Dutch government-in-exile responded to the people's despair by putting pressure on the Allies to act immediately. The government's most valuable contribution, however, was facilitating negotiations on an informal truce with Seyss-Inquart in the final stages of the war: negotiations that could have commenced crucial months earlier if not for serious mistrust and miscommunication. While the eventual wartime shipments made a valuable contribution to the meagre official rations and had an important psychological impact, they cannot be considered the decisive factor to explain why most Dutch survived the famine. The true Allied contribution to relieving the crisis followed more than a week after liberation, in minor part via airdrops, but predominantly through land and sea supply.

This more nuanced revision of the Allied contribution is confirmed by the data presented in this book, revealing that, until the time these Allied relief supplies reached Dutch households, living conditions were indeed harsh and hunger was widespread. Despite the zealous efforts of Dutch food administrators, official rations for all people over four years of age stayed below the life-threatening threshold of 750 kcal during the five-and-a-half months of famine that lasted from late November 1944 until mid-May 1945: slightly relieved for only five weeks with the help of the Red Cross shipments. During the entire crisis period September 1944–July 1945, war-related excess deaths among civilians is estimated at 35,000 in the three famine-exposed western provinces. Of these excess deaths, 8,305 were officially reported as resulting from starvation, thereby forming a large part of the estimated over 20,000 famine-related deaths. Deaths in the large conurbations began to rise sharply after December 1944 and reached a peak in March 1945, and it took until the summer of that year for mortality to reach normal patterns again. Fertility followed similar patterns, with birth rates in the urban west two to three times lower in the famine's wake. The long-term effects of the famine are present even today, in those adults who were conceived or born during the Hunger Winter. In terms of mortality patterns, the Dutch famine showed major similarities to other 'modern' famines, most notably, those experienced elsewhere in occupied Europe during the Second World War. By contrast, the data presented in this book also uncover that the age-specific mortality patterns deviate from most other famines when investigating child mortality. Dutch school-aged children seemed hardly affected by the famine conditions, with the monthly death rate of urban children even remaining below that in the non-exposed parts of the country throughout the famine period.

If it was not official rations or Allied relief that protected the Dutch during the famine – children in particular – then what did? This study has argued that during the food crisis the Dutch food system operated at three main levels: the state desperately trying to keep official rations at subsistence levels, households attempting to obtain food for self-preservation via informal and extra-legal channels, and communities protecting the most vulnerable in their midst. These three levels of food distribution did not operate independently, but evolved and functioned in continuous and dynamic interaction with each other. A systematic analysis of the responses to the famine conditions thus proved vital for understanding the ways in which the Dutch organised the redistribution of food during the crisis – something that would not have been possible by leaving community responses out of the equation.

Bearing the main responsibility for the population's well-being, Dutch food authorities made a conscious decision not only to centralise the rationing system but also to allow grassroots organisations to take over relief responsibilities. The food authorities were aware of their compromised legitimacy and recognised that the supposedly apolitical churches were in a much better position to mobilise and regulate relief. They also understood that local entities would be more capable of identifying those in need of extra food at the individual level. From a policy objective that prioritised maximising consumption levels rather than official rations, it was Director of Food Supply Louwes himself who negotiated with *Reichskommissar* Seyss-Inquart about the establishment of what would become the main NGO for providing relief during the famine – the IKB.

Presenting the 'fairest' approach to food shortage under these specific circumstances, Dutch and German authorities tolerated these relief organisations and even supported them. Other coping strategies were also tolerated to a much greater extent than before the crisis. The CCD and the German *Wehrmacht* condoned food expeditions as long as the yields were meant for household consumption only, and the German authorities did not intervene during the women's food protests. Similarly, Dutch police turned a blind eye to illegal logging, and municipalities and Provincial Food Commissioners encouraged companies to gather food to redistribute among their staff. While the general stance was to not make things any harder for the population than they already were, punishment of economic crimes became much stricter, demonstrating that the authorities created and maintained strict legal and moral standards that differentiated between self-help and profiteering. In doing so, they aligned with the little articulated but clearly demonstrable ideas on what was fair and just among the population.

At household levels, the low rations urged people to obtain food supplies from extra-legal sources. Because of the transportation difficulties, urban black-market prices rose to astronomical levels. Since most households had neither the means to purchase nor to barter on black markets regularly, any man or woman who was able to ventured out into the countryside in search for food. These food expeditions proved to be of great significance in mitigating famine conditions at household levels. During the height of the famine, food outside of legal channels even became more important for household consumption levels than official rations. In addition to having necessary material resources, other factors that determined survival chances included mobility, having the right contacts, skills, willingness, and knowledge to obtain food and fuel. Eventually, the boundaries between right and wrong behaviour blurred during the crisis and grew more towards an understanding of what was acceptable and legitimate given the circumstances. This understanding, in turn, was informed by the main authorities during the crisis – not just the state, but more so by churches and resistance groups.

The basic notions on fairness and justice expressed by these authorities were reconfirmed in practice by the ways in which communities responded to the crisis. Contrary to current views in historiography that often characterise the Hunger Winter as a period of far-reaching social disintegration, this study has shown that there was no severe breakdown of social bonds forcing people back into individual survival mode. Despite the mounting German repression, cooperation was still possible and fruitful even at the height of the famine. State and household strategies left particularly vulnerable groups behind, and this book has shown how vital community responses were in protecting these vulnerable groups from starvation. While individual strategies served those with the best set of 'survival tools', the IKB and other communal relief efforts focused on the most vulnerable in society, children in particular. The collective decision to help school-aged children was supported by both the German and the Dutch authorities and resulted in the extra feeding of approximately a third to half of the children in famine-affected areas as well as the evacuation of another (approximately) 9 per cent of the urban children to the better-off northeast of the country. Because the Netherlands enjoyed an extensive health- and family care system and boasted a strong civil society, many networks were already in place to efficiently organise this emergency relief. Shared ideas on the importance of continuation of family life, even in extreme circumstances, and protecting the future of Dutch society were crucial in the formation of these community efforts.

The ways in which the Dutch coped with food shortage and deprivation is also telling of the crisis itself, with the high level of activity revealing that it was indeed an early-stage famine. As Sorokin has argued: 'We must expect the strongest reaction from the starving masses at the time when hunger is great, but not excessive.'[2] The main reason for this high level of activity and self-organisation was that food supplies in close proximity to the affected urban areas were not yet fully exhausted. Despite the fog of war, this still provided communities and households alike with significant food-gathering opportunities. In the end, the Dutch famine was the result of a transportation crisis, not a decline in food availability, and social conduct during the famine reflected this. Another sign that the Dutch famine should be considered an early-stage famine was the absence of migration. While in most famines large numbers of people leave everything behind in hope for a better food situation elsewhere, in the occupied western Netherlands, migration only took the form of short-term food expeditions. The special circumstances in the Netherlands in 1944–1945 were key to this phenomenon: the Dutch knew the war was drawing to an end, and people preferred to hold out just a little longer and protect their homes than to risk leaving everything behind.

The great efforts made by communities to relieve the famine do not imply that all was truly fair and equal. To a great extent, relief practices during the Hunger Winter reflected the Dutch social order of the 1940s. Because local efforts largely built on infrastructures provided by community networks and established institutions, communal relief was highly

---

[2] Sorokin, *Hunger As a Factor in Human Affairs*, 236.

successful for the targeted groups within community or religious boundaries. Yet this infrastructure also made relief practices very exclusive, not to mention rigid. Not belonging to the right neighbourhood or denomination could have a direct impact on food access during the famine. Denominational boundaries were not only maintained in the crisis period but were sometimes even enforced by those who were convinced that this was the right way to secure the Dutch future. Nevertheless, grassroots interdenominational committees and the constitution of the IKB as an umbrella organisation were clear attempts to overcome social divisions. In practice, however, even the IKB was bound by the limits of religious communities, who offered their homes and food preferably only to children belonging to their own denomination. While the IKB was wary of these conservative practices and the loss of opportunity they presented, they knew that complying would lead to the best possible outcome.

Despite these limits to solidarity, communal efforts achieved considerable success, and, given the strength of evidence accumulated in this study, there can be little doubt about their impact. The Dutch case suggests that, while children may physically be vulnerable to food deprivation and infectious diseases, their strong social position in mid-twentieth-century society also made them particularly resilient to famine conditions. Following this line of reasoning, the main victims of the Dutch famine were those people who solely relied on support by the state: vulnerable groups such as the destitute, people residing in institutions such as prisons and psychiatric wards, and elderly people without a social support network that included community relief.

The special strategy pursued by communities to collectively protect their children makes the Dutch example a relevant starting point for further investigation. This study has argued for a better understanding of the relation between physiological vulnerability to food deprivation and social processes fostering resilience – an understanding that entails abandoning the dualistic focus on the state and the individual with regard to food distributions systems – and instead including community networks operating between these levels. Testing this hypothesis for other food crises and famines that occurred in Nazi-occupied Europe would be a relevant exercise for future research. In addition, collecting anthropometric data on children's height and weight could explain in full detail the extent to which Dutch children were affected by malnutrition, regardless of their mortality rates.

Put together, the main conclusions of this study offer a new interpretation of the causes and effects of the Hunger Winter: the social fabric remained relatively strong; the German civil authorities found reasons to cooperate and allow relief, and, because of the effective action taken by the population, the number of victims remained relatively low. Yet my ultimate goal has not been to debunk the myths surrounding the Hunger Winter. On the contrary, this study has aimed to demonstrate the resilience of the Dutch population during one of the most difficult times in recent history, hence emphasising the agency of the population that the popular narrative of passive victimhood and the scholarly narrative of social disintegration have failed to recognise. With this book, I hope to have brought to the fore the complexity of political and social relations that had ultimately determined the course and impact of the famine.

Appendix: Timeline of Important Events

1940

10 May	German invasion of the Netherlands
13 May	Queen Wilhelmina and Dutch Ministers flee to England State authority transferred to General Winkelman
14 May	Bombing of Rotterdam, killing 850 civilians
15 May	The Netherlands surrenders to Nazi Germany
18 May	Hitler appoints Arthur Seyss-Inquart as head of the new German civil administration in the occupied Netherlands
28 May	Belgium surrenders to Nazi Germany
29 May	Transfer of state authority to *Reichskommissar* Seyss-Inquart and *Wehrmachtbefehlshaber* Friedrich Christiansen
1 June	Dutch army veterans released from internment on Hitler's orders
22 June	France surrenders to Nazi Germany
24 June	Seyss-Inquart dissolves Dutch States General
29 June	Coronation day – first symbolic resistance against the occupation regime
4 July	Ban on listening to foreign radio channels
23 July	Constitution of the Dutch Union
28 July	First radio address by Queen Wilhelmina via Radio Orange
3 September	Formation of the first cabinet Gerbrandy in London
7 September	Start of the Blitz, the German bombing campaign against Great Britain (7 September 1940–11 May 1941)
5 October	Distribution of the Aryan declaration among Dutch civil servants
17 October	Compulsory identification announced
22 October	Constitution of Winter Aid

21 November	Jewish civil servants removed from office
23 November	Student strikes in Delft
26 November	Student strikes in Leiden, famous speech by Professor Cleveringa protesting against dismissal of Jewish colleagues
5 November	Re-election of US President Roosevelt

1941

10 January	Mandatory registration of Jewish citizens
26 January	Episcopal proclamation against the National Socialist Movement (NSB)
11 January	Violence between National Socialists and Jewish fighting squads in Amsterdam
12 January	German and Dutch police encircle and cordon off the Jewish quarter in Amsterdam
13 February	Constitution of the Jewish Council in Amsterdam
19 February	Fights between German *Grüne Polizei* and Jewish/non-Jewish fighting squads
22–23 February	Pogroms in Amsterdam; 425 young Jewish men arrested and deported
25–26 February	General strike in Amsterdam and neigbouring towns in North Holland against anti-Jewish measures and German occupation
1–3 March	Municipal councils in Amsterdam, Hilversum, and Zaandam dismissed; New government commissioners (mayors) appointed, including Edward Voûte for Amsterdam
31 March	Constitution of Central Department for Jewish Emigration
6 April	German invasion of Yugoslavia and Greece
4 June	Freedom of movement for Jews restricted
22 June	Start of Operation Barbarossa, Axis invasion of the Soviet Union
26 July	Formation of second cabinet Gerbrandy in London
28 July	Constitution of Dutch People's Service (NVD)
12 August	Leadership principle introduced in municipal and provincial administrations
8 September	Start of Leningrad Blockade (8 September 1941–27 January 1944)

29 October	Frederik E. Müller appointed as mayor of Rotterdam
1 November	Jews banned from organisations with non-Jewish members
7 December	Japanese attack on Pearl Harbour
8 December	US Congress and the Netherlands declare war on Japan
11 December	Germany and Italy declare war on the US
12 December	Mussert and Seyss-Inquart visit Hitler; Mussert swears oath of loyalty to Hitler
14 December	The NSB becomes the only political party allowed

1942

17 January	Jews from Zaandam forced to move to Amsterdam; start of the concentration of Jews in the capital
17 February	Representatives of the churches protest to Seyss-Inquart
23 February	*Arbeitseinsatz* in Germany made mandatory
9 March	Surrender of Royal Netherlands East Indies Army in Indonesia to Japanese forces
27 March	Implementation of the Nuremberg Laws in the Netherlands
1 May	Constitution of Dutch Labour Front
3 May	Jews forced to wear a yellow Star of David with the word 'Jew' outdoors
26 June	Deportation of Jewish citizens delegated to the Jewish Council
30 June	Evening curfew for Jews set at 8 P.M.
1 July	Start of First Battle of El Alamein (1–27 July 1942), preventing Axis advance into Egypt
15 July	First Jewish deportations from Amsterdam to concentration and transit camp Westerbork
23 August	Start of German offensive to capture Stalingrad (Battle of Stalingrad: 23 August 1942–2 February 1943)
23 November	Start of Second Battle of El Alamein (23 October–11 November 1942), eliminating Axis threat in Middle East

1943

13 January	Opening of Vught concentration camp
27 March	Resistance fighters set fire to the Amsterdam population register
13 March	Announcement of measures against students, including forced signing of declaration of loyalty; about 85 per cent of the students refuse
29 April	Announcement by Christiansen that all veterans are forced to enlist for re-interment
30 April	Start of second general strike in the Netherlands, followed by police state of siege in four provinces
1 May	Police state of siege extended to the rest of the Netherlands
6 May	Students who have not signed the declaration of loyalty are deported to concentration camp Ommen
7 May	First group of veterans summoned to enlist for deportation; all men aged 18–35 years ordered to enlist for the *Arbeitseinsatz*, excluding Reich and government civil servants
13 May	Announcement that radios are strictly forbidden
25 June	Large-scale arrests of Dutch physicians
25 July	Fall of Mussolini's fascist regime in Italy
8 September	Surrender of Italy
29 September	Last deportations from Amsterdam
26 October	The Allied governments adopt proposal from Roosevelt, placing responsibility for relief of liberated Europe with the interim military authorities
3 November	Start of Battle of Kiev (3–13 November 1943)
4 December	Distribution of second rationing card, linking rationing to personal identification

1944

22 January	Seyss-Inquart signs decree, making disruption of the food supply punishable by death
27 January	Last German troops retreat from Leningrad
28 January	Announcement of inundations to delay Allied advance
11 April	Allied bombardment of Registry Office for population registers Kleykamp in The Hague

16 May	Civil Affair Agreement signed between the US, British, and Dutch governments, assigning responsibility for the welfare of the Dutch people to SHAEF
6 June	D-Day, Allied landings at Normandy
3 July	Constitution of the Contact Committee in Amsterdam
2 August	Dutch government in London signs documents for constitution of the Council of Trusted Representatives
25 August	Liberation of Paris
31 August	Liberation of Bucharest
3 September	Liberation of Brussels; Prince Bernhard appointed as Supreme Commander of the Forces of the Interior; Queen Wilhelmina announces via Radio Orange that the liberation is at the door step
4 September	Liberation of Antwerp; Seyss-Inquart announces a state of siege; Major General Kruls appointed Chief of Staff of the Netherlands Military Authority; the Netherlands Government Information Service spreads misguided information that Breda has been liberated
5 September	Massive flight of Dutch and German National Socialists to the east (Crazy Tuesday)
14 September	Liberation of Maastricht (Limburg)
17 September	Start of Operation Market Garden (17–25 September 1944), Allied landings in North Brabant and near Nijmegen and Arnhem; Dutch government announces national railway strike on the request of the Allied Headquarters
18 September	Liberation of Eindhoven (North Brabant)
21 September	Start of German demolitions of harbour installations in Rotterdam and Amsterdam
25 September	Allied troops retreat from Arnhem
27 September	Seyss-Inquart orders embargo on all food transports from the northeast to the western Netherlands
1 October	Raid on adult men in Putten as retaliation for attack on German military officials
2 October	Dutch government announces continuation of the railway strike; Swedish government agrees to send Red Cross relief to the Netherlands; start of

	the Battle of the Scheldt (2 October–8 November 1944)
5 October	Gerbrandy visits Churchill to discuss food relief for the Netherlands
16 October	Seyss-Inquart partially lifts the embargo on inland shipping
18 October	Start of potato harvesting campaign in Drenthe
27–28 October	Liberation of Tilburg and Breda (North Brabant)
1 November	Allied landings near Vlissingen and Westkapelle (Zeeland)
6 November	British Chiefs of Staff discuss possible relief schemes for the Netherlands
8 November	Seyss-Inquart lifts embargo on food transports; Committee for Relief Supply in Western Holland convenes for the first time in London
10–11 November	Raid on adult men 17–40 years in Rotterdam and Schiedam
21 November	Raid on adult men 17–40 years in The Hague, Voorburg, and Rijswijk
21 November	Hunger strike in liberated Eindhoven
25 November	Part of Dutch administration moves from London to liberated territory
28 November	First Allied convoy with relief supplies arrives in Antwerp
31 November	Carel Piek appointed as Secretary General of the Dutch Red Cross, daily board resigns as protest
2 December	The *Wehrmacht* inundates large part of the Betuwe district (Gelderland)
5 December	Constitution of the Central Shipping Company
11 December	Seyss-Inquart approves the constitution of the Interdenominational Bureau for Emergency Nutrition
14 December	First private meeting between Hirschfeld and Seyss-Inquart, during which the latter suggests the possibility of neutralising the western Netherlands; SHAEF transfers relief responsibility for the liberated B2 area (i.e., western Netherlands) to Montgomery's 21st Army group
16 December	Start of the Ardennes Counter-offensive (16 December 1944–25 January 1945)
23 December	Start of period of winter frost (23 December 1944–30 January 1945)

| 24 December | Germans order all Dutchmen aged 16–40 years to register for work in Germany and on fortifying projects in the eastern Netherlands in return for extra rations (*Liese Aktion*) |

1945

2 January	Dutch government forbids people to enlist for the *Liese Aktion* via Radio Orange
14 January	Queen Wilhelmina calls upon President Roosevelt and King George VI to send food relief to the occupied Netherlands
19 January	Agreement reached between the German and Swedish governments on Red Cross relief
23 January	Gerbrandy announces his second cabinet's resignation
25 January	Government announces the continuation of the railway strike
27 January	Liberation of Auschwitz concentration camp
28 January	First Swedish Red Cross food relief ships arrive at Delfzijl
4–11 February	Yalta Conference
23 February	Formation of third cabinet Gerbrandy
26 February	First food distribution of Swedish Red Cross supplies
1 March	Closing of the IJssel bridges for civilian traffic
8 March	Swiss Red Cross ship *Henry Dunant* arrives in Delfzijl
13 March	Queen Wilhelmina sets foot on Dutch soil
3 March	Allied bombing of Bezuidenhout in The Hague
27 March	SHAEF circulates report advising against military operations in the western Netherlands and favouring food relief via air supply
30 March	Start of the liberation of the northeastern Netherlands
1 April	Staff of the Netherlands Military Authority moves from Brussels to Breda
2 April	Hirschfeld meets with Seyss-Inquart to discuss abandoning Hitler's scorched earth order and to neutralise part of western Holland from military activities
12 April	Meeting between Seyss-Inquart, Schwebel, Six, and Van der Vlugt, agreeing that if Allied troops halt before the Grebbe line and commit no further acts of war against the coastal zone, the Germans are

	prepared to forgo further destruction and give full support to relief; President Roosevelt passes away unexpectedly and is succeeded by Truman
16 April	Start of the Battle of Berlin (16 April–2 May 1945)
17 April	Blaskowitz orders the inundation of the Wieringermeer polder (North Holland)
23 April	Combined Chiefs of Staff authorise Eisenhower to negotiate a truce that enables relief without prejudicing the principle of unconditional surrender
26 April	The German authorities agree to the airdrops and accept the invitation to meet with Allied representatives
28 April	Exploratory meeting between German and Allied representatives in Achterveld (Gelderland) to discuss the introduction of food supplies into Western Holland
29 April	The first RAF Lancaster heavy bombers drop food supplies onto the western Netherlands as part of Operation Manna/Chowhound (29 April–8 May 1945); Hitler appoints Grand Admiral Karl Dönitz as his successor
30 April	Second meeting in Achterveld between German, Allied, and Dutch authorities dealing with the provision of food relief; Hitler kills himself in his bunker in Berlin
2 May	The first food transports by truck from liberated Rhenen to occupied Utrecht (Operation Faust)
2 May	Seyss-Inquart meets with Dönitz in Flensburg and is arrested the following day
4 May	Montgomery accepts the unconditional surrender of all German armed forces in northwestern Europe; the first relief ships arrive in Rotterdam
5 May	Foulkes summons Blaskowitz to Wageningen to sign a separate surrender document, which he does the following day; the third cabinet Gerbrandy offers its resignation pending the first post-war elections
10 May	Allied relief supplies begin to reach the population in the western Netherlands
24 May	The third cabinet Gerbrandy officially resigns and is succeeded by the Schermerhorn-Drees cabinet
31 May	The SHAEF Mission Netherlands is formally accredited by Queen Wilhelmina and moves to The Hague

1 July	The Netherlands District hands over responsibility for the civilian supply to the Netherlands Military authorities and Dutch civil authorities
9 July	The Netherlands Military Authority lifts the emergency situation in the western Netherlands
14 July	SHAEF dissolves and the SHAEF Mission to the Netherlands ceases to exist

Bibliography

Archival Sources

STATE ARCHIVES

Bundesarchiv Deutschland, Abteilung Berlin Lichterfelde (BA)
Geschäftsführende Reichsregierung (R62)
Personalarchiv J. von der Wense (R3601)
Polizeistellen in den Niederlanden (R70-NL)
Reichsministerium für Rüstung und Krieg (R3)
Stab Reichsführer SS (NS 19)

National Archives and Records Administration, College Park, Maryland (NARA)
Allied Operational and Occupation Headquarters, World War II (331)

National Archives of the Netherlands, The Hague (NA)
Archief S. L. Louwes (2.21.238)
Centraal Archief van het Ministerie van Economische Zaken 1944–1965 (2.06.087)
Centraal Distributiekantoor (2.06.037)
Nederlandse Volksdienst (2.19.070.01)
Militair Gezag (2.13.25)
Ministerie van Economische Zaken: Directoraat-Generaal voor Prijzen en Voorgangers (2.06.082)
Ministerie van Economische Zaken: Handel en Nijverheid (2.06.001)
Regeringscom. Akkerbouw en Veeteelt (2.11.32)
Rijksbureau Hout (2.06.076.08)
Voedselvoorziening/Massavoeding RBVVO (2.11.30.06)
Voedselvoorziening/Voedingsvraagstukken RBVVO (2.11.30.05)

The National Archives, Kew, London (TNA)
Admiralty (ADM)
Air Ministry (AIR)

Cabinet Office (CAB)
Foreign Office (FO)
Prime Minister Office (PREM)
War Office (WO)

INTERNATIONAL ORGANISATIONS

United Nations Archives and Records Centre, New York City (UN)
United Nations Relief and Rehabilitation Administration (UNRRA) –
Bureau of Areas (AG-018-004)
UNRRA – Bureau of Supply (AG-018-003)
UNRRA – Bureau of Services (AG-018-013)
UNRRA – Office of the Historian (AG-018-040)

SPECIALISED ARCHIVES

NIOD Institute for War, Holocaust and Genocide Studies (NIOD)
Archief H. M. Hirschfeld (212a)
Beauftragte des Reichskommissars (086)
Centraal Distributiekantoor (117)
Centrale Keukens (0145)
Collectie Proces van Neurenberg (458)
Correspondentie (247)
Departement van Justitie (216k)
Departement van Landbouw en Visserij (216h)
Distributie (0198)
Europese Dagboeken en Egodocumenten (244)
Generalkommissariat für Finanz und Wirtschaft (039)
Hongertochten (0331)
Hongerwinter (0332)
Hulporganisatie Amsterdam (1427)
Interkerkelijk Bureau Noodvoedselvoorziening (182f)
Interkerkelijk Overleg (1076)
Kerken (0376)
Kinderuitzendingen (1212)
Regering in Londen (233b)
Reichskommissar für die besetzten niederländische Gebiete (014)
Voedseldroppings (0867)
Voedselvoorziening (0876b)
Vrije Groepen Amsterdam (189)
Wehrmachtsbefehlshaber in den Niederlanden (001: copies of materials held
in the Bundesarchiv Freiburg)
Winterhulp/Nederlandse Volksdienst (179)
Zwarte Handel (932a)

PROVINCIAL AND LOCAL ARCHIVES

Archief Delft (AD)
Interkerkelijk Bureau Noodvoedselvoorziening (217)
Vereniging Armenzorg (8)

Brabants Historisch Informatie Centrum (BHIC)
Militair Gezag in Noord-Brabant (127)
Drents Archief (DA)
Centrale Vereniging Opbouw van Drenthe (0196)
Provinciaal Bureau voor de Nederlandse Volksdienst (0195)

Erfgoed Leiden en Omstreken (ELO)
RBVVO, Onderafdeling Massavoeding (0046)
Verzorgingsraad voor Leiden (0257)

Gemeentearchief Schiedam (GAS)
Collectie Tweede Wereldoorlog (460)
Gemeentebestuur Schiedam (346)
Hulpactie Rode Kruis (108)
Interkerkelijk Bureau Noodvoedselvoorziening (84)
Rode Kruis, Afdeling Schiedam (500)

Gemeentearchief Zaanstad (GAZ)
Vereniging Kindervoeding Zaandam (PA-0033)

Groene Hart Archieven (GHA)
Comité Kinderuitzending en –Voeding Gouda 1944–1953 (0398)

Groninger Archieven (GA)
Gemeentebestuur Groningen 1916–1965 (1841)
Militair Gezag: Provinciale Militaire Commissaris 1945–1947 (63)

Haags Gemeentearchief (HGA)
Centrale Keukens 's-Gravenhage (0655-01)
Crisis- en Distributiedienst (0508-01)
Gemeentebestuur Den Haag 1937–1953 (0610-01)
Huishoudschool Laan van Meerdervoort (0790-01)
Stichting Sociale Wijkcentra (0276-01)

Noord-Hollands Archief (NHA)
Stichting Volksherstel Haarlem (1310)

Regionaal Archief Dordrecht (RAD)

Distributiedienst van de Gemeente Dordrecht, alsmede de Centrale Keuken (260)
Gereformeerde Kerk van Dordrecht (280)
Jaarverslagen Gemeente Dordrecht (576)
Vereniging Kindervoeding en –Kleding (154)

Stadsarchief Amsterdam (SA)

Archief van de Gemeente Amstelveen: Secretarie (30355)
Centraal Secretarie Archief (31010)
Distributiedienst (5257)
Gemeentepolitie (5225)
Gemeentelijk Bureau voor Lijkbezorging (391)
Gemeentelijke Dienst Kinderkleding- en Voeding (5258)

Stadsarchief Rotterdam (SR)

Centraal Evacuatie Bureau te Rotterdam 1940-1949 (336)
Dekenaat Rotterdam (728)
Gemeentesecretarie Rotterdam, Afdeling Algemene Zaken (444-02)
Genootschap Voor Vrouwen Door Vrouwen 1809–1977 (124)
Verzameling Tweede Wereldoorlog (273)

Tresoar Friesland (Tresoar)

Koopmans Meelfabrieken B. V. (101)
Vereniging Friesland 1940–1945 (350)

Utrechts Archief (UA)

Gemeentelijke Voorzieningsdienst (1364)
Militair Gezag Provincie Utrecht (1136)
Nederlands Hervormde Gemeente te Utrecht (816)
Nederlandse Rode Kruis Hulpcorps, Sociale Verbindingsgroep S-1 (831-9)
Stichting Nederlands Volkherstel, Afdeling Utrecht (756)

Waterlands Archief (WA)

Gemeente Purmerend 1930–1974 (0056)

PRIVATE COLLECTIONS

Diepen, Joop van
Lumey, L. H.
Spier, Jan

INTERVIEWS

Jan and Ine Spier, Lopik, The Netherlands, 8 April 2015
Richard C. Hall, Baltimore, USA, 9 November 2016

NEWSPAPERS

Dagblad voor het Noorden
De Courant
De Nieuwe Amsterdammer
De Telegraaf
De Vrije Philips Koerier
De Waarheid
Economist
Het Nationale Dagblad
Het Parool
Lichtflits: Dagelijksch Nieuwsblad
Limburger Koerier
Nieuwe Rotterdamse Courant
Nieuwsblad van het Noorden
Noordhollands Dagblad
Residentiebode
Trouw

WEBSITES

http:/geheugenvannederland.nl
https://nl.wikipedia.org/wiki/Hongerwinter
www.anderetijden.nl/aflevering/95/Hongerkinderen
www.inlichtingendiensten.nl/ambtsberichten/524188.pdf
www.knmi.nl/klimatologie/daggegevens/index.cgim
www.npogeschiedenis.nl/speler.POMS_VPRO_078920.html
www.vpro.nl/speel.POMS_VPRO_079318.html

Published Sources

Bijleveld, H., and L. N. Roodenburg. '*Is het in het Algemeen Wenschelijk aan het Instituut van Schoolvoeding (Schoolkleeding) Uitbreiding te Geven?*', *Prae-Adviezen voor de Algemeene Vergadering van 1, 2, en 3 Juli 1920 te Amsterdam*. Haarlem: H. D. Tjeenk Willink & Zoon, 1920.
Bootsma, George, ed. *Twee Werelden een Hongerwinter: Utrechtse Dagboeken van een Vader en Zoon, 1944–1945*. Hilversum: Verloren, 2010.
Bureau van Statistiek der Gemeente Amsterdam. *Maandbericht van het Bureau van Statistiek der Gemeente Amsterdam, 1939–1946*. Amsterdam: Gemeente Amsterdam, 1939–1946.

Bureau voor de Statistiek en Voorlichting Gemeente's-Gravenhage. *Statistisch Jaarboek 1946*. The Hague: Trio, 1948.

Centraal Bureau Kindervoeding. *Winter 1944–1945: Verslag Centraal Bureau Kindervoeding Haarlem*. Haarlem: Centraal Bureau Kindervoeding, 1946.

Centraal Bureau voor de Statistiek. *De Sterfte in Nederland naar Geslacht, Leeftijd en Doodsoorzaken, 1921–1955*. Zeist: W. de Haan, 1957.

Jaarcijfers voor Nederland 1943–1946. Utrecht: W. de Haan, 1948.

Bevolking der Gemeenten van Nederland op 1 Januari 1944, 1945 en 1946. Utrecht: W. De Haan, 1947.

Economische en Sociale Kroniek der Oorlogsjaren. Utrecht: W. De Haan, 1947.

Geboorte en Sterfte in Eenige Groote Gemeenten in het Westen des Lands: 1e Halfjaar 1945 Vergeleken met 1e Halfjaar 1944. Announcement no. 1006. S.l.: s.n., 1945.

Centraal Comité Hollands-Hælpen. *De Deense Hulp aan Holland*. Copenhagen: Hollands-Hjælpen, 1946.

Charity in War-Time: Final Report of the Local Interclerical Office The Hague and Its Environments. The Hague: Interkerkelijk Bureau, 1946.

Choufour, H. K., and W. G. N. de Keizer. *7 Magere Maanden: Ter Herinnering aan een Moeizame Doorworstelden Oorlogswinter*. Haarlem: Druk Boom-Ruygrok N. V., 1945.

Commissie tot Onderzoek van de Voedings- en Gezondheidstoestand van de Nederlandse Bevolking. *Rapport Betreffende het Onderzoek naar de Voedings- en Gezondheidstoestand van de Nederlandse Bevolking in de Jaren 1941–1945, uitgezonderd de z.g. Hongerwinter (1944–1945)*. Deel 1A Voeding. The Hague: Commissie tot Onderzoek van de Voedings- en Gezondheidstoestand van de Nederlandse Bevolking, 1952–1958.

De Jaarwedden bij't Openbaar Onderwijs in Nederland. Amsterdam: s.n., 1904.

De Nederlandsche Volksdienst: Wat beoogt de N.V.D. en waar ligt het Verschil tussen den N.V.D. en Winterhulp Nederland? S.l: s.n., 194X.

Dongen, W. A. van. *Oorlogswinter 1944–1945: Commissie van de Gereformeerde Kerk van Rotterdam-C, 'Hulp voor ons Allen'*. Rotterdam: Meinema, 1945.

Final Report of the Supply and Economics Branch, G-5/CA of the British and USFET Military Mission to the Netherlands (formerly SHAEF mission to the Netherlands). S.l.: s.n., 1945.

Gemeente Amsterdam. *Dienstverslagen 1944*. Amsterdam: Gemeente Amsterdam, 1945.

Dienstverslagen 1945. Amsterdam: Gemeente Amsterdam, 1946.

Gemeente Hilversum. *Verslag over de Jaren 1939–1949*. Hilversum: Gemeente Hilversum, 1951.

Gemeentelijk Bureau voor de Statistiek Rotterdam. *Jaarcijfers der Gemeente Rotterdam 1942–1947*. Rotterdam: Gemeentelijk Bureau voor de Statistiek, 1949.

Graaff, J. de. *De Eilanden en de Hongersnood: Honger Winter 1944–1945*. Amsterdam: ICLEI Bureau, 1945.

Graaff, J. de, and H. M. Finke. *Herdenkingsalbum: Hongersnood op de Eilanden*. Amsterdam: ICLEI Bureau, 1945.

Groesbeek, J., P. van Roggen, and D. N. de Weerd. *Duizend Wonden Bloeden: Episodes uit het Werk der EHBO-ers Gedurende de Jaren 1940–'45 in Apeldoorn.* Apeldoorn: Nederlandse Vereniging Eerste Hulp bij Ongelukken, 1946.

Hammann, Peter, Eric J. Coolen, Bies van Ede, and Henk Tijbosch. *Lizzy: 126 Dagen Tulpentaart en Appelschilletjesthee.* Weesp: In Blijde Druk, 2015.

Hermans, L. M., and H. van Knol. *Schoolvoeding: Een Aansporing voor onze Wetgevers.* Amsterdam: s.n., 1900.

Het Nederlandsche Roode Kruis in de Tweede Wereldoorlog. Amsterdam: Van Ditmar, 1947.

Hongerend Volk 1945 en Wat Deed het IKB? The Hague: Plaatselijk Interkerkelijk Bureau Den Haag en Omstreken, 1945.

Hoogland, R. *Kindervoeding en – kleding in Nederland: Rapport Samengesteld door het Bureau voor Kinderbescherming (Bond van Nederlandsche Onderwijzers).* Amsterdam: s.n., 1918.

Houben, F. Plaatselijk. *Interkerkelijk Bureau 's-Gravenhage en Omstreken: Verslag Eerste Kwartaal 1945.* The Hague: Interkerkelijk Bureau, 1945.

   Local Interclerical Office: Report First Quarter 1945. The Hague: Interkerkelijk Bureau, 1945.

Jaarverslag van Amsterdam 1944. Amsterdam: Stadsdrukkerij, 1946.

Jaarverslag van Amsterdam 1945. Het Jaar der Bevrijding II. Amsterdam: Stadsdrukkerij, 1946.

Julius, Henri W. *Kinderen in Nood: De Kindervoeding in de Stad Utrecht in de Nood-Winter 1944–1945.* Utrecht: Commissie Kindervoeding voor de Stad Utrecht, 1946.

Kalkman, D. P. *Een Lichtpunt in een Donkeren Tijd: De Geschiedenis van het Noodcomité Moordrecht.* Moordrecht: Noodcomité Moordrecht, 1945.

Köster, Herman J. *Inter Kerkelijk Bureau voor Noodvoedselvoorziening's-Gravenhage en Omstreken: Toelichting der Verstrekkingen op Medische Basis.* The Hague: Interkerkelijk Bureau, 1945.

Kimball, Warren F., ed. *Churchill & Roosevelt: The Complete Correspondence, III Alliance Declining, February 1944–April 1945.* Princeton: Princeton University Press, 1984.

Lagerwey, E. *Utrechts IKO: Een Verhaal van wat de Kerken van Utrecht Deden in den Hongerwinter 1944–1945.* Utrecht: s.n., 1946.

Neve, Ed de (pseud. Willem J. M. Lenglet). *Nederlandsch Roode Kruis Hulpkorps: Zijn Ontstaan en Zijn Arbeid.* The Hague: Van Stockum, 1945.

Nieuwenhuis, G. M. *Vijf Jaren Oorlog over Haarlem: Verslag van de Gemeentelijke Bemoeiingen van 1940-1945.* Haarlem: Gemeente Haarlem, 1947.

Riemsdijk, J. L. van. *Hongerwinter: Dagboek.* S.l.: s.n., s.a.

Seyss-Inquart, Arthur. *Wat Nu? Vragen in Donkere Uren Aan Het Nederlandsche Volk Gesteld,* published radio speech 7 January 1945. S.l.: s.n., 1945.

Staatsbosbeheer, Afdeling Bosstatistiek. 'Verliezen aan onze Houtopstanden, Hoofdzakelijk toegebracht gedurende de Oorlogsjaren'. *Nederlandsch Boschbouw Tijdschrift* 22 (1950): 358–367.

Statistische Mededeelingen der Gemeente Rotterdam 1945-1946. Rotterdam: Gemeentelijk Bureau voor de Statistiek, 1946.

Statistische Berichten der Gemeente Utrecht. Utrecht: Gemeentelijk Bureau voor de Statistiek, 1946.

Vis, J. D. *Rapport over de Nood-Organisatie Koog-Zaandijk: Uitgebracht in de Vergadering van het Bestuur der Nood-Organisatie en het Dames-Comité, gehouden op 15 November 1945.* S.l.: s.n, 1945.

Voeten, Bert H. *Doortocht: Een Oorlogsdagboek 1940–1945.* Amsterdam: Contact, 1946.

Wagenaar, J. H. *Een Jaar Noodcomité.* Amsterdam: Noodcomité Tuindorp Watergraafsmeer, 1946.

Literature

Abbenhuis-Ash, Maartje. *The Art of Staying Neutral: The Netherlands in the First World War, 1914–1918.* Amsterdam: Amsterdam University Press, 2006.

Adamets, Serguei. 'Famine in Nineteenth- and Twentieth-Century Russia: Mortality by Age, Cause, and Gender'. In *Famine Demography: Perspectives from the Past and Present*, edited by Tim Dyson and Cormac Ó Gráda, 158–180. Oxford: Oxford University Press, 2002.

Adams, Alayne. 'Food Insecurity in Mali: Exploring the Role of the Moral Economy'. *IDS Bulletin* 24 (1993): 41–45.

Alfani, Guido, and Cormac Ó Gráda. 'Famines in Europe: An Overview'. In *Famine in European History*, edited by Guido Alfani and Cormac Ó. Gráda, 1–24. Cambridge: Cambridge University Press, 2017.

Amersfoort, Herman, and Piet Kamphuis, eds. *Mei 1940: De Strijd op Nederlands Grondgebied.* 4th ed. Amsterdam: Boom, 2012.

Antonov, A. N. 'Children Born during the Siege of Leningrad in 1942'. *Journal of Pediatrics* 30 (1947): 250–259.

Arnold, David. *Famine: Social Crisis and Historical Change.* Oxford: Blackwell, 1988.

Aykroyd, Wallace R. *The Conquest of Famine.* London: Chatto & Windus, 1974.

Baarle, Willem H. van. *Slag om B2: Een Herinnering in Woord en Beeld aan het Commissariaat Noodvoorziening.* Den Haag: Mouton, 1945.

Bank, Jan, and Maarten van Buuren. *1900: Hoogtij van Burgerlijke Cultuur, Nederlandse Cultuur in Europese Context.* The Hague: Sdu Publishers, 2000.

Banning, Cornelis. 'Voeding en Voedingstoestand'. In *Medische Ervaringen in Nederland tijdens de Bezetting, 1940–1945*, edited by Ite Boerema, 235–267. Groningen: Wolters, 1947.

'Occupied Holland: I Public Health'. *British Medical Journal* 1 (1947): 539–542.

'Food Shortage and Public Health, First Half of 1945'. *Annals of the American Academy for Political and Social Sciences* 245 (1946): 93–110.

'De Gezondheidstoestand in Nederland: De Algemeene Sterfte en Sterfte door Verhongering'. *Nederlandsch Tijdschrift voor Geneeskunde* XXVII (1945): 311–315.

Baranowski, Shelly. *Nazi Empire: German Colonialism and Imperialism from Bismarck to Hitler.* Cambridge: Cambridge University Press, 2011.

Barnouw, David. *De Hongerwinter.* Hilversum: Verloren, 1999.

Barona, Josep L. *The Problem of Nutrition: Experimental Science, Public Health, and Economy in Europe, 1914–1945.* Brussels: P.I.E. Peter Lang, 2010.

Beaumont, Joan. 'Starving for Democracy: Britain's Blockade of and Relief for Occupied Europe, 1939–1945'. *War & Society* 8 (1990): 57–82.

Bedell Smith, Walter. *Eisenhower's Six Great Decisions.* New York: Longmans, Green and Co., 1956.

Beevor, Antony. *Arnhem: The Battle for the Bridges, 1944.* London: Viking, 2018.

Belinfante, August D. *In Plaats van Bijltjesdag: De Geschiedenis van de Bijzondere Rechtspleging na de Tweede Wereldoorlog.* Assen: Van Gorcum, 1978.

Berg, C. van den. 'Over het Ontstaan van de Voedingsorganisatie T.N.O. en van de Voedingsraad en over het Werk van deze Laatste Gedurende de Bezetting'. *Voeding* 26 (1965): 299–308.

Berkhoff, Karel C. *Harvest of Despair: Life and Death in Ukraine under Nazi Rule.* Cambridge, MA: Belknap Press of Harvard University Press, 2004.

Bieleman, Jan. *Boeren in Nederland: Geschiedenis van de Landbouw 1500–2000.* Amsterdam: Boom, 2008.

Blom, J. C. H. 'Vernietigende Kracht en Nieuwe Vergezichten: Het Onderzoeksproject Verzuiling op Lokaal Niveau Geëvalueerd'. In *De Verzuiling Voorbij: Godsdienst, Stand en Natie in de Lange Negentiende Eeuw*, edited by Johan C. H. Blom and Jaap Talsma, 203–236. Amsterdam: Het Spinhuis, 2000.

'Nazificatie en Exploitatie'. In *De Organisatie van de Bezetting*, edited by Henk Flap and Wil Arts, 17–30. Amsterdam, Amsterdam University Press, 1997.

Crisis, Bezetting en Herstel: Tien Studies over Nederland, 1940–1950. The Hague: Nijgh & Van Ditmar, 1989.

Boerema, Ite. 'Inleiding'. In *Medische Ervaringen in Nederland tijdens de Bezetting, 1940–1945*, edited by Ite Boerema, 7–16. Groningen: Wolters, 1947.

Bok, Johannes. *De Kliniek der Hongerziekte: Een Klinische Studie tijdens de Hongerwinter 1944–1945 te Rotterdam.* Leiden: H. E. Stenfert Kroese, 1949.

Bonzon, Thierry, and Belinda Davies. 'Feeding the Cities'. In *Capital Cities at War: London Paris, Berlin 1914–1919*, edited by Jay Winter and Jean-Louis Robert, 305–341. Cambridge: Cambridge University Press, 1997.

Boom, Bart van der. *Den Haag in de Tweede Wereldoorlog.* Den Haag: Seapress, 1995.

Bosma, Elle, Ids Groenewoud, and Sjoerd Veerman. *Eastermar: De Oorlogsevacues en de Hongerkinderen in 1945.* Burgum: Streekmuseum Volkssterrenwacht Burgum, 2010.

Bosman-Jelgersma, Henriette A. 'De Nederlandse Farmacie tijdens de Tweede Wereldoorlog'. In *Geneeskunde en Gezondheidszorg in Nederland 1940–1945*, edited by Marius J. van Lieburg and Wijnandus W. Mijnhardt, 210–221. Amsterdam: Rodopi, 1992.

Bossenbroek, Martin P. *De Meelstreep.* Amsterdam: Bakker, 2001.

Bout, Dirk C. A., and Hendrik Kraemer. *In den Strijd om ons Volksbestaan.* The Hague: Stok, 1947.

Brassley, Paul. 'Food Production and Food Processing in Western Europe, 1850–1990'. In *Exploring the Food Chain: Food Production and Food Processing in Western Europe, 1850–1990*, edited by Yves Segers, Jan Bieleman, and Erik Buyst, 281–289. Turnhout: Brepols Publishers, 2009.

Brink, Thomas van den. 'Birth Rate Trends and Changes in Marital Fertility in the Netherlands after 1937'. *Population Studies* 4 (1950): 314–332.

Broek, Thijs van der, and Maria Fleischmann. 'Prenatal Famine Exposure and Mental Health in Later Midlife'. *Aging and Mental Health* 21 (2017): 166–170.

Brooke Thomas, R., Sabrina H. B. H. Paine, and Barrett P. Brento. 'Perspectives on Socio-Economic Causes of and Responses to Food Deprivation'. *Food & Nutrition Bulletin* 11 (1989): 41–54.

Brown, Alan S., J. van Os, C. Driessens, Hans W. Hoek, and Ezra S. Susser. 'Further Evidence of Relation between Prenatal Famine and Major Affective Disorder'. *American Journal of Psychiatry* 157 (2000): 190–195.

Burger, George C. E., Jack C. Drummond, and H. R. Sandstead, eds. *Malnutrition and Starvation in Western Netherlands: September 1944–July 1945*. 2 vols. The Hague: General State Printing Office, 1948.

Buruma, Ian. *Year Zero: A History of 1945*. New York: The Penguin Press, 2013.

Carmichael, Ann G. 'Infection, Hidden Hunger and History'. In *Hunger in History: The Impact of Changing Food Production and Consumption Patterns on Society*, edited by Robert I. Rotberg and Theodore K. Rabb, 51–68. Cambridge: Cambridge University Press, 1983.

Cary, Richard L. 'Child-Feeding Work in Germany'. *Annals of the American Academy of Political and Social Science* 92 (1920): 157–162.

Cherepenina, Nadezhda. 'Assessing the Scale of Famine and Death in Besieged Leningrad'. In *Life and Death in Besieged Leningrad, 1941–1944*, edited by John Barber and Andrei Dzeniskevich, 28–70. Basingstoke: Palgrave Macmillan, 2005.

Churchill, Winston S. *The Second World War: VI Triumph and Tragedy*. London: Cassell & Col. Ltd., 1954.

Clavin, Patricia. *Securing the World Economy: The Reinvention of the League of Nations, 1920–1946*. Oxford: Oxford University Press, 2013.

Collingham, Lizzie. *The Taste of War: World War Two and the Battle for Food*. London: Allen Lane, 2011.

Conway, Martin. *The Sorrows of Belgium: Liberation and Political Reconstruction, 1944–1947*. Oxford: Oxford University Press, 2012.

Conway, Martin, and Peter Romijn. 'Political Legitimacy in Mid-Twentieh-Century Europe: An Introduction'. In *The War for Legitimacy in Politics and Culture, 1936–1946*, edited by Martin Conway and Peter Romijn, 1–27. Oxford and New York: Berg, 2008.

Christensen, Claus B., and Ralf D. Futselaar. 'Zwarte Markten in de Tweede Wereldoorlog: Een Vergelijking Tussen Nederland en Denemarken'. In *Thuisfront: Oorlog en Economie in de Twintigste Eeuw*. Jaarboek van het Nederlands Instituut voor Oorlogsdocumentatie, edited by Hein Klemann and Dirk Luyten, 89–110. Zutphen: Walburg Press, 2003.

Cox, Mary E. 'Hunger Games: Or How the Allied Blockade in the First World War Deprived German Children of Nutrition, and Allied Food Aid Subsequently Saved Them'. *The Economic History Review* 68 (2014): 600–631.

Croes, Marnix, and Peter Tammes. *'Gif Laten wij niet Voortbestaan'*. In *Een Onderzoek naar de Overlevingskansen van Joden in de Nederlandse Gemeenten, 1940–1945*. Amsterdam: Aksant, 2004.

Cruickshank, Charles. *The German Occupation of the Channel Islands*. London: Oxford University Press, 1975.

Curtis, Daniel, Jessica Dijkman, Thijs Lambrecht, and Eric Vanhaute. 'Low Countries'. In *Famine in European History*, edited by Guido Alfani and Cormac Ó Gráda, 119–140. Cambridge: Cambridge University Press, 2017.

Dabel, Gerhard. *KLV: Die erweiterte Kinder-Land-Verschickung: KLV-Lager 1940–1945*. Freiburg: Schillinger, 1981.

Dam, Peter van. *Staat van Verzuiling: Over een Nederlandse Mythe*. Amsterdam: Wereldbibliotheek, 2011.

Damsma, Josje, and Erik Schumacher. *Hier Woont een NSB'er: Nationaalsocialisten in Bezet Amsterdam*. Amsterdam: Boom, 2010.

Dando-Collins, Stephen. *Operation Chowhound: The Most Risky, Most Glorious US Bomber Mission of WWII*. New York: Palgrave Macmillan, 2015.

Das Gupta, Albert K. *Planning and Economic Growth*. London: Allen & Unwin, 1965.

Davies, Robert W., and Stephen G. Wheatcroft. *The Years of Hunger: Soviet Agriculture, 1931–1933*. Basingstoke: Palgrave Macmillan 2004.

Delft, Antonius J. A. C. van. *Zwarte Handel: Uit de Bezettingstijd 1940–1945*. Amsterdam: Uitgevers-Maatschappij Holland, 1946.

Desai, Meghnad. 'The Economics of Famine'. In *Famine*, edited by Geoffrey A. Harrison, 107–138. Oxford: Oxford University Press, 1988.

Devereux, Stephen. 'Sen's Entitlement Approach: Critiques and Counter-Critiques'. *Oxford Development Studies* 29 (2001): 245–263.

'Famine in the Twentieth Century'. IDS Working Paper 105. Brighton: IDS, 2000.

Theories of Famine. New York: Harvester Wheatsheaf, 1993.

Dirks, Robert. 'Social Responses during Severe Food Shortages and Famines'. *Current Anthropology* 21 (1980): 21–43.

Dols, M. J. L. 'Enkele Persoonlijke Herinneringen aan het Einde van de Hongerwinter, 1945'. *Voeding* 16 (1955): 406–410.

Dols, M. J. L., and D. J. A. M. van Arcken. 'Food Supply and Nutrition in the Netherlands during and immediately after World War II'. *The Milbank Memorial Fund Quarterly* 24 (1946): 319–358.

'De Voedselvoorziening in Nederland Tijdens en Onmiddelijk na den Tweede Wereldoorlog 1940–1945'. *Voeding* 6 (1946): 193–207.

Dols, M. J. L., J. P. van Loon, and H. Zoethout. 'De Centrale Keukens in de Jaren 1940–1945'. *Voeding* 7 (1946): 67–75.

Donnison, Frank S. V. *Civil Affairs and Military Government North-West Europe 1944–1946*. London: Her Majesty's Stationery Office, 1961.

Dyson, Tim, and Cormac Ó Gráda. 'Introduction'. In *Famine Demography: Perspectives from the Past and Present*, edited by Tim Dyson and Cormac Ó Gráda, 1–18. Oxford: Oxford University Press, 2002.

Eisenhower, Dwight D. *Crusade in Europe*. London: William Heinemann Limited, 1948.

Eisenhower's Own Story of the War: The Complete Report by the Supreme Commander General Dwight D. Eisenhower on the War in Europe from the Day of Invasion to the Day of Victory. New York: Arco Publishing Company, 1946.

Ekamper, Peter, Govert Bijwaard, Frans van Poppel, and L. H. Lumey. 'War-Related Excess Mortality in The Netherlands, 1944–45: New Estimates of Famine- and Non-Famine-Related Deaths from National Death Records'. *Historical Methods: A Journal of Quantitative and Interdisciplinary History* 50 (2017): 113–128.

Ekamper, Peter, Frans van Poppel, Aryeh D. Stein, and L. H. Lumey. 'Independent and Additive Association of Prenatal Famine Exposure and Intermediary Life Conditions with Adult Mortality between Age 18–63 Years'. *Social Science & Medicine* 119 (2014): 232–239.

Fasseur, Cees. *Eigen Meester, Niemands Knecht: Het Leven van Pieter Sjoerds Gerbrandy, Minister-President van Nederland in de Tweede Wereldoorlog.* Amsterdam: Balans, 2014.

Feltkamp, C. *De Begrafenismoeilijkheden in 1945 te Amsterdam: Het Opheffen van den Achterstand in het Begraven door het Gemeentelijke Bureau voor Lijkbezorging.* Amsterdam: Stadsdrukkerij Amsterdam, 1945.

Fennema, Meindert, and John Rhijnsburger. *Dr. Hans Max Hirschfeld: Man van het Grote Geld.* Amsterdam: Bakker, 2007.

Fest, Joachim. *Speer: Eine Biographie.* Berlin: Alexander Fest, 1999.

Fock, Cees L. W. 'De Nederlandse Regering in Londen en de Spoorwegstaking'. *De Gids* 188 (1955): 348–356.

Fogg, Shannon L. *The Politics of Everyday Life in Vichy France: Foreigners, Undesirables, and Strangers.* Cambridge: Cambridge University Press, 2009.

Foray, Jennifer L. 'The "Clean *Wehrmacht*" in the German-Occupied Netherlands, 1940–5'. *Journal of Contemporary History* 45 (2010): 768–787.

Frijtag Drabbe Künzel, Geraldien von. *Het Recht van de Sterkste: Duitse Strafrechtspleging in Bezet Nederland.* Amsterdam: Bert Bakker, 1999.

Futselaar, Ralf D. *Gevangenissen in Oorlogstijd 1940–1945.* Amsterdam: Boom, 2015.

'Incomes, Class, and Coupons: Black Markets for Food in the Netherlands during the Second World War'. *Food & History* 8 (2010): 171–198.

Lard, Lice and Longevity: A Comparative Study on the Standard of Living in Occupied Denmark and the Netherlands, 1940–1945. Amsterdam: Aksant, 2008.

'The Mystery of the Dying Dutch: Can Micronutrient Deficiencies Explain the Difference between Danish and Dutch Wartime Mortality?' In *Food and Conflict in Europe in the Age of the Two World Wars,* edited by Frank Trentmann and Flemming Just, 193–222. Basingstoke: Palgrave Macmillan, 2006.

Galesloot, Hansje, and Susan Legêne. *Partij in het Verzet: De CPN in de Tweede Wereldoorlog.* Amsterdam: Pegasus, 1986.

Gentile, Felix M. 'U.N.R.R.A. Child-Feeding in Italy'. *Social Service Review* 20 (1946): 502–522.

Gerbrandy, Pieter S. 'Nogmaals: De Nederlandse Regering en de Spoorwegstaking'. *De Gids* 119 (1956): 39–41.

Eenige Hoofdpunten van het Regeeringsbeleid in Londen Gedurende de Oorlogsjaren 1940–1945. The Hague: Rijksuitgeverij, 1946.

Gerhard, Gesine. *Nazi Hunger Politics: A History of Food in the Third Reich.* Lanham: Rowman & Littlefield, 2015.

286   Bibliography

Gieling, Wilco. *Seyss-Inquart*. Soesterberg: Aspekt, 2009.
Gietema, Marco, and Cecile aan de Stegge. *Vergeten Slachtoffers: Psychiatrische Inrichting de Willem Arntsz Hoeve in de Tweede Wereldoorlog*. Amsterdam: Boom, 2016.
Goudriaan, Buck. *Leiden in de Tweede Wereldoorlog Van Dag tot Dag: Een Kroniek van 10 Mei 1940 tot 15 Augustus 1945*. Leiden: F. G. W. Goudriaan, 1995.
Grazia, Victoria de. *How Fascism Ruled Women: Italy, 1922–1945*. Berkeley: University of California Press, 1992.
Graziosi, Andrea. 'The Soviet 1931–1933 Famines and the Ukrainian Holodomor: Is a New Interpretation Possible, and What Would Its Consequences Be?' In *Hunger by Design: The Great Ukrainian Famine in Its Soviet Context*, edited by Halyna Hryn, 1–20. Cambridge, MA: Harvard University Press, 2008.
Griffioen, Pim, and Ronald Zeller. *Jodenvervolging in Nederland, Frankrijk en België. Overeenkomsten, Verschillen en Oorzaken*. Amsterdam: Boom, 2011.
Groot, Renate H. M., Aryeh D. Stein, Jelle Jolles, Martin P. J. van Boxtel, Gerard-Jan Blauw, Margot van de Bor, and L. H. Lumey. 'Prenatal Famine Exposure and Cognition at Age 59 Years'. *International Journal of Epidemiology* 40 (2011): 327–337.
Guingand, Francis de. *Operation Victory*. London: Hodder and Stoughton, 1947.
Gulmans J. J. 'Operatie Market Garden'. In *De Bevrijding van Nederland, 1944–1945: Oorlog op de Flank*, edited by Christ Klep and Ben Schoenmaker, 118–124. The Hague: Sdu Koninginnegracht Publishers, 1995.
Haas, J. H. de. *Kindersterfte in Nederland/Child Mortality in the Netherlands*. Assen: Van Gorcum, 1956.
Happe, Katja. *Veel Valse Hoop. De Jodenvervolging in Nederland in 1940–1945*. Amsterdam: Atlas Contact, 2018.
Hart, Nicky. 'Famine, Maternal Nutrition and Infant Mortality: A Re-Examination of the Dutch Hunger Winter'. *Population Studies* 47 (1993): 27–46.
Hartog, A. P. den. 'Nutrition Education in Times of Food Shortages and Hunger: War and Occupation in the Netherlands, 1939–1945'. In *Food and War in Twentieth Century Europe*, edited by Ina Zweiniger-Bargielowska, Rachel Duffett, and Alain Drouard, 183–200. Farnham: Ashgate, 2011.
Have, Wichert ten. *De Nederlandse Unie: Aanpassing, Vernieuwing en Confrontatie in Bezettingstijd, 1940–1941*. Amsterdam: Prometheus, 1999.
Healy, Mareen. *Vienna and the Fall of the Habsburg Empire: Total War and Everyday Life in World War I*. Cambridge: Cambridge University Press, 2004.
Heijden, Chris van der. *Grijs Verleden: Nederland en de Tweede Wereldoorlog*. 10th ed. Amsterdam: Olympus, 2009.
Heijmans, Bastiaan T., Elmar W. Tobi, Aryeh D. Stein, Hein Putter, Gerard J. Blauw, Ezra S. Susser, P. Eline Slagboom, and L. H. Lumey. 'Persistent Epigenetic Differences Associated with Prenatal Exposure to Famine in Humans'. *Proceedings of the National Academy of Sciences of the United States of America* 105 (2008): 17046–17049.
Heijmans, Bastiaan T., Elmar W. Tobi, L. H. Lumey, and P. Eline Slagboom. 'The Epigenome. Archive of the Prenatal Environment'. *Epigenetics* 4 (2009): 526–531.

Hemmes, G. D. 'Besmettelijke Ziekten: Epidemiologie en Praeventieve Maatregelen'. In *Medische Ervaringen in Nederland tijdens de Bezetting, 1940–1945*, edited by Ite Boerema, 105–130. Groningen: Wolters, 1947.

Herbert, Ulrich. *Best: Biographische Studien über Radikalismus, Weltanschauung und Vernunft 1903–1989*. 5th ed. Bonn: Dietz, 2011.

Hionidou, Violetta. '"Choosing" between Children and the Elderly in the Greek Famine (1941–1944)'. In *Coping with Hunger and Shortage under German Occupation in World War II*, edited by Tatjana Tönsmeyer, Peter Haslinger, and Agnes Laba, 203–222. London: Palgrave Macmillan, 2018.

Famine and Death in Occupied Greece, 1941–1944. Cambridge: Cambridge University Press, 2006.

'Why Do People Die in Famines? Evidence from Three Island Populations'. *Population Studies* 56 (2002): 65–80.

Hirschfeld, Hans M. *Herinneringen uit de Bezettingstijd*. Amsterdam: Elsevier, 1960.

'De Centrale Reederij voor de Voedselvoorziening'. *Economie* 10 (1946): 1–16.

Hirschfeld, Gerhard. *Bezetting en Collaboratie: Nederland tijdens de Oorlogsjaren 1940–1945 in Historisch Perspectief*. Haarlem: H. J. W. Brecht, 1991.

'Chronology of Destruction'. In *Policies of Genocide: Jews and Soviet Prisoners of War in Nazi Germany*, edited by Gerhard Hirschfeld, 145–156. Boston: Allan & Unwin, 1986.

Hoek, Hans W., Ezra S. Susser, K. A. Buck, and L. H. Lumey. 'Schizoid Personality Disorder after Prenatal Exposure to Famine'. *American Journal of Psychiatry* 153 (1996): 1637–1639.

Hogervorst, Susan, and Patricia van Ulzen. *Rotterdam en het Bombardement: 75 Jaar Herinneren en Vergeten*. Amsterdam: Boom, 2015.

Holmer, A. J. M. 'Verloskunde en Vrouwenziekten'. In *Medische Ervaringen in Nederland tijdens de Bezetting, 1940–1945*, edited by Ite Boerema, 131–158. Groningen: Wolters, 1947.

Hoving, Peter. 'Oorlog en Kriminaliteit'. MA thesis, Vrije Universiteit Amsterdam. Amsterdam: Vrije Universiteit, 1985.

Howe, Paul, and Stephen Devereux. 'Famine Intensity and Magnitude Scales: A Proposal for an Instrumental Definition of Famine'. *Disasters* 28 (2004): 353–372.

Hudig, J. C. 'De Criminaliteit in Rotterdam tijdens den Oorlog'. *Mensch en Maatschappij* 21 (1946): 341–356.

Huizinga T. 'Geneesmiddelenverzorging'. In *Medische Ervaringen in Nederland tijdens de Bezetting, 1940–1945*, edited by Ite Boerema, 187–226. Groningen: Wolters, 1947.

Inglis, Ruth. *The Children's War: Evacuation 1939–1945*. London: Collins, 1989.

Jelliffe, Derrick B., and Eleanor F. Patrice Jelliffe. 'The Effects of Starvation on the Function of the Family and of Society'. In *Famine: A Symposium Dealing with Nutrition and Relief Operations in Times of Disaster*, edited by Gunnar Blix, Yngve Hofvander, and Bo Vahlquist, 54–63. Upsala: The Swedish Nutrition Foundation, 1971.

Jong, Loe de. *Het Koninkrijk der Nederlanden in de Tweede Wereldoorlog* 12. 2 vols. The Hague: Martinus Nijhoff, 1988.

Het Koninkrijk der Nederlanden in de Tweede Wereldoorlog 10a-b. 4 vols. The Hague: Martinus Nijhoff, 1981.

Het Koninkrijk der Nederlanden in de Tweede Wereldoorlog 8. 2 vols. The Hague: Martinus Nijhoff, 1978.

Het Koninkrijk der Nederlanden in de Tweede Wereldoorlog 7. 2 vols. The Hague: Martinus Nijhoff, 1976.

Het Koninkrijk der Nederlanden in de Tweede Wereldoorlog 6. 2 vols. The Hague: Martinus Nijhoff, 1975.

Het Koninkrijk der Nederlanden in de Tweede Wereldoorlog 4. 2 vols. The Hague: Martinus Nijhoff, 1972.

Jongh, C. L. de. 'Ziekteverschijnselen door den Hongersnood Veroorzaakt'. In *Medische Ervaringen in Nederland tijdens de Bezetting, 1940–1945*, edited by Ite Boerema, 233–244. Groningen: Wolters, 1947.

Keizer, Madelon de. 'Hans Max Hirschfeld: De Juiste Man op de Juiste Plaats ...?' *BMGN-Low Countries Historical Review* 123 (2008): 423–432.

Putten. De Razzia en de Herinnering. Amsterdam: Bakker, 1998.

Kemperman, Jeroen. *Oorlog in de Collegebanken. Studenten in het Verzet 1940–1945.* Amsterdam: Boom, 2018.

Kent, George. *The Politics of Children's Survival.* New York: Praeger, 1991.

Kershaw, Ian. *Hitler: Vergelding 1936–1945.* Utrecht: Het Spektrum, 2000.

Key, Ellen. *The Century of the Child.* New York: G. P. Putnam's Sons, 1909.

Keys, Ancel, Josef Brozek, and Austin Henschel. *The Biology of Human Starvation.* 2 vols. Minneapolis: s.n., 1950.

Klemann, Hein A. M. 'De Hongerwinter'. In *Een Open Zenuw: Hoe Wij Ons de Tweede Wereldoorlog Herinneren*, edited by Madelon de Keizer and Marije Plomp, 256–264. Amsterdam: Bert Bakker, 2010.

'Did the German Occupation (1940–1945) Ruin Dutch Industry?' *Contemporary European History* 17 (2008): 457–481.

Nederland 1938–1948: Economie en Samenleving in Jaren van Oorlog en Bezetting. Amsterdam: Boom, 2002.

'Die niederländische Wirtschaft von 1938 bin 1948 im Griff von Krieg und Besatzung'. *Jahrbuch für Wirtschaftgeschichte* 1 (2001): 53–76.

'"Die Koren Onthoudt, wordt Gevloekt onder het Volk ..." De Zwarte Markt in Voedingswaren 1940–1948'. *BMGN-Low Countries Historical Review* 115 (2000): 532–560.

'Mooie Jaarcijfers: Enige Onderzoeksresultaten betreffende de Nederlandse Economische Ontwikkeling tijdens de Tweede Wereldoorlog'. *Utrechtse Historische Cahiers* 18 (1997): 9–25

'De Legale en Illegale Productie in de Landbouw, 1938–1948'. *Neha Jaarboek* 60 (1997): 307–338.

Klemann, Hein A. M., and Sergei Kudryashov, *Occupied Economies: An Economic History of Nazi-Occupied Europe, 1939–1945.* London: Berg, 2012.

Knol, Liefke. *Het Babyhuis: Kinderen en Ouders door Oorlog en Honger Gescheiden.* Amsterdam: Artemis, 2010.

Koll, Johannes. *Arthur Seyss-Inquart und die deutsche Besatzungspolitik in den Niederlanden 1940–1945.* Vienna: Böhlau Verlag, 2015.

Kooij, Pim. 'Geregelde Schaarste: Economische Aspecten van Groningen in Oorlogstijd'. In *Groningen in Oorlogstijd: Aspecten van de Bezettingsjaren*

1940–1945, edited by Elisabeth A. J. Boiten, 153–185. Haren: Knoop & Niemeijer, 1980.

Korppi-Tommola, Aura. 'War and Children in Finland during the Second World War'. *Paedagogica Historica: International Journal of the History of Education* 44 (2008): 445–455.

Kortenhorst, L. G. 'Het Economische Leven'. In *Onderdrukking en Verzet: Nederland in Oorlogstijd II*, edited by Johannes J. van Bolhuis, 201–289. Arnhem: Van Loghum Slaterus, 1950.

Kossmann, Ernst H. *De Lage Landen 1780–1980: Twee Eeuwen Nederland en België II*. Amsterdam: Elsevier, 1986.

Kramer, Nicole. '*Volksgenossinnen* on the German Home Front: An Insight into Nazi Wartime Society'. In *Visions of Community in Nazi Germany: Social Engineering and Private Lives*, edited by Martina Steber and Bernhard Gotto, 171–186. Oxford: Oxford University Press, 2014.

Krips-van der Laan, Hilde. 'Honderd Jaar Landbouwgeschiedenis 1880–1980'. *Kleio-Didactica* 29 (1994): 1-39.

Praktijk als Antwoord: S. L. Louwes en het Landbouwcrisisbeleid. Historia Agriculturae XVI. Groningen: Nederlands Agronomisch-Historisch Instituut, 1985.

Kruijer, Gerardus J. *Hongertochten. Amsterdam tijdens de Hongerwinter*. Meppel: J. A. Boom & Zoon Publishers, 1951.

Sociale Desorganisatie. Amsterdam tijdens de Hongerwinter. Meppel: J. A. Boom & Zoon Publishers, 1951.

Kruizinga, Samuël F. '"Heere God! Straf Posthema!" F. E. Posthuma (1874–1943)'. In *Nederland Neutraal: De Eerste Wereldoorlog 1914–1918*, edited by Wim Klinkert, Samuël F. Kruizinga, and Paul Moeyes, 242–279. Amsterdam: Boom, 2014.

Overlegeconomie in Oorlogstijd: De Nederlandse Overzee Trustmaatschappij en de Eerste Wereldoorlog. Zuthpen: Walburg Press, 2012.

Laurent, Helene. 'War and the Emerging Social State: Social Policy, Public Health and Citizenship in Wartime Finland'. In *Finland in World War II: History, Memory, Interpretations*, edited by Tiine Kinnunen and Villa Kivimäki, 315–354. Leiden: Brill, 2012.

Leeninga, J. J., and E. J. Westra. *En tóch Staat de Martini: Groningen onder Duitsch Schrikbewind*. Groningen: Niemeyer, 1945.

Leersum, E. C. van. *Schoolvoeding*. The Hague: Leopold, 1925.

Lindberg, John. *Food, Famine and Relief 1940–1946*. Genève: United Nations, 1946.

Lingen, Joost van, and Nick Slooff. *Van Verzetsstrijder tot Staatsgevaarlijk Burger: Hoe Progressieve Illegale Werkers na de Oorlog de Voet is Dwarsgezet*. Baarn: Anthos, 1987.

Lise, Jeremy, and Shannon Seitz. 'Consumption Inequality and Intra-Household Allocations'. *Review of Economic Studies* 78 (2011): 328–355.

Lookeren Campagne, J. van, and H. F. Wiers. 'Kinderziekten in Bezettingstijd'. In *Medische Ervaringen in Nederland tijdens de Bezetting, 1940–1945*, edited by Ite Boerema, 277–296. Groningen: Wolters, 1947.

'De Voedselrantsoenen voor Kinderen in den Bezettingstijd'. In *Medische Ervaringen in Nederland tijdens de Bezetting, 1940–1945*, edited by Ite Boerema, 297–306. Groningen: Wolters, 1947.

Louwes, Stephanus L. 'De Voedselvoorziening'. In *Onderdrukking en Verzet: Nederland in Oorlogstijd II*, edited by Johannes J. van Bolhuis, 607–646. Arnhem: Van Loghum Slaterus, 1950.

Loveday, Alexander. *Wartime Rationing and Consumption*. Economic Intelligence Service of the League of Nations. Geneva: League of Nations, 1942.

Lowe, Kevin. *Savage Continent: Europe in the Aftermath of World War II*. London: Viking, 2012.

Lumey, L. H. 'Reproductive Outcomes in Women Prenatally Exposed to Undernutrition. A Review of Findings from the Dutch Famine Birth Cohort'. *Proceedings of the Nutrition Society* 57 (1998): 129–135.

Lumey, L. H., Anita C. Ravelli, L. G. Wiessing, J. G. Koppe, P. E. Treffers, and Zena A. Stein. 'The Dutch Famine Cohort Study. Design, Validation of Exposure, and Selected Characteristics of Subjects after 43 Years Follow-up'. *Paediatric and Perinatal Epidemiology* 7 (1993): 54–67.

Lumey, L. H., and Aryeh D. Stein. 'Offspring Birth Weights after Maternal Intrauterine Undernutrition. A Comparison within Siblings'. *American Journal of Epidemiology* 146 (1997): 810–819.

'Increased Reproductive Success of Women after Prenatal Undernutrition'. *Human Reproduction* 24 (2009): 491.

'In Utero Exposure to Famine and Subsequent Fertility. The Dutch Famine Birth Cohort Study'. *American Journal of Public Health* 87 (1997): 1962–1966.

Lumey, L. H., Aryeh D. Stein, and Henry S. Kahn. 'Food Restriction during Gestation and Impaired Fasting Glucose or Glucose Tolerance and Type 2 Diabetes Mellitus in Adulthood: Evidence from the Dutch Hunger Winter Families Study'. *Journal of Developmental Origins of Health and Disease* 1 (2009): S164.

Lumey, L. H., Aryeh D. Stein, Henry S. Kahn, Karin M. van der Pal-de Bruin, G. J. Blauw, Patricia A. Zybert, and Ezra S. Susser. 'Cohort Profile. The Dutch Hunger Winter Family Studies'. *International Journal of Epidemiology* 36 (2007): 1196–1204.

Lumey, L. H., Aryeh D. Stein, and Ezra Susser. 'Prenatal Famine and Adult Health'. *Annual Review of Public Health* 32 (2011): 237–262.

Lumey, L. H., and Frans van Poppel. 'The Dutch Famine of 1944–45 As a Human Laboratory: Changes in the Early Life Environment and Adult Health'. In *Early Life Nutrition and Adult Health and Development: Lessons from Changing Dietary Patterns, Famines, and Experimental Studies*, edited by L. H. Lumey and Alexander M. Vaiserman, 59–76. New York: Nova Science Publishers, 2013.

Lumey, L. H., Lauren H. Martini, Merle Myerson, Aryeh D. Stein, and Ronald J. Prineas. 'No Relation between Coronary Artery Disease or Electrocardiographic Markers of Disease in Middle Age and Prenatal Exposure to the Dutch Famine of 1944–5'. *Heart* 98 (2012): 1653–1659.

Lumey, L. H., Mykola D. Khalangot, and Alexander M. Vaiserman. 'Association between Type 2 Diabetes and Prenatal Exposure to the Ukraine Famine of 1932–33: A Retrospective Cohort Study'. *The Lancet Diabetes & Endocrinology* 3 (2015): 787–794.

Maas, Walter B. *The Netherlands at War: 1940–1945*. London: Abelard-Schuman, 1970.

Malthus, Thomas. *An Essay on the Principle of Population, As It Affects the Future Improvement of Society*. London: J. Johnson, 1798.

Marshall, Dominique. 'Humanitarian Sympathy for Children in Times of War and the History of Children's Rights, 1919–1959'. In *Children and War: An Historical Anthology*, edited by James Marten, 184–199. New York: New York University Press, 2002.

Mazower, Mark. *Hitler's Empire: How the Nazis Ruled Europe*. New York: Allen Lane, 2008.

Inside Hitler's Greece: The Experience of Occupation 1941–1944. New Haven: Yale University Press, 1993.

Meershoek, Guus J. J. *Dienaren van het Gezag: De Amsterdamse Politie tijdens de Bezetting*. Amsterdam: Van Gennep, 1999.

Meihuizen, Joggli. *Noodzakelijk Kwaad: De Bestraffing van Economische Collaboratie in Nederland Na de Tweede Wereldoorlog*. Amsterdam: Boom, 2003.

Mendlesohn, Farah J. 'The Ethics of Friends' Relief Work in Republican Spain'. *Quaker History* 88 (1999): 1–23.

Mensch, Ed van, ed. *Hilversum in de Tweede Wereldoorlog*. Hilversum: Albertus Perk, 2010.

Mettrop, Georges G. J. *De Kinderuitzending in Nederland: Een Critische Studie*. Nijkerk: Callenbach, 1945.

Miert, Johannes van. '"En Toen kwam het er Eigenlijk op aan": September 1944– September 1945'. In *Een Gewone Stad in een Bijzondere Tijd: Utrecht 1940–1945*, edited by Johannes van Miert, 264–279. Utrecht: Het Spectrum BV, 1995.

Millman, Sara, and Robert W. Kates. 'Towards Understanding Hunger'. In *Hunger in History: Food Shortage, Poverty and Deprivation*, edited by Lucile F. Newman, 3–24. Cambridge: Cambridge University Press, 1990.

Mitchell, Allan. *Nazi Paris: The History of an Occupation, 1940–1944*. New York: Berghahn Books, 2008.

Moore, Bob. 'The Netherlands, 1940–45'. In *The Civilian in War. Occupation and the Home Front in World War II*, edited by Jeremy Noakes, 126–149. Exeter: Exeter University Press, 1992.

'The Western Allies and Food Relief to the Occupied Netherlands, 1944–1945'. *War & Society* 10 (1992): 91–118.

Mouré, Kenneth. 'Réalités Cruelles: State Controls and the Black Market for Food in Occupied France'. In *Food and War in Twentieth Century Europe*, edited by Ina Zweiniger-Bargielowska, Rachel Duffett, and Alain Drouard, 169–182. Farnham: Ashgate, 2011.

Murton, Brian. 'Famine'. In *The Cambridge World History of Food*, edited by Kenneth F. Kiple and Kriemhild C. Ornelas, 1411–1427. Cambridge: Cambridge University Press, 2008.

Nath, Giselle. *Brood Willen we Hebben! Honger, Sociale Politiek en Protest tijdens de Eerste Wereldoorlog in België*. Antwerpen: Manteau, 2013.

Neugebauer, Richard, Hans. W. Hoek, and Ezra Susser. 'Prenatal Exposure to Wartime Famine and Development of Antisocial Personality Disorder in Early Adulthood'. *JAMA* 282 (1999): 455–462.

Neuman, Henk J. *Arthur Seyss-Inquart: Het Leven van een Duits Onderkoning in Nederland*. Utrecht: Ambo, 1967.

Neurdenburg M. G. 'Algemeene Statistiek der Mortaliteit en der Morbiditeit'. In *Medische Ervaringen in Nederland tijdens de Bezetting, 1940–1945*, edited by Ite Boerema, 321–408. Groningen: Wolters, 1947.

Nieuwendijk, Caroline. *De Schiedamse Bleekneusjes: Kinderuitzendingen tussen 1900 en 1979*. Schiedam: Stichting Musis, 2012.

Nieuwenhuis, Frans J. M. *Naar de Boeren! Kinderuitzendingen tijdens de Hongerwinter*. Rotterdam: Donker, 2010.

Nijs, Thimo de. 'Food Provision and Food Retailing in The Hague, 1914–1930'. In *Food and Conflict in Europe in the Age of the Two World Wars*, edited by Frank Trentmann and Flemming Just, 65–87. Basingstoke: Palgrave Macmillan, 2006.

Nolzen, Armin. 'The NSDAP's Operational Codes after 1933'. In *Visions of Community in Nazi Germany: Social Engineering and Private Lives*, edited by Martina Steber and Bernhard Gotto, 87–100. Oxford: Oxford University Press, 2014.

Ó Gráda, Cormac. *Eating People Is Wrong, and Other Essays on Famine, Its Past and Its Future*. Princeton: Princeton University Press, 2015.

Famine: A Short History. Princeton: Princeton University Press, 2009.

Black '47 and Beyond: The Great Irish Famine in History, Economy, and Memory. Princeton: Princeton University Press, 2000.

Onderwater, Hans. *Operatie 'Manna': De Geallieerde Voedseldroppings April/Mei 1945*. Weesp: Romen Luchtvaart, 1985.

Ossendorp, Frans L., and E. J. van Det. *Kindervoeding en – kleeding in Nederland en in het Buitenland*. Amsterdam: Edelman en Barendregt, 1913.

Oudheusden, Jan A. van, Marian Omtzigt, and Ria van den Heuvel-Habraken. 'Feest en Frustratie: Het Leven achter het Front'. In *Tussen Vrijheid en Vrede: Het Bevrijde Zuiden, September 1944–Mei 1945*, edited by Jan A. Oudheusen and Henk Termeer, 45–91. Zwolle: Waanders, 1994.

Overmans, Rüdiger. 'The Repatriation of Prisoners of War once Hostilities Are Over. A Matter of Course?' In *Prisoners of War, Prisoners of Peace. Captivity, Homecoming, and Memory in World War II*, edited by Bob Moore and Barbara Hately-Broad, 11–22. Oxford: Berg, 2005.

Painter, Rebecca C. *The Pathophysiology of Cardiovascular Disease after Prenatal Exposure to Maternal Undernutrition during the Dutch Famine*. Amsterdam: Buijten en Schipperheijn, 2006.

Painter, Rebecca C., Susanne R. de Rooy, Patrick M. Bossuyt, David I. Phillips, Clive Osmond, David J. Barker, Otto P. Bleker, and Tessa J. Roseboom. 'Blood Pressure Response to Psychological Stressors in Adults after Prenatal Exposure to the Dutch Famine'. *Hypertension* 24 (2006): 1771–1778.

Pauw, Jeroen L. van der. *Rotterdam in de Tweede Wereldoorlog*. Amsterdam: Boom, 2006.

Peereboom Voller, Dirk H. *Distributiewetgeving in Nederland*. Groningen: Rijksuniversiteit Groningen, 1945.

Petrow, Richard. *The Bitter Years: The Invasion and Occupation of Denmark and Norway, April 1940–May 1945*. New York: Morrow, 1974.

Petterson, Anne. 'Aardappelnood: Amsterdamse Arbeiders en het Socialisme tijdens het Aardappeloproer van 1917'. *Tijdschrift Holland* 42 (2010): 18–39.

Piersma, Hinke, and Jeroen Kemperman. *Openstaande Rekeningen: De Gemeente Amsterdam en de Gevolgen van Roof en Rechtsherstel, 1940–1950.* Amsterdam: Boom, 2015.

Pitkänen, Kari. 'Famine Mortality in Nineteenth Century Finland: Is there a Sex Bias?' In *Famine Demography: Perspectives from the Past and Present*, edited by Tim Dyson and Cormac Ó Gráda, 65–92. Oxford: Oxford University Press, 2002.

Pitkänen, Kari, and James H. Mielke. 'Age and Sex Differentials in Mortality during Two Nineteenth Century Population Crises'. *European Journal of Population* (1993): 1–32.

Poiger, Uta G. 'Imperialism and Empire in Twentieth-Century Germany'. *History and Memory* 17 (2005): 117–143.

Randwijk, Hendrik M. van. 'Hongertochten tijdens de Hongerwinter'. In *Onderdrukking en Verzet: Nederland in Oorlogstijd II*, edited by Johannes J. van Bolhuis, 647–660. Arnhem: Van Loghum Slaterus, 1950.

Ravelli, Anita C. J., Jan. H. van der Meulen, R. P. Michels, Clive Osmond, David J. Barker, and Otto P. Bleker. 'Glucose Tolerance in Adults after Prenatal Exposure to Famine'. *Lancet* 351 (1998): 173–177.

Ravelli, Anita C. J., Jan H. van der Meulen, Clive Osmond, David J. Barker, and Otto P. Bleker. 'Obesity at the Age of 50 Y in Men and Women Exposed to Famine Prenatally'. *American Journal of Clinical Nutrition* 70 (1999): 811–816.

Ravelli, G. P., Zena A. Stein, and Mervin W. Susser. 'Obesity in Young Men after Famine Exposure in Utero and Early Infancy'. *New England Journal of Medicine* 295 (1976): 349–353.

Ravallion, Martin. *Markets and Famines.* Oxford: Clarendon Press, 1987.

Ravesloot, J. *De Houding van de Kerk in de Bezettingstijd, 1940–1945.* S.l.: s.n, 1946.

Ravesteyn, T. L. W. van. 'Studies over de Follikelrijping: Histologisch Onderzoek over de Follikel van de Graaf in de Praeovulatiephase, Klinisch Onderzoek over de Oorlogsamenorrhoe te 's-Gravenhage in 1944 en 1945, met een Inleiding over de Geschiedenis van het Onderzoek van de Follikel van de Graaf', Thesis, Rijksuniversiteit Utrecht. Utrecht: Utrecht University, 1946.

Reid, Anna. *Leningrad: The Epic Siege of World War II, 1941–1944.* New York: Walker & Company, 2011.

Reve, Gerardus K. van het. *Tien Vrolijke Verhalen.* Amsterdam: G. A. van Oorschot, 1961.

Ribbens, Kees R. *Bewogen Jaren: Zwolle in de Tweede Wereldoorlog.* Zwolle: Waanders, 2005.

Rigter, R. B.M. 'De Gezondheids – en Voedingsraad in Oorlogstijd'. In *Geneeskunde en Gezondheidszorg in Nederland 1940–1945*, edited by Marius J. van Lieburg and Wijnandus W. Mijnhardt, 228–239. Amsterdam: Rodopi, 1992.

Riet, Frank A. M. van. *Handhaven onder de Nieuwe Orde: De Politieke Geschiedenis van de Rotterdamse Politie tijdens de Tweede Wereldoorlog.* Zaltbommel: Aprilis, 2008.

Rijksen, Rijk. *Criminaliteit en Bezetting*. Assen: Van Gorcum, 1956.

Rivers, Joan P. W. 'The Nutritional Biology of Famine'. In *Famine*, edited by Geoffrey A. Harrison, 57–106. Oxford: Oxford University Press, 1988.

'Women and Children Last: An Essay on Sex Discrimination in Disasters'. *Disasters* 6 (1982): 256–276.

Roland, Charles G. *Courage under Siege: Starvation, Disease, and Death in the Warsaw Ghetto*. New York: Oxford University Press, 1992.

Romein, Jan M. 'The Spirit of the Dutch People during the Occupation'. *Annals of the American Academy of Political and Social Science* 245 (1946): 169–180.

Romijn, Peter. 'Liberators and Patriots: Military Interim Rule and the Politics of Transition in the Netherlands, 1944–1945'. In *Seeking Peace in the Wake of War: Europe, 1943–1947*. NIOD Studies on War, Holocaust and Genocide, edited by Stefan-Ludwig Hoffmann, Sandrine Kott, Peter Romijn, and Olivier Wieviorka, 117–144. Amsterdam: Amsterdam University Press, 2015.

Burgemeesters in Oorlogstijd: Besturen tijdens de Duitse Bezetting. Amsterdam: Balans, 2006.

Snel, Streng en Rechtvaardig: De Afrekening met 'Foute' Nederlanders 1945–1955. 2nd ed. Amsterdam: Olympus, 2002.

Roodhouse, Mark. 'Popular Morality and the Black Market in Britain, 1939–1945'. In *Food and Conflict in Europe in the Age of the Two World Wars*, edited by Frank Trentmann and Flemming Just, 243–265. Basingstoke: Palgrave Macmillan, 2006.

Roodt, Evelyn U. de. *Oorlogsgasten: Vluchtelingen en Krijgsgevangenen in Nederland tijdens de Eerste Wereldoorlog*. Zaltbommel: Europese Bibliotheek, 2000.

Rooij, Sieneke de. *De Boot naar Lemmer: Een Verhaal uit de Hongerwinter*. Leiden: De Witte Uitgeverij, 2009.

Rooij, Susanne R. de, Hans Wouters, Julie E. Yonker, Rebecca C. Painter, and Tessa J. Roseboom. 'Prenatal Undernutrition and Cognitive Function in Late Adulthood'. *Proceedings of the National Academy of Sciences of the United States of America* 107 (2010): 16881–16886.

Rooij, Susanne R. de, Rebecca C. Painter, Tessa J. Roseboom, D. I. W. Phillips, and Clive Osmond. 'Glucose Tolerance at Age 58 and the Decline of Glucose Tolerance in Comparison with Age 50 in People Prenatally Exposed to the Dutch Famine'. *Diabetologia* 49 (2006): 637–643.

Rooij, Susanne R. de, Rebecca C. Painter, Tessa J. Roseboom, D. I. Phillips, Clive Osmond, David J. Barker, M. W. Tanck, R. P. Michels, Patrick M. M. Bussuyt, and Otto P. Bleker. 'Glucose Tolerance at Age 58 and the Decline of Glucose Tolerance in Comparison with Age 50 in People Prenatally Exposed to the Dutch Famine'. *Diabetologia* 49 (2006): 637–643.

Rooy, Piet de. 'Een Zoekende Tijd: De Ongemakkelijke Democratie, 1913–1949'. In *Land van Kleine Gebaren: Een Politieke Geschiedenis van Nederland 1780–2012*. 8th rev. ed., edited by Remieg Aerts, Herman de Liagre Böhl, Piet de Rooy, and Henk te Velde, 177–262. Amsterdam: Boom, 2013.

Republiek van Rivaliteiten: Nederland sinds 1813. Amsterdam: Mets & Schilt, 2002.

Roseboom, Tessa J. *Prenatal Exposure to the Dutch Famine and Health in Later Life.* Enschede: Ipskamp Printing Partners, 2000.

Roseboom, Tessa, and Ronald van de Knol. *Baby's van de Hongerwinter: De Onvermoeide Erfenis van Ondervoeding.* Amsterdam and Antwerp: Augustus, 2010.

Roseboom, Tessa J., Jan H. van der Meulen, Anita C. J. Ravelli, Gert A. van Montfrans, Clive Osmond, David J. Barker, and Otto P. Bleker. 'Blood Pressure in Adults after Prenatal Exposure to Famine'. *Journal of Hypertension* 17 (1999): 325–330.

Rossem, P. V. J. van. *Tietjerksteradeel 1940–1945.* Burgum: Stichting Streekmuseum Tytsjerksteradiel, 1995.

Het Ontstaan van het Inter Kerkelijk Bureau en zijn Organisatie. Amsterdam: s.n., 1984.

Rüter, Adolf J. C. *Rijden en Staken: De Nederlandse Spoorwegen in Oorlogstijd.* The Hague: Martinus Nijhoff, 1960.

'De Nederlandse Spoorwegen'. In *Onderdrukking en Verzet: Nederland in Oorlogstijd IV*, edited by Johannes J. van Bolhuis, 633–648. Arnhem: Van Loghum Slaterus, 1954.

Schaarschmidt, Thomas. 'Mobilizing German Society for War: The National Socialist Gaue'. In *Visions of Community in Nazi Germany: Social Engineering and Private Lives*, edited by Martina Steber and Bernhard Gotto, 101–115. Oxford: Oxford University Press, 2014.

Schaik, Th. van. 'Voedingsmiddelen door den Mensch tijdens de Oorlogsjaren 1940–1945 Gebruikt, die Voordien in Nederland Vrijwel Onbekend Waren'. *Voeding* 6 (1946): 93–109.

Scheepmaker, Nico. *Het Zweedse Wittebrood.* Baarn: Erven Thomas Rap, 1979.

Schierbeek, Abraham. *Den Haag 1945: Een Documentatie over de Jaren 1940–1945.* The Hague: De Hofstad, 1945.

Schoonoord, Dick C. L. *Het 'Circus Kruls': Militair Gezag in Nederland, 1944–1946.* Amsterdam: NIOD, 2011.

Schouw, Tineke van de. *Opdat de Kinderen Leven.* Amsterdam: Nederlandse Vrouwen Beweging, 1957.

Scott, James C. *The Moral Economy of the Peasant: Rebellion and Subsistence in Southeast Asia.* New Haven: Yale University Press, 1976.

Sen, Amartya. *Poverty and Famines.* Oxford: Clarendon Press, 1981.

'Starvation and Exchange Entitlements: A General Approach and Its Application to the Great Bengal Famine'. *Cambridge Journal of Economics* 1 (1977): 33–59.

Sereny, Gitta. *Albert Speer: His Battle with the Truth.* London and Basingstoke: Macmillan, 1995.

Seyle, Hans. *The Stress of Life.* New York: McGraw-Hill, 1956.

Shephard, Ben. 'Becoming Planning Minded: The Theory and Practice of Relief 1940–1945'. *Journal of Contemporary History* 43 (2008): 405–419.

Sijes, Ben A. *De Arbeidsinzet: De Gedwongen Arbeid van Nederlanders in Duitsland.* 2nd ed. The Hague: Nijhoff, 1990.

De Razzia van Rotterdam: 10–11 November 1944. The Hague: Nijhoff, 1951.

Sindram, I. S. 'De Invloed van Ondervoeding op de Groei van de Vrucht'. *Nederlands Tijdschrift voor Verloskundige Gynaecologie* 53 (1953): 30–48.

Sintemaartensdijk, Jan. *De Bleekneusjes van 1945: De Uitzending van Nederlandse Kinderen naar het Buitenland.* Amsterdam: Boom, 2002.

Slager, Kees, Nienke Feis, and Paul van der Graag. *Hongerwinter: Verhalen om te Onthouden.* Amsterdam: Link, 1985.

Smith, Clement A. 'Effects of Maternal Undernutrition upon the Newborn Infant in Holland, 1944–1945'. *Journal of Paediatrics* 30 (1947): 229–243.

'Effects of War-Time Starvation in Holland upon Pregnancy and Its Product'. *American Journal of Obstetrics & Gynecology* 53 (1947): 599–608.

Snyder, Timothy. *Bloodlands: Europe between Hitler and Stalin.* London: Vintage, 2011.

Sorokin, Pitrim A. *Hunger As a Factor in Human Affairs.* Gainesville: University Presses of Florida, 1975.

Man and Society in Calamity: The Effects of War, Revolution, Famine, Pestilence upon Human Mind, Behavior, Social Organization and Cultural Life. 4th ed. New York: E. P. Dutton & Co., 1946.

St. Clair, David, Ming Qing Xu, Peng Wang, Yaqin Yu, Yourong Fang, Feng Zhang, Xiaoying Zheng, Niufan Gu, Guoyin Feng, Pak Sham, and Lin He. 'Rates of Adult Schizophrenia Following Prenatal Exposure to the Chinese Famine of 1959-1961'. *JAMA* 294 (2005): 557–562.

Steege, Paul. *Black Market, Cold War: Everyday Life in Berlin, 1946–1949.* Cambridge: Cambridge University Press, 2007.

Stein, Aryeh D., Henry S. Kahn, A. Rundle, Patricia A. Zybert, Karin M. van der Pal-de Bruin, and L. H. Lumey. 'Anthropometric Measures in Middle Age after Exposure to Famine during Gestation: Evidence from the Dutch Famine'. *American Journal of Clinical Nutrition* 85 (2007): 869–876.

Stein, Aryeh D., Patricia A. Zybert, Margot van de Bor, and L. H. Lumey. 'Intrauterine Famine Exposure and Body Proportions at Birth: The Dutch Hunger Winter'. *International Journal of Epidemiology* 33 (2004): 831–836.

Stein, Zena, and Mervyn Susser. 'Fertility, Fecundity, Famine: Food Rations in the Dutch Famine 1944/45 Have a Causal Relation to Fertility, and Probably Fecundity'. *Human Biology* 47 (1975): 131–154.

'The Dutch Famine, 1944–1945, and the Reproductive Process. I. Effects on Six Indices at Birth'. *Pediatric Research* 9 (1975): 70–75.

Stein, Zena A., Mervyn W. Susser, Gerhard Saenger, and Francis Marolla. *Famine and Human Development: The Dutch Hunger Winter of 1944–1945.* New York: Oxford University Press, 1975.

'Nutrition and Mental Performance. Prenatal Exposure to the Dutch Famine of 1944–1945 Seems Not Related to Mental Performance at Age 19'. *Science* 178 (1972): 708–713.

Stinnis, Yvonne. 'Lijfsbehoud: Vrouwen in het Verzet tegen de Honger'. *Skript Historisch Tijdschrift* 10 (1988): 25–33.

Stuijvenberg, J. H. van, and C. Van den Berg. 'Zwarte Prijzen van Consumptiegoederen gedurende de Bezettingsjaren'. *Economisch-Statistisch Kwartaalbericht* I (1947): 27.

Susser, Ezra S., and Shang Lin. 'Schizophrenia after Prenatal Exposure to the Dutch Hunger Winter of 1944–1945'. *Archives of General Psychiatry* 49 (1992): 938–939.

Susser, Ezra, Richard Neugebauer, Hans W. Hoek, Alan S. Brown, Shang Lin, Daniel Labovitz, and Jack M. Gorman. 'Schizophrenia after Prenatal Famine: Further Evidence'. *Archives of General Psychiatry* 53 (1996): 25–31.

Swift, Jeremy. 'Understanding and Preventing Famine and Famine Mortality'. *IDS Bulletin* 24 (1993): 1–15.

Tames, Ismee. 'Innocence and Punishment: The War Experiences of the Children of Dutch Nazi Collaborators'. In *Restaging War in the Western World: Noncombatant Experiences, 1890–Today*, edited by Maartje Abbenhuis and Sara Buttsworth, 87–108. New York: Palgrave Macmillan, 2009.

Taylor, Lynne. 'Food Riots Revisited'. *Journal of Social History* 30 (1996): 483–496.

Thompson, E. P. 'The Moral Economy of the English Crowd in Eighteenth Century'. *Past & Present* 50 (1971): 76–136.

Tobi, Elmar W., Jelle J. Goeman, Ramin Monajemi, Hongcang Gu, Hein Putter, Yanju Zhang, Roderick C. Slieker, Arthur P. Stok, Peter E. Thijssen, Fabian Muller, Erik W. van Zwet, Christoph Bock, Alexander Meissner, L. H. Lumey, P. Eline Slagboom, and Bastiaan T. Heijmans. 'DNA Methylation Signatures Link Prenatal Famine Exposure to Growth and Metabolism'. *Nature Communications* 5 (2014): 1–13.

Tobi, Elmar W., L. H. Lumey, R. P. Talens, D. Kremer, Hein Putter, Aryeh D. Stein, Eline Slagboom, and Bastiaan T. Heijmans. 'DNA Methylation Differences after Exposure to Prenatal Famine Are Common in Timing- and Sex- Specific'. *Human Molecular Genetics* 18 (2009): 4046–4053.

Tobi, Elmar W., Roderick C. Slieker, Rene Luijk, Koen F. Dekkers, Aryeh D. Stein, Kate M. Xu, Biobank-based Integrative Omics Studies Consortium, P. Eline Slagboom, Erik W. van Zwet, L. H. Lumey, and Bastiaan T. Heijmans. 'DNA Methylation as a Mediator of the Association between Prenatal Adversity and Risk Factors for Metabolic Disease in Adulthood'. *Science Advances* 4 (2018): 1–10.

Tönsmeyer, Tatjana. 'Supply Situations. National Socialist Policies of Exploitation and Economies of Shortage in Occupied Societies during World War II'. In *Coping with Hunger and Shortage under German Occupation in World War II*, edited by Tatjana Tönsmeyer, Peter Haslinger, and Agnes Laba, 3–23. London: Palgrave Macmillan, 2018.

Tönsmeyer, Tatjana, Peter Haslinger, and Agnes Laba, eds. *Coping with Hunger and Shortage under German Occupation in World War II*. London: Palgrave Macmillan, 2018.

Tooze, Adam. 'The Economic History of the Nazi Regime'. In *The Short Oxford History of Germany: Nazi Germany*, edited by Jane Caplan, 168–195. Oxford: Oxford University Press, 2008.

The Wages of Destruction: The Making and Breaking of the Nazi Economy. London: Allen Lane, 2006.

Touw, Hendrik C. *Het Verzet der Hervormde Kerk*. The Hague: Boekencentrum, 1946.

Trentmann, Frank, and Flemming Just. 'Introduction'. In *Food and Conflict in Europe in the Age of the Two World Wars*, edited by Frank Trentmann and Flemming Just, 1–12. Basingstoke: Palgrave Macmillan, 2006.

Treub, Marie W. F. *Herinneringen en Overpeinzingen*. Haarlem: H. D. Tjeenk Willink & Zoon NV, 1931.

Trienekens, Gerardus M. T. 'The Food Supply in The Netherlands during the Second World War'. In *Food, Science, Policy and Regulation in the Twentieth Century: International and Comparative Perspectives*, edited by David F. Smith and Jim Phillips, 117–134. London: Routledge, 2000.

Voedsel en Honger in Oorlogstijd 1940–1945: Misleiding, Mythe en Werkelijkheid. Utrecht: Kosmos Z & K, 1995.

Tussen ons Volk en de Honger: De Voedselvoorziening 1940–1945. Utrecht: Stichting Matrijs, 1985.

Tuntler, J. 'Onderzoek naar Den Voedingstoestand van Schoolkinderen te Amsterdam 1935–45'. *Tijdschrift voor Sociale Geneeskunde* 23 (1945): 106–124.

Vallin, Jacques, France Meslé, Serguei Adamets, and Serhii Pyrozhkov. 'A New Estimate of Ukrainian Population Losses during the Crises of the 1930s and 1940s'. *Population Studies* 56 (2002): 249–264.

Vanhaute, Eric, and Thijs Lambrecht. 'Famine, Exchange Networks and the Village Community: A Comparative Analysis of the Subsistence Crises of the 1740s and 1840s in Flanders'. *Continuity and Change* 26 (2011): 155–186.

Veenendaal, Marjolein V. E., Rebecca C. Painter, Susanne R. de Rooij, Patrick M. M. Bossuyt, Joris A. M. van der Post, Peter D. Gluckman, Mark A. Hanson, and Tessa J. Roseboom. 'Transgenerational Effects of Prenatal Exposure to the 1944–45 Dutch Famine'. *BJOG* 120 (2013): 548–554.

Verhagen, Jessica A., *Vergeten Kinderen: Kroniek van een Kindertransport vanuit Reeuwijk naar Drenthe tijdens de Tweede Wereldoorlog, 19 Maart–23 Juni 1945*. Soesterberg: Uitgeverij Aspekt, 2017.

Verhoeven, Dolly. '"Verder hebben we Heel Gewoon Geleefd": Dagelijks Leven in Utrecht tijdens de Bezetting'. In *Een Gewone Stad in een Bijzondere Tijd: Utrecht 1940–1945*, edited by Johannes van Miert, 163–195. Utrecht: Het Spectrum BV, 1995.

Vermaat, Emerson. *Anton Mussert en zijn Conflict met de SS*. Soesterberg: Aspekt, 2011.

Verwey, Marcus G. *Leiden in Bezettingstijd: Herinneringen van een Gemeentebestuurder*. Leiden: A. W. Sijthoff's Uitgeversmij NV, 1946.

Vincent, C. P. *The Politics of Hunger: The Allied Blockade of Germany, 1915–1919*. Athens: Ohio University Press, 1985.

Voglis, Polymeris. 'The Politics of Reconstruction: Foreign Aid and State Authority in Greece, 1945–1947'. In *Seeking Peace in the Wake of War: Europe, 1943–1947*. NIOD Studies on War, Holocaust and Genocide, edited by Stefan-Ludwig Hoffmann, Sandrine Kott, Peter Romijn, and Olivier Wieviorka, 277–296. Amsterdam: Amsterdam University Press, 2015.

'Surviving Hunger: Life in the Cities and the Countryside during the Occupation'. In *Surviving Hitler and Mussolini: Daily Life in Occupied Europe*, edited by Robert Gildea, Olivier Wieviorka, and Anette Warring, 16–41. Oxford: Berg, 2006.

Vorländer, Herwart. *Die NSV: Dastellung und Dokumentation einer nationalsozialistischen Organization*. Boppard am Rhein: Boldt, 1988.

Vorstenbosch, Tom, Ingrid J. J. de Zwarte, Leni Duistermaat, and Tinde R. van Andel. 'Famine Food of Vegetal Origin Consumed in the Netherlands During World War II'. *Journal of Ethnobiology and Ethnomedicine* 13 (2017): 1–15.

Vrints, Antoon. 'Alles is Van Ons: Anonieme Brieven over de Voedselvoorziening in Nederland tijdens de Tweede Wereldoorlog'. *BMGN-Low Countries Historical Review* 126 (2011): 25–51.

Waal, Alex de. *Mass Starvation: The History and Future of Famine.* Cambridge: Polity Press, 2018.

'Famine Mortality: A Case Study of Darfur, Sudan, in 1984–1985'. *Population Studies* 43 (1989): 5–24.

Wachsmann, Nikolaus. *KL: A History of Nazi Concentration Camps.* New York: Farrar, Straus and Giroux, 2015.

Warmbrunn, Werner. *The Dutch under German Occupation, 1940–1945.* Stanford: Stanford University Press, 1963.

Wassenaar, Aart W. *Van Winterhulp via Oost-Compagnie en Marseille naar Rode Kruis: De Loopbaan van Carel Piek Voor, Tijdens, en Na de Bezettingstijd 1940–1945. Een Geschiedenis van Idealisme en Collaboratie.* Soesterberg: Aspekt, 2016.

Watson, Fiona. 'Why Are There No Longer "War Famines" in Contemporary Europe? Bosnia Besieged, 1992–1995'. In *The New Famines: Why Famines Persist in an Era of Globalization*, edited by Stephen Devereux, 269–289. London: Routledge, 2007.

Watts, Michael J., and Hans G. Bohle. 'Hunger, Famine and the Space of Vulnerability'. *GeoJournal* 30 (1993): 117–125.

Welshman, John. *Churchill's Children: The Evacuee Experience in Wartime Britain.* Oxford: Oxford University Press, 2010.

Wemheuer, Felix. *Famine Politics in Maoist China and the Soviet Union.* New Haven: Yale University Press, 2014.

Wheatcroft, Stephen, and Cormac Ó Gráda. 'The European Famines of World Wars I and II'. In *Famine in European History*, edited by Guido Alfani and Cormac Ó Gráda, 240–268. Cambridge: Cambridge University Press, 2017.

Whitaker, William H. 'Food Entitlements'. In *The Cambridge World History of Food*, edited by Kenneth F. Kiple and Kriemhild C. Ornelas, 1585–1593. Cambridge: Cambridge University Press, 2008.

Wielinga, Anne, and Johan Salverda. *De Lemmerboot: Levenslijn tussen Amsterdam en Lemmer.* Leeuwarden: Friese Pers, 1983.

Willering, Bert. *Rotterdammertjes in Stadskanaal: Kinderen in de Hongerwinter 1944–1945.* Assen: Alwil, 2015.

Winstone, Martin. *The Dark Heart of Hitler's Europe: Nazi Rule in Poland under the General Government.* New York: I. B. Tauris & Co. Ltd, 2015.

Winter, Jay. 'Paris, London, Berlin 1914–1919: Capital Cities at War'. In *Capital Cities at War: London, Paris, Berlin 1914–1919*, edited by Jay Winter and Jean-Louis Robert, 3–24. Cambridge: Cambridge University Press, 1997.

Wirsching, Andreas. 'Volksgemeinschaft and the Illusion of "Normality" from the 1920s to the 1940s'. In *Visions of Community in Nazi Germany: Social Engineering and Private Lives*, edited by Martina Steber and Bernhard Gotto, 149–156. Oxford: Oxford University Press, 2014.

Withuis, Jolande. *Opoffering en Heroïek: De Mentale Wereld van een Communistische Vrouwenorganisatie in Naoorlogs Nederland, 1946–1976.* Meppel: Boom, 1990.

Woltjer, Jan J. *Recent Verleden: Nederland in de Twintigste Eeuw.* Amsterdam: Balans, 1992.

Xu, Ming Qing, Wen Sheng Sun, Ben Xiu Liu, Guo Yin Feng, Lan Yu, Larry Yang, Guang He, Pak Sham, Ezra Susser, David St. Clair, and Lin He. 'Prenatal Malnutrition and Adult Schizophrenia. Further Evidence from the 1959–1961 Chinese Famine'. *Schizophrenia Bulletin* 35 (2009): 557–576.

Young, Liz. 'World Hunger: A Framework for Analysis'. *Geography* 81 (1996): 97–110.

Zanden, Jan Luiten van. *Een Klein Land in de 20ᵉ Eeuw: Een Economische Geschiedenis van Nederland 1914–1995.* Zeist: Het Spectrum, 1997.

Zee, Henri A. van der. *The Hunger Winter: Occupied Holland 1944–45.* London: Jill Norman & Hobhouse, 1982.

De Hongerwinter: Van Dolle Dinsdag tot Bevrijding. Amsterdam: Becht, 1979.

Zoethout, H. 'De Dieetkeukens in de Jaren 1944–1945'. *Voeding* 8 (1947): 237–240.

Zoon, J. J. 'De Huid- en Geslachtsziekten in Oorlogstijd'. In *Medische Ervaringen in Nederland tijdens de Bezetting, 1940–1945,* edited by Ite Boerema, 467–482. Groningen: Wolters, 1947.

Zwarte, Ingrid J. J. de. *De Hongerwinter.* Amsterdam: Prometheus, 2019.

'Fighting Vulnerability: Child Feeding Initiatives during the Dutch Hunger Winter'. In *Coping with Hunger and Shortage under German Occupation in World War II,* edited by Tatjana Tönsmeyer, Peter Haslinger, and Agnes Laba, 293–310. London: Palgrave Macmillan, 2018.

'De Voedseldroppings van 1945: Waarom duurde het zo Lang?' *Geschiedenis Magazine* 3 (2017): 26–29.

'Save the Children: Social Self-Organization and Relief in Amsterdam during the Dutch Hunger Winter'. *Food & History* 14 (2016): 51–76.

'Coordinating Hunger: The Evacuation of Children during the Dutch Food Crisis, 1945'. *War & Society* 35 (2016): 132–149.

'Commissie Kindervoeding hielp Utrechtse Kinderen de Hongerwinter Door'. *Oud-Utrecht* 89 (2016): 32–37.

'Samen tegen de Honger: Hulpverlening aan Kinderen in Amsterdam Tijdens de Hongerwinter'. *Ons Amsterdam* 67 (2015): 16–21.

'Voedsel, Spoedig en Radicaal! Voedseldistributie en Hulpverlening in Amsterdam, Eindhoven en Groningen tijdens de Hongerwinter, 1944–1945'. MA thesis, University of Amsterdam. Amsterdam: University of Amsterdam, 2013.

'Grenzen Vervagen: Economische Criminaliteit in Amsterdam, 1940–1945'. *Ons Amsterdam* 63 (2011): 202–207.

Zwarte, Ingrid J. J. de, and Debbie Varekamp. '"Vrouwen, Eist Meer Eten!" Protest tijdens de Hongerwinter'. *Historisch Nieuwsblad* 25 (2016): 78–83.

Zweig, Ronald W. 'Feeding the Camps: Allied Blockade Policy and the Relief of Concentration Camps in Germany, 1944–45'. *The Historical Journal* 41 (1998): 825–51.

Zweiniger-Bargielowska, Ina. *Austerity in Britain: Rationing, Controls, and Consumption 1939–1955.* Oxford: Oxford University Press, 2000.

Index